# A HISTORY OF MODERN PALESTINE
*One Land, Two Peoples*

Ilan Pappe's book is the story of Palestine, a land inhabited by two peoples, with two national identities. It begins with the Ottomans in the early 1800s, the reign of Muhammad Ali, and traces a path through the arrival of the early Zionists at the end of that century, through the British mandate at the beginning of the twentieth century, the establishment of the state of Israel in 1948, and the subsequent wars and conflicts which culminated in the intifadas of 1987 and 2000. While these events provide the background to the narrative and explain the construction of Zionist and Palestinian nationalism, at center stage are those who lived through these times, men and women, children, peasants, workers, town-dwellers, Jews and Arabs. It is a story of coexistence and cooperation, as well as oppression, occupation, and exile. Ilan Pappe is well known as a revisionist historian of Palestine and a political commentator on the Israel–Palestine conflict. His book is lucid and typically forthright. It is a unique contribution to the history of this troubled land which all those concerned with developments in the Middle East will have to read.

**Ilan Pappe** teaches politics at Haifa University in Israel. He has written extensively on the politics of the Middle East, and is well known for his revisionist interpretation of Israel's history and as a critic of its policies towards the Palestinians. His books include *The Making of the Arab–Israeli Conflict, 1947–1951* (1992, 1994) and *The Israeli/Palestine Question* (1999).

# A HISTORY OF MODERN PALESTINE

## PALESTINE

*One Land, Two Peoples*

ILAN PAPPE

*University of Haifa, Israel*

CAMBRIDGE
UNIVERSITY PRESS

PUBLISHED BY THE PRESS SYNDICATE OF THE UNIVERSITY OF CAMBRIDGE
The Pitt Building, Trumpington Street, Cambridge, United Kingdom

CAMBRIDGE UNIVERSITY PRESS
The Edinburgh Building, Cambridge, CB2 2RU, UK
40 West 20th Street, New York, NY 10011–4211, USA
477 Williamstown Road, Port Melbourne, VIC 3207, Australia
Ruiz de Alarcón 13, 28014 Madrid, Spain
Dock House, The Waterfront, Cape Town 8001, South Africa

http://www.cambridge.org

First published 2004

Printed in the United States of America

*Typeface* Adobe Garamond 11/12.5 pt.     *System* LATEX 2$_\varepsilon$   [TB]

*A catalogue record for this book is available from the British Library*

*National Library of Australia Cataloguing in Publication data*
Pappe, Ilan, 1954– .
A history of modern Palestine.
Bibliography.
Includes index.
ISBN 0 521 55406 3.
ISBN 0 521 55632 5 (pbk.).
1. Arab–Israeli conflict.   2. Jewish–Arab relations.   3. Palestine – History.   I. Title.
956.94

ISBN 0 521 55406 3 hardback
ISBN 0 521 55632 5 paperback

*To Ido and Yonatan, my two lovely boys. May they live not only in a modern Palestine, but also in a peaceful one.*

# Contents

# Figures

# Maps

# Chronology

| | |
|---|---|
| 1699 | Austro–Ottoman War ends; Peace of Karlovitz |
| 1703–30 | Sultanate of Ahmet III |
| 1710–11 | Russo–Ottoman War |
| 1725–30 | Ismail Pasha governor of Damascus |
| 1730–54 | Sultanate of Mahmoud I |
| 1745 | First Wahhabiyya state founded in Arabian Peninsula |
| 1746–75 | Dahir al-Umar rules Galilee |
| 1754–57 | Sultanate of Uthman III |
| 1757–74 | Sultanate of Mustafa III |
| 1767–74 | Further Russo–Ottoman War |
| 1770–73 | Ali Bey al-Kabir rules Egypt |
| 1771 | Dahir al-Umar and Ali Bey occupy Damascus |
| 1774–89 | Sultanate of Abdul Hamid I |
| 1774 | Kaucuc Kainerge Agreement between Russia and Ottoman Empire |
| 1775–1804 | Ahmad al-Jazzar rules *vilayet* of Syda from Acre |
| 1783 | Russia occupies Crimean Peninsula |
| 1787–92 | Further Russo–Ottoman War |
| 1789–1807 | Sultanate of Selim III |
| 1789 | Austrian army invades Bosnia and Serbia; Russian army invades Moldavia and Wallachia |
| 1789–1840 | Bashir II Amir of Mount Lebanon |
| 1798 | Napoleon invades Egypt |
| 1799 | Napoleon in Palestine and Syria |
| 1800 | French army retreats from Egypt |
| 1801 | Wahhabis occupy Karbala |
| 1802 | Mecca and Medina taken by Wahhabis |
| 1805–48 | Muhammad Ali rules Egypt |
| 1806–12 | Further Russo–Ottoman War |
| 1807–08 | Sultanate of Mustafa IV |

| 1808–39 | Sultanate of Mahmoud II |
| 1818–32 | Abdullah Pasha rules *vilayet* of Syda and Acre |
| 1820 | London Society for the Promotion of Christianity among the Jews begins activity in Palestine |
| 1820–30 | Greek War of Liberation |
| 1824 | First modern hospital opens in Palestine |
| 1826 | Massacre of Yeneceris in Istanbul |
| 1828–29 | Further Russo–Ottoman War |
| 1830 | French invade Algeria |
| 1830 | British consulate opens in Jerusalem |
| 1831–40 | Ibrahim Ali rules Syria and Palestine |
| 1834 | Revolt in Palestine against Egyptian rule |
| 1834 | First Arab printing house opens in Beirut |
| 1838–58 | Mustafa Rashid is Grand Vizier |
| 1839 | British occupy Aden |
| 1839–61 | Sultanate of Abdul Magid II |
| 1839 | Hat-I-Sharif of the Gulhana lifts discrimination against non-Muslims in Ottoman Empire; beginning of the Tanzimat period |
| 1840 | Treaty of London ends Egyptian rule in Syria and Palestine |
| 1843 | Lebanon divided into two sub-districts: Maronite and Druze |
| 1850 | Riots in Aleppo against Tanzimat |
| 1853 | Sahayun Anglican School opens in Jerusalem |
| 1853–56 | Crimean War |
| 1856 | Berlin Conference ends Crimean War |
| 1857 | Land Law of the Ottoman Empire |
| 1858–61 | Civil war in Lebanon |
| 1858–71 | Ali Pasha is Grand Vizier |
| 1860 | Massacre of Christians in Syria and Lebanon; French forces land |
| 1861–69 | Fuad Pasha is Grand Vizier |
| 1861 | Organic Law of Lebanon |
| 1861–76 | Sultanate of Abdul Aziz II |
| 1864 | New *Vilayet* Law of the Ottoman Empire |
| 1868 | Young Ottoman Movement founded; first Templars' colony founded in Haifa |
| 1869 | Suez Canal opened; Fuad Pasha dies |
| 1870 | Mikveh Israel, first Jewish agricultural school, founded in Palestine |

| 1871 | *Sanjaq* of Jerusalem autonomous; Templars' colony founded in Sharona, near Jaffa |
| 1875 | Partial bankruptcy of Ottoman Empire; newspaper *Al-Ahram* founded in Egypt; first Muslim and Jewish neighbourhoods outside Old City of Jerusalem; first national associations appear in Arab world. |
| 1876–1908 | Sultanate of Abdul Majid II |
| 1876 | New constitution for Ottoman Empire and first parliament |
| 1877–78 | Further Russo–Ottoman War |
| 1878 | Zionist colony Petach Tikva founded |
| 1878 | Dissolution of Ottoman parliament |
| 1879 | Britain takes over Cyprus; full bankruptcy of Ottoman Empire |
| 1880 | Urabi Pasha revolt in Egypt |
| 1881 | American colony founded in Jerusalem |
| 1882 | British occupation of Egypt; foundation of Rishon le Ziyon, Zichron Yaacov and Rosh Pina; Pinsker publishes *Auto-emancipation* |
| 1882–1903 | First wave of Zionist immigration (First Aliya) |
| 1885 | First newspapers in Hebrew (*Ha-Shahar* and *Ha-Megid*) founded in Europe |
| 1892 | Railway opened between Jaffa and Jerusalem |
| 1893 | Founding convention of Hibat Ziyon in Katowitz |
| 1896–1904 | Herzl precursor and leader of Zionist movement |
| 1897 | First Zionist Congress in Basel |
| 1898 | St George's School opened in Jerusalem; Kaiser Wilhelm II of Germany visits Palestine |
| 1902 | El-Arish plan of Herzl |
| 1903 | Herzl's Uganda plan; first Palestinian women's association convenes in Palestine |
| 1903–14 | Second Aliya |
| 1905 | Final determination of line dividing Egypt and Palestine |
| 1907–20 | Hashomer movement in Palestine |
| 1908 | Sharif Husayn appointed Guardian of Mecca and Medina; oil discovered in Persia; Young Turks come to power |
| 1909 | Building of Tel-Aviv |
| 1911 | Al-Fatah founded |
| 1911–13 | Balkan wars |

| | |
|---|---|
| 1913 | Enver Pasha, Talat Pasha and Jamal Pasha ('the Trio') take over Ottoman Empire |
| 1915–16 | McMahon–Husayn correspondence |
| 1916 | Sykes-Picot agreement between Britain and France; Sharif Husayn's revolt in the Hejaz against Ottomans |
| 1917 | Balfour Declaration; Allenby's troops occupy most of Palestine and enter Jerusalem and Damascus |
| 1918–20 | British military rule in Palestine |
| 1918 | Muslim–Christian Association founded; first Palestinian National conference |
| 1919 | King-Crane Commission visits Palestine; upper Galilee ceded from Syria to Palestine; Ahdut Ha'Avoda and Beitar movements founded |
| 1920 | Palestine becomes mandatory entity; clashes between Jews and Palestinians in Jerusalem; Faysal declared King of Greater Syria; San Remo Conference; Hebrew University built in Jerusalem; Jewish Agency established; Palin Commission |
| 1921 | Transjordan separated from Palestine; clashes in Jaffa between Jews and Palestinians |
| 1922 | Britain recognizes Transjordan as separate political entity and Amir Abdullah as its ruler; Amin al-Husayni appointed Grand Mufti; Supreme Muslim Council founded; Egypt gains independence |
| 1923 | Lausanne Conference finalizes borders of Palestine |
| 1925 | Histadrut founded |
| 1926 | Major earthquake in Palestine |
| 1927 | Palestine currency (pound) introduced |
| 1928 | British resident appointed to Transjordan to guide Amir Abdullah in foreign and defence policies |
| 1929 | Violent clashes between Jews and Palestinians |
| 1930 | Shaw Commission and White Paper of Lord Passfield; Ha-Poel founded; Arab Workers' Union founded |
| 1931 | Pan-Islamic Conference in Jerusalem |
| 1932 | Louis French Report |
| 1933 | Assassination of Haim Arlosaroff by Jewish right-wingers; Izz al-Din al-Qassam operates in Palestine until his death in 1935 |
| 1934 | Arab Higher Committee founded; al-Difa' Party founded |
| 1936–39 | The Arab revolt |

| 1937 | Peel Royal Commission |
|------|------------------------|
| 1938 | Grand Mufti flees Palestine |
| 1939 | White Paper restricting Jewish immigration and land purchase |
| 1946 | Amir Abdullah proclaimed King of Jordan; new Arab Higher Committee appointed; King David Hotel blown up by Jewish terrorists |
| 1947 | British Cabinet decides to refer question of Palestine to UN; UN General Assembly Resolution 181 proposing partition of Palestine between Jewish state and Palestinian state |
| 1948 | State of Israel proclaimed; Arab armies enter Palestine, and uprooting of Palestinian population begins; pro-Hashemite notables in Jericho declare wish for union between Palestine and Transjordan under Hashemite rule; Resolution 194 orders Israel to allow repatriation of refugees expelled from Palestine and the internationalization of Jerusalem; David Ben-Gurion becomes Israel's first prime minister; Herut founded |
| 1949 | Armistice agreement signed between Israel and the Arab states, apart from Iraq |
| 1950 | West Bank officially annexed to Jordan; tripartite declaration by USA, Britain and France recognizes borders in Middle East as final |
| 1954–55 | Moshe Sharett replaces Ben-Gurion as prime minister |
| 1954 | Lavon affair (Ha-Parasha); espionage and sabotage plan exposed by group of Jews in Egypt under orders from Israeli defence minister, Pinchas Lavon |
| 1956 | Suez Campaign |
| 1957 | Eisenhower Doctrine ignites cold war between Nasser and the West; national religious party, Mafdal, founded |
| 1958 | British forces land in Jordan, American marines in Lebanon; Hashemite rule in Iraq ends |
| 1959 | Wadi Salib riots |
| 1963 | End of Ben-Gurion era; Levi Eshkol elected prime minister |
| 1964 | First Arab summit; PLO founded; al-Ard movement in Israel outlawed |
| 1965 | The Fatah and Gahal founded |

| | |
|---|---|
| 1967 | The Six Day War; Israel occupies the West Bank, the Gaza Strip, the Sinai Peninsula and the Golan Heights; 200,000 new Palestinian refugees; Resolution 242 adopted by UN Security Council |
| 1968 | The Fatah takes over PLO; Karameh campaign; hijacking of El-Al aeroplane to Algeria; PFLP and PDFLP founded |
| 1969 | Golda Meir becomes prime minister of Israel |
| 1969–70 | USA attempts to resolve conflict |
| 1970 | Civil war between Jordanian army and PLO; mass killing of Palestinian guerrillas in Jordan and subsequent expulsion to Lebanon of many of them as part of agreement between Arafat and King Hussein; Nasser dies |
| 1972 | Russian advisers leave Egypt; Husayn plan for federation between Palestine and Jordan |
| 1973 | October War between Egyptian, Syrian and Israeli forces; superpower intervention ends fighting; during war, Arab oil countries impose embargo on West (apart from Britain and France); Resolution 338 adopted by UN Security Council affirming Resolution 242, with added reference to need to solve refugee problem |
| 1974 | UN includes Palestine on its agenda and PLO invited as observer; Arab summit in Rabat recognizes PLO as sole legitimate representative of Palestinian people; Jordan abrogates parliament representing two banks of River Jordan; Agranat Report leads to fall of Meir government and election of Rabin as prime minister; Kissinger's 'shuttle diplomacy' in Middle East to seek bilateral peace between Israel and neighbours; Gush Emunim, settlement movement in occupied territories, founded |
| 1975 | Arafat addresses UN General Assembly; outbreak of civil war in Lebanon; first disengagement agreement between Israel and Egypt; partial Israeli withdrawal in Palestine |
| 1976 | Syrian army enters Lebanon |
| 1977 | President Anwar Sadat of Egypt visits Jerusalem and begins bilateral peace talks with Israel. Likud and Begin come to power; Peace Now movement founded in Israel |
| 1978 | Peace treaty signed between Israel and Egypt on White House lawn; PLO attack on northern entrance to Tel-Aviv reciprocated by Litani operation, in which Israel occupies part of southern Lebanon |

# Foreword

The idea of this book germinated in my Haifa University class entitled 'The history of the Palestine conflict'. Very alert and eager Palestinian and Jewish students demanded again and again a narrative of their country's history that did not repeat the known versions of the two conflicting parties; one that respected the other, included those who are not part of the story, and above all was more hopeful about the future. I began writing the book in the twilight of the Oslo Agreement and found it difficult to comply with the last request. But then I realized that, by then, industrious researchers had already provided us with new perspectives on Palestine, but they were never presented in one narrative. What these novel approaches had in common was that they attempted to tell the story of the people and the land, and not just that of high politics, dogmatic ideologies or rehearsed national narratives.

The fact that the students, Palestinians and Jews, wanted to hear the story told from a humanist, and not nationalist, ethnic or religious, perspective was itself a hopeful sign for the future. It is this perspective that dictates the tone of this book, It is a narrative of those in Palestine who were brutalized and victimized by human follies well known from many other parts in the world. The abusive power used by people against other people in the name of one ideology or another is condemned in this book for being the source of much evil and few blessings. These human ambitions wrought invasions, occupations, expulsions, discrimination and racism on Palestine. The heroes of this book are therefore the victims of these calamities: women, children, peasants, workers, ordinary city dwellers, peaceniks, human rights activists. The 'villains' to a certain extent are the arrogant generals, the greedy politicians, the cynical statesmen and the misogynist men. Many of the victims were, and still are, the indigenous people of Palestine, the Palestinians; but many of them also belong to the community of the newcomers, now evolving into a second generation of natives, the Jews.

We are constantly warned that we should not be slaves of our history and memory. This book is written with the view that in order to perform this liberation act in Israel and Palestine, you need first to rewrite, indeed salvage, a history that was erased and forgotten. The violent symbolic and real exclusion of people from the hegemonic narrative of the past is the source of the violence of the present. Various historians who came directly from the forgotten and marginalized communities in Palestine provided with their original and pioneering works the bricks with which I could attempt the present project of redrawing the historical picture of Palestine. This is done not for the sake of intellectual curiosity, but out of a wish to disseminate a more expanded narrative of what happened in a country that never ceases, to the great dismay of its inhabitants, to capture the global headlines, even if its population does not exceed that of London or New York and its territory is smaller than that of any of the Great Lakes of North America. It is both an introduction to those interested for the first time in the country – if there are still such fortunate persons – and a suggestion for an alternative narrative for those who think, quite understandably, that they have read everything they need to know of the torn and tortured land of Palestine.

# Acknowledgements

Many people made this book possible. All of them had to be above all patient with someone who felt, rightly or wrongly, that he was writing from the trenches. Being in Palestine at one of its most dramatic moments and writing about its past was beneficial to the book, but not for those who needed manuscripts in time, speedy answers to crucial questions, or the usual last bits and pieces that make a manuscript a book. I would like to thank them all: Marigold Acland, Karen Hildebrandt and Amanda Pinches.

Equally important for someone whose mother tongue is not English (and is actually a dormant German, but whose native tongue is Hebrew, and who today converses more and more in Arabic) is the help of linguistic and stylistic editors. I am most grateful to Mary Starkey who did the bulk of the work, to Dick Bruggman who, as always, had a thorough and constructive look, and Donna Williams, who did the copy editing. I thank them all for the excellent work they have done.

Finally, as always, to Revital and the kids for paying the price of my love for the country, my dislike of the state, and my devotion to my work.

# Introduction: A New Look at Modern Palestine and Israel

From my classroom at Haifa University, up on the Carmel Mountains, there is seldom a clear view of the city below. On a rare day, when smog and pollution are miraculously absent, I can see the Jewish and Palestinian neighbourhoods of Haifa. The city stretches from the seacoast to the Carmel Mountains. The Palestinians live below, in the areas adjacent to the harbour, but in recent years have moved up to the slopes of the mountains, to parts of the town in which they lived before 1948. In Haifa, the standard of living improves as one moves up the slopes; poverty decreases with altitude.

Socio-economic well-being is closely entwined with national and ethnic affiliations and topography. This forms a pyramid which encapsulates the stratification of Israeli society and, more importantly, the history of the land. Given this geographical polity, it is not surprising to find the university at the top of the mountain, marked by a tower of thirty storeys and overlooking the Palestinians, Mizrahi Jews and the less fortunate socio-economic classes of the town. Like all other national institutions in Israel, the community of Haifa University is predominantly Jewish, European and middle class.

Haifa University, however, has a large share of Palestinians, 20 per cent to be exact; more than their share of the population at large. My class consists of both Palestinian and Jewish students; and the course deals with the history of the land. In this very politically charged country of mine, both groups regard history as just another prism through which to view present rather than past reality. I often ask my students, on those unexpected clear days, to associate the view from the window with history. Palestinian students will describe a town that was once a flourishing Palestinian city but was then emptied and destroyed by the Jews in 1948; Jewish students will see a flourishing town built where emptiness and destruction once reigned. Everywhere else in the country the same two conflicting views exist. They represent historical narratives, powerful versions of history accepted as truth, whether told by child carers to kindergarten children or by university professors to students of history. The thickness of the narrative varies, but not its sequence or its heroes and villains.

A concise history of Israel and Palestine must take into account these narratives, but cannot accept them as 'historical truth', if only because each is the mirror image of the other. If one version is the historical truth then the other has to be a lie. If both are correct then there is no historical truth, only fictional versions of the past. Something else is needed: an alternative narrative that recognizes similarities, criticizes overt falsifications, and expands the history of the region to the areas not covered by the two national narratives.

Bridging conflicting narratives is difficult enough, but this book also attempts to tell a chapter in 'modern' history. (The two narratives, by the way, accept more or less the same definition of what is 'modern'). Approaching the concept of modernity critically is thus one possible way of deconstructing both narratives without discriminating against either. There are therefore two hurdles to be crossed before setting off on our journey to the past. The first is coping with, and even struggling against, two very distinct versions of the country's history deeply planted in the minds of most of its people. These are the two opposing national historiographies of Israel and Palestine, which are of course better told in two distinct textbooks. Here they appear in one, where they are sometimes rejected for their pretensions and criticized for their ethnocentricity and elitism, and at others respected for their epic chapters while being ridiculed for their absurdity.

The second hurdle is challenging the principal paradigm of history accepted by national historiographers. This paradigm is based on the theory of modernization, which produces a story with a clear beginning, a distinct present and a reasonably predictable future. Adherents of modernization, whether advocates of the Palestinian or the Israeli view, can pinpoint readily the departure point for the history of modern Israel and Palestine. This is always the first contact with Europe. Challenging this paradigm may help produce alternative departure points for our story.

The term 'modern' is no longer taken for granted as a 'reality', nor is 'modernization' still a universally understood concept. Therefore, a discussion of the question of beginnings, of where and when one begins a journey back into the 'modern' past of Palestine and Israel, is no mere discussion of periodization. Any attempt at it raises complex and interrelated issues ranging from the definition of modernity to the role of national ideology in the writing of history. This introduction is not the place for an elaborate discussion of these problems, but they are too important to be pushed aside. Historiographical reconstructions are deeply affected by historians' definitions of 'modernity', 'progress' and 'nationalism', especially where the history of Asian and African societies is concerned.

While recent theoretical debates on history, modernity and nationalism have to be taken into account in any introduction to such an intricate subject as the history of Palestine and Israel, I have chosen an indirect treatment. This is to present a summary of how modern histories of either Israel or Palestine usually begin. My aim is not to show that the theoretical approach is 'wrong' or 'right', but that it exposes only part of the historical reality, albeit a significant one. Books on the region are abundant because of its high profile in the global media, but the narratives are similar due to the dominance of modernization theory in Middle Eastern studies. This introduction tries to explain why, despite extensive scholarly and popular endeavours, there is room for a new account of the region's modern history that differs from the common version.

### THE EMERGENCE OF MODERN PALESTINE – THE COMMON VERSION

In the common narrative, the historiography of Palestine begins with the incursion of Napoleon's army into Palestine and Syria at the end of the eighteenth century. But his stay was too short to be regarded as an 'influence'. The role of modernizing Palestine was kept for the Egyptian ruler Muhammad Ali, who held Palestine between 1831 and 1840. Muhammad Ali was a general in the service of the Ottoman sultan, and had worked his way up through intrigues and coalitions to become Egypt's ruler at the beginning of the nineteenth century. His ambitions stretched beyond the Nile, perhaps even to overthrowing the sultan. As part of his bid to widen his power in the area, he annexed Palestine and Syria.

It was Muhammad Ali's son Ibrahim Pasha who became Palestine's most impressive modernizer. Ruling the lands in his father's name, he introduced agricultural reforms, centralized taxation, safer roads and a constitutional system that gave fair representation to the local elite (for the first time in the history of the Ottoman Empire, the new representative bodies included Christians and Jews).[1]

The old system was restored when, with the help of the European states, the Ottoman reformers of Palestine defeated and replaced Ibrahim. The Europeans returned the status quo ante to Palestine, but enabled modernization to continue in full force. It began, according to most models suggested by modernizationists, with technology and economics. More structural reforms from Europe were implemented, first in the capital,

Istanbul, then in the principal provinces, and finally in marginal areas. The Ottoman reformers, at work from the 1830s until at least 1876, created new social and political realities in Palestine. The reforms, known as the Tanzimat, were mainly a centralizing and reorganizing effort designed to hold together an empire that threatened to disintegrate under the pressure of ambitious local rulers, embryo national movements and greedy European imperialists. In Palestine, their implementation began in the 1840s. The agents of change in Palestine were thus the reforming governors of Beirut and Damascus, the two regional capitals, which between them shared power. Other agents of modernization were the European consuls, who had been there since the late 1830s, and European merchants and bankers who began arriving in the wake of the Crimean War (1853–56). From a modernizationist point of view, this war was a catalytic event, facilitating and accelerating the process of change. The Tanzimat signified the decline of Ottoman power in Palestine and the rise of European interest in the region. The result was economic integration with Europe, and greater interference by European consuls in both local affairs and central politics.

The most important consequence of integration with Europe, from a modernizationist point of view, was the emergence of a national and secular society in Palestine. This was possible only after a fundamental change in the relationship between Palestine's Muslim majority and Christian minority. Under European pressure, exacerbated by the Ottomans' dependence on British and French aid during the Crimean War and afterwards in the face of the ongoing Russian threat, the sultans promised improvement in the status of their Christian subjects. This promise was fulfilled to some extent by the creation of a basis for the secularization of society, and coincidentally of a common base for future Arab nationalism.

At the point where nationalism emerges, the common narrative is very much in line with modernization theories, according to which nationalism is the penultimate stage in the process of becoming 'modern' and follows the importation of Western technology and military know-how and the emulation of Western administrative structures and institutions. This stage is said to appear only when a society is 'ripe' enough to be transformed conceptually with the help of Western ideology and moral political philosophy.[2] A very particular group of people facilitated Palestine's entry into this phase of perceptional transformation: American missionaries teaching in schools opened in the second half of the nineteenth century. Through these schools, the future leaders of Palestinian nationalism were introduced to nationalism, democracy and liberalism. At first only Christians were interested in this secular education, but with the admission of Muslims these schools became the private schools *par excellence* for the elite.

While Egyptian rulers, Ottoman reformers and European consuls, advisers and bankers were all bringing the message of Europe to the local elite in Palestine and Syria, there was reaction by guardians of the old ways. These 'reactionary' forces prevented the completion of the process. As with everywhere else in the Middle East, Palestine was frozen in what modernizationists call a 'transitional' period, namely between tradition and modernity. This means that only parts of the elite were modernized, and that most of the land was still 'primitive'. This would have continued were it not for the arrival of new agents of modernization in Palestine in 1882, the early Zionists. Zionism was a European phenomenon, and so, from a modernizationist point of view, its influence in Palestine was part of Westernization. Zionism acquired the power and motivation for change previously accorded colonialism.

The British Mandate after World War One consolidated European influence in Palestine, and was the last modernizing factor in the narrative of pre-1948 Palestine. It was due to its presence and policies on one hand, and Zionist plans and ambitions on the other, that the Arab community in Palestine regrouped under traditional leadership, headed by Amin al-Husayni, and became a new national Palestinian movement. In fact, at the juncture of 1918, most history books diverge and divide the region's history into two distinct parts, Palestinian and Zionist. As for the post-1948 period, I doubt whether more than a handful of books deals with the two national histories as a single subject, except in the specific context of the Arab–Israeli conflict.

The narrative thus presents a linear history of the modernization of Palestine from a primitive to a modern era. In the Zionist narrative, Zionism is part of that progress, and in the Palestinian one, Palestinian nationalism is the message and outcome of modernity. The conflict is seen almost as the inevitable, but temporary and dispensable, product of these two conflicting consequences of modernization, to be brought to an end by the completion of the modernization process.

## DECONSTRUCTING THE EMERGENCE OF MODERN PALESTINE

Modernization theory presupposes that there is a detectable moment in history, in this case 1799, when societies cease to be traditional and stop living in the past. In this view, Palestine left the past behind with the help of the West. With Europe's magic touch it was exposed to enlightenment and progress. As in other cases of Westernization, whether this exposure was a tale of success or failure has yet to be determined.

In the modernizationist view, local Palestinians, the subaltern society, are not valid subject matter for historians unless they were, or until they are, modernized. It happened that Palestine's elites succeeded in becoming Westernized, which is why the narrative of the country's modernization is more their story than a 'people's' story. The elite left behind written evidence of their world, which helped historians to reconstruct the elites' history as if it were Palestine's history. In other words, the conventional history of Palestine and Israel is one that is extrapolated from the political archive.

But the local elites are not the heroes in the drama of modernization; theirs is a secondary role. The principal players are the foreigners who facilitated the fusion between the West and Palestine. These external facilitators are referred to in the modernization literature as 'agents'. As we have seen, several agents of modernization entered Palestine after Bonaparte's brief invasion in 1799. In the eyes of the conventional historians, all these agents had one thing in common: they succeeded in transforming Palestine beyond recognition. So in their view the history of modern Palestine is both Eurocentric and highly dramatic.

It would be natural to assume, at the present stage, that Israeli historiography will subscribe to the modernizationist narrative and that Palestinian historiography will challenge it. The Israeli (and before that the Zionist) version of past events adopts and echoes what I call the 'common version'. Israel's self-image as a Western entity in the midst of an Arab wilderness, and its perception of the Palestinians as 'Other', feeds this view. But the present state of affairs is not that simple.

At first glance, the nationalist Palestinian version might be seen as an alternative to the Eurocentric, or colonialist, view. On the contrary, however, the emergence of nationalism in Palestine is an integral part of the Westernization story. A side-effect of modernization is the nationalization of local traditional societies. It is written into the story of modernization that a society will be nationalized under the influence of the Western modernizer, only to rebel against the modernizer in the name of Western ideals such as the right to independence and freedom.

Therefore we can say that the hidden hand of the national narrative has written the history of the land of Palestine/Israel or, more to the point, has produced two conflicting historical narratives that quite conveniently fall into the paradigm of modernization theory. Fortunately for the Israelis, due to their closer identification with the West, their national historiography has until recently been more respected as academic research, more loyal to the 'truth' than to ideology. Palestinian researchers were less fortunate. Without a state of their own, they lacked an appropriate academic infrastructure, and although their works adhered to the same scholarly rules as in the West, they were generally portrayed as mere propagandists. This academic evaluation has recently been reversed; a swing of the pendulum that owes as much to politics as to the transformation that has taken place in human sciences. Nevertheless, the histories of the region have until very recently been telling either a pro-Israeli or a pro-Palestinian story. The historians may have wished to be neutral and objective, but they either belonged to, or identified strongly with, one of the two parties in the conflict.

National historiographical writing, on both sides, has assumed that a history of the land is synonymous with its history of nationalism. Nationalism, as a concept, is seen as encompassing the lives of everyone in a given land; in reality, it is a story of the few not the many, of men not women, of the wealthy not the poor. In that sense, it has been much more than just taking sides. The history of either the Palestinian national movement or of Zionism has been tantamount to the history of the land of Palestine and Israel. Nationalist historiographers do not differentiate between land and nation; these are the same and become an essence at the same historical time. The nation, like the mother- or fatherland, is portrayed as an essentialist entity. Nationalist historians are not concerned with dates of birth but with dates of discoveries. The question is not when a nation was born but rather when was it reborn. As Homi Bhabha so felicitously put it: 'Nations, like narratives, lose their origins in the myths of time and only fully realize their horizons in the mind's eye'.[3] So the origins of nations and their lands can only be found in a distant or ancient past: a nationalist convenience noticed and ridiculed by Benedict Anderson.[4]

## WRITING THE HISTORY OF ONE LAND, TWO PEOPLES

Even more encompassing, in the case of Palestine and Israel, is the history of the intra-national conflict, which became the essence of the region's history, the history of Palestine and Israel. Can this history be reconstructed differently? In this book I attempt a new approach. I hope to do this without marginalizing the importance of the West, political elites, nationalism and the intra-national conflict, or ignoring the importance of some of the main changes chronicled by modernization theorists. These processes include developments such as the industrialization, urbanization, hygienization, secularization, centralization and politicization of what I call 'non-Western' societies which came in contact with the West.[5]

All these factors are included, but they are viewed more sceptically than in the past. This new approach, therefore, does not question the actual occurrence of the processes described above, but rejects the logic of the way modernizationists construct the connections between them. Against the structural and teleological pattern of change and development caused by contact with the West, an alternative view finds a fragmented and fractured process of transformation, in which local societies move with equal fervour 'back' (into the past) or 'forward' (into Europe) along the line drawn by modernization theory. Contact with a powerful 'Other' is as much a negative as a positive factor. It destabilizes and polarizes local society before nationalism tries to cement it back together. Society is transformed, and the external impact produces kaleidoscopic and modular instances of continuity and reform, unpredicted by theory and not fitting any European historical example.

This is an approach that owes much to the lessons learned from case studies in Asia and Africa in the 1960s and the 1970s. Thus, both inductively and deductively, the a priori view of Palestine's recent past is bound to be more post-structuralist than before. But before I deter the reader with the prospect of post-modernist jargon, I wish to add that this is not why I turned to the critique on modernization and nationalism. I was more interested in how a new approach introduces to the historical scene actors who were absent, or totally marginalized, in the modernizationist approach. In attempting such an approach, this book argues that the history of these actors is no less the history of the place than is the history of nationalism, of conflict, of elites, or of Westernization.

In this 'de-modernized' history, a new leading actor is the subaltern society, which refers to the groups that as a rule live outside the realm of politics and power, and are willing to rely on the state and elites in some, but not all, aspects of life. The narrative is clear; it begins with a society in Palestine as remote as possible from politics in the late Ottoman period and ends with its condition in the post-Oslo reality of the 1990s. In between, it is invaded, seduced, and moulded by elites, politics, ideology, nationalism, colonialism and Zionism. New factors, such as mass media and state education, appear with time, complicating the interaction even more.

This society makes brief appearances in books subscribing to modernization theory, where it is presented as the 'masses': pawns, passive beings to be judged by their obedience to some or other elitist policy or decision. They are accorded in this book a very different identity and pattern of behaviour. They are not one mass of people. They are grouped according to choice in small social units, usually households. But, with time, they prefer to define themselves via ethnicity, gender, occupation, class or culture. They change at will, but at times are forced to, not always to their advantage. Their world is a mix of material necessity and spiritual solace. Many of them are closely connected to the land where they live or chose to settle on. They cling to the land or to their property not from a national imperative to protect the mother/fatherland, the entity, but for much more mundane and at the same time humane reasons.

These local actors are leaders as well as ordinary members of the community. They are Palestine's women and children, peasants and workers, town dwellers and farmers. They are defined according to their religious or ethnic origins as Armenians, Druzes, Circassians, or Mizrahi and Ashkenazi Jews, as well as to their views on religion, whether secular, orthodox or fundamentalist. In writing about them, definitions call for a balance between their own claims and the author's understanding of what groups them together. Feeding a family, staying on the family land or attempting to make a new life on foreign soil can be portrayed as patriotism or nationalism: for most people it is an existentialist and survivalist act.

The second new actor is the past in its garb of tradition and religion. As conventional modern history has it, the past is an obstacle to the progress brought by the West to Palestine. Its presence is the best explanation of why parts of Palestine and of Israel have not completed the process of modernization. This negative intrusive past is widely present in Palestine or among the Palestinians, but less so in Israel. In Israel, it is a feature of life among Jews from Arab countries but not from Western countries. It is a stronger factor among women than among men, among peasants than among land owners, and among workers than among employers. In the conventional view, the history of modern Palestine and Israel is the history of the disappearance of this past from all disadvantaged groups waiting to realise a better future. Pessimists such as the late Elie Kedourie believed that for many that future was unattainable; optimists such as the late Albert Hourani asserted it was just a matter of time. But a whole generation of historians of Palestine and Israel assumed that the past, represented by tradition, religion and customs, had to disappear in order to give way to the emergence of a modern, developed Palestine or Israel.

In this work, I wish to reintroduce the past, and show that it was and still is a vital factor in the lives of the people of Israel and Palestine. The past is not always regressive, as the present is not always progressive. In

Palestine, as elsewhere in the Middle East, the past contained egalitarian patterns of behaviour that were lost in the present. Similarly, the encounter with the West did not always improve women's status or invariably reduce clan power. Rather, the past proved adaptive and resilient, with the basic relationships within society remaining what they had been, despite dramatic political changes brought by colonialism, Zionism and later by Palestinian nationalism.

That is why, in this history of Palestine and Israel, secularization is not described as an inevitable consequence of encounter with the West. Religion is presented here as elastic: adapting successfully to a changing technological and even political world. Tradition appears not as the last obstacle to becoming 'modern', but as a defensive and adaptive mechanism of those who found themselves caught within the turmoil of a changing reality. Religion and tradition became – remained – formidable forces affecting politics, society and culture.

When the past plays such a role, it also affects our understanding of change. Change in this book is not linear, and definitely not harmonious. At times, the meeting with the West strengthened traditional modes of behaviour, and broke them at others. For some, change was fast, for others moderate, and for the rest barely existent. Perhaps even 'change', but definitely 'continuity', are terms we ought to rethink. The post-colonialist critique and subaltern studies, which seek alternative ways of reconstructing the past of the colonized and the natives, have already suggested a reappraisal. They abhor the description 'pawns of the past' and do not view Westernization as inevitable or positive. They look for a new way of describing the local actors in the history of Asia and Africa as human beings who, cautiously and painfully, carved a path in a world that had been theirs before its invasion by others.

In national historiographies, the past is generally romanticized. The past that nationalism tries to bring back into the story is a distant and magnificent past, reinvented by national movements as the cradle or dawn of their existence to claim a hold over the present. I have tried to dissociate myself from that kind of historical reconstruction, first by giving the area a bi-national name, and second by not referring to an obscure, splendid past. The 'ancient' past, so important for national movements, seems to me irrelevant to most of the people. I would rather begin with the more recent, relevant, 'ordinary' human past, not the version favoured by either the Palestinian or Israeli histories. Nor is the nation described here as it would be in a nationalist chronicle, as something eternal. It is a human invention, which appeared relatively recently to serve particular purposes and benefited some but destroyed others. Above all, it was never the essence of life that it pretended, and still pretends, to be. Life is determined by physical factors, such as climate, the locust, economics and tradition, no less than by nationalism.

Most of the histories of Palestine and Israel are histories of the conflict. But life in Palestine and Israel is not determined by conflict alone. In this book, in treating Israel and Palestine as one subject, I have to include an analysis of the conflict, but by offering one history I also refuse to view the conflict as the essence of life in the land of Palestine. I understand that the sub-title of the book may raise a few eyebrows. But readers familiar with the region will agree that the people living there use the two names with the same conviction and emotion. The history I am presenting is that of one land which became Israel and Palestine, and my task is to examine the implications for the people of this land with two names.

Naming the land was a political act in Ottoman Palestine at the end of the nineteenth century. Before that, there had been no dispute over a name, and whatever the land was called by its rulers, inhabitants or visitors was apparently accepted as one option of many used for religious or administrative purposes. What the land was called did not play an important role in the lives of those who lived there.[6] It was only with the arrival of Zionism and European colonialism on one hand, and the emergence of Palestinian nationalism on the other, that the name assumed importance and meaning. Instead of merely describing an area, the name came to represent a claim over it. And so, from the end of the nineteenth century, different groups of people at different historical junctures, when they had the will and the power to do so, named the land in a forceful act aimed at creating a new reality. Such is the power of nationalism. By 'bi-nationalizing' the history and even 'de-nationalizing it', I hope in this book to loosen the firm grip of nationalism on historiography.

Furthermore, titles or names of places are not the only components of a nationalist historiography. As an author living in the region, I am only too well aware of the difficulty of reconstructing history outside one's own national ethos and myths. While one may wish to write a detached and neutral history, one's own sympathies and affiliations remain. The reader of this book will find instances and descriptions that fit many of the claims of one national narrative, the Palestinian one, but fewer of the Israeli one. This is not because the writer is a Palestinian: I am not. My bias is apparent despite the desire of my peers that I stick to facts and the 'truth' when reconstructing past realities. I view any such construction as vain and presumptuous. This book is written by one who admits compassion for the colonized not the colonizer; who sympathizes with the occupied not the occupiers; and sides with the workers not the bosses. He feels for women in distress, and has little admiration for men in command. He cannot remain indifferent towards mistreated children, or refrain from condemning their elders. In short, mine is a subjective approach, often but not always standing for the defeated over the victorious. At most historical junctures of this history, the Palestinians were in the inferior position, and the Zionists and later the Israelis had the upper hand. This book is not a national Palestinian historiography, but it tries to show, at most junctures, the force, destruction, coercion, abuse and other means of power used by Palestinians on Palestinians, by Israelis on Israelis, or jointly by Palestinians and Israelis on other Palestinians and Israelis. As mentioned, this book assumes that national identity was and is only one of many factors determining the interrelations between the people of the land. It sees national identity as reductionist, as ignorant of factors, such as social status, gender, political situation and distribution of economic and technological means, that have affected human life in Palestine and Israel. Therefore, the past appears in this story also as a coercive tool employed by national movements to manipulate people. As such it is in the hands of a few who want their own selfish actions made to look as though they were done only for the benefit of the coerced.[7]

To sum up, I suggest that the history of modern Palestine/Israel should be a history of both its subaltern society and its elite groups; of those wishing to change and those happy with what they have; and of external as well as internal dynamics of change. This history seeks to combine the narratives of the exploiters with those of the exploited, the invaders with the invaded, and the oppressors with the oppressed. Its subject matter is the people of Palestine and Israel, and their departure points from known patterns of life; departure points collectively referred to as the beginning of the modern history of the land of Palestine and Israel. This means that I cannot choose one specific departure point. Indeed, the second chapter of this book proposes several beginnings, which represent significant changes in the lives of people brought about by formidable processes such as disintegrating empires, nationalism, colonialism, capitalism. Rather than overshadow one another, these different beginnings illuminate the possibilities open to historical research as well as the arbitrary hand given to the historian as an expositor of a land's history. As each of these beginnings represents a group of people, the book tries to remain faithful to their chronicles by steering away from a history that turns into a case study of either modernization or nationalism.

However, as we move to the British Mandate period and the post-1948 era, we find that politics and nationalism are allowed to become what they cannot truly be – the essence of life. This was particularly true for the period 1948–1967. Politics invaded every echelon of society, hunting down those who wished to ignore it, and capturing even the free spirits of poets and novelists who were now recruited to nationalism, the ideology of the day.

Moving on from 1948, the book focuses on how the different groups constituting society in Israel and Palestine reacted to high politics. Each event initiated or produced by the elites, be it a war or a peace agreement, is described and examined against the claim usually made for it as being an encompassing human event. We will see that wars did not affect everyone, nor was their impact on everyone the same. Peace agreements fared much the same. It was the economic and social policies that were often crucial to the lives of those inhabiting the land. The ideological tide ebbs only towards the end, with the emergence of 'mini-societies' throughout the land of Israel/Palestine that challenged nationalism in the name of ethnicity, gender and human rights, only to be cruelly washed away again, at the end of 2000, by politics and national ideology.

# CHAPTER I

# Fin de Siècle (1856–1900): Social Tranquillity and Political Drama

## THE RURAL LANDSCAPE AND ITS PEOPLE

On the eve of the Crimean War, about half a million people lived in the land of Palestine.[1] They were Arabic-speaking. Most were Muslims, but about 60,000 were Christians of various denominations, and around 20,000 were Jews. In addition, they had to tolerate the presence of 50,000 Ottoman soldiers and officials as well as 10,000 Europeans. Their administrative life revolved around the *sanjaq*, the Ottoman sub-province, of which Ottoman Palestine had three: Nablus, Acre and Jerusalem. To some extent these administrative divisions corresponded to the topography. Palestine had four hilly regions: the Jerusalem mountains, the Nablus mountains, and two other areas: Hebron in the Jerusalem district, and Galilee in the Acre sub-province. Each geographical and administrative area had a major town as its capital, so that some of Palestine's most famous cities were foci of social and cultural life. Acre, Jerusalem, Hebron and Nablus were among these important towns, as were the smaller coastal towns of Haifa, Jaffa and Gaza.

Outside the official activities of the *sanjaq*, people lived an autonomous, pastoral life, with relative homogeneity of style and purpose. About 400,000 people inhabited the rural areas in small villages scattered mainly on the slopes of the mountains or at the entrances to the small valleys between them.[2] Visitors were rare, although not unheard of. Intruders and thieves were also infrequent, but that they were an integral part of life was recognized by the authorities, who allowed the village men to possess arms. Not unexpectedly, these weapons were sometimes used against greedy tax collectors or uninvited Ottoman soldiers.

Life revolved around the family, and each family's affairs were governed by its clan (*hamula*). These varied in size, and some were divided into sub-clans. A clan could extend over one or two villages, while a single village could contain several clans. The clan determined the way of life unless outside forces intervened. The most impressive feature of communal life was the musha' system, a voluntary method of cultivation based on the rotation of collectively owned plots of land among villagers, so that all would in turn have the benefit of the more fertile parcels.[3]

Each Ottoman administrative sub-unit (*nahiya*) consisted of several villages. Each sub-unit was controlled by a sheikh, the head of the strongest clan. Although a kind of semi-feudal baron, a sheikh belonged to the poorest socio-economic stratum in the land. First among equals, he represented his own clan and others before the authorities, and disseminated to his people the policies from above.[4] Unlike the urban notables, these destitute leaders were often in a precarious position. They were judged according to their capabilities as tax collectors, but no less important was their ability to reconcile conflicting clans and clamp down on blood feuds. The problem was that, while it was in their interest to prevent local conflicts, such conflicts served the interests of the urban notables or official clerks who either owned the villages or were responsible for them administratively. However, many of the sheikhs fulfilled their role successfully. One of the best known, even notorious, was Mustafa Abu Gosh. Based in a village overlooking the Jaffa–Jerusalem road, he remained powerful despite urban intrigues against him and the authorities' dislike. By the end of the nineteenth century, however, most of the rural leaders had fallen prey to centralization efforts directed by the reformers in Istanbul.

In rural Palestine, good harvests and successful agricultural ventures signified happiness. Cotton was grown on the western plains and their higher elevations, but most of the terraced hills of central Palestine were planted with olive trees, suited to the climate and the soil. In the valleys, wheat, corn, barley and sesame were grown.

The least agreeable aspect of life was poor health, often the result of inadequate housing.[5] The traditional dwellings, although suited to the climate, did not always provide protection. Poor construction made houses cold in winter. In summer, people spent hot nights on rooftops, but their sleeping quarters attracted vermin. Traditional customs and practices also encouraged poor health. Marriage within the family or the clan was a widespread traditional custom among both Muslims and Christians. This increased the prevalence of hereditary diseases, still common well into the 1970s in rural Palestinian areas.

Life and death were more strongly determined by health and nature than by economics and politics. Poor health meant a high death rate, among children and adults alike. Against that, religion and tradition were the prime defence mechanisms. The terms 'religion' and 'tradition' are misleading here. Some of these 'defence mechanisms' were ancient spiritual practices that had little to do with the religious traditions accepted by the Islamic, Christian or Jewish clergies. The spiritual world, the religious network and the customs of habitation thus provided the basis for the cycle of life in Palestine.[6] The strong belief in the supernatural served as a buffer against the diseases and plagues that broke out at intervals, and even against the follies of one's neighbours: casting the 'evil eye' was a common practice.

The accepted date for the emergence of a modernized Palestine has little relevance to some aspects of the history of society and culture. The metaphysical world was firmly connected to what Clifford Geertz called the 'popular interpretation' of religion, an interpretation usually at variance with that provided by the religious authorities.[7] In late Ottoman Palestine, as throughout the region's history, popular interpretations of the three monotheistic religions survived and still survive today despite all attempts by their custodians to crush them. In late Ottoman Palestine, while the peasants followed a cult of traditional religious customs in which spiritualism played an important role, the establishment was involved in intellectual exercises aimed at adapting religion to a developing reality. Other senior clerics worked in the opposite direction, adapting reality to a fundamental and inflexible interpretation of religious texts.[8]

While the role of established religion in providing solace and guidance should not be underrated, it was more a regulating force than an interpreting entity. But the society was not a passive player in this interaction. Recent research on Palestine in the period when the country became 'modern' has revealed that the areas in which the religious elite communicated with the population, such as the shari'a (religious law) court, were interactive and dynamic. Not only did the population receive religious rulings (fatwas) from the muftis, the clerical authorities on the law, they also engaged in dialogue with them on how to interpret the holy scriptures.[9]

This interaction is also informative about the affairs of non-Muslims and women. For example, Jews and Christians preferred to seek rulings on land and estate disputes in Muslim courts if they found their own structures inadequate.[10] But it is mainly in relation to women that we see how wrong the conventional histories can be, especially in depicting their lives as passive. Recent monographs have introduced case studies in which women took bold stances in court, demanding the right to have some say in choosing a husband or on their share in inheritance disputes.[11]

Taking women as a subject for research, one can see how continuity and change are not easy terms to grapple with. It is most difficult to see dramatic changes in the lives of rural women in Palestine, although, to be fair, we know very little about them before the seventeenth century. Women were only registered in the population during the Tanzimat reforms, around the 1870s. From that time onwards, the register was detailed enough to enable demographic historians to assess the number of men, women and children in a given period in the land of Palestine.[12]

However, the quantified research does not dramatically challenge what can be learned from graphic representations and travellers' accounts. Rural women were subject to a patriarchal regime that affected their lives in matters of marriage, divorce and inheritance, usually to their disadvantage. European painters, admittedly not always accurate conveyers of reality, drew images of peasant women in Palestine lagging at some distance behind their husbands, carrying on their heads the heaviest loads on the way to the local market, and sometimes with the added burden of babies tied to their backs.

The gender-based distribution of labour in rural Palestine was quite common in the Middle East at the time, with the men working in the fields and the women in the home. Much depended on the type of agriculture. Where wheat was grown, women worked in the fields weeding and gathering the sheaves. Where corn was grown, the men's work ended only when the corn was finally stored in the house. Generally speaking, there was differentiation in income within the villages, which affected the status of women. Ethnographers noted that the very poor women went to the fields to glean. They could be seen, after the harvest was gathered, carrying home on their heads pitifully small sheaves. In more fortunate families, women and men worked jointly when growing wheat or barley. The men did the work on the threshing floor itself, while the women selected lengths of straw. The straw was woven into large trays, called tabaka, for carrying heavy loads. The straw was dyed with various colours, a lengthy business that kept the women busy until sunset.

In the villages, and to some extent among the lower classes in the towns, Muslim women went unveiled, until the exposure of these villages to frequent foreign visitors. Among the better classes, however, veiling was the general rule, but exceptions became more frequent as the incorporation of Palestine into the world economy proceeded. In the matter of veiling, a longstanding custom but not a law, Palestine lagged behind Syria and Egypt, according to some observers at the time.

Wives of rural chieftains are hardly mentioned in scholarly research on Palestine, so we can only speculate that their position was, at least officially, little different from that of their peasant sisters. They may, however, judging from accounts by European women who had access to the female sanctuaries, have had some behind-the-scenes influence on their husbands' activities.[13]

## URBAN PALESTINE AND ITS SOCIETY

Throughout the Ottoman period, Palestine's rural life was closely interconnected with that of the urban centres. Surplus agricultural produce was bartered in the towns as part of that lifeline. This interconnection was later interrupted, and eventually destroyed, by the integration of the Palestine economy into the world economy.

The towns were also well linked to the life of the nomadic people, the Bedouins, who roamed the western and southern areas. They were the nucleus of the trading infrastructure connecting the towns with the villages and the outside world. The Bedouins supplied the raw materials and were the main customers, apart from the villagers, of the products manufactured in the towns.[14] This arrangement remained intact until modernizationist zeal forced permanent settlement on the Bedouins. A case study exists that shows this reciprocity in detail. Over a long time, the Bedouin Bani Shakr tribe supplied raw material to the soap industry in Nablus in return for commodities. The study on Nablus teaches us also that, around 1700, the barter economy was intensified and even assumed a new aspect, when commodities, as well as land, were treated as though privately owned, thus creating an economic model that could easily be called modern long before the arrival of Europeans. European influence only accelerated these processes; it did not invent them.

Economic change was also an influential factor for women in Palestine. While integration with the European economy settled the Bedouin and ended their barter relationship with the towns, it also exposed the towns to the market forces of supply and demand. The opening up of the market dramatically decreased the authority of public officials responsible for regulating urban economies, which in turn affected women's status and well-being. One example was the decline in the authority of the local judge (*qadi*). They were the only town officials that the Ottomans appointed from abroad. In the second half of the nineteenth century, these judges were stopped from intervening, as they had done for centuries, in the city's prices, which included dowries. In the absence of regulation, fathers demanded higher dowries. But the higher price had the effect of postponing marriage, which many would see as an improvement in the status of women.

Life in urban Palestine, and not just the economy, was affected by history. Some of Palestine's towns, such as Jerusalem and Hebron, had a long and ancient history, while others, such as Haifa, were newer. History mattered because it was a factor in the life of the *a'ayan*, Palestine's urban nobility. An elite family had a genealogy stretching back to the days of early Islam, with such a family tree more likely to be found in the old towns. The Muslim elite consisted of families that owed their position both to such ancient familial connections, and also to the good relationship they maintained with the ruling powers.[15] Before the Ottoman reforms, these families conducted a political life described by the late Albert Hourani as the 'politics of notables'.[16] This term explains the success of certain families in the Arab world in maintaining their position as the urban social elite. Nobility was gained by the double legitimacy granted to these families by their own society and the central authority in Istanbul. Their high standing led the Ottomans, who had avoided direct rule as much as possible, to entrust these notables with important positions within the provinces. This required negotiation and balancing skills, which became the essence of the 'politics of notables'. During the Ottoman period, their tactics formed the ethical and political code of urban society in the Arab world, and remained so during the years leading to the emergence of local nationalism and eventually of independence. The key to the notables' success was moderation, a virtue that safeguarded their high rank throughout the political dramas of the eighteenth and nineteenth centuries, a time when the area became an arena for colonialist competition and when insurgent local rulers tried to implement their dreams of independence and sovereignty.

As in the rural areas, urban society was governed by religion as well as by history. The difference was that cities and towns were more influenced by state religion, which, in the Ottoman Empire, was a bureaucratic tool for ensuring loyalty to the state rather than to God. It was thus less prescriptive in fundamental issues of belief but more in performance of the religious duties to the house of the Ottomans.[17] This may also help to explain the change in the status of urban women that occurred as early as the latter part of the nineteenth century. European travellers reported anecdotes demonstrating the erosion of the patriarchal structure in urban Palestine. Travellers recorded that girls were asked about their choices in marriage, and that courtship was quite common.[18] This practice persisted throughout the late Ottoman and British Mandate periods. Negotiations between the families of bride and groom were lengthy and complicated, involving dowries and legal agreements, and the bride certainly had a say in them. It also appears that, in the towns, there was a privileged group of women belonging to the notables. They moved about more freely and had a say in the marriages and education of their children. Marriages were an important means of strengthening political coalitions between notable families, so for women to have influence in the matter of marriages indicated political status as well.

Thus social status, custom and tradition, the ecological unit and, one suspects, the personalities of individual patriarchs, determined the welfare of women more than their affiliation to Judaism, Islam or Christianity. This was true of elite life in the urban centres in general, where the culture of Christians and Jews was like that of Muslims: determined not just by religious affiliation, but by geographical and social location. The elites of all religious groups were still part of an Arab Ottoman society, with proximity to the corridors of power determining how 'Ottoman' one became. Each ecological unit – tribe, village and town – expressed individually a mixture of Arabism and Ottomanism in its language, customs and way of life. For example, as far as we can tell, people generally conversed in Arabic, while all official correspondence was in Ottoman Turkish.

## A SOCIETY WITHOUT POLITICS

During this period, politics hardly touched the lives of the overwhelming majority of the people. Outside the economic sphere, local populations were clear in their wish to avoid upheaval in their lives. At certain times in the eighteenth and nineteenth centuries, popular revolts and uprisings occurred sporadically, and seem to contradict our assumption of a pastoral and stable Palestine. But these uprisings were not so much a call for change as a protest against it.

Some uprisings have been appropriated as national history. One was the famous 1834 revolt against Egyptian rule in Palestine (an occupation that began in 1831 and ended in 1840). This revolt, like its predecessors, was the peasants' way of protesting against excessive taxation, compulsory military conscription, and excessive central intervention in their affairs manifested in a demand that they surrender their arms to the authorities. The peasants had resisted before, and felt that they had the ability to overcome the abusive and coercive power of particularly callous and inhumane Ottoman governors and the local households in their service. In an unusual sequence of events, the rebels would first be punished and then the ruthless governor or tax collector removed from his post. As a recent book on Ottoman Syria has shown, the inability of the Ottomans in the eighteenth and nineteenth centuries to administer vast and complex territories properly led to the pursuit of a coercion policy.[19] In Syria and Lebanon particularly, less so in Palestine, Ottoman power was based on clannish dynasties that used their power to oppress the local peasants. In 1834, although the Egyptian rulers replaced these clans with other clans, the mode of reaction to oppression and abuse remained the same, and the desire for improvement remained the motivating force behind uprisings.

The new Egyptian policies were an unwelcome change for the Palestinian population, which had been largely left alone by the Ottomans. The urban and rural notables of Palestine had been especially autonomous, but were being harassed by the Egyptian rulers who demanded money, weapons and, worst of all, wanted to recruit their children into the Egyptian army. The 1834 uprising was a rare moment of elite and popular solidarity, which led the authors of one book to define it as not only a national rebellion, but even as the birth of Palestinian nationalism. It seems to me that the revolt actually signified a wish to become Ottoman again, rather than independent.[20] Similar dramatic collective urges for fundamental change, if indeed this is what this event was about, were not recorded until the British Mandate period.

### GLOBALIZATION OF THE LOCAL ECONOMY

During this time, no political force emerged in the rural areas to spur the peasants to change their familiar way of life. However, there was a slow move towards change, caused first by the transformation of local economies into more private modes of production and trade, and second by the hesitant integration of Palestine into the European economy, a process much desired by both European capitalists and Ottoman reformists. This latter process hung like a shadow over the clear skies of rural Palestine. 'Process' is an enigmatic term, easily chartable on a diagram but more difficult to see in daily life. Although foreigners were behind the 'processes', personalities more familiar to the population of Palestine, the Ottoman rulers, also took part.

The obscure nature of the term 'process' explains why, unlike the conventional version of the 'emergence of modern Palestine', we do not have a clear date for the beginning of modern life in the region. Change occurred where the urge to transform the way of life existed. Whenever and wherever such development occurred, it could be called the beginning of a new phase in the life of Palestine in the modern era. The first group seeking change came from the outside; the second belonged to the local elite.

The urge of European forces to enter Palestine or to join it to the European economy began in earnest after the Crimean War ended in 1856. The Berlin Congress that ended the war opened the Middle Eastern provinces of the Ottoman Empire to European investment and profiteering. From that date, foreigners were permitted to buy land and property, and pilgrimage societies became flourishing real estate and banking businesses. Foreign bankers, merchants and other agents of economic transformation followed the flow of capital to Palestine, seeking easy profits. The new economic order that began to take shape had a two-fold impact on the social structure of Palestine. It redefined the country as a geo-political unit, and changed its modes and means of production.[21]

The external pressure corresponded with a natural wish to improve standards of living by relatively wealthy families, successful members of the urban elite already involved in the money trade. In several places in Palestine, traders, land owners and notables attempted continually to enrich themselves, and every now and then the existing equilibrium, between city and village, rich and poor, consumers and producers, shifted. Until 1856, however, these moves had taken place within a known social system where the codes were recognizable and the underlying balance of power was maintained. The first to override these codes and take heed of the European challenge were the merchants of Palestine, who were mostly Christians with a few Jews. The awakening of this hitherto dormant sector of the population was manifested not by an embarrassment of riches but rather in an increase in their numbers. Among them, the Greek Orthodox community of Jerusalem was the first to adopt a European lifestyle, which led to a lower mortality rate and higher birth rate in the urban centres.[22]

The Greek Orthodox not only adopted a new way of living; they developed a different Weltanschauung, shaped by the commercialization of the local economy. It was an outlook in which money and finance came uppermost, and it was in joining this that the Muslim nobility procrastinated. Society needed bankers, but they could not be Muslims given the prohibition in the shari'a against making a profit through interest on loans. Foreign trade increased the need for finance and credit, so peasants and traders alike turned to those who were allowed by tradition and trusted by the Europeans to run a local banking system. In quick succession, branches of foreign banks opened, run by local Christians mostly from the Greek Orthodox community or by foreigners. In a short time, the Greek Orthodox community became a pillar of the economic elite in Palestine, a position which enabled it to influence politics with relative ease once less religious and more ethnic variants of secular nationalism had emerged. To this day, the Greek Orthodox community plays a pre-eminent role in Palestinian politics, not only in Israel and Palestine but also in the Palestinian diaspora.[23]

Christian merchants, Jewish entrepreneurs and small industrialists from Greece and Lebanon began a period of economic prosperity that was accompanied by a greater sense of security and at times condescending self-confidence towards the Muslim 'Other'. Elsewhere in the empire, the newly gained Christian and Jewish self-assurance provoked the anger of dissatisfied Muslim leaders and a large number of less fortunate city dwellers. In Damascus this anger turned into a wave of violence that swept through the city's Christian quarters in 1860. In Jerusalem and the rest of Palestine, however, it never went beyond random infrequent attacks on individuals.

It was in the towns more than in the countryside that the revolution in the life of Palestine could be sensed. In both new and old urban centres, the population grew steadily, and a minor process of urbanization can be detected in those years. Some of these changes, however, were hardly visible at the time; only with hindsight can we detect their potential to threaten or damage the social life of Palestine. The majority of the population had to integrate itself into a larger economic system by adjusting to the different laws of land ownership, taxation and subsistence instigated by this process. The chronology of change and the formation of a new reality differ greatly from the conventional narrative outlined in the introduction to this book.

The impetus for change existed before the integration of the local economy into the global one, which is why it is so difficult to assess or analyse the external force. Before the Crimean War, the balance of power between urban notables, merchants, rural chieftains, peasants and Bedouins shifted several times. From the beginning of the eighteenth century, the merchants took a larger share of the profits from agricultural produce, and were not content with merchandizing alone. The notables did the same, while the rural chieftains lost some of their control over the peasant economy. The opportunity to become rich was connected to changes in taxation policies, which led to a redivision of the surplus produce in pre-globalization Palestine. What made this transformation different from the later European-sponsored one is that it did not involve immigration, the uprooting of peasants, or a cessation of commercial ties with the Bedouins. The advent of European financial and commercial interests caused much more damaging consequences in the long run, such as internal migration, loss of land, and the breaking up of traditional social structures. It did of course benefit some, mainly traders and notables, but not the majority.

## THE POLITICAL ECONOMY OF 'MODERN PALESTINE' IN THE 1880S

The first results of the interaction with outside forces were apparent less than thirty years after the Crimean War. In the 1880s, the economy of Palestine became irreversibly dependent on and connected to the world economy. Exports to and imports from Europe increased dramatically as large ships, including steamers, arrived with products manufactured in industrialized Britain and France, and left again with raw materials, most of which originated outside Palestine but had to pass through there. Palestine became a clearly defined station on the world economic map, subject neither to Beirut nor Cairo. More importantly, Palestine provided convenient access to the markets of Lebanon, Syria and Egypt. It was no longer simply biblical Palestine.

Modern Palestine began in the rural areas when the market became a source in itself, and not just a transitory exchange mechanism. The change was obvious where it mattered most for the majority of Palestinians: the cultivated field. Palestinian agriculture began bowing to powerful external market forces. Local agriculture was now locked on marketing, which meant that subsistence crops gave way to cash crops. However, agriculture that concentrated on one marketable crop undermined its peasants' self-sufficiency, which was guaranteed by growing a variety of crops. The peasants of Palestine paid a high price for economic globalization.

Ottoman reforms and global economic processes also worked jointly to transform the means of production. The Ottoman land law of 1858 had, among other things, banned the musha' system. This form of cultivation, however, persisted in spite of the Ottomans, to be finally abolished during the mandate by the British, who saw it only as a primitive form of agriculture. As a result, life became unsustainable for poorer peasants totally dependent on their land.

The Ottoman land reforms had one dramatic and damaging effect on the musha' system. They produced the first ever pockets of hired labour in Palestine. Whereas, in the past, land had been leased from the state against services to the sultan, such as taxes, the reforms allowed anyone to become a small-property owner, not only in the countryside but also in towns, provided they paid the increased taxes. Private ownership became a new and expensive privilege, forcing small land owners and shopkeepers in the city to sell their ownership rights to the big land owners and rich urban families. The peasants could not pay the higher taxes, and surrendered the land to those who could.

Rural Palestine became more accessible to private ownership, and those who could profit from this accessibility had no use for subsistence agriculture. They wanted cash crops that could be translated into wealth in the form of raw materials for the European market. Peasants had not owned the land before, so this was not what was different. However, they had had, in normal times, access to plots of land that for most of the year provided minimal subsistence, particularly where the musha' system was in place.

Steady, but not dramatic, population growth also acted as a push factor from the villages. Economics, trade, late marriages and better health conditions all contributed to Ottoman Palestine's increasing population, which almost doubled from 350,000 in the 1870s to an estimated 660,000 in 1914.[24] From today's perspective, this may strike us as unimpressive; even by 1947, Palestine's population was no larger than an average American city today, i.e. almost two million. But if we consider that the world population explosion only began after the First World War (in fact after 1920), Palestine's demographic transformation was remarkable.

The peasants were not just moving away from known modes of production or losing their traditional means of production; they were abandoning a way of life, a set of beliefs that had helped them make sense of their lives, but without a blueprint for the future. It was in these circumstances that nationalism became an attractive option, particularly the brand that had its roots in a spiritual or religious interpretation of reality. The gap left by the end of an old social system still exists in today's Israel and Palestine, as does the attraction of spiritualism.

## INVADING CIVIL SOCIETY: THE MAKING OF THE MODERN OTTOMAN STATE (1876–1900)

Lest the impression be given that the whole rural life of Palestine was changing, I should say here that the process seems not to have affected all of the peasants, and also that it was slow. In terms of the rhythm and pace of life, there was little change in rural Palestine before the 1930s. Life in rural Palestine continued to be measured by death, rites of passage, and religious festivals.

The first disruption to this rhythm occurred when the Ottomans sought the construction of a centralized state on a French model. Not content with economic transformation alone, they wanted to rule in a more 'modern'

(European, i.e. French) way. The French model meant at least a desire, if not the ability, to infiltrate the autonomous rural parts of Palestine, and to restrict the sphere of operations of the urban notables. From their return to Palestine as rulers in 1840, the Ottomans engaged in reorganizing the region, perhaps less from an urge for change as from a wish to control the two powerful administrative centres of Beirut and Damascus, which between them ruled Palestine. The new policy was finally formulated in the late 1860s, and amounted to the limitation of Damascus's unchallenged dominance in Palestine by allowing Beirut to share administrative control of the region. The sub-provinces of Nablus (which included the towns of Nazareth and Safad) and Acre (which included the town of Haifa) were annexed to the newly created province of Syda, of which Beirut became the capital. Damascus continued to enjoy influence in the sub-province of Jerusalem (which included the towns of Jaffa, Beersheba, Hebron and Gaza), but had to tolerate the rising power of Beirut.

The reorganization of the geo-political map is a formative act preceding the creation of a modern state. This was true for almost every state created in the Middle East, but seems not to have occurred in Palestine, unless we regard the creation of the state of Israel as a natural progression from Ottoman policy. Incidentally, this view of Israel as Palestine's successor is accepted by Zionist historiography, but totally rejected by the Palestinian view. The Ottoman reformist trend in Palestine reached its peak in 1872, when Istanbul made a final attempt to redefine Palestine and turn it into a more cohesive geographical unit. One historian at least has suggested that this had a significant impact on the formation of modern Palestine, proposing yet another possible starting point for the history of modern Palestine: the creation of the independent *sanjaq* of Jerusalem.[25] This was an outcome of the 1864 *vilayet* (provinces) law, which reorganized the division of the empire, turning sub-districts into independent districts, and placing them directly under Istanbul's authority. For Jerusalem, this meant, at least officially, that it would no longer be under the direct rule of a powerful regional centre such as Damascus or Beirut. This was part of a general move to restrict the power of these two administrative centres. The elevation of Jerusalem's status was also meant to turn it into a buffer zone against two secessionist rulers in the south: the Wahhabiyya in the Arabian Peninsula and the house of Muhammad Ali in Egypt.

These regional policies had a limited impact on the local population. In essence, it meant that all their dealings with the authorities were now conducted within the administrative and economic borders of the sub-province of Jerusalem. A Jerusalem resident gradually ceased to be a Shami

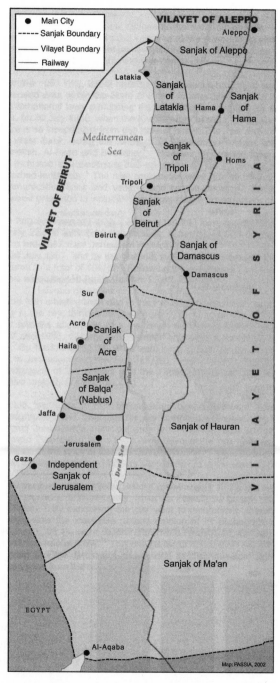

Map 1. Administrative boundaries under the Ottomans

(Damascene) and became a Qudsi, a subject of the *sanjaq* of al-Quds (Jerusalem).

The new *sanjaq* of Jerusalem included the sub-districts of Jaffa, Hebron, Gaza and Beersheba, together with thirty-seven villages and the living areas of five Bedouin tribes. The notables and heads of the local religious and ethnic communities were represented in a council supervising the financial concerns of the *sanjaq*. While this was no more than a rubber stamp of the governor's decisions, it meant at least that the new municipality of Jerusalem was a much more effective and energetic body. The municipality eventually contributed significantly to the transformation of the city's social, architectural, and sanitary aspects. The Jerusalem municipality, by the way, was only the second to be created in the empire after Istanbul.

For a brief moment, the reformers in Istanbul toyed with the possibility of adding the sub-provinces of Nablus and Acre to Jerusalem. Had they done this, they would have created a geographical unit in which, as happened in Egypt, a particular nationalism might have arisen. However, even with its administrative division into north (ruled by Beirut) and south (ruled by Jerusalem), Palestine as a whole was raised above its previous peripheral status. The north and the south would become one unit in 1918 with the onset of British rule. In a similar way and in the same year the British established the basis for modern Iraq when they fused the three Ottoman provinces of Mosul, Baghdad and Basra into the state of Iraq. In Palestine, unlike in Iraq, familial connections and geographical boundaries (the River Litani in the north, the river Jordan in the east, the Mediterranean in the west) worked together to weld the three sub-provinces of South Beirut, Nablus and Jerusalem into one social and cultural unit. This geo-political space had its own major dialect and its own customs, folklore and traditions.

These similarities had all along been recognized by the people themselves, which is why the people of Nablus had made every effort to remain connected to Jerusalem. When Nablus was officially annexed in 1858 to the province of Beirut, a protest movement arose, so massive that it turned into a blood-bath in which, according to the British consul in Jerusalem, 3,000 people were killed. (He was, however, known to exaggerate, so the number could have been much lower.)

In this way, Ottoman reformist zeal directly affected the lives of some of the people, and they reacted, as in the case of the Jerusalem municipality and the loss of Nablus from the Jerusalem *sanjaq*. In Palestinian history books, these two events are presented as the early buds of nationalism. But it was hardly a crisis that penetrated deeply into the lives of the majority, and villagers were still left to themselves, even if the reforms brought with them a new system of direct taxation, more strict registration and more frequent visits by administrators.

The new pattern of intervention by the state in rural life also included some benefits for the general population. The Ottomans, and later with greater success the Zionists, contributed to the struggle against some of the epidemics by draining the swamps that were havens for mosquitoes. Thus they achieved particular success in their fight against malaria, a disease feared in all Palestine and which European travellers called the 'Jerusalem fever'. Nevertheless, improvements were slow; the population grew faster than the availability of modern medicine imported from Europe and Istanbul.

## END OF AN ERA: RURAL CHIEFTAINS AND THE *A'AYAN*

In the 1840s, the sheikhs, the rural chieftains who had run people's lives for centuries, were engaged in a battle for power with the urban elite. The balance of power finally shifted to the elite in a division of loyalties triggered by the Ottoman reforms. In Palestine, it was mainly the centralizing aspect of these reforms that led to the demise of the sheikhs, who fell prey to the government's drive for direct political and economic rule. As the sheikhs fought back, the most famous of them, Mustafa Abu Gosh of the Jerusalem mountains, invoked an ancient allegiance which classified the people of Greater Syria (what is now Syria, Lebanon, Jordan, Palestine and Israel) according to a genealogy that dated back to the tribal configuration of the pre-Islamic Arabian peninsula. The descendants of the southern tribes in the peninsula were the Yamani, and those of the northern tribes the Qaysi. Abu Gosh, as the informal leader of the Yamani faction in the Jerusalem area, called upon the other local families, regarded as Yamanis, to join forces. Traditionally, their most important ally was the house of the Husaynis in Jerusalem. (The rival family in the city, the Khalidis, belonged to the Qaysi faction).

The Husaynis had, however, grown tired of the allegiance and decided to ignore Abu Gosh's call to join an anti-Ottoman coalition. Many other urban families in Palestine followed suit and remained faithful to the Ottomans, despite the reforms. The result was a significant change in the balance of power. The urban notables began replacing the rural chieftains as the leading social force in the land.

After all, the *a'ayan* of Palestine adapted easily to the new policies. The old politics of notables proved a very helpful tool in facing the new reality. The notables learned how to join and gain control of the new organizations the Ottomans introduced, such as municipalities and regional councils, and they continued their mediating role, this time as officially paid clerks of the empire. In the second half of the nineteenth century, Palestinian names traditionally associated with religious positions were now to be found even in secular places: Yusuf Diya' al-Khalidi became the first mayor of Jerusalem; Musa Kazem al-Husayni attained the governorship of Yemen; Haj Tawfiq Hammad of Nablus became the first mayor of his city and represented his district in the Ottoman parliament. Before the reforms, these urban notables would not have been able to climb beyond the lower rungs of the bureaucratic ladder; by the end of Ottoman rule, they held ever higher positions in Jerusalem and Beirut, and even in Istanbul.[26] Thus, 'the politics of notables' prevailed. The reformers, after all, needed the urban notables to help them implement their reforms, and the population needed them as a protective shield against excessive conscription and tax abuses.

The notables' changed status was reflected in the towns. The architecture changed as towns expanded beyond their traditional walls and slowly adopted European features. This transformation was particularly dramatic in the coastal towns, Haifa being a prime example. The rise in Haifa's importance as the country's northern port sharply reduced its dependence on Beirut and added wealth and territory to the little town originally built by Dahir al-Umar, a Galilean chieftain who had rebelled against the Ottomans in the late eighteenth century. The growth of the other port town, Jaffa, was not only due to its status as an important gateway to Europe but also to its position as a junction on the new rail network. The Christian and Jewish pilgrimage route to Jerusalem started at these ports, and this mixture of business and 'religious' pleasure in a single trip expanded their fortunes.

The new economic and financial reality spawned new social realities. A number of families and individuals benefited and helped propel the country's integration into the world economy while translating their wealth into political power. Palestine's integration into Europe's capitalist monetary system created new patterns of social mobilization, introducing newcomers into the local elite.[27] These nouveaux riches had neither respectable genealogies nor high religious standing. Not only were they now able to join the elite, but also in many respects they became the leading social, if not political, force in the country. A prominent example was the Nashashibis in Jerusalem, whose fortune had been made through commerce.

For the old elites, confronting the rise of upstarts required capital. They did this by dismembering the religious endowments (*awquf*). These were quite valuable real estate assets such as shops and businesses. Muslim notables had dedicated such endowments in the names of their families, and the profits were used for the benefit of religion and society. Administering

such endowments had been a main source of income for the religious hierarchy, the *ulama*. Supervision of these endowments had been taken over
by the central government, which through a special ministry hoped to
divert the profits its way. The not unnatural response was a widespread
tampering with the *awqaf*, with the financial assets being returned to their
founders.[28]

As in Europe, the new regulation of land ownership and cultivation led
to a redistribution of the means of production. Unlike in Europe, however,
a far greater proportion of this means, such as land, property and the workforce, was accumulated by a few. The new ruling elite, consisting primarily
of large land owners and agricultural producers, discovered that the most
attractive way to increase their capital was through land speculation. The
Zionist movement, arriving in Palestine at this precise moment, quickly
assessed the situation and began exploiting it.

### NEW BEGINNINGS AND NEW INFLUENCES

During the Tanzimat, a new Palestine transpired for the urban elite,
Muslims, Christians and Jews alike, in other spheres of life, such as law
and education. Although, to the Ottomans, legal and educational reforms
were of lesser importance than taxation and administration, reforms were
nonetheless carried out with zest. A closer look at law in the Ottoman
Empire shows that constitutional and judicial transformation seems to
have been more impressive in its goals than in its implementation. At the
constitutional level, the reforms amounted to little more than a codification
of the existing Islamic law, while at the judicial level they entailed a genuine
effort at secularizing the Islamic penal code. What is significant for our purposes is that they brought a separation of the criminal and civil law from
the religious law. Cases were no longer dealt with by the old religious courts
but by new administrative courts, and the shari'a was restricted to matters
of marriage, divorce and burial. The reforms thus brought to Palestine a
new breed of secular judges, who presided in new courts, while in ad hoc
tribunals cases involving foreign citizens were often judged by foreigners.
The new judges and mixed tribunals much reduced the previous powerful position of the shari'a authorities. The European consuls in Jerusalem,
for instance, now participated in cases, and their interference could sway
the judges to convict locals and acquit Europeans. The most successful in
bringing about such results was the British consul in Jerusalem, James Finn,
whose reputation in this regard exacerbated his already tense relationship
with the city's notables.

In education, the Ottoman reforms included the restructuring of the school system to allow some, but never more than a few, members of the local elite to pursue careers in the Ottoman bureaucracy. Elementary education expanded to absorb more children and opened for them a window, albeit narrow, onto subjects that had not formed part of the traditional curriculum. This was true for the empire as a whole but particularly evident in the Levant.

While educational reform may at first have done little to raise the overall level of literacy in Palestine, it did enable more people to join the social elite if they could afford it. It also altered the orientation of that section of society from which the elites were recruited, its 'core group'.[29] This helped create a kind of Muslim middle class whose members graduated either from the new reformed schools, which aimed at professionalism in the service of Istanbul, or from the private Christian schools where education was Western and indirectly nationalist.[30]

For the urban elite, the joint attendance of Muslims, Christians and Jews in similar schools in Jerusalem, Jaffa and Haifa constituted a new reality. In these schools, the young generation was absorbing the same images and formulating a common outlook on the world, which made for a kind of cosmopolitan worldview which would disappear again with the rise of militant nationalism in Palestine.[31] But before nationalism could become a dominant feature of life in Palestine, the country was to become the object of foreign ambitions, always a vital factor in the making of a national movement.

The economic integration of the local market was one motive for fresh interest in the region. A rise in interest in the Holy Land towards the end of the Christian century also played a role, increasing the exposure of Palestine to foreign intervention. This came on top of the increased political and strategic interest in the country due to the Crimean war, the disintegration of the Ottoman Empire, and the growing appetite for land and influence among the five leading powers in Europe. A constellation emerged that suited Europeans wishing to visit, occupy, settle or radically transform the land.

Even those from humble positions in their own societies could fulfil their desires in a foreign land due to the political processes, described in the introduction, that annexed Palestine to the European sphere of influence. These newcomers varied in origin, ideology and purpose, and yet all were colonizers, Christian missionaries and Zionist settlers alike. Colonialism is not just a catchword explaining motivation; it also implies certain consequences. So depicting all the new arrivals in the formative period of Palestine as wishing to turn it into a 'modern' entity also shows something about the way they perceived the indigenous population. There was a distinct and common attitude displayed by Europeans towards the local Palestinians, forged by shared assumptions about the natives' future role in whatever kind of Palestine the newcomers wished to build.

The foreign outlook was at best oblivious and at worst condescending. The indigenous population would either be modernized for its own good or make way for the newcomers and their ideas. Some of the foreigners, of course, do not deserve such harsh judgement, but they were few and their presence did not divert the principal route colonization took in Palestine's modern history. The newcomers wished to change the world and themselves. Among them the most ambitious and energetic were the German Templars and the Zionists. In many historical accounts, this urge for change and its successful implantation became synonymous with the history of the land. By now readers will appreciate that most Palestinians led a different life and had other aspirations.

In 1837, the Reverend Michael Russell, a British traveller, published a guidebook, one of about thirty such appearing at that time. His book, like the others, presented Europeans as modern people discovering the old land of Palestine and transforming it into a new entity: 'The country to which the name of Palestine is given by the moderns, is that portion of the Turkish Empire in Asia which is comprehended within the 31st and 34th degrees of north latitude, and extends from the Mediterranean to the Syrian desert, eastward of the River Jordan and the Dead Sea.'[32] This empirical and cartographic definition became the official reference to the area for foreigners, inside and outside Palestine. This was not the way the Ottomans, or the Egyptians for as long as they ruled the country, referred to the area. When Russell published his guidebook, the region was still under the sovereignty of the Ottoman Empire, and was described as one of the many administrative provinces ruled by the Ottomans since the beginning of the sixteenth century.

Travellers were not the only foreigners eager to redefine Palestine. Other harbingers of a modern Palestine were missionaries, who flocked to the area from the beginning of the nineteenth century, especially after the Crimean war, when better roads and security made the land even more accessible and attractive. They were pushed by their expansionist governments to form a presence in the Holy Land, but even without such encouragement many of them wished to witness the possible eschatological events predicted for the end of the century.

The Jesuits and other Catholics already had a foothold in Palestine, but were joined by a variety of other denominations. First came the representatives of the Orthodox churches, followed by American and British Protestants. Notable among the latter were the members of the London Society for Promoting Christianity among the Jews, which had begun its work in 1820. In 1824, one member, a Dr Dalton, became the first European physician to open a practice in Palestine. He worked mainly in Jerusalem and it was he who, after twenty years of raising funds and circumventing Ottoman red tape, opened the first modern hospital in the city. Dalton's work, as well as that of the Society, was assisted by the first British consulate to be established in Jerusalem, in 1839, which had a clear mandate from London not to confine itself to diplomatic affairs but to help the missionaries in their conversion efforts.[33]

The British efforts were greatly helped by close co-operation with the Prussians or, more precisely, between the Lutheran Prussian Church and the Church of England. In 1841, the British parliament passed the Bishopric Law, which decreed that the Bishop at Jerusalem (not of Jerusalem, as the bishop was subordinate to the Archbishop of Canterbury and his sphere of activity included the whole of Syria, Egypt and Ethiopia) would be elected alternately by the monarchs of England and Prussia.[34]

Dr Michael Solomon Alexander from Prussia was the first Bishop at Jerusalem. Although himself a Jewish convert, he was not successful at converting others. He fell from grace because of his constant disagreements with the British consul, James Finn. He died while visiting Egypt shortly after his appointment. His successor was a French Swiss, Samuel Gobat. He serves as a model of 'modernization'. His Arabic was impeccable, as was his honest interest in the welfare of his community. Although a missionary at heart, his main concern seems to have been expanding education in Jerusalem and beyond. His relevance to our story is his opening of a boys' school on Mount Sahayun in 1853, and soon afterwards a girls' school. The boys' school was a private school, and converted many of its students to Anglicanism by the sheer force of Gobat's charisma and the level of the education he offered.[35] It was at these schools, as we shall see in the next chapter, that the first nationalist perceptions were nurtured. These developments were not confined to Jerusalem. In 1908, the Valley of the Cross School (a Christian Missionary Society school) for girls was opened in Haifa. One hundred Muslim girls attended the school, including daughters of the local notables.

The foreign visitors were prolific writers. More than three thousand books and travelogues on Palestine were written by Europeans throughout the nineteenth century, all painting a picture of a primitive Palestine wait-ing to be redeemed by Europeans. In the more pious travelogues there is a sad lament over the tragic disappearance of the biblical Holy Land brought about by the inevitable Europeanization of Palestine. Most visitors, how-ever, wanted to change Palestine. With the power of money and land they carved out a new beginning for themselves; few thought they were doing the same for the local population. One group of 'do-gooders', however, was the Palestine Exploration Fund, a nineteenth-century British archaeological body recording the topography and ethnography of Palestine. Its members reported to readers back home that they had all had a 'jolly good time' in Palestine. According to its Quarterly Statements, the Fund's members regarded modernization as not unlike a salvage operation. Palestine stood in urgent need of modernization since the people the European explorers encountered were obviously miserable in their pre-modern world. As one of the explorers, Thyrwhitt Drake, noted: 'I have seldom in this country heard a genuine laugh from a man, woman or child; the great struggle for existence seems to have crushed all but fictitious mirth'. We cannot quan-tify misery or joy, but Palestinian biographies from a short time later, and subsequent anthropological research, tell us that this picture represents the distorted view of European colonists. Inevitably, this encounter between the first representatives of European modernity and Palestine's peasantry was also part of the formation of modern Palestine. It reveals the degree of presumption, not to say arrogance, on the part of Europeans who thought they were providing not just material benefits but also the key to human happiness.

## THE ZIONIST IMPETUS

The early Zionists arrived at roughly the same time as the missionaries. Zionism was a European phenomenon and so shared other Westerners' disregard for the local population. It also adopted a cautious attitude to-wards the Ottoman rulers, relying instead on the goodwill of European colonial powers. Like the other colonizers, the Zionists carved out territory to create a haven for persecuted Jews from Europe. Zionism began as a European national movement but turned into a colonialist one once its leaders decided to implement their vision of national revival in the land of Palestine.

Zionism had emerged in two ways in Europe. It appeared first in the cen-tral parts of the continent as an intellectual conceptualization of European Jewry's predicament, and second in eastern Europe as a practical solution to this predicament. At the heart of the intellectual movement stood Theodor Herzl, a Viennese Jew who at the age of thirty abandoned an unsuccessful career as a playwright and journalist to lead the Jewish national movement on a course that would end with the colonization of Palestine at the end of the nineteenth century.

Herzl's vision of a national solution for European Jews was not original. It owed much to an intellectual Jewish proto-nationalism that had begun in the 1850s in eastern Europe. This quasi-national scholastic, but by no means political, revolution was part of an exciting period of unprecedented Jewish cultural revivalism and renaissance. Its practitioners abandoned centuries of religious dogmatism for reason and science in search of solutions for the particular problem of Jewish existence in Europe. These scholars had preceded Herzl in their reinvention of Judaism as the ideology of a nation rather than a religion; they thus sought guidance not from holy scripture but from ancient Jewish history as a model for the future. They wrote in the ancient Hebrew language, and retold the stories of the biblical kingdom of Solomon and the last Jewish republic of the Hasmoneans.

Herzl had the sense of urgency and the common touch that the scholars lacked. According to his own account, now questioned by leading Israeli scholars, it was the Dreyfus affair that made him abandon his former career for the sake of Zionism. Alfred Dreyfus was a French officer of Jewish origin, who was accused in 1894 of treason, an unsubstantiated allegation motivated by anti-Semitism. The 'Affair', as it was called in France, convinced Herzl, at the time a correspondent in Paris for an Austrian journal, that there was no hope in assimilation, which was the solution suggested by leading Jewish secularists. The false conviction and abuse of a French officer just because he was a Jew made a profoundly pessimistic impression on Herzl. The only solution, he thought, was to leave Europe for a new life, in Zion, the land of Israel. His role was clear: to warn the Jewish people of the inevitability and implacability of anti-Semitism in Europe and to lead them to their ancient homeland where they could rebuild themselves as a European nation outside Europe. The term 'Zionism' was not his – it had been invented a few years earlier – but his name became synonymous with that of the Jewish movement for return to Palestine.

Herzl's initial inclination was to recruit the Jewish elite in the West for the Zionist cause. The well-established Jewish bankers and industrialists whom he met failed to take him seriously and, apart from a few friends, he remained isolated in his efforts. He did much better in the eastern parts of Europe. In Poland, Russia and Romania he found wretched, persecuted and underprivileged Jewish communities eagerly awaiting the arrival of a saviour, preferably religious, but secular if necessary. Herzl was greeted as 'the new David' by enthusiastic crowds who flocked to hear him on his lecture tours.

When Herzl returned frustrated from his lack of success with statesmen and bankers but elated by the popular reaction in eastern Europe, he found that the Zionist cause had at least attracted a large number of intellectuals in western and central Europe. These thinkers and their equivalents in Eastern Europe were the horses that pulled the Zionist wagon.[36] His circle of these friends grew into a substantial political movement. They helped him to conceptualize and articulate the new national ideology in an accessible manner for a wider audience of Jewish communities.[37] With 200 friends and delegates from eastern Europe, Herzl convened the first Zionist Congress in Basle in 1897. Here, Zionist ideologues from all over Europe not only discussed the making of a Jewish Athens but also expressed a desire for a Zionist Sparta. It became clear to the leaders of the movement that a vast array of national traits had to be acquired before the Jews could 'retake' Palestine and build their own homeland there. Moreover, there was a need to confront quite a few Jewish personalities and organizations that stood against Zionism. Many traditional rabbis forbade their followers to have anything to do with Zionist activists. They viewed Zionism as meddling with God's will that the Jews should remain in exile until the coming of the Messiah.

The visionaries carried the day. They echoed Herzl's dreams of a mass movement to Palestine of Jewish farmers, labourers, managers, technicians, engineers and other skilled workers. The early leaders realized that such a movement depended on the prior expansion and differentiation of Jewish occupational life in Europe, a process that would establish the human infrastructure needed for building a nation. When Jewish socialism in eastern Europe sought national avenues, its main spokesmen elaborated on the need for the social and economic transformation of the Jews from their traditional occupational world into a more productive one suiting the project of colonizing Palestine.

The Zionist or Basle Programme was the main product of the first Zionist Congress. The manifesto explained that 'the Zionist movement aspires to create an asylum for the Jewish people in Eretz Israel which would be guaranteed by international law'.[38] The second Zionist Congress, in 1898, added the imperative of colonizing Eretz Israel (Land of Israel) for that purpose. At the third congress, in 1899, Herzl suggested replacing the search for international legitimacy with a chartered lease from the Ottoman sultan. He believed that money and European pressure would induce the sultan to grant such a charter. Herzl then travelled to Istanbul, but failed to meet the Ottoman sultan Abdul Hamid II (r. 1876–1908). The sultan's aides flatly rejected Herzl's request to lease Palestine to the Jews. Even his offer to pay an enormous sum of money to the bankrupt Turkish government, money he did not have, did not help. He fared no better in the courts of European monarchs or in the antechambers of presidents.

In the eyes of the politicians, Herzl was a charlatan whose ideas were far removed from reality. Leaders of Jewish communities took him more seriously, but feared his ideology. They were disturbed by his call for Jewish sovereignty in a foreign land with equal status to other sovereign states in the world. For the more established sections of western and central European Jewry, this was a provocative vision that called into question the loyalty of English, French and German Jews. Ever since the Napoleonic Code had been accepted in France, and later made its influence felt in other countries, Jews had felt themselves more and more assimilated into, and confident within, these areas of Europe. The horrible fate of these communities and their leaders half a century later explains the magnetic force that the arguments of people such as Herzl exerted on Zionist thinking, and particularly on Israelis, after the Second World War. Herzl came to be seen as the prophet of wrath, unheeded by blind assimilationism, a saviour who had been rejected.

Towards the end of the nineteenth century more practical figures took the lead in the Zionist movement. They created their own Zionist dream, quite different from Herzl's, and one that to some extent had been on the eastern European Jewish agenda even before Herzl. While he was still preaching, they began settling in Palestine. They enjoyed the support of the younger generations within the Russian Jewish communities, and had a leader, Haim Weizmann, a young Russian Jewish émigré living in Manchester. Known as the 'territorial Zionists', they were inspired by a mixture of romantic nationalism and socialist revolutionary ideology to be enacted in the land of Palestine. Their most pressing need was to combat the wave of anti-Semitic violence sweeping Poland and Russia in the second half of the nineteenth century. The persecution aroused in many the will to rebel and to transform their existence. Before focusing on Palestine, their interest was eastern Europe, where their major organization, Hovevi Zion (Lovers of Zion), had formed the nucleus for the proto-nationalist Zionist movement a few decades before Herzl's appearance. The sense of urgency of these young Jews was accentuated by a particularly cruel wave of pogroms in 1881 in southern Russia. In that year, Tsar Alexander II was assassinated. His liberal policies had been attributed partly to the influence of Jewish capitalists. His heir, Alexander III, pursued a reactionary policy, blaming the Jews for both the follies of his predecessor and the assassination. The Russian policy makers and secret police suspected the Jews of playing a leading role in the clandestine revolutionary organizations that were mushrooming in late nineteenth-century Russia under the spell of socialist and communist ideas. Jews in south-western Russia were attacked in an unprecedented wave of violence.

Fear of annihilation spurred Jews to leave Russia, the great majority emigrating to the United States. In Europe, others, mainly Jewish students, joined the newly formed national organizations. A few went beyond talking and opted to experience nationalism in reality. In 1882, they were the first wave of Jews to arrive in Palestine. Those who came in 1882 are referred to in Zionist historiography as the 'First Aliya'. Aliya means 'ascent', and is used because immigration to Palestine was seen as an act that elevated the Jew to a higher form of living and existence. (This is why emigration was, and still is, called *yerida* 'descent'.)

These early immigrants saw themselves as *haluzim* (pioneers), emulating, or at least borrowing from the reservoir of images common among, the white settlers who drove into the west of North America. The best known of the first pioneers were the biluim, a movement of young Russian Jews who built the first Zionist settlements in Palestine. They were led by charismatic spiritual leaders such Moshe Lilienblum and Leon Pinsker, who were the great prophets of ideological immigration to Palestine. In their writing, they explained why Jews should leave Europe and what should lead them to Palestine, although neither specified Palestine as the only acceptable haven. The few hundred Jews who heeded their advice gave Palestine exclusivity as a haven, and became leaders directing the rest of the Russian and eastern European Zionist organizations to become Palestine-orientated.

The 'territorial Zionists' who reached Palestine were few, and many did not stay long. But they laid the foundations for a future Jewish community in the land. They prepared for the new life in special centres in Europe and were organized in several unions that had their first convention in 1884 in Russia. The different groups became a registered legal society in Russia in 1890, working openly for the Jewish colonization of Palestine.

In Palestine, they settled mainly as farmers, but some also entered urban centres where they opened their administrative headquarters. The names they gave to the first settlements echoed their aspirations and dreams: Rishon le Zion (First to Zion), Zichron Yaacov (Yaacov's Memorial), Rosh Pina (Cornerstone), Petach Tikva (Ray of Hope). Their main difficulty was money, so they turned to the richest Jew in Europe, Baron Edmond de Rothschild, who was one of the Jewish bankers who had refused to assist Herzl but was persuaded by the early settlers' enthusiasm. He set up vineyards and farms for them in Palestine.[39] Rothschild not only funded the settlers, he also sent agriculturists and experts to help the settlers plan and structure the colonization of the land. Soon after he started his project, however, his own interests clashed with those of the colonists. The settlements that developed did not fit his notions. His managers felt overruled by the settlers, and were not impressed by their diligence or rate of production. The Zionist colonization took a different turn when two colonies (Hadera and Rehovot) were built without Rothschild's help. In 1899, Rothschild withdrew, and his support was replaced by that of a new organization, the Zionist Organization for the Settlement of the Land of Palestine.

The Ottoman government at first did all it could to stop the Zionists. In 1882, a law was passed prohibiting Jewish immigration. In 1888, however, due to British pressure via its embassy in Istanbul, the restrictions on Zionist immigration were eased, but not removed altogether.

A NEW CRUSADE: TEMPLARS, COLONISTS AND PROFITEERS

As the Zionists began settling in Palestine, they encountered not only the local population, whom they ignored, but also Christian colonization, structured in a way very similar to their own. This colonization, termed by one historian the 'Quiet Crusade', sprang from an unprecedented flood of Christian pilgrims to Palestine. It reconnected the old Eastern Christian churches to the Western church, and changed the outlook on life of local Christians living in holy places such as Bethlehem, Nazareth and Jerusalem. Their religious festivals were now celebrated, at least until the outbreak of the First World War, in great numbers and with much ardour as thousands of pilgrims made their way to the Holy Land. At Easter, the Holy Sepulchre in Jerusalem would be crowded, the surrounding streets hardly able to contain the masses of people passing through, while others hovered dangerously above them on makeshift balconies or even in wooden boxes suspended from the houses. This time the pilgrims were officially protected by the Turkish police, but this meant that Istanbul inadvertently helped to strengthen the European hold over the city of Jerusalem and the towns of Bethlehem and Nazareth.

The missionary effort in Palestine grew in pace and intensity with the arrival of the German Templars. A missionary order from the German state of Württemberg, its leaders envisioned a German colony in the Holy

Land. Christians would cultivate the land, convert the local inhabitants and create a new Eden. The Templar order was highly organized. The result was a system of German colonies, whose typically northern European houses are still a distinctive feature of local architecture in Galilee, Haifa and Jerusalem.

At first a refuge for German Protestants, the Templar colonies became one of Germany's many assets in the Ottoman Empire. A far more important and visible aspect, in Palestine at least, of the new German imperialist aspirations was a Turco-German military alliance struck in the 1890s, which meant the presence of German officers in the region. In 1892, Yoachim Fast, a German, opened a hotel near the Jerusalem railway station with a German bar and a billiards club. It was a place where German officers could escape the Oriental world and, for a while at least, feel at home. 'Modern' Palestine, like 'modern' Egypt, meant a chain of such hotels providing European islands that reminded foreigners of home but also accentuated the colonial reality they were creating of master and native.

The Templars left a bad impression on the local population because of their arrogant and racist attitude. However, not all foreign visitors feature negatively in the local collective memory. The American colony in Jerusalem, for example, is recorded as having a high reputation. It was a philanthropic religious organization run by a Chicago family, the Spaffords. They settled outside Jerusalem's walls and created the American colony (today a hotel of that name). Their daughters contributed to the local community by supervising the spread of education among Muslim girls, an initiative begun by a close friend of the family, Ismai'l al-Husayni, who was then a director of the education department in the city.[40]

The foreign presence in Palestine created islands of introverted settlers who viewed the local population as one of the physical hardships they were forced to cope with. The reformist zeal in Istanbul, combined with the arrival of a substantial number of foreigners, either in a private capacity or as representatives of their governments, undoubtedly contributed to the changing face of Palestine. But did the Europeans modernize Palestine? Were they agents of change? Not always and not in everything. Like the Zionists who were to follow them, most Europeans settling in Palestine in the nineteenth century were more concerned about the land than about its people, and modernizing and cultivating the land could also have meant getting rid of its 'primitive' native population. In effect, settlers introduced new techniques and equipment and increased agricultural production, but seldom shared these modern benefits with the local population. Moreover, while contributing to the positive statistics of production in Palestine in economic terms, they set themselves above the Palestinian population. Some Palestinian notables in town and country succeeded in exploiting the new technology for their own benefit, as did the owners of the citrus groves who used the new developments for increasing their yield and their marketing capabilities, but they were the exception. Local industrialists did not benefit at all, and their way of life or production saw hardly any transformation at all. The rest of the population seemed to suffer from the intrusion, even when the impressive improvements in health, sanitation and communication are taken into account. These processes were a mixed blessing, helping to fight death and disease but bringing with them European control and exploitation.

It would be just as wrong to assume that 'modern' Palestine was defined only in the rediscovery of the Holy Land as to see all the Europeans who came as missionaries. Foreigners were also attracted to Palestine as profiteers and financial speculators. Thus becoming 'modern' in Palestine for Europeans was either re-enacting the past or totally erasing it for the sake of a fresh beginning.[41]

However, nothing could compare to the colonizing energy brought by the Zionists, evident already in that early period of modernization. Although their number was small, it was with hindsight a colonizing immigration. It was not a proper colonization, as Palestine was not occupied by a European power. But like colonialism elsewhere, it was a European movement, with people entering Palestine for the sake of European interests, not local ones. The locals were seen as a commodity or an asset to be exploited for the benefit of the newcomers or an obstacle to be removed. For the Christian missionaries, the locals were spiritual commodities, with which they hoped to enlarge the community of Christian believers. For the early Zionists, the indigenous people were cheap labourers or producers of cash crops. For the more ideological Zionists, Palestinians were an enigma. They were defined as the *shela neelama*, the 'hidden question', both invisible and a puzzle.

# CHAPTER 2

# Between Tyranny and War (1900–1918)

In the first decades of the new century, the changes discussed above became an integral and accepted part of life for almost everyone living in Palestine. Palestine was already 'modern', or at least modernized. A further upheaval was looming however. Palestine was about to enter the Great War, in which it was a secondary arena, but a bloody one nonetheless. The war was an all-encompassing event, whereas the impact of the political activity before and after would be felt only later.

The period began with the last years of Abdul Hamid's reign, which ended in 1908. He was a reactionary tyrant, who resented many of the reforms introduced by his predecessors after 1839. Some of the reforms were almost lost when Abdul Hamid expelled, executed or simply marginalized the reformers. But he was no conventional reactionary. He transformed the empire, but in his own way. He expanded the railway infrastructure, introduced direct taxation and conscription, and promoted the idea of Ottoman citizenship.[1] Unlike his predecessors, he was concerned about the loyalty of his Arab citizens. By then he was losing the loyalty of many groups within the empire, Greeks, Bulgarians and Armenians, to name a few, and hoped that by presenting himself as a reborn Muslim caliph he would induce the Arabs to remain within his grip. His empire was shrinking at an alarming pace. It had become prey to both European colonial greed and the national aspirations of ethnic and religious groups. Abdul Hamid himself contributed to nationalism as a divisive force within his empire by trying to promote to the many peoples comprising the Ottoman world the notion of 'Ottoman nationalism'. This strategy not only failed to arouse any sympathy among his subjects, but also the idea of an externally imposed official identity sharpened the already fragmented counter-identities. When his pan-Islamism and pan-Ottomanism failed to persuade, Abdul Hamid employed more coercive methods. He established a police state that used violence to centralize the empire, clashing with and destroying any forces threatening to take it apart.[2]

Figure 1.  Palestinians and Jews in the Jerusalem market near the Jaffa Gate, circa 1900

Within this police state, the integration of the local Palestinian economy into the world economy marched on unhindered. This meant that the peasants of Palestine continued until the moment the war reached their doorsteps to struggle against an inevitable loss of self-sufficiency, whether on their own land or on land leased from others. In the first fourteen years of the twentieth century they moved in greater numbers into hired agricultural work, while many were transformed into an unskilled labour force, building their lives on the periphery of Palestine's urban centres.

Abdul Hamid's regime also became more interventionist in the lives of its citizens, peasants and city dwellers alike. This meant increased and unwelcome contact with tax collectors and recruiters for public works. There was also more contact with foreigners, which in the case of women generated a momentum towards modesty in dress that had not existed earlier, to judge by paintings and travellers' accounts. Nonetheless, among Christian women, the encounter with a foreign milieu began modest politicization, leading to the founding of the first-ever women's association in Palestine in 1903, and the exit of women from their restricted domestic existence.[3]

The state also demanded recognition and gratitude. Eyewitness reports from the period tell us that people were angered by Abdul Hamid's megalomaniac style. One of his most hated whims was the annual celebration on 19 August of the anniversary of his accession to power (following the suspicious death of his brother, Abdul Aziz II). Palestine was required to rejoice in remembrance of this shameful incident, with colourful displays and dancing to the loud music of military marches. Those who refused to take part were suspected of being enemies of the state, and risked arrest and even death at the hands of the secret police.[4]

But in more than one respect Abdul Hamid also tried to encourage co-operation from the local population, which opened the way for the politicization of the urban elite in Palestine. In his last years as sultan, the towns of Palestine changed radically, and a new Palestine emerged for the urban notables and dignitaries. The ruler encouraged them to seek higher administrative positions, to enhance their standing and improve their economic position. He also regarded himself, under the influence of the great Islamic reformer Jamal al-Din al-Afghani, as a champion of modern Islamic thought. This meant for the more learned and scholarly sections of the elite, in Palestine as elsewhere in the Arab and Muslim world, the adoption of a new pan-Islamic identity. Although failing to save Abdul Hamid's sultanate, this marked the beginning of a new phase in Middle Eastern history.

The first decades of the new century produced more marked change in the life of the urban nobility. Or, to be fairer, we should say that we have more detailed evidence about them, which perhaps contributes to a more rounded description of their way of life. As a group that included *a'ayan* families, well-to-do urban families and big landlords, they seemed to undergo a process of politicization from 1914 onwards. The rural lords were now a new breed of people. They can no longer be viewed as semi-feudal sheikhs, but as large owners of rural real estate, with many of them residing outside Palestine in the cities of the Levant. The eve of war found them consolidating their wealth, and attempting to translate it into political power, albeit with very little success.

The most adventurous group within the elites consisted of young members of the urban families, who at this time began toying with the concept of nationalism. The construction of a national consciousness is an almost mystical process. It is particularly difficult to discern its beginnings and mechanisms. Its history in Palestine, or rather of its birth in Palestine, is not much different from that of Arab nationalism in general. According to some accounts, it was in the 1870s that a growing number of Arab intellectuals in various towns in Syria, Lebanon and Palestine challenged Ottoman rule in their countries. (These accounts have been questioned recently. It has been suggested that their number was not that great and that, for many intellectuals, the Pax Ottomana was an acceptable reality.) Those who did contest Ottomanism began reinterpreting the world around them in Arab, not Ottoman, terms. This re-identification of Palestine as an Arab country did not at first lead to open rebellion against the Ottomans, but it was enough, when articulated openly, to cause friction. When these new ideas appeared in pamphlets and petitions, they expressed an ambivalent wish to leave the empire and yet a desire to remain within its sphere of influence. It was the kind of ambiguity recognized by many theoreticians of nationalism: the simultaneous and contradictory need of a national movement both to rely on, and disassociate itself from, history. This has been eloquently described by Homi Bhabha in reference to the mechanism found in the national narrative, even after maturation: 'History may be half made because it is in the process of being made'.

But it was more than just a perception of reality. It was, much as in the case of the early Zionists in Europe, a sensation shared by only a few and discussed in secret national associations convened for the first time probably around 1875 in Lebanon, Egypt and Syria. A very small number of Palestinians participated in these meetings at first, but gradually their numbers grew. They were a large enough group to be able to preach these ideas and spread them to other Palestinians. Moreover, this was now an open country, and those who could travel became very influential, with easy access to Istanbul, Beirut and Damascus.

National consciousness produced the first aspirations for autonomy within the empire and fired the imagination with visions of independence and of a reconstructed glorious pan-Arab past. It took some time before these ideas were turned into a political platform with which people around the Arab world could identify. At the end of the previous century, only in Egypt had these ideas matured and nationalism become both a discourse and a reason for political action.

### PALESTINE IN THE LAST YEARS OF ABDUL HAMID (1900–1908)

The situation in Palestine was very different. As hated as was Abdul Hamid, the house of Ottoman and Ottomanism were an integral part of life, known and accepted. An exceptionally bad Ottoman ruler had to be resisted, reformed or removed, but this did not mean the removal of Ottomanism from Palestine altogether. Moreover, Abdul Hamid was not anti-Arab, as the Young Turks would be. And so he could always rely on the support, if not the sympathy, of the urban Arab elite, who did not want to lose their place in the Pax Ottomana. So, if we seek nationalism in pre-1908 Palestine, we find it on the margins. Its most significant site of operation was the private missionary education system. This system has quite often been described as secular, but this term is somewhat misleading. It was secular in so far as it did not provide Muslim education; it was religious as Christian missionaries managed an important part of it. The missionaries' success in attracting converts is difficult to assess, but it was probably very low compared to the original aspirations of the churches involved. They were, however, successful in introducing the European world to Muslim students, an introduction that opened the way to the rise of secular Islam, so characteristic of many Muslim Palestinians today (notwithstanding the counter-rise of Islamic fundamentalism). Oxymoronic terms such as 'secular Muslims' and 'secular Jews' can be added to the long list of paradoxes produced by nationalist realities developing in the modern world.

Private schooling in Palestine was a by-product of a protest by local priests, both Catholic and Anglican, who demanded independence from Rome and Canterbury, respectively. The Anglican Arabs were more successful than their Catholic or Orthodox counterparts, and it was in their midst that the mini-rebellion occurred. Probably because they themselves did not object to local control of church infrastructure in Palestine, the British representatives gave in to the teachers who wished to Arabize the Anglican colleges. The Anglican schools had been intended as purely missionary establishments but changed their designation in the wake of this initiative and passed into the hands of the Palestine Native Church Council, an organization of Palestinian priests, answerable to the bishop in spiritual affairs but not in social or educational matters.[5]

By the end of the Hamidian era, the Anglican church had thirty schools in Palestine, mainly in Jerusalem, Nablus and Nazareth. On a more individual level, teachers in the Orthodox and Catholic private schools served as precursors of nationalism by introducing materials that went beyond the requirements of a missionary school, adding, like the Anglican schools, to the dissemination of European education, secularizing and politicizing the local educated elite. I am focusing on Jerusalem, as this was the centre of embryo Palestinian nationalism. More specifically, St George's College in Jerusalem deserves a particular place in the pantheon of formative national Palestinian institutions. The sons of the Muslim elite attended this school in great numbers. Among them were the Husaynis and the Khalidis, the two clans that between them shared the most powerful social, political and economic positions given to the local elite by the Ottomans. St George's and its like in Jaffa, Haifa, Nablus and Nazareth shaped the *Weltanschauung* of those who would form the social elite of the Palestinian national movement. It was for a few years the school of Amin al-Husayni, the Grand Mufti of the Mandate years and the acknowledged leader of the Palestinian national movement up to 1948.

These schools produced the future generation of national leaders; they also planted other, more universal, values in their pupils' minds. This led those who chose careers as engineers, doctors, writers and academics to adopt a moderate attitude towards tradition and modernity. The more politically orientated graduates, however, began to take an active part in public life after the revolution of 1908. In this time of political turmoil and change, the usual inertia and indecision were simply not feasible for anyone belonging to the elite.

Those in the older generation were busy exploiting the new avenues the Hamidian regime opened up for them. The Pax Ottomana meant that certain career paths were exclusively in the hands of the notables. What is remarkable about this group is that in a short span of time it was able to react swiftly to the high political drama of the day. It had to change long-standing patterns of behaviour, first in the face of the revolution by the Young Turks and later under the British occupation. This group now assumed a political role, as distinct from its previous religious and social functions. They assumed this role in the name of Arab nationalism. In short, the leading notables of the Hamidian era would become agents of nationalism during the Mandate. They would both oversee the nationalization of their society and contribute to its destruction. This is why their image in the contemporary Palestinian national ethos and narrative is so ambivalent.

Each notable family deserves an individual history, but so much of the transformation was identical for the families that common trends can be seen. Two individuals from these families exemplify this similarity in patterns of continuity and progress. Haj Tawfiq Hammad, from Nablus, managed in a short span of time to become a member of the Ottoman parliament, mayor of his city, and then a leading figure in three parties with conflicting ideological orientations (pro-Syrian, pro-Husayni and anti-Husayni). The period in which he moved was unstable, but there was an openness that encouraged individuals to try more than one political orientation and to switch ideological positions with relative ease. The second example, Musa al-Husayni of Jerusalem, managed to become chief clerk in the Ottoman health ministry in Istanbul, then governor in Jaffa, Safad, Aleppo, Acre and Ajlun, all between 1881 and 1892. He rose even higher in the Ottoman ranks, serving in Iraq, the Arabian Peninsula, Anatolia and Huran. In 1918 he became mayor of Jerusalem, was deposed by the British, and then served as chair of various Palestinian national conferences, heading their delegations to negotiations in London with the British government, until his death in the 1930s.

The notables' loyalty to the Hamidian order was widespread and was challenged only by what might be called nationalist intellectuals, not, as was the case in Egypt, by 'nationalist notables'. Only with the demise of the Ottoman Empire did the notables unequivocally join the national movement and lead it. This behaviour was not peculiar to Palestine. In quite a few places around the Arab world, the urban notables accepted Abdul Hamid as the legitimate ruler, thus postponing, in a way, the emergence of Arab nationalism.

In Palestine, Abdul Hamid was supported by the local *a'ayan* thanks to his perception of their traditional role. They were not affected by his centralizing zeal, which was directed against the sheikhs of rural Palestine and the Bedouin tribes in the more arid areas. The Bedouins were left alone for most of the Tanzimat period, but their time also came during Abdul Hamid's era. They were forced to turn their *dira*, as their sphere of habitation was called, into land registered in the *tapu* (the land and property state register still in use in Palestine and Israel today), a process that reduced the area which they could call theirs.[6] Some of them were tempted to settle and a process of sedentarization began, leaving them in an unsatisfactory and disturbing limbo between old and new ways of life, a predicament still suffered by the Bedouins in Israel.

The urban elite benefited from the decline of the sheikhs and the Bedouin. Thus, by not alienating the *a'ayan*, Abdul Hamid soothed a potential proto-nationalist group. Their only source of grievance seems to have been the relatively free hand Istanbul gave the foreign consuls in Palestine, but this was not enough to arouse the kind of common nationalist feeling that leads to a rebellion against authority. The movement took time to materialize because the urban notables had never accepted Egyptian rule in the 1830s and did not wish to depart from the Arab-Ottoman world they knew in the 1890s.

## THE ARRIVAL OF ZIONISM

The *a'ayan* were aware of, but not strongly active against, the challenge of Zionism in the Hamidian era. It was perceived as yet another wave of European settlers, not very different from the European missionaries, consuls and entrepreneurs who had preceded it and were seen as a potential danger to the economic and social status of the nobility and the elite. Whenever they tried to push into new territory, such as building an Anglican school in Nablus, or claiming land in the valleys, as the Zionists did, local resentment would appear in the form of demonstrations or petitions to the government, and only in extreme cases of physical attacks on the newcomers.[7]

The Palestinian nobility as a whole, probably more than the peasantry or the city dwellers, were the first to come into contact with both the Zionist diplomatic effort and their more pragmatic activities on the ground. They learned about the former from the Egyptian, Lebanese and Turkish press. The latter they tackled as land owners when confronted by Zionist offers to buy land, or as religious leaders, such as when the Mufti of Jerusalem, Taher al-Husayni II, was asked to issue fatwas (religious rulings) against them. Other notables' first encounters with Zionism were as members of local municipalities, where they passed resolutions calling on the authorities to halt Jewish purchase of land. However, some of them also sold land to Jews when good offers were made. If Zionism accelerated the crystallization of Palestinian nationalism, it did not as yet create the coercive national atmosphere necessary to force individuals to compromise their personal interests in the face of a collective will.

It is only we, with hindsight, who can appreciate the significant change of orientation that occurred within Zionism; one doubts whether the urban leadership of the Palestinian community knew of these developments. The movement became a more potent factor in Palestine's affairs after Herzl's unique success in allying it to Britain, and his failure to persuade the Zionists to agree to settling in Uganda.

To the end of his life, Herzl believed that Zionism could not succeed without the blessing of a European power. We can see now that he was correct, and that he chose the right ally in Britain. It was a logical choice given the recent British interest in the Middle East, a colonialist interest that began with the occupation of Egypt in 1882, but did not end there. The British residents in Cairo, and an expansionist school of thought in the Colonial Office at home, had looked to Palestine as a future British acquisition, should the Ottoman Empire collapse. Such a collapse was now a feasible scenario, once dreaded by British policy makers as a formula for a European war, but by the 1880s one to which Britain itself contributed with the occupation of Ottoman Egypt. If the Jews, like the Anglican missionaries, could ease British expansion into the land of Palestine, they should be welcomed. The pro-Zionist bent in British Middle Eastern policy at the end of the nineteenth century was produced by a mixture of new colonial perceptions of global reality and old theological concepts connecting the return of the Jews to Palestine with the second coming of the Messiah. Herzl succeeded in inflaming the British colonialist and evangelist imagination when he offered the British government the opportunity to turn the arid area of El-Arish, near Gaza, into a Zionist oasis. All that was lacking, he explained, was a canal bringing fresh water from the Nile. However, the British governor of Egypt, Lord Cromer, an ardent utilitarian, was not impressed by these visions, and his objection led to the plan's demise.[8]

Herzl was now desperate. He tried another avenue, the last before his death in 1904. He attempted to enlist British help in installing a temporary Jewish state (i.e. one that would eventually be moved to Palestine) in British Uganda, an offer which was seriously considered by some in Whitehall. He proposed Uganda for tactical reasons, but his offer seemed to many in the movement a betrayal of Zionism. Haim Weizmann, leader of the 'territorial Zionists', foiled the Uganda plan. After all, it was Herzl who had sanctified Palestine by defining Jewish nationalism as Zionism, irrevocably connected to settling Palestine (Zion). He had created a yardstick by which patriotism or loyalty to Jewish nationalism would be judged. Any unpatriotic act was dealt with as in any other national movement – with contempt and hostility.[9]

Something of the new Zionist vitality and energy must have left a mark on those in the urban elite interested in politics. This is probably why the Palestinian protests against Zionism became more conspicuous after 1904 and were quite well orchestrated by Palestine's few representatives in the Turkish parliament, re-opened in 1908 after being suspended by Abdul Hamid. These representatives tried, sometimes successfully, to pass legislation curbing Jewish expansionism in Palestine. The settlers continued to arrive, however, and laid the foundations for the Zionist community. They would meet serious opposition only after the end of the First World War.

By the beginning of the twentieth century, there were twelve Zionist settlements in Palestine. The land was bought from rich land owners in and outside Palestine. In 1903, on land bought near the village of Zamarin on the Mediterranean coast, at the colony of Zichron Yaacov, the first assembly of Benei Israel in Eretz Israel convened under the chairmanship of Menachem Usishqin. Usishqin was the ultimate Zionist, a Russian Jew in his early forties who had been one of the early Hovevi Zion, the first Jewish society to contemplate settlement as a nationalist group in the land of Palestine. Usishqin laid the foundations for the organizational infrastructure of the

Jewish community. Under his guidance, professional organizations sprang up next to the political ones, preparing the way for a more permanent Zionist presence in Palestine.

After Herzl's death, different personalities dominated the Zionist scene, quite a few of them German Jews, as the headquarters of the Zionist movement was in Berlin until the First World War. One figure was Arthur Rupin, whose arrival and subsequent activity in Palestine accelerated the pace of Jewish settlement.[10] He was an economist, a sociologist and head of the Zionist colonization effort in Germany. He emigrated to Palestine in 1908 and founded some of the principal Zionist groups dealing with settlement. Rupin used these new structures for the energetic purchase of land. The jewel in the crown of the project was the acquisition of a large part of Mount Scopus in Jerusalem. In 1913 Rupin bought the plots from Lord Grey-Hill, a pro-Zionist Englishman who had arrived there in 1875 and built a summer resort. The Hebrew University of Jerusalem was built in the grounds of his mansion in 1920.

Rupin represented the people of the Second Aliya. The first wave (1882–1903) had not led to any significant change in the lives of either Jews or Palestinians in Ottoman Palestine. The second, however, coincided with the disintegration of the Ottoman Empire and its replacement by a modern Turkish political system. It thus came at a more appropriate historical moment, a lull between the old and the new worlds, and was able to influence the situation in Palestine. The settlers combined Jewish nationalism with socialism, and argued among themselves as to which of the two should take priority, a debate that created the first two Zionist parties in Palestine.[11] The debate also produced different modes and types of collective settlement, the most famous of which was the kibbutz. It should be said, however, that most Zionists were not attracted to agriculture or village life and preferred to settle in Palestine's towns, where collectivism was practised not so much as a way of life as through affiliation to strong trade union organizations.

Zionism on the eve of the First World War remained a colonialist project motivated by national emotions. The prescription of ideologies varied according to the newcomers' economic interest in land. The collective settlements stressed the national aspect. The private land owners wanted a muted version of nationalism; they desired a large Jewish territory but were content with a measured flow of immigrants. This position stemmed from their wish to employ Palestinian, in preference to Jewish, workers, who were more conscious of their rights as labourers. The Palestinian workers did not demand high wages and were better qualified for plantation work.[12]

For national purposes, the leaders of the Zionist enterprise included the old Jewish *millet* of Palestine as belonging to the community, which was called the Yishuv (settlement). With hindsight, given the way the intra-national conflict in Palestine developed, this strategy seems justified. However, at the time these were two distinct communities. The veteran Jews of the *millet* were an urban indigenous population and strictly religious. They resented newcomers, and could not accept in particular the secular way of life of the immigrants who entered Palestine after 1905 (many of them Russian Jews escaping after the failed revolution of that year). It should not be forgotten that the Zionist leaders and ideologues wished to reform the veteran Jews as much as they desired to reinvent the new Jew of Europe on Palestine's soil.

That there was no single Jewish community is shown by the constant struggles and small wars between the newcomers and the veterans. Also, the intricate relations between the Zionists and the authorities complicated life for the existing Jewish community. This group, anything but revolutionary in its outlook, had felt much safer since the introduction of the Tanzimat, and was even better off under Abdul Hamid II and the Young Turks.[13] The veteran Jews saw Zionism as heresy, and a threat to the ethical code of Judaism in that it cherished secularization as the means of salvation. Secularization for the old Jewish community in Palestine, however, represented an immoral development. They therefore looked for any signs of moral degradation in the conduct of the newcomers. This cannot have been easy, since as far as we can tell the first Zionists were quite puritan. The Orthodox Jews, nonetheless, decided that the appearance of Jewish prostitutes, in their eyes for the first time in history, could only be attributed to Zionism.

In Jaffa, the constant fights between Ashkenazi Jews (newcomers from Eastern Europe) and Sepharadi Jews (veteran members of the Ottoman Jewish *millet*) were barely containable. The Ashkenazis made their presence felt by expanding Jaffa, adding two new neighbourhoods and some small businesses and workshops. However, in Jaffa as in other Jewish communities, the main disputes were caused by political rivalries between rabbis in the guise of religious legal debates, for example over slaughtering methods, burial rites and so on. In reality, this was competition for domination of the community's life and politics.

Orthodox Jews had a particularly strong presence in Jerusalem and did not welcome Zionists there, nor did the Zionists wish to go. They built their own secular, modern town of Tel-Aviv. Sixty-six eager Zionists, who were among the first to settle the colonies with the help of the Baron de

Rothschild, founded the city on a Saturday morning in July 1907. It started as a manor house called Ahuzat Bayit, which was renamed Tel-Aviv. Qeren Ha-Qayemet (the National Fund), the principal Zionist funding agency, lent the money. The next summer the first buildings were erected. Almost a century later, at the beginning of the twenty-first century, after a meandering history, Jewish society in Israel would once more be divided between Orthodox Jerusalem and secular Tel-Aviv, as if time had stood still.

In 1909, the Zionists took another loan from a local bank, bought land and started building additional houses. Soon the first children were born, a school was added, Gimnazia Herzlia, which was for a long time the leading high school in the country. A very particular insular Zionist presence in Palestine thus began. Tel-Aviv was the heart of Zionist activity, much more so than Jerusalem, and because it was exclusively Jewish it enabled the energetic Zionist leadership to fulfil its dreams for the country as a whole.

The immigrants from Russia were the motivating factor in the new town. They were mostly Jews who had escaped conscription into the Tsar's army or who, like Aharon Eitin, the founder of the first printing house in Tel-Aviv, had spent years in the army before reaching Palestine.[14] Their subsistence was based on craftsmanship. Their expertise was either brought from Russia or acquired locally, which gave them a basis for an independent economy which, while needing interaction with the indigenous population, turned the Zionists into providers and not just receivers. This was a process of integration into the land of Palestine that could not be opposed by hostile policies like those used by the Turks against land purchase or immigration.

The protocols of the early Tel-Aviv council reveal a bureaucratic world in which members inquired busily about proper usage of lease contracts, payment of loans, and permits for new enterprises. Sabbath was observed, but not in a fanatical way. It was forbidden to keep chickens indoors, nor could dominoes be played in the new open cafes and the hotel on the promenade. There were also many musicians among the first Tel-Aviv residents, and they were asked to stop playing at 10 p.m. Beggars were not allowed to roam the city. The first cinema opened in 1914. Parts of the city could have been in Central Europe. Even during 1948, some bohemian and hedonistic parts of Tel-Aviv did not participate in the war of survival.[15]

Tel-Aviv was the antithesis of the socialist communal life offered in the settlements. Its importance was due also to the fact that many of the pre-1905 immigrants sought employment rather than land. This is understandable if we consider their meagre existence in the Jewish townships in Eastern Europe, where they had been allowed only a limited number of occupations:

as brokers, agents, bankers, money lenders and so on. This occupational spectrum itself, as much as the Christian religion and xenophobia, can account for the anti-Semitism prevalent in Europe at the time.

Those who came after 1905 wanted to turn settlement of the land into the main thrust of Zionism in Palestine. They were veterans of the socialist movement of Eastern Europe and sought to implement not only a national dream but also a communal one. The situation on the ground meant that the balance of power between newcomers and the indigenous population had to be considered. There was no more room for the kind of plantation colonies of the pre-1905 period, and there was no hope of surviving with too much insistence on privacy and individual indulgence. Strict communal and Jewish-centred colonies were the answer. In consequence, a serious and violent struggle commenced against Jews who employed Arab workers. In Galilee near Mount Tabor, five Arabs were found among forty Jewish workers in a joint farm called Sejra. The owner was threatened with violence and gave in. Later he was murdered, probably by one of the Palestinians he dismissed.[16] To circumvent the ban on employing Palestinians, it was decided to employ Arabs of a different kind, Arab Jews. The first batch was imported from Yemen. This was an ingenious as well as a racist solution; the workers were Jews, but also Arabs who could be hired cheaply. Their history is a sad story of people who were employed temporarily in a settlement and then dispensed with. They had been deceived, and were eventually crammed into slums near the newly developing Jewish towns in the heart of the Zionist settlement.[17] The political leadership had to cope with the dual issues of high politics and unemployment. With the British occupation, purchasing land and combating unemployment would be combined in a colonialist attempt to extract land and jobs from the local population for the growing numbers of Jewish immigrants.

Zionism moved confidently into the twentieth century, not only building towns, creating colonies and imposing taxes, but also providing an independent monetary system that would in coming years direct the flow of Jewish capital into Zionist projects in the land of Palestine. The immigrants also needed their own financial basis because of instability in the local fiscal and monetary economy. The currency at the end of the Ottoman period was Turkish, but the values of some coins varied in different parts of Palestine. Investment was both erratic and insecure, and susceptible to manipulative banking. Foreign banks existed in Palestine before the close of the century, but the Zionists were the first to open a bank with a local headquarters. They also established credit cooperative societies in the early twentieth century.

The local perception of the growing Zionist project is difficult to reconstruct. Although still fewer than fifty thousand people at the time, the Zionists antagonized the population at large, a feeling that found expression in physical resistance by Palestinians. The settlers defended themselves, and later discovered that military force could be employed to obtain important goals, including non-defensive ones. On the rural Palestinian community, however, the effects of Zionism would be felt only after the First World War, even though there were local community leaders who as early as the 1880s sensed danger and destabilization from Jewish immigration. Indeed, for most of Palestine's population, Zionism was still a storm in a teacup. The Jewish colonies were few, and only a handful of Palestinian villages came into contact with them. The pastoral worldview owed much to the dominance of rural life, and it was not until the First World War, and the major Zionist drives for land purchase, that the rural population witnessed events that changed their lives beyond recognition.

## PALESTINE IN THE AFTERMATH OF THE YOUNG TURK REVOLUTION (1908–1916)

In 1908, the Young Turks, a group of anti-Ottoman officers and students, commenced the toppling of Abdul Hamid. At first they contemplated replacing the empire with a liberal republic, but soon gave in to the intoxicating power of romantic nationalism and admiration for the forces of modern centralist government. At the end of 1908, the Young Turks succeeded in forcing Abdul Hamid to restore the constitution and recall parliament, which he had suspended on coming to power in 1876. The success of the new constitutional regime was, however, immediately undermined by a series of territorial losses to the Empire's rivals in the Balkans and elsewhere. Abdul Hamid tried and failed to exploit these disasters in a counter-revolution in April 1909. A month later, the Young Turks' army marched into Istanbul, dethroned the sultan, and effectively ended Ottoman rule.

The Young Turks outlawed any association in the Arab world wishing to promote Arab autonomy or independence. These associations went underground, and increased their numbers by recruiting teachers, students and army officers. Some of them were from Palestine, and all were inspired by the dream of a united, independent Arab entity. The Young Turks responded with a policy of Turkification aimed at forcing a new Turkish national identity on anyone living within the shrinking Ottoman Empire. This policy was coupled with strong secular tendencies, almost to the point of separating religion from state.

Notables and intellectuals alike faced a new situation with the Young Turks revolution of 1908. The older generation among the local Palestinian elite was, to put it mildly, unenthusiastic about the sudden change in their world. Secularism undermined their religious standing, the abolition of the sultanate weakened the influence of those owing personal allegiance to the sultan, and Turkish nationalism could not offer anything positive for those who were regarded as Arabs. In a way, the taking of sides created a generation gap within the leading urban families of Palestine. The old guard wished to stay away from politics, the younger generation to be more active. Some were excited by the revolutionary zeal of the Young Turks, but the majority wanted to be the avant-garde of the embryo national Arab movement. They therefore joined the various national associations operating in Greater Syria. These organizations were unable to surface as official parties until the end of the First World War, which also marked the appearance of the first official national Palestinian organizations. Before that, Palestinians toying with nationalist ideas did so secretly and at risk to themselves. In 1912, the Turkish government decreed that there would only be one national identity in the empire – Turkish. Those active in nationalist politics, many of them graduates of the Ottoman schools and of the private Christian schools, rejected this dictate, but did little to express their resentment.

The years immediately after the 1908 revolution were a watershed for the local social elite. In 1930, the Palestinian leader Jamal al-Husayni told a Central Asian Society conference in London that, for people like himself, the year 1908 had not only been the end of Ottoman rule in Istanbul, but also the end of the Ottoman era in Palestine. In his words, the 'Liberty of Palestine' had taken place at that moment. A more accurate account would have pointed to 1912 as the unequivocal turn towards Palestinian nationalism, when a coup inside the Young Turks regime brought the ascendance of anti-Arab Turkism.[18]

The political energy of the Young Turks affected not only the Muslim urban elite, but also all the Christian and veteran Jewish urban groups. Abdul Hamid's rebirth as a fundamentalist Islamist towards the end of his reign had created fears of a radical change for the worse in the status of Christian notables and Jewish city dwellers, which had hitherto been improving. The Young Turks, with their overt secularism, seemed to promise a more relaxed way of life and better chances for political involvement. In Palestine, the old Jewish *millet* adapted immediately to the secular state, while the elite Christians, in particular the intellectuals, were already slowly absorbing and mildly articulating a national Arab consciousness. They were readily joined in this by members of *a'ayan* families, the Muslim social elite.

However, there was another, anti-Turkish, Christian reaction. This came from products of the Anglican education system, which had motivated Christians to seek identity with a new secular Muslim Arab civilization in which nationalism would unite the religious groups, unlike the Ottoman world, which had divided them. Reformist Islamists and other members of the Muslim intellectual elite went through a similar process, influenced also by the Young Turks' blatant Turkish nationalism. The war provided a chance for this intellectual nationalism to claim to represent a mass political movement at the head of an anti-Turkish coalition. Damascus was the vibrant intellectual centre of Syria, and acted as a magnet for anyone in Palestine, Christian or Muslim, wishing to redefine themselves in secular national terms and prepare for a post-Ottoman future where the local Arab elites would have the final say in their societies' affairs.

During the First World War, this new-found politics, still mostly clandestine and under the guise of cultural and literary clubs, must have been an exciting experience for local urban elites. The town was the centre, in fact the exclusive territory, in which these new games were played. But most people in the towns did not belong to the elites, nor were they strong or organized enough to add weight to the process of politicization. Their lives changed not because of politicians, but because of engineers, builders and capitalists. They found new livelihoods within the new service infrastructure offered by towns early in the twentieth century: railways, sanitation, and the maintenance of lighting and water. There was nothing particularly 'Palestinian' about this way of life. Only after the First World War would the existential struggle for a reasonable living become associated by many locals with struggle against either Zionism or the British occupiers. When that happened, political discourse became more accessible and relevant to the majority.

A development did occur among ordinary people in urban Palestine, however. Local, as distinct from national, politics became an arena where town dwellers, not necessarily belonging to the elite, could play a role. The people of the towns seemed to discover the importance of legislative and representative bodies, especially city councils, which had been given new life after the Young Turks revolution, when more interest was shown in the welfare of the local population than ever before. The local Palestine press of the time gives the impression that the 'people' were asking for better municipal services.

This press was itself a new feature of the social and political scene in Palestine under the Young Turks, and played a progressive role in transforming the society, even though their survival was precarious and dependent on their owners' wealth. In one case, the press reported demands, made by that mysterious group 'the people', that the governor and the city council of Jerusalem intervene in the rising prices of essential commodities, bread being one. This was a demand, in fact, to broaden the terms of reference of the council. This may have come from members of the council who spoke in the name of the people; it is doubtful that it indicated a more sensitive attitude on the part of the notables. By law, the council was allowed to supervise the price of bread (as most people baked bread in their own homes, this was not much of a concession by the government). Other commodities were in fact not under supervision, and their prices had risen and fallen erratically. Some supervision was introduced as a result of this complaint.[19] That this was not necessarily a power struggle between the council and the governor can be seen from the Jerusalem press. In 1914, the press gave vent to the first criticism from below against the governor's corruption and the municipality's negligence. Both were accused of exploiting the city's budget for their own benefit. The council was criticized for its failure to maintain the water and sanitation systems.[20]

The press also gave the impression that the Turkish governor's hostile attitude towards foreigners was not always shared by members of the municipality or by those whose livelihood depended on tourists. The newspaper *al-Quds* made a clear distinction between tourists and more permanent visitors. The former in particular were now embraced: 'Tourists are welcome', it declared, '[as] they provide business for tourist guides, shop keepers etc'. However, these were exceptional cases; ordinary urban Palestinians were still far from having a meaningful say in their own social and economic welfare.[21]

Women too – but the elite only – began attempting to change their lives. At the beginning of the century, they organized on a gender basis for the first time. It was a small beginning, but an indication that politicization of elites extended to the women, and presumably also to life within elite families. Women workers were recruited only within the new Zionist community, but even here rhetoric was more abundant than fundamental change in gender relations. Ironically, in the less well-to-do sections of society, the increase in the number of tenants produced improvement of another sort in women's lives. The tenured life altered the traditional distribution of labour, although it did not curb the dominant role of the husband within the old patriarchal structure of the family.[22] This was manifested in women and men doing the same jobs for the same hours. Although this equality did not release women from their domestic tasks, it did expose them to the world outside their homes.

It is also possible to say that 1908 marked a new beginning for children in Palestine. Change depended less on their parents' decisions than on transformation occurring from above, such as when education became more universal and secular under the Young Turks. Although still harsh (corporal punishment remained the norm in Palestine in the first half of the century), education served as an alternative preparation for work in the adult world. Their progress was temporary, however, as they found themselves the main victims of the First World War.

In that very short period of Young Turk rule in Palestine, much was invested in the world of children. This had already begun in the late Ottoman period under Abdul Hamid's enthusiastic educational reforms. Generally speaking, Ottomans controlled the education system.[23] Local Palestinians, however, were given more say in supervising the schools, in that notables and religious dignitaries were members of the councils that ran schools in each sub-district. In Gaza, for instance, the local mufti headed the educational council, and Ismai'l al-Husayni's introduction of girls' education in Jerusalem has already been mentioned.

Education under the Young Turks was free, which meant little in the case of the Jerusalem *sanjaq*, where much of the education was in the hands of foreign missionaries who were not subsidized by the government. The districts of Acre and Nablus, being part of the *vilayet* of Beirut, benefited more from the policy. The Young Turks imposed a special tax on villagers and city dwellers for the construction of new schools. Despite their almost fanatical zeal for Turkification, the Young Turks expanded the study of Arabic in schools to counter the attraction of the secret nationalist societies and to support their claim to represent genuine Arab culture.[24] The societies, ironically, were able to exploit the new curriculum to increase national consciousness. In 1913, Turkish officials fought back against this surge in nationalism with new centralizing decrees that gave them direct supervision over the school system.

At the end of 1914, there were ninety-five elementary schools in Palestine and three junior high schools, the equivalent of the French lycée, in Acre, Nablus and Jerusalem. Just over two hundred teachers took care of about nine thousand pupils, of whom a little over 10 per cent were girls.[25] The traditional system, the *kutab*, was still functioning, with about three hundred schools and eight thousand pupils, of whom one hundred and thirty were girls.

During the First World War the school system was in chaos; yet the Turkish government decided at that time to build a *sultaniyya* school, rather like an American college, in which Arabic was the language of instruction and Turkish only a special choice. This became a teachers' college. Jamal Pasha, the governor of Palestine, took special interest in the school, and personally made sure it acquired laboratory equipment from Germany. It was built within a Jerusalem monastery and marked the last Turkish contribution to culture and society in Palestine after four hundred years of rule.[26]

Lest the impression be given of the Young Turk period as a comprehensive move towards a different Palestine, it should be stressed that the main actor in this book, the society at large, remained unaffected by high politics. Apart from foreigners and a few notable families in the principal towns, the peasants and land owners of Palestine took no interest in affairs in Istanbul. In the years between the revolution and the outbreak of the First World War, the people of Palestine who were not part of the political elite had other troubles. These were probably old troubles, but they appear in history books as new because Palestine became more open to the world at that time and therefore more accessible to the historian. For example more epidemics seem to have been reported in Palestine after the revolution than before it. So while Turkish secularism, Jewish colonialism, and Palestinian nationalism made their presence felt in Palestine in those first years of the twentieth century, for most of the people the annual episodes of cholera and plague remained a much more significant part of life. In 1910, the areas around Jerusalem were badly hit by a locust attack. The infestation followed a harsh winter in the Jerusalem mountains. In 1912, a cholera epidemic severely affected the town of Haifa and its vicinity. A local Jewish paper reported that all the people of Haifa lived in tents for the duration of the epidemic. These were rehearsals for two even worse years, 1915 and 1916, when natural disasters were overshadowed by human actions, which brought with them unprecedented death, hunger and unemployment. In this human catastrophe, villages fared better than towns, and densely populated cities such as Jaffa and Jerusalem suffered more than anywhere else the horrors of a war fought between foreign powers on Palestine's soil.[27]

The outbreak of the war destroyed the early buds of social and economic improvement undergone by a significant portion of the population. Ottoman citizens elsewhere in the empire had also demanded a larger share in the welfare system and policies. Specific groups in Palestine had become more assertive and critical. Women had procured political positions, and children been granted a higher level of literacy. The war, at first a European affair waged in the Balkans and Western Europe, took half a year to reach Palestine and, when it did, it brought with it hunger and death, the victims of which, apart from foreign soldiers, were the townspeople of Palestine, especially the children.[28]

The news of the outbreak of war was received with indifference in Palestine, by Muslims, Christians and Jews alike. The newspaper *Filastin* commented: 'Let the Europeans wash their own laundry. Our laundry we will wash in the Balkans' [i.e. the Balkans was a Turkish problem]. In December 1914, however, the Ottoman Empire abandoned its neutral position and joined Germany and Austria-Hungry in the war. Masses of soldiers arrived in Palestine, turning its cities into huge military camps. For most people in the cities this was the beginning of a terrible period. The military, like locusts, consumed everything in sight, including the meagre wealth and limited food the population possessed. Palestine began to starve, but all protest was silenced.

Banks closed their doors, so account holders could not gain access to their money. People had to cope with prices rising to unprecedented levels, particularly those of subsistence commodities such as flour, kerosene and sugar. Food imports stopped completely, and essential commodities became so dear that no one could afford them. Unemployment was rife. The Jewish community in Jaffa demonstrated its strength by teaching other Jews to adopt a campaign of self-sufficiency and solidarity. This was impressive in its scope, as it included the imposition of taxes on the wealthy, work for the unemployed, and the organization of medical help.[29] Only the very rich could maintain a decent lifestyle, particularly those who held money in British currency.

The people of Palestine were expected to conceal their despair. Muslim, Christian and Jewish leaders were recruited by the Turks to voice their unconditional support for the government in the frequent rallies held from the start of the war.[30] People who failed to rejoice in public, notwithstanding their hardships, risked the wrath of Jamal Pasha. This man and his actions are synonymous, in the collective memory of Jews and Arabs alike, with the evils of the war. Jamal was one of the most powerful people in Istanbul and a founder of the Young Turks movement. He was appointed commander-in-chief of the Turkish war effort in the Middle East just before fighting began. He based himself in Damascus, and frequently visited Greater Syria. His rule is remembered as a time of brutality, and Palestine was not spared. Whenever Jamal Pasha came to Palestine, he insisted on being received by large crowds as if he were the saviour of the common people. He was always seen in the company of the supreme commander of the German forces, General von Schellendorf, a sight that must have reinforced the perception of foreign rule by those who chose to oppose him in the name of Arab nationalism.

One of Jamal Pasha's main tasks was to recruit young men into the army. Very few Palestinian Arabs had served in the conscripted forces of the Ottoman army before the First World War.[31] As the war dragged on, soldiers became an acute need, but few young men in Palestine were interested, despite Jamal's fearsome presence. His ruthlessness towards deserters knew no boundaries. In 1914, he had three deserters, a Muslim, a Christian and a Jew, hanged in public in Jerusalem, and he continued mass executions for two years. Jews and Christians avoided military service by paying the *badaliya* (a fee levied to avoid conscription during the Ottoman period), but those who did not pay were considered deserters and forced to hide.

Muslims were victims of another of Jamal's personal crusades. He showed a growing paranoia about the secret associations of Syrian and Arab nationalism. Notables suspected, rightly or wrongly, of being associated with these groups were executed on charges of treason. For some reason, probably partly because he had a Jewish wife, Jamal could be more benevolent towards the Zionist settlements than towards the urban Muslim elite.

This is not to say that the Turkish position in the war was considered unacceptable. In particular, one feature of Turkish policy was welcomed: the abolition of the European capitulations. These were mainly trade concessions and judiciary privileges granted to European nationals and also bestowed on local Christians and Jews during the last years of Ottoman rule. The expansion of the capitulatory status had undermined the Muslim character of the country and the Muslims' position in it. Even Zionist leaders such as Yizhak Ben-Zvi (who would be the second president of the state of Israel) spoke against capitulations. But most Zionists, such as the leader of the pro-British underground and the founder of Zionist agronomy, Aharon Ahronson, saw their abolition as an unwelcome move which 'allowed every Arab shoe-polisher to feel equal . . . '.[32]

Jamal Pasha was, in a way, persecuting the wrong group. With hindsight it seems that Ahronson's anti-Turkish activities in Palestine were probably more damaging to the Turkish war effort than were those of the Palestinians. At first, Ahronson offered his services to the Turks, as part of the settlers' aim to be on the winning side in the war. When this was rejected, he found the British more than happy to accept his offer of intelligence assistance, which bound Zionism even more closely to the British. The Zionists' timing was perfect, as it would be throughout the Mandate. This practice in intelligence gathering and military life benefited the Zionists in an additional way by helping to shape the military strength of the Jewish community in Palestine. This embryo infrastructure would grow in the 1920s into an impressive defence organization that would enable the community finally to stand on its own, independent of the British.[33]

There was of course a silent majority of the population not involved in the war. At first, the Turks appeared to be heading for victory, which made it seem prudent to be passive and survive Jamal Pasha's dictatorship. In April 1915, the victory at Gallipoli was celebrated all over Palestine. But sadder images were to follow. The roads were filled with *tabur amliyeh*, the forced-labour battalions that were sent south to toil in inhuman conditions in the service of the Turkish army. They paved roads and cut down the forests until, by the end of 1915, Palestine was barren. The wood was used for railway lines to the south, where Jamal planned to transfer the bulk of his military force in preparation for the invasion of Egypt via the Sinai Peninsula. Nothing was spared; oaks, cedars and olive trees disappeared, not to mention the beautiful variety offered by the natural forests. This was an act of annihilation that undermined the livelihoods of many Palestinians. The destruction was in vain. Jamal's armies were defeated, and the railway lines were used two years later by the British Expeditionary Force coming from Egypt under the command of General Allenby. To Jamal Pasha's credit, however, it should be mentioned that this erratic general had unaccountable bursts of humanity. When a locust plague wiped out the wheat crop, he established a general grocery company on a commercial basis for the benefit of all the inhabitants, to combat price speculation. However, the famine was of a magnitude unprecedented in the history of Palestine, and by 1917 it had decimated the towns in particular. In that year, in Jerusalem alone, 300 people a month died of hunger.

The war finally ended, and with it the deprivation, the executions, and the killings. It had delayed but not ended the slow processes of change that had begun in Palestine in the nineteenth century but was most significant between 1908 and 1918. It had begun with the replacement of the Ottoman Empire by a secular state in the wake of the revolution, and with the transfer of the centre of Zionist activity from Europe to Palestine. It culminated in the First World War, the 'Great War', and the British occupation. The latter development resulted in the British policy of support for the Zionist movement, in which Britain shared the vision of Palestine as a Jewish homeland.

Palestine's political future was determined without any local participation in the discussion. The intensive colonial negotiations on the country's structure and development moved in three discrete directions. The first was the Hashemite connection. The Turks' anti-Arab and anti-Islamic policies generated anti-Turkish reactions from religious figures in the Arab world, such as Sharif Husayn of Mecca, Guardian of Mecca and Medina, the two holy cities of Islam in the Hejaz, and from the various members of the secret Arab associations.

The Hashemites were notables, descendants of the Prophet Muhammad. The family had strong ties with Abdul Hamid, but these ceased to be of use when the Young Turks came to power. From the outset, the Young Turks made it clear that they preferred to control Mecca and Medina directly, and in 1908 threatened to depose Sharif Husayn. It is no wonder that when the British, with the help of the legendary T. E. Lawrence, contacted the Sharif and offered an anti-Turkish alliance, the head of the Hashemite family did not hesitate. He insisted, however, on defining the quid pro quo. At the end of 1915 and throughout the first months of 1916, a correspondence was conducted between Sharif Husayn and the British high commissioner to Egypt, Sir Henry McMahon, in which the Hashemites were promised a leading role in the new Middle East. In return, they led an Arab revolt against the Turks in 1916.

The British had not been open with the Hashemites, however, who could not have known that the British had other plans for the Middle East. These plans had been concocted with the French in 1912, and were the second axis on which politics in the area developed. At that time, Palestine was seen as a buffer zone to protect the Suez Canal, its occupation complementary to the annexation of the Sinai Peninsula to Egypt, which had been accomplished by Britain in 1906. Palestine was discussed as part of the diplomatic hyperbole involving the European powers, which became entangled in pre-war alliances and counter-alliances. This web of treaties deeply involved the European powers in the Balkans, a part of the Ottoman Empire that gradually became independent with the help of the European powers, particularly Russia, France and Britain. Against this trio, Germany and the Austro-Hungarian Empire continued to support the Ottoman presence in the area, or at least preferred to have it under their control. Therefore, with the intensification of competition and hostility between the Germanic powers and the Allies (Britain, France and Russia), the Ottoman Empire drew closer to the former. The Ottomans needed German help against expansionist tsarist tendencies. Russia was still looking for an outlet to a warm sea (its northern ocean was frozen for most of the year), as it coveted a superior position in the continent. Its war plans included the occupation of Anatolia, the heart of the Ottoman Empire. This balance of powers meant that the Ottoman–Arab Middle East was a potential site for a European confrontation, which came to pass in the First World War.

In 1912, the British and French had not yet discussed the division of the spoils, should they win the war. They contemplated a different political configuration for the Arab Middle East via the establishment of new political units in the place of the Ottoman provinces. Thus Syria, Iraq and Palestine would come into existence as political entities, to be joined later by Lebanon and Transjordan. When the war finally began, France and Britain moved to implement their plan to take over the Arab Middle East. In a meeting in May 1916, Sir Mark Sykes of the British Foreign Office and his counterpart in the French Foreign Ministry, George Picot, divided the Arab Middle East between them into two spheres of influence and into new political entities.

This division broke promises made by the British government to Sharif Husayn. In his letters, Husayn had stated that he wished for an extended reign, for himself and his four sons, and possibly for representatives of the embryo Arab national movement, over all the Arab former provinces of the Ottoman Empire. The British agreed in principle, but cautioned Husayn that in certain areas, which they defined vaguely, they had to consider other interests, such as those of the French and the non-Arab minorities. These considerations became the major criteria in the Sykes-Picot Agreement.

Under the pressure of political events, Husayn paid little attention to these qualifications. He learnt later that the Sykes-Picot Agreement removed a sizeable chunk from the area that to the best of his understanding had been designated part of a future Hashemite kingdom. Quite a few historians agree that Husayn was cheated. T. E. Lawrence shared the Hashemites' sense of humiliation, and tried in the last stages of the war to extend the Hashemite area at the expense of the French sphere of influence, but to no avail. Lawrence was responsible for the attempt to enthrone one of Husayn's sons, Faysal, as king of Greater Syria (to include Transjordan, Palestine and Lebanon as well as Syria). This attempt was foiled by the British Foreign Office, which gave precedence to the Anglo-French alliance over agreement with local Arab forces. So Britain allowed French troops, in accordance with the Sykes-Picot Agreement, to land in Lebanon in 1918 and from there invade Syria in 1920, expel Faysal's small army, and end his short-lived kingdom.

The Hashemites realized that they had been deceived even before the war was over. The Bolshevists, who overturned the Russian Empire in

November 1917, published secret agreements to which the Russian government had been a party. One such document was the Sykes-Picot Agreement, as it had involved conceding to the Russians, lest they should object, some areas in Armenia and northern Anatolia. The contradiction between the Sykes-Picot Agreement and the Husayn–McMahon correspondence now became public knowledge.

At first these developments did not seem to touch the fate of Palestine, but with the Balfour Declaration, the third aspect of the colonial strategy for Palestine, the connection was all too obvious. It took some time before the Hashemites and Palestinians learned of the promise made by the British government to build a Jewish homeland in Palestine, but when they did hear about it they hastened to ascertain whether this posed an additional limitation on the promises made to Husayn.

The Balfour Declaration was part of a British attempt to revise an earlier proposition to rule Palestine jointly with France. In November 1917, the British forces were already occupying Palestine; there was not a single French soldier in the region. The British therefore became *de facto* rulers, with no intention of sharing it with anyone. The Sykes-Picot Agreement was not applied to Palestine, and the British remained there until 1948.

At the start of the war, the Zionist leadership had quickly tried to persuade the British government that the establishment of a Jewish colony in Palestine was a superior British interest. In London, politicians such as Herbert Samuel and the foreign secretary, Arthur Balfour, took it upon themselves to help the new president of the movement, Haim Weizmann, to carry out his propaganda campaign. They eventually succeeded in bringing about a change in British policy. Their main success was in building a stable lobby group of both Jewish and non-Jewish public figures, centred on the Rothschild family. In 1916, the government began official negotiations with the heads of the Zionist movement. On 2 November 1917, Lord Balfour declared British commitment to the establishment of a Jewish homeland in Palestine.

What caused the British government to support the Zionist cause? The documents of the period reveal that a central factor in its decision was the important role its ministers attributed to the Jews of Russia in formulating the new reformist tsarist government there. Without Russia, there was very little hope of successfully surrounding Germany with a ring of enemy states, a strategy it was hoped would cause Germany to surrender. The British government expected that Russian Jews would become the agents of pro-British propaganda that would persuade the tsarist government to come out clearly in support of the Allies' effort to subjugate Germany. This was an exaggerated evaluation of the role of Russian Jewry in the empire; there is no evidence of Jewish influence at the Tsar's court at that time. The British Foreign Office was also aware of the importance of Jews in the Bolshevik movement, and hoped that support for Jewish nationalism would build pro-British sentiment in the Bolshevik organization. In hindsight, the Bolshevik Jews were a-nationalist in their outlook; certainly not Zionist. British hopes were wrongly placed.

Other factors encouraged the British in their efforts. Both their allies and their enemies hinted that they were interested in linking the Zionist movement to their own colonialist interests, thus accelerating the decision in London to issue the Balfour Declaration. In addition, an unrealistic view of the role of Jews in shaping American policy contributed to the British pro-Zionist orientation. The British government was eagerly awaiting handsome American financial aid in its war effort. This aid, in the form of a loan, was postponed due to objections from many members of Congress. Finally, we should not exclude the possibility that pious Christians, such as the British prime minister David Lloyd George, were motivated by a wish to facilitate the return of the Jews to precipitate the second coming of the Messiah.

In November 1917, the Zionist movement was rewarded with the Balfour Declaration. This document promised a benevolent British attitude towards the establishment of a national home for the Jews in Palestine, provided it did not clash with the interests of the local population. The honeymoon between Arab nationalism and Britain during the Great War did not therefore produce Arab sovereignty in Palestine, which became part of the British Empire in the Middle East and remained, as it had always been, the homeland of the indigenous population of Palestine. This population was not interested in British imperialism, Zionist colonialism, or even local proto-nationalism. This did not prevent their becoming victims of these three phenomena.

In summary, the negotiations on Palestine's future produced three documents: the Husayn–McMahon correspondence, the Sykes-Picot Agreement and the Balfour Declaration. Each included a promise for the local population. In ambiguous language, each promise contradicted the other two. The first associated the future of Palestine with that of an Arab Hashemite kingdom in the Arab world; the second proposed placing Palestine under Anglo–French colonial rule; and the last envisaged it as a future Jewish state. The only group represented in this game of high politics was the foreign community in Palestine, which now consisted of three distinct groups: the most important was the Zionist settlement; the second was the Templars;

and the third the European consuls and their social milieu, which included long-term visitors from the countries they represented.

For the Zionist movement, the First World War was a turning point. The Balfour Declaration and similar statements by the Allies accentuated the sense among the movement's leaders that history was on their side. For a while during the war, the project had seemed endangered. Shortly after the defeat of the Turks at El-Arish and the evacuation of Gaza early in 1917, Jamal Pasha ordered the removal of Jaffa's population in preparation for an imminent British landing from the sea. It seems that he imposed the order mainly on the Jewish population, as well as on the small community of Jews in Tel-Aviv. Altogether 9,000 poor and hungry Jews had to leave their homes and jobs for eighteen months before being allowed back by the new occupiers of Palestine, the British.

The Zionists were undeterred by this, and instead focused their energy on high politics. For them, rhetoric and visionary scenarios were no less important than their implementation. Leo Mozkin, a leading intellectual, ideologue and leader of the Zionist movement, summarized the Zionist position on the Palestine question in 1918 in a manner that was accepted by almost all his colleagues in the movement's leadership. It was based on an assumption made by a German expert at the time that Palestine could absorb six million Jews without the need to expel the local population. The same expert had also stated that much depended on the consent of local Arabs to live under Jewish sovereignty and a future Jewish majority. Expulsion was thus not considered a necessary part of the plan for a new home for Jews, unless the Zionist project was resisted by the local population.

However, the Zionist reality on the ground in Palestine was far from satisfying. The community that historians now call the Yishuv (the settlement), a term that would be used during the Mandate, had suffered severely from war and Turkish oppression. This was a poor community that was starving as a result of the war. Veteran Jews and newcomers alike barely survived the shortage of food and the absence of essential commodities. Their number had been reduced to 60,000 by war's end.

This was not the final act in the theatre of the absurd that was unfolding in the wake of the disintegration of the Ottoman Empire. Two additional actors made their voices heard. One was the Hashemite family, in the form of Faysal, Sharif Husayn's son, who based himself in Damascus, thereby challenging the Sykes-Picot Agreement. Even before the end of hostilities in the Middle East in the spring of 1918, Husayn and his family faced the harsh reality of broken promises in the age of modern imperialism. Husayn's sons and their tribes had joined the British forces, contributing to the general

Figure 2. A rural family from the Ramallah area at the end of the Ottoman era

Allied military effort by waging a kind of guerrilla warfare in the wake of the conventional forces. They did not change the military balance, but the fact that Husayn, who held one of the most important positions in the Muslim world, was on the British side was significant in counterbalancing the Turkish attempt to raise a holy war with the help of the Muslims of India. At first, Husayn had contemplated the division of spoils between his sons. He allocated Baghdad, and whatever would be attached to it, to his eldest son, Abdullah, and Damascus and its environs to his second son, Faysal. Husayn had two others sons, who were promised positions in his own kingdom in the Hejaz. In 1916, this part of the Arabian Peninsula became an independent state, recognized at the Versailles peace conference in 1918.

· The second actor was the USA, specifically President Woodrow Wilson, who had in 1914 stipulated the conditions for American entry to world politics, whether in war or peace. Wilson, a democrat, wished to dismember colonial empires and grant their oppressed peoples the right of self-determination. As we shall see, he demanded the same for the people living in the area divided by Britain and France as their new colonial possessions.

As the drums of war sounded in Damascus and Cairo, rural Palestine lived, as it had for centuries, on terraced hills and mountain slopes, and in new locations slowly edging towards the coast. The villages, much like the Mediterranean islands today, were painted white, adorned with strong blue ornaments against the evil eye, and ringed with fruit trees and bougainvillea. In the centre of a typical village, a square and a mosque served as the meeting point for public discussion and interaction. The clan was still the dominant point of reference, much more so than sect or religion. The community remained patriarchal and yet egalitarian in its attitude to possession, quite abusive in its treatment of women and children, and yet it included mechanisms for improvement and change from within. The village's main source of survival was still the cultivated field. This was a meagre but secure existence. Abuses of power, whether by Turkish tax collectors or military press-gangs, were infrequent enough to enable a routine-filled lifestyle to go on.

Palestine's cities were also growing steadily, enabling several groups to improve their status and standard of living. Women belonging to wealthy families fared better than before, and their children were accorded a reasonable level of education. Both cities and villages were as autonomous as they had been when the Ottomans occupied the land at the beginning of the sixteenth century. This autonomy entrenched the dominant position of the city notables in their own society and in the forefront of Istanbul's memory. This elite, consisting of different categories according to religious genealogy, wealth and history, successfully negotiated a path for themselves between Istanbul, the regional capitals of Beirut and Damascus, the intrusive foreign consuls, and the demands from society inside and outside the city walls. It was a Palestine lost to the rural sheikhs and to the heads of Bedouin tribes, who had realized earlier than anyone else in the nineteenth century that whatever modern Palestine meant, it offered them few prospects. However, perhaps surprisingly, some future role in politics would be found, at least for the sheikhs, as will be seen in the following chapters.

# CHAPTER 3

# The Mandatory State: Colonialism, Nationalization and Cohabitation

## ALLENBY'S PALESTINE

On 9 December 1917, General Allenby, the commander in chief of the British Expedition Force from Egypt, occupied Jerusalem and established a temporary political framework for administering Palestine, the occupied enemy territory. In September 1918 the north of Palestine was taken quietly and, once upper Galilee was ceded from French Syria in 1919, Palestine and Israel as we know them today were one geo-political unit and an integral part of the British Empire in the Middle East.

Allenby envisaged himself as a reborn crusader, or a quasi-monarch, whose 'realm' was run very much like other new British possessions in the area, with the help of Arabists from the British Arab office in Cairo. With their guidance, Allenby laid the foundations for a new political dispensation in Palestine. A few months after his arrival, his small entourage of experts was augmented by colonial officials who had gained their experience in India, Africa or Egypt. They shared a common perception of the new British possession as an Arab country.

General Allenby and the two military governors who replaced him between 1918 and 1920 were hampered by the commitment in the Balfour Declaration to make a Jewish homeland in what they saw as an Arab country. While senior and junior members of the administration may have had reservations about this, their personal views mattered little. They were functionaries of a policy formulated in London's corridors of power. There was also a group of pro-Zionist officials within the local British administration who helped to further the Zionist cause. Whether military governors or colonial clerks, pro-Arab or pro-Jewish, the Britons were all committed to serving British interests in Palestine. Not only was this interpreted according to events in the Middle East, but it also reflected a more global British strategy.

Allenby's Palestine was battered, its landscape scarred by war, particularly in and around the coastal areas. Nearly a third of it was still densely cultivated, another third was urban, and the rest was a mixture of desert, small natural reservoirs, and what were flourishing forested areas before being erased by the Turkish war machine. The 800,000 inhabitants were immediately classified by the new rulers according to religious affiliation: 650,000 Muslims, 80,000 Christians, and 60,000 Jews, including the veteran Jewish *millet* and the Zionist settlers.

The immediate consequence of the war was the disappearance of Turkish officialdom and language, as if the Ottomans had never been in charge. The urban Muslim elite constituted the country's leadership as far as the new occupiers were concerned. The people of Palestine had paid dearly for the European decision to use their land as a theatre of war. Almost forty thousand Muslims, more than ten thousand Christians and more than a thousand Jews had died by tyranny, arms, famine and disease. Dry statistics talk about a 'decline of 6 per cent in the population'.[1]

In this Palestine, as under the Ottomans, most people were peasants who lived in about a thousand villages, whose houses were built, as in previous centuries, from materials found around them: stone in the hills; mud, clay and straw on the plains. There was a certain symbolic quality to the materials selected for the houses; the stony ones in the hills withstood the wrath of war, while the clay ones on the coast succumbed. Not everyone in rural Palestine was a cultivator of land. About 15 per cent of the community made a living indirectly from agricultural production (traders, mule drivers, middlemen etc.). They all competed with each other, and with the Zionist settlers, for water. Few agriculturists used irrigation; 90 per cent of them waited for rain or drew on, with varying degrees of efficiency, the rivers and springs – by then polluted. Those who did use modern methods of irrigation were growing citrus fruit or producing vegetables and fruit for sale.[2]

The human capacity for resuming life once the winds of war had subsided was apparent everywhere. The same patterns that dictated the village economy in the late Ottoman period occurred in British Mandate Palestine. The capitalization of the agriculture market intensified. Wheat, sesame and sorghum were now grown everywhere, reducing the variety and narrowing the spectrum of colours in the local fields.

The villages remained safe spaces for their inhabitants. They were also autonomous, as British interference was slow in coming and restricted to certain spheres of life. There were two schools of thought in Britain about how far and in what manner London should rule its colonies: a generous one, which prevailed in the early years of British rule, and a more austere, which dominated later policy. The first strategy assumed a long British stay in Palestine and appears euphemistically in the documents as 'the commonwealth approach'. Its logic was that there was a need to invest in the local infrastructure so that economic autonomy would benefit colonized and colonizer alike.

On the ground, the choice between investment, i.e. intervention, and autonomy was unclear. In the early stages the government wished to follow the Indian example, allowing villages autonomy according to traditional hierarchy and custom. But a mixture of additional influences, particularly officials who came from Egypt where British colonialism was far more involved in infrastructure development, made the Mandate government more invasive than it had originally wished or declared itself to be.

Despite theoretical autonomy, there was a higher level of colonial intervention by the end of the first decade of British rule. The British tried to influence local agricultural policy, educational infrastructure, medical services, and political orientation. The clear aim was limited modernization: improvement in rural life with the help of existing local tradition so as to avoid the dangerous leap forward that had produced anti-British nationalism in Egypt and India. Similarly, expansion of elementary schools was encouraged, but there was no need for high schools, and certainly not for universities. The colonial officials thus allowed only a slow process of change, which left the rural economy unable to cope with the economic competition of the Jewish market.

More than anything else, the officials wanted to keep the villagers in the rural areas, and they hoped that traditional agriculture would do this. Full urbanization was deemed a dangerously uncontrollable process. The local social elite was to be left intact but subordinate to the British officials, who would mediate between village and government.

The British educational policy provides a good illustration of this. It led the foundation for a rural education system under governmental supervision. Special stress was put on teacher training. Two new colleges for teachers were opened in Jerusalem. The *sultaniyya* school was closed and its sophisticated German equipment, the pride of Jamal Pasha, moved to the new colleges. Girls' education was enhanced too on a grander scale than in the days of Ismai'l al-Husayni.[3] Within a year, results were visible. In every village and town there was an elementary school, and each village received 30 pounds, provided it allocated a similar sum for the opening of new schools. In 1919 alone, fifty-two schools were opened in rural Palestine.[4]

Figure 3. The Girls' College of Jerusalem, 1920

When civil administration was brought in, Humphry Bowman, a quintessential colonialist educator, took charge of education. He viewed the local people in the same way as he had those for whom he had previously been responsible in Egypt and India, as primitive, illiterate and, above all, too poor to pay for their education. And yet, his approach was motivated by more than contempt and scorn. He wished sincerely to make improvements, and indeed contributed to the local education system. He opened an additional college for teachers in Ramallah in 1920 and an agricultural college, the Kedourie College, in Tul-Karem in 1931 (not be confused with the Jewish Kedourie College, on the slopes of Mount Tabor, which was a kind of preparatory school for the next generation of Zionist leaders, such as Yigal Alon and Yitzhak Rabin). Bowman's idea was to expand elementary schooling, to widen the high school system slightly and to open up limited opportunities to a more general, non-nationalist education. In short, Bowman wished the villages to continue in their traditional way of life and production with no incentive for change or urbanization (in his eyes a recipe for politicization and nationalization).[5]

In one respect, the British newcomers were most welcome – as healers and doctors. At the end of the First World War, Palestine was still a breeding ground for many diseases, mainly due to the total absence of hygiene. Several European doctors who served the local community should be mentioned in any history of Palestine. Most came after the war as part of the British army health corps in Palestine, and did much to reinforce health and hygiene regulations, so that Palestine became one of the healthiest societies in the eastern Mediterranean.[6]

The motives for this were less altruistic than may at first appear. Thousands of Allenby's soldiers suffered from what he called 'unhealthy conditions', and action was taken primarily to save British lives.[7] The worst health conditions were experienced by Bedouins, whose goat-hair tents and clothing were insufficient protection against the extremes of nature, and who were defenceless against lice and mosquitoes. Even in the wealthier sections of society, however, money and ample food were no shield against malaria and pulmonary tuberculosis. Had it not been for the culture of outdoor life, the instances of smallpox, typhus and measles would have been even higher. When the British introduced their own system of public health and medicine to Palestine, the mortality rate fell. Some British doctors even felt that rural Palestine had something to teach them. They reported with astonishment how easily and naturally childbirth was treated. In addition, contrary to their prejudices, recovery from injury with the help of herbal treatments was swift, provided acute diseases did not affect patients.

Although colonization meant control and exploitation, the infrastructure put in place to achieve this had useful by-products. There was investment in communication and infrastructure, which made rural Palestine less isolated. Trains and trucks brought the telegraph and the mail service to almost every corner. During the late Ottoman period, foreign mail had been taken to Jaffa to be shipped to Europe, but now post office branches were opened everywhere. A public telephone network was installed early on, old roads were fixed and asphalted, and the railways extended to many new destinations.[8]

Most government effort, however, in terms of time and energy, was directed to high politics. The goal was clear: to build an Arab–Jewish mandate modelled on British rule in Egypt and Iraq, with a high commissioner to rule over Arab–Jewish executive and legislative authorities. Development and welfare were left to follow. The most pressing issue on the political agenda was the developing conflict between the Zionist settlers and local people, in which rural Palestinians felt more threatened than the urban elite. This began in 1919 with the early tours by Zionist officials responsible for the purchase of land. These officials came to inspect land owned by urban notables. In their wake, new Jewish settlements appeared, mostly on the coast, with modern methods of irrigation and their new habitations fenced and guarded.

To the rural people of Palestine, however, their colonial rulers were largely at arm's length, although they would have seen the face of the far distant British sovereign on coins and notes when the Anglo-Egyptian pound was made an official currency. (In 1927 this was replaced by a Palestinian pound, equal in value to sterling but looking like the Egyptian pound.)[9] Also, in the Ottoman period, rulers had been accessible on tax-collection days, but local heads of villages now collected taxes, and for quite some time the British rulers left the chief Turkish taxes intact. The main burden as far as the peasants were concerned was the tithe, which was demanded by the British with the same vigour as had the Turks.

When Allenby left for England and was replaced by a civil government, a period of stagnation was over. In 1920, commerce in the towns resumed, and with it the autonomy of the villages was eroded. In a very measured way, over more than fifteen years, market forces, or rather the human beings behind them, invaded the apolitical environment of the villages. Those engaged in agricultural production no longer limited their selling to the nearby town or city; they now exported goods outside their known world to the ever-growing Jewish population of Palestine, with its unprecedented level of consumption. The proportion of Palestinian agricultural produce marketed outside the Palestinian economy went from 50 per cent in 1921 to 65 per cent in 1935.[10]

The new customers, British and Jewish, needed labour as well as fruit and vegetables. Between 1921 and 1935, the number of Palestinians employed in the Jewish economy tripled from 4,000 to 12,000. This figure is all the more impressive when one considers that, according to national narratives, the Zionist determination to exclude Palestinian labour was strengthened, formulated and turned into a proper ideology in those very years, with any deviation punished. And yet, despite efforts by the Zionist leadership to pursue an exclusively Jewish labour policy, it is evident that the Palestinian and Jewish markets remained interdependent, and the people themselves acted against the demands for segregation made by the political elites of both sides.

This is in many ways the untold story of Mandate Palestine. The familiar account of events charts a dramatic story of British colonialism confronting local nationalisms; a spectacle of intrigue and power relations that affected the population as a whole. While not contradicting this, I am suggesting that, before that process was completed, those who were neither local elites or leaders, nor the British ruling class, attempted a different way of life.

Most books on Mandate Palestine would begin with the early days of conflict that culminated in the first wave of violence in April 1920. However, we should take into account the reductionist nature of this description. In the relatively autonomous spaces in which most people lived, religion and spiritualism were still much more common influences on life than were British officials or Zionist colonialists. In fact, some of the newcomers, who were ethnographers by heart or profession, reported on various aspects of life in a Palestinian village. It seems that the metaphysical world was still occupying a powerful position in rural life (and continued to do so until the end of the Mandate).

In rural Palestine, villagers still trusted their saints more than the new rulers or would-be national leaders. Pilgrimages to the burial sites (*maqam*) of holy people were as widespread in Palestine during the Mandate as before, except that, in the Ottoman period, most of these sites had been visited jointly by followers of the three monotheistic religions. As they were often in difficult terrain, sites were visited collectively, with donkeys and mules carrying provisions for a long stay. Almost every Palestinian village had such a *maqam*, some several. Heroic mythical or real warriors from the time of the Arab conquest, quranic and biblical figures, and even people who had fought against Muhammad Ali in the 1840s, were included in the saintly community buried in these holy places. Some urban notable families claimed to be and were recognized as descendants of these saints, such as the Dajani family, which was responsible for many sites associated with King David in Jerusalem. There were also some female saints. The Bedouins in southern Palestine worshipped heroines such as Fatima, the daughter of the saint Ahmad Abu Shabib, known for her healing abilities both during her lifetime and after her death. However, during the Mandate, the sites were politicized and therefore segregated.

Living in Palestine now meant belonging to a more cohesive geo-political unit than ever before. This was the product of colonialist effort, corresponding somewhat to the harmonious ethnic and religious fabric on the ground. This was a break from the past, as Palestine had not been a well-defined entity before. By 1918, Palestine was more united administratively than in the Ottoman period, since the war fused the three sub-provinces into one administrative entity. While waiting for final international approval of Palestine's status in 1923, the British government negotiated the final borders of the land, creating a better-defined space for the national movements to struggle over, and a clearer sense of belonging to the people living in it. The final shaping of the borders helped the Zionist movement to conceptualize geographically its concept of Eretz Israel, the land of Israel.

## THE NATIONALIZATION OF THE CITIES (1918–1920)

Two chapters in the political drama were followed closely by the urban elite: the inclusion of the Balfour Declaration in the Mandate, and the French struggle against Faysal's claim to be king of greater Syria, made after his entrance to Damascus at the end of 1918. Whereas politics was encroaching slowly on rural Palestine, it was galloping at speed into the world of the urban Palestinian elite. In the towns, a new force was emerging: nationalism. It was disseminated by the religious notables, who quickly became nationalist notables.

As elsewhere in the world, nationalism meant a powerful bond between people sharing a story of the past, an interpretation of the present, and a vision for the future. People in different walks of life imagined or invented themselves and the reality around them in a similar way. As such they were able to become a political collective. How much of this was new is hard to say. The people involved in this process continued much of their previous lifestyle as an Ottoman nobility, and had a blurred notion of what nationalism demanded in terms of solidarity and commitment.

The new interpretation of life as a national experience was formulated within the familiar clannish circles of Palestine's principal towns. When the British came, they found the notable families in control over social, cultural and religious life as before, with added economic power that had come into their hands since the Crimean war. The names of the local leaders were familiar to the British from their consuls' reports in the Ottoman period: they were all listed as *a'ayan*, the urban notables of late Ottoman Palestine.[11] There was nonetheless one conspicuous difference. The end of the Ottoman era in Palestine closed a chapter in the political life of one generation but opened the way into politics for the younger one. The leaders were now young men in their twenties belonging to the *a'ayan* families of Jerusalem, Jaffa, Nablus, Hebron and Haifa. They were much more suited to dealing with the new rulers, given their more secular and, to a certain extent Europeanized, education. These people could more readily engage in nationalist politics, having as youth at the end of the Ottoman period been genuinely attracted to the idea of Arab nationalism. Very few of them had translated this support into actual membership of the secret Arab national societies of Damascus, Beirut or Cairo, partly from fear, but mainly because their elders had wished the Ottoman world to remain the same. But now there was no longer a Turkish state and, far more importantly, there was a genuine, albeit virtual, Arab state, in the form of Faysal's Greater Syria. National discourse could be toyed with, articulated and propagated. The British impact on the urban education system was at first closely in accord with the dreams of the young nationalists. The British made Arabic the official language, thus contributing to a further formulation of national identity. They allowed secularism to supersede religious education, and were regarded by the national elite as helping to foment a national force and combat sectarian affiliations.

Faysal's claiming of Palestine as an integral part of an independent Arab kingdom caught the novice nationalists unprepared. Their country was ruled by the British, desired by the Zionists and, until 1920, claimed by the Hashemites. This is not to say that they were passive. They shared a sense of a historical moment that could be influenced by anyone who chose to enter the political arena of Arab nationalism in Palestine. The more perceptive among them understood the power of the printed word and, although playing a subaltern role in their country's politics, gained access to it by starting up newspapers to communicate their ideas on the future of the country to their peers.[12]

The new activists used newspapers, first in Jaffa and Haifa, then in Jerusalem, to mobilize a common response to the first anniversary of the Balfour Declaration. This was dictated by the fact that almost all the early journalists were Christians, who promoted nationalism as a bi-religious movement. The discussions in the press turned into real political action when, in 1918, young Palestinian enthusiasts from the notable families established the Christian–Muslim Association, Palestine's first-ever political party. The society opened branches all over the country, aiming to organize a national show of power against Zionism and for Faysalism.

On that first anniversary, a national day of protest was declared, and strongly supported, even by relatively marginal members of the leading families. Its success induced more Muslim notables to join in enthusiastically. Although capable of enlisting hundreds and at times thousands of people for protests during the years in which Palestine's political future was decided, the elites lacked the will to organize on a more consistent basis in order to erect the infrastructure for a future state. While Zionism was moving from small intimate communities to an anonymous and impersonal modern structure, Palestinian politicians left the reins of politics in the hands of Faysal, rather than entrust them to the Mandate.

The British were now about to play a strange role in completing the process of turning the *a'ayan* into nationalist leaders. The main problem for the British rulers was that the community they called the 'Muslims of Palestine' had an elite, but no leadership, let alone a leader. The British tried to impose the Ottoman concept of a *millet*, a community represented by a titular religious head, on the Muslim majority in Palestine. Their experts on Islam reinvented the mufti, who held the highest position in the Muslim social hierarchy. A mufti was a Muslim priest who delivered judgements on the basis of his scriptural and religious knowledge. His judgements applied to both mundane and critical aspects of life, and affected communal as well as individual behaviour. The potency of the role position had already impressed the British in Egypt, where they regarded the Mufti of Egypt as the highest religious authority in the land, before the secular national movement took over. Ironically, Palestine was the only British possession in the Middle East to be led by a mufti who became an enemy of Britain in the region.

Palestine had many muftis. There was one for each major town and each school of Islam. The Hanafi school, which was favoured by the Ottomans, was dominant in Palestine. The British therefore appointed the Hanafi mufti of Jerusalem to be the Mufti of Palestine and the leader of its Muslim majority. This was Kamil al-Husayni, a descendant of the city's leading family, whose ancestors had held that position, with few interruptions, since 1700. Al-Husayni was an Anglophile, and at least until the spring of 1920 seemed to be uninterested in politics, which served the British well. But other members of his family, particularly his younger brother Haj Amin, had approved of the creation of Greater Syria, and revered Faysal as the future king of Palestine. The younger generation, like their peers among the urban Christians, formed the nucleus of an active cadre of Palestine's future politicians.[13]

### THE END OF 'SOUTHERN SYRIA'

During the process of appointing a suitable leader, the local elite was asked to voice its opinion on Palestine's future. This request came from the American president, in those days an unimportant actor in Middle Eastern politics. President Woodrow Wilson sent a commission of inquiry, which was told that Palestinians wanted to be part of Greater Syria, opposed the Balfour Declaration vehemently, and if they had to consider foreign guardianship at all would prefer it to be American. Nothing came of this as Wilson was losing ground at home and the US was withdrawing into isolation.

The American initiative served as a catalyst for three national groups. They differed little in their responses to the Americans, but enough to divide them. The Christian–Muslim Association expanded its branches, while two new national clubs with opposing views enlivened the political scene. They were al-Nadi al-Arabi and al-Muntada al-Adabi, an Arab club and a literary club respectively. The former was dominated by the Husayni family, and the latter by their opponents, the Nashashibis. This conflict among the notables was echoed later when the Husayni elevation by the British was opposed by the Nashashibis, who established, with British help as part of a divide and rule policy, an official opposition group, al Mu'arada. However, the tension was less obvious since the sons of both families, as with other notables and intellectuals, were members of more than one, and at times of all three, organizations.

In all, only a few dozen urban notables and intellectuals were involved in nationalism in Palestine when the Americans inquired into the will of the people. This is not meant as irony. There is no way of telling whether what the Americans were told was indeed the will of the people; but this was elite politics in practice, and was therefore limited to the self-interest of the elite groups.

The withdrawal of the Americans left King Faysal of Greater Syria alone in his struggle with European colonialism. Britain and France concurred after lengthy negotiations that the French had the right to oust the Hashemite prince from Syria, which they did in the summer of 1920. In return no one challenged British rule in its new Middle Eastern possession that provided economic gains to the mother country and served imperial interests such as in the case of Palestine the route to India and access to the oilfields of Arabia.

The Palestinian nationalist notables made a last effort to save Greater Syria, using mass rallies, theatre productions and newspapers in an attempt to show widespread support for Faysal in Palestine. The most vociferous among them were two enthusiastic young men, Arif al-Arif and Amin al-Husayni. Arif al-Arif was one of Jerusalem's most reputable teachers, and later became one of Palestine's leading historians. Amin al-Husayni was the Mufti's brother. In the twilight of Greater Syria, the two published a newspaper called *Southern Syria*, the name Palestine was to take in Faysal's future kingdom. The Nashashibis and their allies were not recruited to Faysal's side and, in a newspaper called *Filastin*, founded by an Orthodox Christian in Jaffa in 1909, they called for an independent Palestine.

Zionism, however, was universally condemned as evil and dangerous. The notables earmarked the Christian Easter and the Muslim feast of Nabi Musa, both near the Jewish feast of Passover, as an appropriate time at which to express public wrath against the decision of the British government to recognize the Zionist claims over Palestine. In April 1920, a Nabi Musa rally clashed with the most aggressive of the Zionist organizations, Beitar, whose members marched provocatively in the streets of Arab Jerusalem at the time of the feast, and a day of violence ended with deaths on both sides. Despite the relatively few casualties, however, the British government seemed to take the incident seriously, so much so that it tried al-Husayni and Vladimir Jabotinsky, whom they regarded as instigators. Al-Husayni fled to Transjordan, whence he would return, pardoned by Herbert Samuel, who wished to balance his otherwise pro-Zionist policies.

A commission of inquiry, the Palin Commission, concluded the obvious: that there was growing dissatisfaction among the Palestinian elite with the British pro-Zionist, anti-Faysal policy. In order to prevent further incidents, it recommended that British policy be revised and the Balfour Declaration reconsidered.

By April 1920, there was little reason for Palestinian nationalist notables to continue fighting for Faysal. He had, from the beginning of his reign in Damascus, been looking anxiously for help, even at the expense of the Palestinian cause. In desperation, he turned to the Zionist movement. In January 1919, he had met Haim Weizmann and signed an agreement with him. In return for Faysal's recognition of a Jewish homeland in Palestine, the Zionist movement would persuade Britain to keep its promise to the Hashemites. However, the Zionist movement could not keep this promise, and Faysal could not for long afford to be seen as anti-Palestinian. The agreement became a historical document void of any political significance. By the summer of 1920, Faysal's future in Syria was doomed. In July, the arriving French troops met a small, makeshift army of Faysal's supporters on the Maysalun plateau, on the present Lebanese–Syrian border. The French won easily, and Faysal fled, finding asylum in Haifa until he was compensated by the British with the throne of Iraq.

Palestine saw changes too. In 1920, the British replaced military rule with a civil administration. They sent a high commissioner instead of a military governor, then waited until 1922, when their mandate over Palestine was affirmed by the League of Nations. They then gave Palestine a charter, a constitution of a sort, articulating British aspirations and plans for the land and its people.

With Abdullah of Transjordan safely installed in Amman (at the time a small Circassian village of about five thousand people), the French in control of Damascus, and the Americans out of the way, nothing could stop the British from realising their colonial aspirations in Palestine. The Zionist movement gained a victory in the form of a British mandate committed to the Balfour Declaration. This was not achieved without effort. A Zionist campaign to turn the vague promise of 1917 into a *fait accompli* had begun in April 1920, when discussions on the final map of the Middle East began in San Remo in Italy. From that time until the conclusion of the deliberations, Zionist diplomacy was at its height. It recruited Lord Balfour to head an Anglo-Zionist committee to lobby for the implementation of his 1917 declaration. With such support, it was possible to convince the Americans not to oppose the inclusion of the Balfour Declaration in the charter for the mandate of Palestine. In September 1922, a clause was added to the charter excluding Transjordan from Palestine and defining the Mandate as extending from the River Jordan to the Mediterranean Sea. This revision in the charter created the first significant ideological schism in the Zionist movement. The right-wing organizations, led by Jabotinsky, left the main body of the movement in protest against the leadership's concession of Transjordan, which they regarded as a vital part of the Jewish homeland.

The inclusion of the Balfour Declaration created a fundamental contradiction within the charter, in that it was phrased in ambivalent language that gave the British room for manoeuvre between the promise of a Jewish homeland and the pledge of Palestinian independence.

On the ground, the political elites on both sides were seeking to impose their interpretation of the charter on the other. The main thrust of this embryonic Palestinian diplomacy was directed towards renegotiating with the British government the exceptional status granted to Palestine in comparison to other Arab provinces, which became states after the war. They had to be content, however, with an autonomous existence within the British Mandate and a future Jewish state. Against this anomalous background, we can better understand the Palestinian leadership's disinclination to compromise in the first years of the Mandate. They represented 90 per cent of the inhabitants, who were treated as if they constituted only 50 per cent. Had the Mandate sponsored democratic elections for local government and parliament, as it had in Egypt and Iraq, the Arab–Palestinian character of the land would never have been in doubt.

The generous term 'Palestinian leadership' should be treated cautiously when discussing the first years of British rule. It was some time before, aided by the British, a more cohesive leadership emerged. The making of a national elite was focused on one person, Amin al-Husayni. His rise to power was facilitated by, among other things, changes in Palestine, when in 1920 the British gave Palestine a civilian government and a new political chapter in the country's history began.

### EARLY YEARS OF THE MANDATE (1920–1929)

The first high commissioner, Sir Herbert Samuel, had pardoned Amin al-Husayni in July 1920 as part of a transparent British attempt to balance its pro-Zionist policies. A month earlier, Samuel had landed unceremoniously in the Holy Land. To avoid anti-British demonstrations, he had been taken ashore in a small boat at Jaffa, and then rushed to the governor's house in Jerusalem.

In March 1921, a few months after al-Husayni returned home, his brother the Mufti, Kamil al-Husayni, died, leaving Amin as the Husayni candidate to replace him. His membership of an influential family, as well as a clever campaign of petitions, intrigues and sympathetic intervention by local British officials, paved his way to power. He was appointeds Mufti despite coming fourth in the elections conducted among all the religious Muslim dignitaries of the country.

Samuel established al-Husayni at the centre of Palestinian politics, but the actions of the high commissioner were far from satisfactory to the local elite. A pro-Zionist ruler in more ways than one, he enabled the Zionist movement to carry out a systematic land survey that was the basis for its expansion throughout the Mandate. He facilitated the employment of a higher proportion of Jews than Muslims in the new civil government (the number of Jews equalled the number of Christians). Nevertheless, Samuel seemed to have a rapport with al-Husayni, and helped the Mufti to become the head of a new body of Muslim religious dignitaries, the Supreme Muslim Council, established in 1922, which supervised and controlled religious courts, endowments and charities. The council was a powerful political and economic base which gave al-Husayni not only religious authority but also leadership of the national bodies arising out of anti-Zionist fervour.

Al-Husayni was joined at the top of the political pyramid by members of his family and representatives of other Jerusalemite families, such as the Nashashibis and Khalidis, and notables from other cities as well. Their earlier divisions remained, however, and factions began to form. Those supporting the Mufti and the council became the Majlisiyyun (the coalition), and those opposing him the Mu'aridun (the opponents). This simplistic division was further complicated by the appearance in the 1930s of ideological parties supporting pan-Arabism – al-Istiqlal (Independence); political Islam (Muslim Youth) – and other trends typical of the contemporary Arab world. But the basic coalition–opposition rift was the most important one in the high politics of the day. When active, which was usually the case, it weakened the national movement as a whole.

Both sides wished to free Palestine from the Zionist presence and were willing to tolerate British control to achieve this. They differed on tactics and in self-confidence. The Husaynis hoped that pan-Arabism would help them to resist any compromise with the Zionist leadership, while the Nashashibis relied on Abdullah in Transjordan to assist them in countering Jewish power and to influence British policies in Palestine's favour. They did not hesitate, when they deemed it necessary, to follow the pragmatic stance of Abdullah who, from the early 1920s, was prepared to divide Palestine between himself and a small Zionist entity under a British umbrella. (This was when he was not harbouring much more grandiose visions, as he did in 1940, for becoming the ruler of Greater Syria).[14]

All the notables involved seemed to be pro-British, or at least against the pro-Zionist policy of Britain without necessarily being against the idea of the Mandate. The Mufti in particular displayed a pro-British stance, which was quite often criticized by newspapers close to opposition circles. His stance explained the visions of the Mandate government for the future of Palestine. The British wished it to be ruled by a local government, underwritten by a shadow cabinet of British officials and supervised by a British high commissioner. The Mandate's structure was the facade of an independent state that was in fact a colony, with one exception in the case of Palestine: local government had to be based on the principle of parity. At first, between 1923 and 1928, the Palestinians rejected parity. The Zionist leaders, using an efficient intelligence service, reciprocated by consenting to parity, although it was a far cry from their dream of a Jewish state in Palestine. Their consent was given as long as they were confident that the Palestinians would reject it. The Zionist position changed in 1928, when the pragmatic Palestinian leaders agreed to the principle of parity in a rare moment in which clannish and religious differences were overcome for the sake of consensus. The Palestinian leaders feared that without parity the Zionists would gain control of the political system. The unexpected Palestinian agreement threw the Zionist leaders into temporary confusion. When they recovered, they sent a refusal to the British, but at the same time offered an alternative solution: the partitioning of Palestine into two political units.

The nationalist notables were thus facing their first serious challenge. They needed to proceed cautiously against the changing politics of the Zionists, pay heed to growing discontent among their own community, and watch helplessly as the growing numbers of new Jewish immigrants turned Zionism from a mere footnote into a threatening chapter in the region's history. Although still recognized as leaders, the Palestinian notables did not succeed in expanding their power base beyond their towns of origin. One of their attempts was to reach out to the long-forgotten rural chieftains in order to create a joint, perceived, community of notables via an appropriate nationalist discourse. The rural chieftains were continuing the steep decline that had begun with the Ottoman reforms of the 1840s. They were now looking for a new role in nationalist politics in Mandate Palestine. The nationalist notables needed to show an ability to establish durable alliances and enlist large numbers of supporters. This could only be done with the aid of rural chieftains. So we find many of their names among the opposition and in the bodies which the Husaynis dominated, the most important of which was the executive committee of annual meetings of the various Palestinian political organizations (a body that was replaced by a more permanent executive body in 1934, the Arab Higher Committee). Such manoeuvres did little to forge an expanded leadership. Instead, they allowed the various factions to clash, not only in the conference halls but also on the ground. The clan and not the ideal, the chief and not the land, were the primary concerns of those peasants who were recruited into political life in the early 1920s.

As the decisive year of 1929 approached, nationalist politics looked much the same as they had in 1918. The Zionist community, by contrast, had achieved more in terms of solidarity and leadership. Its members had moved with relative ease from communal life in small Jewish towns in Eastern Europe to participation in a nationalized community. It used colonialism, both its own and the British version, for this purpose, while the Palestinian leadership needed more time to cope with the dual colonialist designs on the country. The Palestinian leaders, semi-feudal in the countryside and authoritarian in the cities, were unable to transcend the narrow world of the politics of notables. In a situation where political elites fought each other vehemently, this narrowmindedness was tantamount to paralysis and stagnation.

The Zionist leadership, by contrast, concentrated on mobilizing its community towards one clear goal: the construction of an infrastructure for a

Jewish state in Palestine. It was a homogeneous group, predominantly eastern European, but including a fair number of native as well as central and western European Jews. The Jewish Agency was almost entirely Eastern European, as were most of the political institutions of the community.[15] The eastern Europeans, who had arrived during the second wave of Zionist immigration and produced the first strata of leaders, formed the core from which the political elite of Israel was drawn until the 1970s.

East Europeanism was also at the heart of the construction of a new culture for the settlers. The cultural elite expanded into meaningful proportions in the 1920s, formulating the cultural code, canons, ambitions and pretensions of the Jewish community in Palestine. This community aspired to be an integral part of Western culture and looked for ways of eliminating any Middle Eastern or Arab characteristics in their society.

The Zionist leaders were most impressive, however, in politics. This dynamism baffled the British rulers and paralysed the Palestinian notables. The Zionists had a holistic approach to their role, which permeated every sphere of their communal life with force and determination, just as it invaded every neglected or empty space in the land it could reach. It was led by a trio, David Ben-Gurion, Eliezer Kaplan and Moshe Sharett, who benefited from the advice and guidance of active ideologues such as Berl Kazanelson and were promoted by brutal colonizers such as Menachem Usishqin and Yeshosua Hankin. Their desire for absolute control stood in stark contrast to the readiness of Palestinian leaders to leave the social and economic life of their community in the hands of the British government. Their greatest success was in extracting the Zionist community from the colonial state in significant spheres of life, to the extent that even non-Zionist Jewish sections, such as the ultra-orthodox Jews, were subject to the Zionist leadership's executive and legislative bodies. One of the earliest examples of this was education.[16] The Zionist educational unit, founded in 1914, was an essential tool in creating this new reality. With the help of the Mandate, the Jewish leadership effected the segregation of the education system as early as 1923, and, although there was still bilingual and bi-national education, it was all private.

The British consent to autonomous Zionist education is understandable, if we remember that those colonial officials dealing with education in the Mandate had gained their experience in Africa and India, where the local population was considered 'uneducated' and 'primitive', and had to be modernized through education. This could not apply to a community of Europeans. Humphry Bowman, the first director of education in the Mandate, was an ardent supporter of the Zionist desire for educational autonomy. He claimed that their high level of modern education and their European background meant they were 'mature' enough to run their own education system. The large share of self-finance also convinced Bowman that this situation should persist. The money brought by the Jews from abroad for education matched that granted by the government. (The most surprising act by government was to appoint several Zionists to the general directory of education, which was responsible only for the Palestinian public, i.e. government, schools).[17]

The system was in full operation by the 1930s. The Jewish community's parliament, the Vaad Leumi, had an education department, which was superficially supervised by the government. It had some private schools, but most were what could be called public schools, divided into three major ideological streams: orthodox, agricultural training, and national. Almost half of the pupils were in the national stream, with the rest divided equally between the other two.[18] The educational effort was particularly impressive in its comprehensive approach. The kindergarten became an important tool of indoctrination, first in order to teach Hebrew, which was of course not the mother tongue of most of the children, and second to inculcate the new narrative of the land's history in the minds and hearts of veterans and newcomers alike. Almost all the children of the Zionist community were at school, at a time when education was not yet compulsory or universal anywhere else in the world.

Other areas in which the Jewish community achieved an early semi-independence were in the health and legal systems. The health services were first run on a voluntary basis, organized by the American Jewish women's organization, Hadassa, but were soon assisted by government funds.[19] Independent courts were established to deal with local community matters according to, among other sources, Hebraic (i.e. biblical and Talmudic) law. This was in addition to religious courts, which, like the Muslim and Christian ones, dealt with matrimony and other aspects of religious life.[20]

In one important sphere, the economy, the Zionist movement took a long time to create new structures in Palestine. Well into the 1930s, the indigenous Palestinian population and the newcomers shared an economy, a government and a social milieu. This changed gradually from 1936, and abruptly in 1948.

The Zionist political leadership engineered a new society through its control of the flow of the 'new Jews', for which purpose it had constructed an efficient and centralized organization. The first significant step in that direction was expropriating any say in Palestine's Jewish affairs from the Zionist organizations outside Palestine. By 1929, Zionist politics were run by the 'government' of the local community, the Jewish Agency in Jerusalem. The Agency's executive consisted of both Zionists and non-Zionists (mostly ultra-orthodox Jews and representatives of global non-Zionist, but not anti-Zionist, organizations). The presidency was a titular position, and Haim Weizmann, who also became the first figurehead president of Israel, occupied it for most of the Mandate. The chairman of the executive was David Ben-Gurion, who became Israel's first prime minister The second-in-command was the head of the political department, the foreign office of the Agency. This was Haim Arlosaroff until his assassination by Jewish extremists in 1933. He was succeeded by Moshe Chertock (renamed Sharett after 1948), who became Israel's first foreign minister. Many members of the executive were ministers in the first government, ensuring a swift transition from a community into a state in 1948; strictly speaking, this was a state within a state that gained official status in 1948.

Four major ideological interpretations of Zionism competed for control and leadership. The most powerful was the Labour movement, followed by the more socialist Hashomer Hazair, the religious national Mizrahi movement, and finally the right-wing revisionists. Much of Israeli politics until 1992 was coloured by these four ideologies. Their influence in the various bodies was determined by democratic elections, political machinations and personal manipulation.

The nationalist notables and the Zionist leaders had one thing in common: they made and wrote their own history. They constructed a narrative of the people of Palestine that fitted the agendas of their respective elites. The power of these two contradictory views became increasingly evident between 1882 and the 1948 war, and they still dominate historiographical narratives in Israel and the Palestinian communities. On the political level, each day brought political drama, which mostly affected a small number of people but were written into history as collective calamities or victories.

WHERE POLITICS AND SOCIETY MET: THE 1929 WATERSHED

By 1928, the British realized that constructing a modern state in Palestine was an impossible task, given the perpetual state of conflict between the two political elites. They concentrated instead on finding ways to rule indirectly while containing the developing conflict. The British attempt to bypass the question of a 'solution' and induce the two communities to concentrate on the joint construction of a British protectorate failed for several reasons. One was the hardening of Zionist policy. The inflexible position of the Jewish Agency was directly connected to its new dominant position in Zionist circles. The Palestinian leadership, on the other hand, was confronted by an unwillingness on the part of its constituency to collaborate with the British. While centralization and consolidation were Zionist priorities, the nationalist Palestinian notables were compelled to work out their relationship with the deprived elements of their community. They now experienced the explosive power of economic deprivation and political despair, which were combining to create an uncontrollable (as far as the elite was concerned) protest movement. Amin al-Husayni was sucked into this maelstrom, at first watching, then approving, and finally inciting even more turmoil and action against Jewish settlers and settlements. He formed his own paramilitary youth movement, which instigated violence, particularly in densely populated urban areas where Jews and Arabs lived in dangerous proximity, such as in the old quarters of Jerusalem, Safad and Hebron. These youths would later be joined by shanty-town dwellers in a powerful groundswell of unrest, culminating in a countrywide revolt against the Mandate in 1936.

Palestinian politics was driven not only by poverty but also by religion, particularly in Jerusalem. The religious nature of al-Husayni's own leadership as the highest religious dignitary in the land, whose authority stemmed from a Jerusalemite genealogy, turned the attention of many Palestinians to Zionist activity in that city. In 1929, when sporadic acts of violence surrounding the issue of holy places in Jerusalem turned into days of rioting, al-Husayni was unprepared. He had sensed rising tension in Jerusalem in 1928, in the face of a suspected Jewish drive to expand the Wailing Wall area, which would have undermined the holiest place for Islam in Jerusalem, Haram al-Sharif, the site of the al-Aqsa mosque. He hoped to exert control by establishing a committee for the defence of Jerusalem in 1928, to counteract any Zionist attempts to build a third Temple there.

Ironically, al-Husayni lost control because he was now trusted by a wider range of Palestinians than anyone in his family before him. The *a'ayan* traditionally valued ambiguity and caution as the best means of navigating their communities through times of trouble. In 1928, this meant simultaneously calling for the defence of Jerusalem and discouraging direct action on the ground. But the Palestinian masses found this kind of co-opted nationalism impossible. They lived near the holy places and saw Jews praying there in unprecedented numbers, which they saw as part of a larger scheme to 'de-Islamize' Palestine. A minor incident concerning prayer arrangements near the Wailing Wall, the western wall of the Haram, sparked violence that soon swept through Palestine as a whole in 1929. In all, 300 Jews and a similar number of Palestinians were killed.

The spillover of anger from Jerusalem into the countryside and other towns was not a co-ordinated plan by the leadership. Rather, it started with uprooted Palestinians who had lost their agricultural base for various reasons, including the capitalization of crops and the Jewish purchase of land. These former peasants lived on the urban margins, from where they participated in what to them was their first ever political, and violent, action. Their dismal conditions were not the fault of Zionism, but it was easy to connect Zionist activity in Jerusalem with the purchase of land or with an aggressive segregationist policy in the labour market.[21]

The Jewish leadership had won concessions in major industries, such as phosphates and electricity. The significance of this infiltration was conveyed by the press and recognized by the more educated and politicized Palestinians. We can see how this was presented to the poor and unfortunate as part of a grand, infidel design, a political or colonialist menace to which violence was the only reply. In retrospect, this was not an inaccurate assessment.[22]

The British army was slow to respond to the unrest. The 1920s had been quiet, apart from limited outbursts of violence in Jerusalem in 1920 and Jaffa in 1921. These had seemed inevitable in a mixed community, and quite normal in the vast British Empire. But the events of 1929 exceeded the level of containable violence, and the British government decided in 1930 to appoint a commission of inquiry, the Shaw Commission. After touring the country, its members pointed out the deterioration in the peasants' living conditions and reported the growing frustration among a large number of Palestinians with British pro-Zionist policy. This harsh report should be read in the context of Britain's involvement in other parts of the Middle East. These were uneasy days for the British Empire in the area. In Egypt and Iraq, voices of resentment and dissent were being raised, and the partial independence offered by Britain to these countries, instead of appeasing the malcontents, seemed to anger them even more. The abolition of the Iraqi mandate in 1930, and the Independence Act for Egypt in 1922, merely disguised continued British rule in the two countries. The appearance of yet another anti-British national movement was something policy makers in London wished to avoid. In response, the Shaw Commission recommended the exclusion of the Balfour Declaration from the Mandate charter and a limitation on Jewish immigration and land purchase. The colonial secretary at the time, Sidney Webb, Lord Passfield, turned these recommendations into a government White Paper.

The report described Amin al-Huysani as having tried to halt mob action, which he had originally intended as a protest movement, and as having very little control over events elsewhere in Palestine. He was acquitted by the commission, rightly so it seems, but he never fully recovered his position as a leader. His greatest failing was the massive selling of Palestinian lands for Jewish settlements. The sales continued to the end of the Mandate, but had declined somewhat by the mid 1930s. This decline temporarily patched over the rifts within Palestinian society, but the pace of political mobilization and organization was slow, especially compared to the dynamic developments by the Zionists.

The Zionist leadership reacted to the violence by organizing a paramilitary force, the Hagana ('defence'), and increasing Jewish expansion within, and immigration to, Palestine. Its leadership succeeded in persuading the British prime minister, Ramsey MacDonald, to scrap the 1930 White Paper. Simultaneously, they made what seemed to be a final effort to reach an understanding with some Arab leaders outside Palestine, as well as a few inside it, over the basic Zionist demand for a limited state on the land of Palestine. This attempt was futile.

The rise of Nazism and Fascism in Europe pushed more Jews into Palestine and further toughened the Zionist position vis-à-vis the Arab and British positions: Ben-Gurion clarified in his diary that settlement and, when circumstances would allow it, the transfer of the indigenous population would ensure the realization of the Zionist dream. The Zionist leaders' most urgent task, however, was to win economic and political autonomy within Palestine.

## THE MAKING OF THE ZIONIST ENCLAVE (1929–1936)

Until 1929, the Mandate was a single economic unit, the result of ad hoc government monetary policy rather than ideology. Palestine belonged to the sterling bloc and, without an independent bank, was run from London. This uniformity was also due to the focus of the Mandate, at least until 1929, on the integrative development of social services and local economic activities. The British decision, somewhere around 1929, to allow a division of the unitary economic system was purely pragmatic, as had been the decision to build an integrated system in 1918. One of the utilitarian reasons for this policy shift was financial: the government as a tax collector benefited much more from the Jewish community; Jews paid twice as much tax as Palestinians did.[23]

The making of an independent Jewish enclave, and a change in leadership that allowed Ben-Gurion to marginalize the moderate Haim Weizmann, entrenched the Zionist leadership in its inflexible position. The separation and segregation that occurred benefited those within the enclave, but disadvantaged the indigenous population around it. By consenting eventually to the bifurcation of the country's economy, and by helping to create a Jewish privileged enclave, the British enhanced the chances of Zionist success in Palestine. The Jewish settlement, the Yishuv, became a separate economic entity. This profited the Jewish settlement, as it prevented foreign exploitation of the country's natural and human resources and speculation in its financial assets or fiscal markets.[24]

Even during the integrated economy, the Jewish had gained some advantages, such as the authorization of a Zionist protectionist policy which allowed Jewish labour, industry and agriculture to grow at the expense of the Palestinian population. Allowing such concessions to the Jews meant not only that the British had deviated from their conventional colonial practices, but they had also violated commitments made in the Mandate charter; the British government, like any mandatory power, had promised to work for the progress and well-being of the population of Palestine as a whole.

For the British authorities in Palestine, the Jews were not a typical group of 'natives', but rather acted as a competing colonial movement. However, unlike other such movements, Zionism did not originate in a single home country. It was an international movement, unconcerned with profit and, above all, ideologically bound to nationalism. It aspired to turn the 'colony' into the new home country. This meant that it could not be patronized, as were indigenous populations in the empire, nor could it be challenged as if it were another colonial power. British officials were divided in their attitude to Zionism. Those in sympathy helped it to further its cause, whereas antagonistic officials tried to tip the balance and assist the Palestinians, thereby unwittingly strengthening Zionism as a national movement.

To the Zionist movement, the timing was perfect. Before 1929, its leaders had not wished for economic independence, as the movement lacked the resources to build the foundations for a state, and depended on the British Mandate to supplement its relatively small budget. After 1929, money from external Jewish investment in Palestine enabled the Yishuv to prosper, a process helped greatly by middle-class Jews coming from Central Europe with their own capital.

The principal motivation for the Zionist drive for independence was a desire to have as much control as possible over the land and labour markets. The key interest, almost an obsession, was land. The constant worry about having 'enough land', which grew into a national hysteria in the state of Israel, had existed since the early 1920s. For Ben-Gurion, land was everything; it was the resource on which young Jews would settle and train as soldiers, workers and farmers. In 1929 he came to the conclusion that land should have spending priority. By the end of the 1930s, 40 per cent of the overall expenditure of the Jewish Agency was on purchase of land and agricultural colonization, and about 75 per cent of overall investment was appropriated for that purpose. The concentrated effort towards grasping as much as Palestine had to offer drove the process of capitalization. This was particularly evident in the property market, where plots were trading assets, and in the construction business, which could offer the most accessible jobs. Money was also easily made by importing and later manufacturing modern technology for cultivation and construction.

The leadership of the Yishuv, with the help of the slogan 'Hebrew labour', took over the labour market of the mixed towns, purchasing land from the big land owners, many of whom were absentees. The Jewish Agency fully exploited the (mostly Ottoman) ownership laws to take over lands that had been cultivated by the same families for centuries without ownership.

This awareness of the link between money and land helped the Zionists to focus on building foundations. The leadership included a group of settlers who took it upon themselves to find the best investments for the Yishuv's capital resources and growing manpower. Thus national considerations, from the start, took precedence over purely economic ones: Jewish labour was more expensive than Arab labour, but more important nationally; imported goods were of higher quality, but local goods contributed to the nation-building process.

Economic policies based on national considerations also meant that the general trade union of the Zionist community, the Histadrut, was more concerned with expanding the community's political borders than with workers' rights. This expansion took place in the 1920s, despite the economic depressions of 1923, 1926 and 1928, and the wretched conditions of the immigrants. The Histadrut was run by the Zionist Labour party, Mapai, and served as an additional power base for Ben-Gurion in his almost total control of the Jewish political system. Mapai itself absorbed most of the socialist Zionist groups, for example Ahdut Ha-Avoda and Ha-Poel Hazair, which had been active in the early years of Zionism. (Only the communists, the hard-core socialists, Hashomer Hazair, the Liberals and the religious parties remained independent bodies until the end of the Mandate). This centralized political and economic power facilitated the Yishuv's independence.[25]

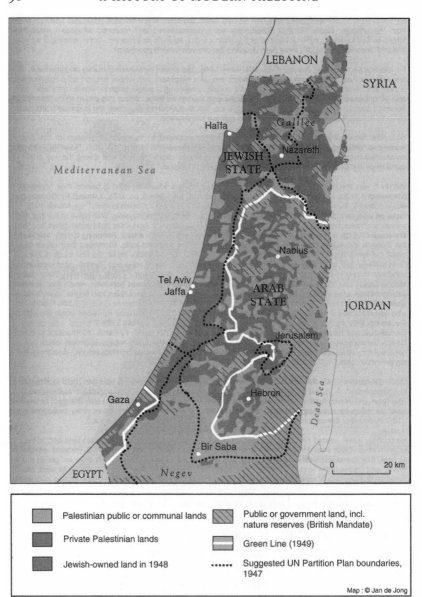

Map 2.  Land ownership in Palestine, 1948

Such managerial capabilities were absent on the Palestinian side. The nationalist notables ran the agricultural and economic lives of their clan-based tenants at best in an ad hoc manner, and were unable to provide economic leadership for the society as a whole. This imbalance is yet another explanation for the Zionist success in the crucial clash of May 1948, as a result of which Palestinians lost their homeland. Welfare institutions, agricultural communes (kibbutzim), collective cooperatives, construction companies and large factories were all part of the Mapai enterprise. The momentum embraced cultural networks (theatre, literary clubs and children's books) and the education system. Later Israeli historians said that socialism was highly spoken of in Mapai, but rarely adhered to as a way of life or as a political programme; party Bolshevism was enacted in full force.

The need to be economically active and alert served an additional purpose. Intensive economic activity was presented by the Zionist movement as proof of the country's ability to absorb a large number of immigrants without disadvantaging the local community, a consideration which at least until 1933 influenced the British policy makers. It seems that official Zionist reports even exaggerated the level of activity to impress the British with the benefits of Jewish immigration.

The Jewish Agency had its own state bank, so to speak, the Anglo-Palestine Bank, established in 1903. It was the principal credit institution for the building of towns and settlements. Another important financial body, the Jewish National Fund, contributed largely to the Zionist project, through taxation and donations, throughout the Mandate. The Palestine Foundation Fund was in charge of distributing the money given by the national fund and lent by the national bank. During the Mandate, the Fund spent almost 20 million pounds on expanding the Jewish settlement in Palestine. The British had spent more than 55 million pounds on Mandate Palestine, but this was partly also to meet Jewish needs.

Only after the Second World War did the nationalist Palestinian notables make an attempt to grant economic independence to their communities, but it was too little and too late, and even this attempt was divided along clan lines and did not serve the nationalist cause. For most of the time, the leadership focused on high politics rather than economics. The construction of an independent Zionist enclave did not escape their attention and was one of the reasons for the great revolt of 1936. But far more important in explaining the 1936 uprising, which lasted until 1939, was the impoverishment of rural Palestine under colonialism. This was a socio-economic calamity that at first politicized the Palestinian countryside, giving new life and meaning to Palestinian nationalism, but later crippled the society when the decisive moment of the Mandate's end arrived.

## THE PAUPERIZATION OF RURAL PALESTINE (1929–1936)

Rural Palestine was devastated by colonial policies. These policies enabled exogenous actors to exploit the villages to breaking point. It was a disastrous mix of agricultural commercialization, of Zionist drive for land purchase, and of the notables' greed, which left rural Palestine, where 60 per cent of the population lived, in ruins. Even without Zionism, however, the impoverishment of villages could have only been prevented by agrarian reform. The economic interaction between the Zionist movement and the big land owners provided the infrastructure for Zionist expansion, which led, exclusively and solely, to the expulsion of the indigenous population in 1948. The Zionist approach during the Mandate was to buy land from the big landlords and evict the tenants. The government hoped that a mass transfer of the tenants from Palestine could be organized, preferably as part of a general solution to the situation, but was prepared, in the short term, to put up with small evictions here and there. When the 'mass transfer' happened, in 1948, it affected Palestinians from almost all walks of life. In the meantime tenants were losing their land without any compensation or work elsewhere.[26] The easiest course for the Zionists was to buy land from the most a-national of the notables, the absentee landlords, who during the Mandate owned more than 20 per cent of private land.[27] The largest landowner in Palestine was Abdul Rahman Pasha, who lived in Damascus and owned 200,000 dunams (the richest of the local notables, such as the Husaynis in Jerusalem, owned just 50,000 dunams).

While this was a crucial factor in the movement of peasants from the villages to the towns, it was not the only one. Other factors included the demand of an ever-increasing urban population for more cash crops, a demand potent enough by itself to make former peasants into hired workers on their own land on commercial-type farms.

Complaints about the harsh economic situation were directed at the colonial government rather than the national leaders or the Zionist movement. The British were, after all, in charge, although they ruled by 'remote control'. British officials, apart from a few eccentrics, lived not in rural areas but in urban enclaves, where they created a sort of British Raj, a little England consisting of houses, official residences, sports clubs, and military camps. From here the Mandate civil service pursued a policy of limited modernization. On the ground, this meant government indifference towards the peasants' dwindling self-sufficiency. There was very little hope for improvement, as the state no longer invested in the necessary infrastructure.

As previously mentioned, the British, from the beginning of the Mandate, adopted what they called a 'commonwealth approach' to development in Palestine. Although this meant controlling the country through development, it necessitated a comprehensive policy designed to improve life in rural Palestine. In reality this was never a priority, or even a serious objective, for the British rulers, who seem instead to have been more interested in high politics.

After the 1929 uprising, officials in London were convened for lengthy discussions over development policies in Palestine. When development was first mentioned as a policy, it was promoted as the solution to the problems that had caused the uprising. For a short while, development became a catchword in London. It appears several times in the Shaw report of 1930, which demanded a new 'development' policy in rural Palestine. The report suggested intensification of agricultural production that would, so it was hoped, save the livelihoods of the villagers.

The British experts on agriculture who were sent to Palestine were deeply shocked by their government's neglect of the rural areas. Upon their return they sent determined reports in which they appealed to the government to intervene in market forces in the rural areas, and warned against leaving the situation to supply-and-demand factors. They indicated that the gap between the pace of economic development on the Zionist and British sides was such that the rural economy of Palestine was able to serve only as a supplier of raw materials, without any benefit or improvement for the peasants themselves.

A few of these experts were particularly critical, stating forcefully that Palestine did indeed have a development policy, but that it only fitted Zionist and imperial interests. It made rich Palestinian landowners richer, while most of rural Palestine was impoverished. Not content with rhetoric, they quantified exactly what was missing: a budget of 7 million pounds to shift the focus to investment in the rural areas.

Their recommendations fell on deaf ears. This was due less to a pro-Zionist lobby in London than to the decline of the so-called commonwealth approach to British colonies in general; a wish to make the colonies self-sufficient for the benefit of the British Empire. This change resulted from growing socialist tendencies in domestic British policies. While the new Labour government there identified with de-colonization, it adopted a policy that can be defined as 'social imperialism', as one of the leaders of the Zionist movement called it. The new policy amounted to a clear desire to increase public expenditure in Britain itself, and correspondingly to cut down on spending in the colonies and mandate territories.[28]

This was not a novel idea. Throughout the history of the British Empire, there had been an anti-commonwealth school of thought, called by contemporaries the 'Greater Britain' policy, represented in the nineteenth century by Benjamin Disraeli and by Winston Churchill during the time of the Mandate. The essence of this approach was that empire building consisted of extracting as much out of the colonies as possible while investing as little as possible in their welfare. But a mandate was not officially a colony, and the visible lack of investment in Palestine was tantamount to a breach of the Mandate charter. Nevertheless, Palestine was treated like a colony, perhaps because Britain's responsibility for its welfare was to the League of Nations, an international body that carried little weight in global politics after the American withdrawal.

The 'Greater Britain' approach united conservatives and socialists alike. Socialists wanted more money for the home front, while capitalists objected to the industrialization of the colonies or the expansion of productive economic activities there. For Palestine, this meant that economic growth, new jobs, agricultural planning and modernization were all unimportant goals, even when for a moment the powers in London put aside discussion about the political future and vowed to deal with social and economic problems.

It is difficult to assess how a more balanced policy of subsidies, profits, ownership and trade would have influenced agricultural life. For the historical record, I would say that Labour Party politicians were ambivalent, and realized where the lack of investment would lead. Labour's ambiguity was revealed in the appointment in 1931 of the thrifty and utilitarian Louis French as the head of Palestine's development project. By the time he reached Palestine, however, he had new bosses in London: Labour had won the 1931 election but had entered a coalition with the Liberals. The latter's impact on policy was to cut down foreign spending even further, and replace it with laissez faire economics. Free-market forces, argued a new secretary of state for the colonies, Conlif Leicester, would eventually be 'good news for Palestine's peasants who would one day integrate to the new capitalist reality that the Jewish immigration would build in the land'.[29] The new high commissioner, Arthur Wauchope, explained that the British policy would now be to encourage Jewish capitalists to immigrate to Palestine. Their fortunes would be used to assist their destitute brothers and sisters, fleeing in their thousands from Nazi Germany, and would benefit the country as a whole.

Not surprisingly, French and Wauchope disliked each other. Also, to French's dismay, none of the Palestinians, and certainly none of the Zionists, saw him as a potential ally. The Palestinians missed a genuine opportunity there. It would be fair to state that even before their own leaders realized the full scope and significance of land sale and purchase in Palestine, French had already seen that this would be the focus of the conflict and the principal source of the Palestinian tragedy. It is possible that his work helped some nationalist notables to be more firm and focused in their campaign against land sales. But the land take-over was already a substantial base from which the Zionist movement would acquire most of western Palestine by 1948.

French's correspondence on the need to invest and intervene in the rural economy continued until the end of 1932. From 1933, rural Palestine was not mentioned as a priority or a target of investment. Ironically, one thing mentioned with great satisfaction in London in 1933 was that the government of Palestine was one of the richest in the British Empire. Furthermore, it rejoiced in the success of the free-market policy by pointing to the failure of the Palestinian politicians to recruit peasants for orchestrated action against the government in 1933; this was an unheeded call for a joint strike and riots.

Out of this rich government's budget, 11 per cent was allocated to education and health services. However, education was a coercive and manipulative tool, and health, although important, did not ensure economic survival. The government gave limited loans to small numbers of peasants and at times relaxed taxation, but this was not enough. The gap between the city, especially its Jewish constituents, and the village became more acute and more visible. That something could have been achieved can be seen from a British pilot development project that was never continued. This was Tel al-Suq near Beisan (on the ruins of which the Israeli development town of Beit Shean was built in 1948), where on a local level a different infrastructure and a system of self-sufficiency were put into place, followed by a marketing and trading network. This type of development improved the standard of living of a few fortunate peasants.

For a growing number of Palestinian peasants, it was becoming clear that their lack of capital rendered them vulnerable in their struggle for survival against the growing and greedy cities. They demanded the right to establish joint credit cooperatives in the villages. The government and the banking authorities responded favourably, as they knew they could, and indeed did, appropriate the idea and turn it to their advantage. This was done by allowing credit only to those peasants who were known to have the means to pay high and immediate interest on loans. The advice given by Charles Strickland, one of the more positive British experts sent from London, to allow a land policy based on trust, a basic feature of economic interaction in the villages, went unheeded. Instead, mistrust deepened, and became rooted in the villagers' relationship with the government.[30]

The 'successful' financial policy of the Palestine government in the 1930s was the result of a conscious decision to prefer the urban centres and the coastal areas, where most of the Jews lived, to Galilee and the mountains, where the Palestinians lived. The main result was migration to Palestine's urban centres. The increasing flow of peasants into the towns began in the economic depression of the mid-1920s, but peaked in the years following the events of 1929. Migration was not the first choice, even for those who found it difficult to live off their land. Many peasants tried tenancy before giving up agriculture altogether. The tenancy system was complex, and depended on ad hoc agreements struck between the tenant and the land owner or the *wakil*, the agent representing an absentee land owner. Tenancy was abandoned only in the face of economic hardship. Former peasants, no longer tenants, became a rural proletariat, offering their labour, agricultural or not, to any takers. They were called the *harath*, and their numbers grew steadily around 1936. Their frequent unemployment also determined their political behaviour, erratic and easily led by anyone offering a radical solution to the general Palestinian predicament. In 1931, a government census estimated them at 30 per cent of the peasant population.[31]

Unskilled agricultural work was not a long-term option either, as land cultivated by hired labourers was the most susceptible to sale. The *harath* moved to the cities and towns, where they found menial work serving both the urban Palestinian bourgeoisie and Jewish immigrants. The latter arrived in increasing numbers after 1929, fleeing a hostile Europe, and less in search of a new Jewish kingdom than a haven from persecution. As other destinations, including the United States, became inaccessible, a small Jewish bourgeoisie found a new home in Palestine's cities and towns.

By 1936, those peasants still living from their land, or at least on their land, were in dire circumstances, unable to translate commercial agriculture into profit. Those leaving the land were crammed into the inhospitable towns and cities. They waited for guidance, knowing, even without being well informed in high politics, that conditions were bound to deteriorate further. In addition, they now recognized that they had no leadership to rely on.

## QUESTIONS OF LEADERSHIP AND NATIONALISM (1930–1936)

By the beginning of the 1930s, the Zionist movement had a distinct body of leadership, the Jewish Agency, and by 1934 the Palestinians had their own embryo government, the Arab Higher Committee. It was now clear, even to the British, that politically Palestine comprised not three religion-based groups, but two national movements with two respective 'governments'. This almost created the illusion of a satisfactory arrangement in Palestine, with each community having an executive body responsible to a government of British officials under a high commissioner, the effective ruler of Palestine. But this semblance of control was soon shattered by demographic and economic developments: Jews escaping in large numbers from Europe; and a rural Palestinian hinterland simmering with resentment at the loss of land and livelihood.

In the early 1930s, the nationalist notables widened their scope of activity, and thus politics, i.e. nationalism, infiltrated the world of the uprooted, unemployed peasants living near Jewish settlements and in the shanty towns encircling cities such as Haifa and Jaffa. The notables also made an effort to recruit support from rural Palestine. This proved very difficult, however. For one, the notables were themselves either exploitative landowners or liberal professionals, whose world had very little in common with that of the peasant. The former rural chieftains had exercised a semi-feudal system that bonded owners and tenants, but was based not only on exploitation but also on mutual commitment. Nothing of that was left in the 1930s.

Economic exploitation continued, even after the urban notables succumbed to the lure of nationalism, and adopted its discourse of solidarity and concern for the people as a whole. Few recognized that their control over the economic life of rural Palestine gave them a role in rural social structure that could have been a basis for a new kind of solidarity. Only the Nashashibi family, in 1934, made an apparent effort to take a greater interest in rural Palestine and its predicaments when it established a 'peasants' party'; but this was not a serious or significant bid to create a new common identity.[32]

This lack of identification with the rest of the population made the nationalist notables leaders, but not representatives, of their community, as the situation in Palestine became polarized. They were unable to advise their people on how best to confront the Jewish community and its ambitious expansionist plans. They failed to curtail Zionist expansion, but encouraged their rural, peasant communities to clash, unprepared and disorganized, with the Jewish settlers. Open confrontation occurred twice. The first, in 1936, was momentous but not disastrous, as the Zionist movement was still weak. The second, in 1948, when the Zionist movement was stronger and already well established, was catastrophic.

Lest I read history from the present backwards, I would hasten to caution that at the time of the dramatic events of the 1930s, rural Palestine was off the national stage. Rural society, at least half the Palestinian population at the time, did not anticipate the catastrophe awaiting it in 1948, and continued to live more or less according to an unchanging rhythm and routine.

One of the problems was the leadership vacuum in rural Palestine, and the failure of most attempts to fill it. One of these attempts was that of Izz al-Din al-Qassam, a Syrian preacher who settled in Haifa in the mid 1920s. Many history books assert that Izz al-Din al-Qassam ignited the 1936 revolt by fusing Islamic dogmas with national ideology. But his recipe for revolution was welcomed only among a particular segment of the population. This was the poor of the cities and the unfortunate inhabitants of *harat al-tanc*, the shanty neighbourhoods that surrounded towns such as Haifa. In 1933, Izz al-Din al-Qassam initiated a guerrilla war in the north, recruiting fighters from around Haifa and leading them to the surrounding hills, attacking any Jews or British soldiers they encountered on the way. In 1935, al-Din al-Qassam was killed by the British army, but this was enough to make him a martyr and provide an example of a new kind of resistance.

However, the brand of nationalism invented by al-Qassam failed to impress rural Palestine as a whole, where custom, not religion, determined daily morality, conduct and routine. Moreover, despite al-Qassam's short-lived success with some inner-city migrants around Haifa, most of these had not cut their ties with their clans and villages, which made them less receptive to his preaching. The hierarchy in the village was clear: first the clan, then the village, then everything else.[33]

Today, al-Qassam is associated with militant political Islam resisting the Israeli occupation of the West Bank and the Gaza Strip. It is the name of units of suicide bombers, who have tried since 1987 to force an Israeli withdrawal. He was a much more cherished and popular hero than any of the national leaders, but the revolt when it took place in the countryside had more to do with the pauperization of the land than with political Islam. Politics in the villages was local, not national, in 1935, and would still be so in 1948.

This attachment to locality rather than to nationality did have political manifestations. When villages were threatened by political movements such as Zionism, or by government policies, they acted from what could be termed 'local patriotism'. Once nationalist notables succeeded in constructing a solid association of such centres of local patriotism to oppose Zionist land purchase or government policies towards the Jewish presence in Palestine, then Palestinian nationalism became a potent force; but this seldom happened. Rare also were the occasions when villages tried to join forces without the intervention of the notables. In the 1920s, several conferences took place at which the mukhtars (village headmen) called for such synchronized action against both Zionism and taxation policies, but these produced no real action.[34]

While the expansion of Zionist settlement gave the nationalist notables a chance to reach a wider audience, there was still no genuine solidarity with the peasants, apart from rare displays of unity and firmness of purpose. Such a moment took place in March 1933 in Jaffa, where leaders of all the political factions joined in a united call for a concrete campaign of sustained pressure on the British government to change its policy. Five hundred representatives of the Palestinian elite, in a rare show of resolve, declared their intention of boycotting British and Zionist commodities, and for the first time ever rejected the legitimacy of the Mandate in the land of Palestine.

However, the ties that bound them for a few days in Jaffa soon dissolved, and factionalism took over again. I will spare readers the names of those involved. It will suffice to point to two axes dividing the political scene: clannish affiliations, and the ideological friction between Qawmi (pan-Arabist) and Watani (territorial nationalist) orientations. The former divide was the more important, and poised the Husayni family and its allies against other notable families, such as the Nashashibis.

### THE 1936 REVOLT

The short but impressive phenomenon of a leader such as Izz al-Din al-Qassam, who sacrificed his life for the struggle, impressed the notables of nationalism for a time. The Mufti, Amin al-Husayni, ignored al-Qassam's widow at first, but, on hearing of the mass participation in the man's funeral, he paid his respects at the end of the forty days of mourning.

On a less symbolic level, there was an attempt after al-Qassam's death to show unity of leadership and purpose. Finally, in the autumn of 1936, the hesitant Arab Higher Committee finally took firm action against the explicit clarity of purpose it saw on the Zionist side, brought home after an abortive attempt to negotiate a principled settlement with the Jewish Agency.

The nationalist notables tried to persuade the disgruntled masses that the best weapon of the weak was industrial action. In October 1936, the Arab Higher Committee declared a general strike and organized nationwide demonstrations, the principal one held in Jerusalem, where about two thousand demonstrators gathered inside the walls of the Old City. The demonstrations became more violent three weeks later, when British police opened fire on demonstrators in Jaffa.

At first the magnitude and nature of the protests impressed the British. They appointed a commission of inquiry, headed by Lord Peel, who visited Palestine in 1937 before making his recommendations. His commission recommended the annexation of most of Palestine to Transjordan, and urged the maintenance of a direct British presence in vital strategic positions such as Haifa and the newly built airport in Lydda, as well as in the Negev. A small portion of the land was designated as a future Jewish state. This plan was rejected, not of course by Prince Abdullah in Transjordan; but in a way it was endorsed by Ben-Gurion, who had the foresight to understand that you take what you are given when the balance of power is not yet in your favour. For Ben-Gurion, the proposal was a basis for negotiations, not a final map, hence his willingness to be content with such a small portion of Palestine.[35]

The failure of the Peel plan, and a revised version of it offered by yet another commission, the Woodhead Commission, reinforced the wave of protest against, and condemnation of, British policy. The Palestinian leadership was pitiable in those days, unable to provide solace or guidance to its population. It is no wonder that the younger generation of notables was searching for a more imaginative brand of Palestinian nationalism, one built on a determination to cease negotiating with the Zionists, and not to succumb to British pressure. Prominent within this group stood the Mufti's own nephew, Abd al-Qader al-Husayni (the father of Faysal al-Husayni, a prominent Palestinian politician of the 1990s), who chose alternative courses of action and became more attuned to the population at large. These young notables became mythical heroes, no less than Izz al-Din al-Qassam himself. Their boldness was matched by local rural mukhtars, who in 1937 began a punitive guerrilla war against British convoys and installations. This activity commenced in the wake of the release of Peel's report and of an abortive peace mission attempted by external Arab leaders. The pressure from rural and urban areas alike was intense, and the more militarily inclined youth intensified their attacks on the British army.

This was not the time for a small national movement to fight against a mighty empire. On the eve of the Second World War, British policy makers had no scruples in quelling the rebellion. They saw it as a German- and Italian-inspired scheme to promote anti-British activity, against which they acted with all the force they possessed in the area. In Palestine, the assassination in August that year of Major Andrew, the senior British official in charge of Galilee, marked a turning point for the Mandate government; it used the assassination as an excuse for a general attack on the nationalist notables, arresting them and exiling many. Amin al-Husayni escaped before being arrested, and devoted his early months in exile to creating a network of volunteers and organizing, together with other members of his family, a large-scale arms-supply operation to the guerrillas. The further he was from Palestine, the closer he came to cooperating with Britain's new enemies in Europe, the Italians and the Germans. At first this led him to support an abortive pro-German coup against the British in Iraq in the summer of 1941, and later during the war he helped the Nazis with their propaganda machine in Muslim communities.[36] Meanwhile, the community in Palestine remained in effect leaderless. The British had effectively destroyed the nationalist notables. The resulting vacuum was filled by politicians from neighbouring Arab states.

Many of the younger participants in the rebellion, quite a few of them women, died in the uprising. Those who survived the confrontation with a superior army and air force formed the backbone of paramilitary organizations after the Second World War. They gave the Palestinian cause a limited but vital military capability, in preparation for the inevitable clash with Zionism. But, like the politicians, these guerrilla commanders were not autonomous and after the Second World War were subordinated to Arab politicians in the neighbouring states, each of whom used the situation in Palestine according to his own national, or at worst personal, agenda.

### THE 1939 WHITE PAPER

A British White Paper of 1939 tried to make provision for Palestinian sensibilities. It repeated the promises made in 1930 of withdrawal from the Balfour Declaration and limits to Jewish immigration and land purchase. The objective was to maintain the status quo until the situation in Europe was clear. The limitation on immigration came at a time when

Nazi expansion in Europe was making life for Jews there unbearable and impossible. The Yishuv now waged its own kind of rebellion, a clandestine operation of illegal immigration, land take-over, and formation of a paramilitary organization, helped by sympathetic British officers such as the legendary Orde Wingate.

The British gesture towards the Palestinians and the Arab world came too late. The Palestinian side, politicians and rebels alike, felt that the British, in their brutal suppression of the 1936 revolt, had already exposed their real agenda. Their conduct was documented in the local press, and included horrific stories of abuse, hanging, torture and callousness, mostly, but not exclusively, between 1936 and 1939. Even without this brutality, the nationalist notables felt betrayed by Britain, which had constantly violated its promises to the Palestinians since 1916.

The Zionist community emerged from the revolt fortified and more determined than before. More than anything else, its leaders were mesmerized by the power of military force. These were days when military solutions to the Palestine problem received precedence over negotiated solutions, and in which a particular brand of Zionist, and later Israeli, militarism emerged.

The objective threat, the genuine fear, inspired and justified the consolidation of an army as well as of more extreme positions towards both the British authorities and the Palestinian population. The military effort went in two directions, one infrastructural and the other more provocative. The infrastructure was created by pushing aside more moderate members of the elite, such as Haim Weizmann, who advocated prudence and a piecemeal build-up of the Yishuv's military power. He was replaced by tougher characters, such as David Ben-Gurion, who moulded the Zionist community along more Spartan lines, and forsook the Athenian visions harboured by early Zionists such as Ehad ha'Am. After all, the backbone of the Yishuv was not only the Histadrut, but also the Hagana. The spearhead of this military body was the Palmach, which had no more than seven hundred members in 1941. By 1948, it consisted of seven thousand well-trained soldiers. It was the permanent wing of the military force of the Yishuv, and between 1946 and 1948 it fought against the British, experience that it put to good use in the 1948 war.

The more provocative military direction was represented by the Stern Gang, which terrorized first the British and later the Palestinian population. The Palmach, the Stern Gang, and Menachem Begin's Irgun would merge at the end of the Mandate.

At the time, the Stern Gang and the Palmach represented two different wings of Zionism. Both, however, disregarded the local population before the revolt, but afterwards did all they could to drive as many of them as possible out of Palestine. The socialist mainstream was willing to confine the Palestinians to a small portion of the country; the revisionists to offer them the choice of either transfer or co-optation. Ultimately, both ideological wings of Zionism visualized Palestine as the land of the Jewish people. The socialist majority strove to realize the Zionist dream by Realpolitik, while the revisionist minority occupied themselves with utopian visions of past grandeur, employing an extremist rhetoric about the need to create a future kingdom of Israel stretching as far as the eastern border of Transjordan.

### ENCOUNTERING NATIONALISM: THE URGE FOR COHABITATION

During and after the Second World War, the politicians could not predict the exact moment of the final clash, but seemed to sense it coming. The national ideologies were therefore even more ferociously put forward in an attempt to empower both leaderships and unite their communities behind them. This did not develop naturally, as national historians would have us believe. Nevertheless, the Mandate created a space in which a basic human urge towards cohabitation and cooperation could exist. It surfaced at times that nationalists considered mundane and unimportant, such as when natural disasters like earthquakes occurred (1926), and when businesses were declining at times of economic crisis or booming in times of prosperity. Such calamities or blessings engendered human responses that transcended national identities. In Palestine these joint responses occurred where people who lived with occupational hazards realized trade union options, shared anti-government sentiments, coped with bad harvests, or faced famine and epidemics. These, and many other, circumstances led people to coexist and cooperate on non-national levels of class solidarity, common occupations, or common problems such as employers and unemployment.

This natural urge was far more detrimental to the nationalist project than was British colonialism. The urge for cohabitation came from below, and competed with two other human drives towards transformation that operated from above in Palestine: nationalism, both Palestinian and Zionist, and colonization. The nationalist activity from above was not directed only at those living on the land; for them a new identity was constructed, mainly by negating those who were excluded from the new imagined community. The British tolerated this elitist project to a point, but more on the part of the Zionists than of the Palestinians. The two elites had the same goal of nipping in the bud any human impulses not orientated towards serving the two new meta-identities of Mandate Palestine – Zionist or Arab

Palestinian. The extinction of such urges is an untold story and deserves more attention. An existential wish to build a common life for the sake of occupational security, economic prosperity, higher levels of education and a better life generally was not naturally connected to the cause of nationalism in Mandate Palestine.

On the face of it, the nature of Zionism should have made cohabitation an impossibility. The construction of a Zionist identity in Palestine was not a mere intellectual exercise. It was implemented by such an extensive colonization of the land that even the elitist, quasi-aristocratic Palestinian national leadership could impress upon the nation the danger now lurking at the door of every Palestinian home. Palestinian resistance to the Zionist takeover in its turn made the personal hardship of Jewish immigrants into a 'national' problem: being a Jew in Palestine made one a target of Palestinian hostility; at least that was how the Zionist elite explained the developing conflict to its community.

At times this rhetoric contradicted the reality on the ground. The British colonial state could be a trigger for a different interpretation of the situation. It was, unlike the Ottoman Empire, a foreign power, colonialist and exploitative. It was also the principal employer, tax collector, policeman, judge and developer, and so attracted the attention of society at large, beyond the demands of the elites to join in the intra-communal conflict. The state as such was quite often opposed on occupational and professional grounds that transcended national boundaries. There was plenty of such action in Palestine, but it does not fall within a Whiggish perspective of history as the history of the victorious. The history of the defeated needs to be included in the successful, at times callous and destructive, story of nationalism in Palestine.

This alternative history does not begin with the Mandate. Late Ottoman Palestine had a tradition of integrated economic activity on ethnic and religious lines. However, in its first decade the Mandate did even more to shape an integrated and unitary economic system. The British state was such a powerful factor in the life of people, a fact hardly mentioned in the national historiographies of the conflict, that it disabled the national elites in one of the most important aspects of life – economic control. As long as Palestine was administered as a single economic unit, consumers did not have to abide by national affiliations. Local Palestinian producers could have met the growing demands of the Jewish immigrants, who needed channels of investment and expenditure for the capital that they brought with them. Instead, segregation resulted from the political elites' enlistment of their respective communities in their mutual struggle. However, neither the Jews nor the Palestinians could have hoped to dominate the economy of Mandate Palestine without British consent.

The urge among ordinary people on both sides to cohabit persisted even after the Zionist establishment of a separate economic enclave in 1929. The segregationist policy did not fulfil the needs of either Jewish or Palestinian workers, farmers, traders and consumers. The few who persevered in prioritizing occupational over national considerations were strongly opposed by the Zionist leaders, who regarded segregation as a prerequisite for the creation of an independent Jewish state in Palestine.

The entire history of Mandate Palestine is dotted with instances of cooperation between workers. Although there is no clear chronology to document this history, it was there in the early years of the Mandate, it was there when the independent Jewish enclave became a fait accompli, and it was there during the bloodiest years of the intra-communal strife towards the end of the Mandate. At every escalation of violence – 1920, 1929, 1936 or 1948 – I can find a case study of economic or social cooperation that was strongly opposed and destroyed by the national leaderships, especially the Zionist one.

In many of these instances, courageous people tried to prevent the clash between the Jewish proletariat (which was turning into a lower middle and working class) and the impoverished indigenous rural and unskilled town dwellers (who were slowly becoming a proletariat in their own country). The political elites on both sides, who did not share the miserable conditions of their communities, found it easy to depict the poor as a 'national mass' that could be exploited during the successive waves of violence and bloodshed. In other cases, the elites themselves were engaged in cohabitation practices that defeated the claims made in their fiery speeches and sermons.

It is worth mentioning briefly some of the more striking examples, noting that this type of history has yet be written. The first example is from Haifa in 1920. That Haifa became the site of the most exciting experience of class solidarity and bi-national, or even a-national, cooperation is not surprising. It was a city whose Jewish, Christian and Muslim communities were similar in size. It was the most prosperous town in Palestine, containing the major government factories, such as the oil refineries, and many Palestinian and Jewish industrialists decided to open their plants in its vicinity. The army had large camps in and outside the city, and once the harbour-building project was commenced in the 1920s, the level of activity intensified. Moreover, both communities included immigrants: Jews from Europe and Palestinians from the rural hinterland. It was also an attractive destination for several thousand workers from Syria and Egypt.

Although there was much to compete for in Haifa, there was also much to be gained by the people themselves from occupational cooperation. In 1920, Palestinians, Jews, and Arabs from Syria and Egypt established the first trade union in Palestine in the yards and workshops of the railway, telegraphic, and postal services. Faced with long working hours, underpayment, inhumane living conditions and, above all, cruel treatment by their employers (the British government), they united in demanding a fundamental improvement in their conditions. They were failed by the Histadrut. Its protocols reveal statements by its leaders claiming that there was danger in joint Arab–Jewish unions. The local Histadrut leader in Haifa, David Hacohen, rebuked Jewish workers who joined forces with Palestinians: 'The railway workers forget that the mission of the Hebrew workers who are part of the movement for settling Palestine, is not to be bothered by mutual assistance to Arab workers, but to assist in the fortification of the Zionist project on the land.'[37]

By 1929, the Histadrut had succeeded in coercing most of the Jewish workers in the union to put national interest above class solidarity. The Histadrut established a union of exclusively Jewish workers in these services and demanded that all the Jewish workers recognize it as their sole legitimate representation. The Palestinian workers responded with the establishment of their own union, which soon emerged as a general union of Palestinian workers. The union was declared in 1930 in a building in Wadi Nisnas in Haifa, which today serves as the headquarters of the Israeli Communist Party.[38]

Apart from class consciousness, the routine of life succeeded in generating almost unimaginable instances of cohabitation. The politicians themselves sometimes engaged in such intercommunal interaction, even at the height of conflict. In the bloody year of 1929, for example, in the middle of his campaign for the defence of Jerusalem, Amin al-Husayni was looking for ways to raise the regional and international profile of the Palestinian problem. His campaign was to climax in 1931 with a pan-Islamic conference to enlist Muslim and Arab support against what he saw as Zionist encroachment on Haram al-Sharif. In 1929, he began by building the Palace Hotel for the dignitaries. The project was tendered to two Jewish builders, one of them Haim Weizmann's brother-in-law. The beautiful building, near the Jaffa gate, was designed by a Turkish architect in the late Ottoman style. The Mufti was so pleased with the work that he employed the same builders to finish some unsatisfactory work done on his new house by Palestinian builders.[39]

However, it was mainly among workers and employees that existentialist instinct encouraged people to bond on occupational rather than a national

basis. One such case was of Palestinian and Jewish truck drivers who organized, in 1931, a very effective strike. The British government in Palestine
was extremely efficient in expanding motor traffic and road infrastructure.
In the late 1920s traders and commuters began to prefer buses and trucks to
trains, and the government, which had the monopoly on the railway network, began losing money. To cut its losses the government imposed heavy
taxes on motorists, especially truck drivers. Most of these were Palestinians,
but a substantial number were Jews. For eight days in November 1931,
Palestinian and Jewish drivers stood shoulder to shoulder in a strike that
paralysed the country. In 1932 the government lowered the taxes.

The Palestinian truck drivers usually owned their trucks and were part of
a growing urban middle class, willing to find ways of cooperating with the
Jews on a professional basis. The Histadrut at first endorsed the strike, and
considered the chairman of the truck drivers, Hasan Sidqi al-Dajani, as a
moderate, closer to the Palestinian opposition led by the Nashashibi family.
Al-Dajani saw the strike as an opportunity to build a joint infrastructure
that could benefit truck drivers as well as traders on both sides of the
divide. The Histadrut invited him to join Brit Po'alei Eretz Israel, its sister
organization for Palestinian workers, but he declined. The Brit was a co-
optive, rather than cooperative, body, intended to submit the Palestinian
workers to the Zionist interpretation of reality. When al-Dajani tried to
expand the strike to include trade boards and institutions, the Histadrut
leaders changed their opinion of his 'moderation' and suspected him of
organizing what they called a 'political strike'. This meant expanded bi-
national industrial action. In this instance, the Histadrut leaders did not
indulge in overt coercion, but rather in a slow process of protraction that
rendered any meaningful continuation of the week's strike futile.[40]

The nationalist notables used the local press to condemn Palestinians
collaborating with their Jewish comrades, even against government employment policies. Both political leaderships, realizing the importance of
traffic and roads, over the next few years forced drivers from their communities to take a national rather than a professional position. The result was
that in 1936 the truck drivers stood in the forefront of the clashes between
the Zionists and Palestinians.

Although the 1936 revolt hindered the pattern of cohabitation, cooperation continued in many significant areas of life. The communists, which
included the Arabs and Jews most committed to coexistence, split over
the uprising. But outside the areas where the actual guerrilla warfare was
taking place, cohabitation continued. For example, the municipality of
Haifa was run jointly by Jewish and Arab clerks. Throughout the revolt,
islands of cohabitation also existed in the labour and land markets. Jewish

employers found it hard not to employ cheap Palestinian labourers, although the Zionist elite fought back, reinforcing the process of national indoctrination to prevent the phenomenon from expanding. Even more dangerous from the Zionist perspective were political movements such as the Palestine Communist Party, or the very radical leftist Zionist movement Poalei Zion Small, which advocated cohabitation as the norm. The Palestinian nationalist notables fought with similar vigour. When persons such as Fawzi al-Husayni or Fakhri al-Nashashibi joined Arab–Jewish organizations advocating a bi-national political structure, they paid with their lives. In 1937, a leader of the Palestinian labour union was assassinated. In 1947, another union leader named Sami Taha was murdered. Both were killed for subordinating national solidarity to class awareness. Like other workers, they regarded the national cause as a limited venture run by and for the nationalist notables. The hand of Amin al-Husayni was visible in both assassinations.

In all, however, the Zionist elite tried more than its Palestinian counterpart to kill the instinct for cooperation. The Palestinian elite seemed indifferent towards socio-political developments that did not fit their *Weltanschauung* or agenda, while the Jewish leadership was busy undermining Arab–Jewish professional organizations.

The urge to cohabit persisted in the remaining years of the Mandate. It is even possible to suggest that it matured in a very different way from nationalism. It moved beyond the labour market into the state and private sectors. It even penetrated areas crucial for national triumphalism, such as industry. A high level of cooperation was maintained during the Mandate in the citrus industry, mainly due to the energetic Palestinian chairman of the Arab Citrus Industry, Shuqri Taji al-Faruqi. Similarly, Jews and Palestinians co-ran the salt plant of Atlit, a profitable business then and today.

While employers found it difficult to cooperate, the urge persisted among industrial workers to stand together against employers. Clerks, too, found cooperation expedient. A final example of this dates from 1947. Eighteen months before the Mandate ended, when politicians from each side of the divide, as well as those in London and in the Arab capitals, seemed to be preparing for a Greek tragedy on Palestine's soil, several groups of workers and employees across the divide decided to put occupational expediency above national solidarity. For two weeks a strike by government clerks paralysed official business. Their success was so overwhelming that the two segregated national unions, the Histadrut and the Arab Union of Workers, were obliged to join in. In April 1946, postal services were brought to a halt by a joint Arab–Jewish strike. Even in May 1947, when the drums of war could be heard once Britain relinquished its obligation to rule the country, Palestinian and Jewish workers in the telegraph service embarked on a joint strike.[41]

In both the public service and industry, strikes were the preferred modus operandi for bi-national industrial action. Quite frequently during the Mandate, Arab and Jewish workers in the oil and petroleum industry, the cigarette factories, and the bakeries struck jointly. The pattern of strikes increased after 1936. Between 1938 and 1943 there was an average of two joint strikes a year, mainly in the railway system, the municipalities and the British army camps. Action peaked in 1943, with a strike declared by Palestinian workers, who gathered with their Jewish colleagues in front of the Jerusalem municipality. The Histadrut tried to control this strike by claiming it as its own, but to little avail. One year later, in February 1944, the Histadrut did not even try to intervene in a joint strike in the railway workshops, where the main strikers were Jews, encouraged by a show of solidarity from Palestinian colleagues, who demonstrated, gave food and provided coats for the cold nights spent in the plant.

To the very last days of the Mandate, local consumers from both communities frequented each other's shops in Palestine's cities. An astonished Jewish reporter noted the prevalence of this custom even during the time of an official boycott declared by the Arab Higher Committee in March 1946.[42]

In rural Palestine too, the cooperative urge continued. As the Mandate drew to its end, Jewish settlements provided more organized and structured aid to Palestinian villages, unprecedented joint agricultural cooperatives sprang up in the Marg Ibn 'Amr in the 1940s between kibbutzim and villages, and in the city new joint commercial boards were established.

Cohabitation was not only practised in a few isolated circles in Palestine: it was an ideology. It had very little political support, as it did not enjoy a significant institutionalized political leadership, but it was a basic tenet of the Palestine Communist Party. This body was predominantly Jewish until 1936 when, in what the party's chronicle termed a process of 'Arabization', more Palestinians began joining. The party, despite its marginal nature, contributed to an alternative course of social development by engaging in a-national discourse in its leading journals. There was also a socialist discourse within the Palestinian community, outside the party, within the rank and file of Palestinian trade unions.[43]

The most outspoken political body to endorse bi-nationalism as a way of life was a small Jewish group called Brit Shalom. It was the brainchild of one person, Yehuda Magness, an American Jew who had immigrated to Palestine in 1922. A member of the American Reform movement within Judaism, he was not interested in Jewish sovereignty in Palestine, but in maintaining Jewish life there in a unitary bi-national state. Until his death in 1948, he tried to convince both sides of the logic and practicality of his solution. He created a political body for this purpose. One of his greater successes towards the end of the Mandate was in recruiting Fawzi al-Husayni, a leading member of the Husayni family, to the Brit Shalom movement. Al-Husayni was assassinated soon afterwards by the more nationalist wing of the family. Magnes was a founder of the Hebrew University and its first president, but his prominent position did not help move him from the margins of Zionist activity.[44]

The survival of cooperation and joint ventures did not mean the decline of politicization or violent interaction, or that rural Palestine remained immune from nationalization. On the contrary, politicization, nationalization and cohabitation coexisted in parallel. The elites were ever willing to employ force and violence in their pursuit of national goals, and now there were younger and more extreme groups of leaders snapping at their heels, pre-empting the elite's indecision by bold and aggressive activity.

Cooperation was unable to stem the course of nationalist segregation, which won the day with disastrous consequences for the indigenous population of Palestine. But as far as short-term achievements went, much of the industrial action was successful; particularly after the Second World War. At times the gains were unevenly divided between the two groups, with Jewish workers usually winning more from the negotiations that followed industrial action. Overall, however, Palestinians and Jews were often able to work together to change their terms of employment, including reducing working hours, gaining paid leave, and expanding insurance and compensation.

From a historiographical point of view, the impression is left of an alternative history. One particular fact recorded in the British documents serves as an epilogue to this parallel development. The British government in Palestine reported that, throughout the Mandate, 1,400 commercial partnerships between Jews and Arabs were forged on what the government defined as an 'Inter Racial Basis'.[45]

## PALESTINE IN THE SECOND WORLD WAR

The Second World War affected Palestine at various times and with differing intensity, with Rommel's speedy progress in North Africa generating a web of rumours of a possible Nazi occupation, of Italian air bombardment of the coastal towns, and of flirtation between the Axis powers and the Palestinian leadership. Jewish youth joined the British army, not only to fight in Europe but also to topple pro-German Arab regimes, such as that established in Baghdad in the summer of 1941 (with the blessing and assistance of the former Grand Mufti). But more than anything else, the war was made visible by an unprecedented number of British soldiers and military personnel in the land, turning it into a vast logistics centre. It should be stressed that, unlike in the First World War, Palestine was not a war zone. Instead, it was an enormous army camp, which both increased the number of foreign soldiers and provided jobs.

In more mundane terms, the war meant an economic boom and the loosening of social and traditional hierarchies and structures. Prosperity did not come at once; in fact at first it looked as if the economy was going to collapse. The banking system was particularly vulnerable. The first year of the war almost crippled the local economy. Heavy withdrawals destabilized the local banks, some of which went into liquidation.[46]

In 1942, the Mandate government decided to introduce subsidized elementary commodities. A wise government monetary system prevented the hyperinflation usually associated with commodity shortages, enabling the society as a whole to recover after the war. Palestine in 1946 was quite different from at the beginning of the Mandate. Thousand of cars, buses and trucks appeared on the new network of asphalt roads, where previously horses and carriages had transported passengers in a slow and haphazard manner.[47]

In wartime Palestine, also, more working women than ever before hurried to jobs women had never held before, or walked unaccompanied to coffee-houses and public gardens they had not frequented in the past. Those were good days for independent urban Palestinian women who, until the war, had worn veils over their Western clothing in public. Now they could be seen on the beach in bathing costumes, and in the latest fashions on the promenades of the main cities, a change of dress that signified more independence and assertiveness. Tel-Aviv acquired the enviable image of a liberated city, which probably attracted women from Beirut who were willing to marry Jews in order to enjoy life in the new city.[48]

The war transformed the lives of Jewish women as well. At the beginning of the 'Zionist Revolution', the founding fathers promised to create a new 'Hebraic woman'. For an exceptional few, this meant sexual freedom, which was preached and practised in exclusive circles. For the majority, it signalled the end of the traditional family structure, especially in the kibbutzim, but also in urban communes.

However, the new jobs and freer lifestyle did not seriously undermine the dominant role of men in the economy. They occupied the best-paid jobs and had exclusive control over the most productive workplaces such as construction sites and factories. The equality of women was part of the pseudo-socialist discourse of Zionism, but the reality was rather different. The terms 'member wife' and 'member's wife' were used interchangeably, implying a double duty for the sake of the Zionist and socialist revolutions – a housewife bore the additional burden of being a labourer, worker or farmer.[49]

The Zionist leadership made the best of the war years for the Jewish people. Most important of all was its ability to exploit the war to give the youth vital military experience. When the Second World War was in its most crucial stages, and notwithstanding its overt aim of ending the Mandate and even fighting against it, the Jewish leadership offered its military capability to the British in the service of the struggle against Nazism. This was not a hypocritical political act. At certain stages of the war, Palestine itself might have fallen into Nazi hands, were it not for the bravery and resilience of the British forces facing the Germans. The Yishuv leaders could not openly fight those who had the power to stop the Nazi death machine in Europe. This dilemma was solved by Ben-Gurion, who said, 'We shall fight alongside the British army against the Germans as if the anti-Zionist White Paper of 1939 did not exist, and fight against the White Paper as if the war with Germany did not exist'.

For the Zionists, the focus of their activity during and after the war remained on immigration. For the first time in the history of the Zionist settlement, vast numbers of Jews abroad demanded to enter Palestine. This came at a time when Britain, as a consequence of the 1936 revolt, had decided to limit Jewish immigration. The leadership exhausted its legal permission to bring Jews into the country, and then started a successful campaign of illegal immigration. This was selective, in which the physically fit and those with the right ideological bent were given priority and, at times, exclusivity. This mode of selection was abandoned for a while when the horrific news of Nazi exterminations reached Palestine around 1942. The news even prompted the symbolic act of sending Zionist parachutists into Nazi Europe as a gesture of support to the Jews dying in the death camps rather than as a real attempt to save them. Little Zionist energy was invested in saving Jews, as the priority in those difficult days remained the survival of the Jewish community in Palestine. When the war ended, selection was resumed, but it undermined a Zionist desire to prove the connection between the Holocaust and the Jewish project in Palestine. Indeed, if all the survivors of the Nazi horror, especially those placed by the Allies in displaced persons' camps all over Germany, had chosen Palestine as their destination, they would have vindicated Zionist arguments to the international community. The leading diplomats of the Yishuv claimed that only a future Jewish state could be a haven for those people and a buffer against another Holocaust. In the event, many survivors wished to go to the United States. It took a serious effort of persuasion, to the point of intimidation by Zionist envoys, together with a strict American immigration policy, to create at least the impression that most of the Holocaust survivors wished to settle in Palestine (eventually only 10 per cent of the 3 million Jews left in Europe did so).

But an important diplomatic battle was won, helped greatly by the British insistence on controlling and minimizing immigration, highlighted by the *Exodus* incident, when a Jewish refugee ship was not only refused entry to Palestine, but was also turned back to Germany, an act condemned all over the world. In parallel to illegal immigration, land was purchased and new settlements erected.

As with immigration, the continuation of the settlement policy also ran contrary to the 1939 White Paper. *Homa* and *migdal*, 'fence' and 'guard tower', was the Zionist method. These tactics were based on an Ottoman law, still intact in Mandate Palestine, which ruled that the erection of elementary infrastructure for a potential settlement produced a *fait accompli*. The British government was without the resources to evict settlers.

After the war, the Zionist elite prepared its community well for the eventuality of a British evacuation. It paved the way for successful Zionist negotiations with Abdullah in Transjordan over the division of Palestine between Hashemites and Zionists in the post-Mandate era by tightening up its control over the community in terms of taxation and army enlistment and by creating the sense of life-or-death struggle in an imminent war with the Arab world at large.

The Palestinian leadership went through very different experiences during the Second World War. Amin al-Husayni was wandering as an exile from one Arab capital to the other, but made his way to Berlin, where he served the Nazi propaganda war machine and alienated the cause of his national movement in the eyes of the victors. He was accompanied by other members of the Arab Higher Committee, some having served terms in British prisons, where, ironically, they met extremist Jewish terrorists who had fought the British. In their absence, others had replaced them. The political scene had already been affected by politicians from neighbouring Arab countries and their local protégés. The result was the establishment of two conflicting official leaderships of the community: the old Arab Higher Committee, sanctioned by the Arab League and still dominated by the Husaynis (headed by Jamal al-Husayni), and the National Authority, headed by Raghib al-Nashashibi and supported by the Hashemites. This disunity affected the political structure from top to bottom, and was evident in every sphere of life. It crippled the financial organization which had recently been erected to counter Zionist economic power; it weakened the paramilitary outfits, which were in any case poorly armed and totally outnumbered by the Zionists; and it prevented solidarity within the national committees established to run local communities. These committees were particularly active in urban areas, and tried to prepare their communities for autonomous life during the transition at the end of the Mandate. The committees were, however, less loyal to their communities, and much more in debt to their clans or political groups, rendering the communities defenceless before a Zionist determination to take over Palestine, should the diplomatic solution offered by the British, or later by the UN, allow it, or an ensuing war enable it to do so. Had it not been for the military intervention of the Arab armies on 15 May 1948, not one fragment of Palestine would have remained outside Jewish control.

During the Second World War, the Palestinian nationalists became nationalist diplomats, although not effective ones. Some became irrelevant like al-Husayni, who travelled around the Axis powers, hoping to recruit those he erroneously thought would be the next masters of the Middle East, or at least allies in the war against the British. Some remained in Palestine, or returned from exile after being pardoned by the British. They were helpless in the face of the committees the British had set up to find a solution for a place they were determined to leave, or if necessary rule only indirectly or by proxy. The Palestinian notables felt so insecure that, on one occasion, they recruited a young scholar from the Arab Office in London, Albert Hourani, to present their case before one such committee, the 1946 Anglo-American Commission of Inquiry.

This frenzied Palestinian activity was futile. Their flirtations with the Germans left foreign governments with the impression that the leadership, particularly al-Husayni, was pro-Nazi, a designation that made his return to Palestine impossible. This also alienated the British policy makers from supporting the idea of an independent Palestinian state, which they now contemptuously called a 'Mufti state'. The episode of al-Husayni's connections with the Nazis did a great service to Zionist propaganda after the war.

Figure 4. The Atlit stone quarries, where Arabs and Jews were jointly employed
by the Mandate government

At the same time, the British offered a rapid succession of peace programmes, the general theme of which was a hybrid between partition and
continuing British control, all rejected by the opposing parties. The last one
was put forward in January 1947 by the then foreign secretary Ernest Bevin.
It recaptured the spirit of all the previous plans. It called for American
involvement, allowed for a large number of Jewish immigrants into the
country, and envisaged autonomous Jewish and Arab cantons for most
of Palestine, apart from areas to be directly ruled by Britain. It was flatly
rejected by both sides.

By February 1947, Britain had had enough. It had more soldiers in Palestine than on the Indian subcontinent, and had been constantly involved
in direct clashes with both political leaderships. The number of British
casualties had also risen, mainly due to a terror campaign waged by Zionist
extremists, the most notorious being the Stern Gang. This terror campaign
peaked with the blowing up of British headquarters in the King David
Hotel in Jerusalem in 1946. But it was not terror that forced the British
out. A particularly bad winter in 1946–47, and a harsh American attitude

towards Britain's debt to the United States, created an economic crisis in Britain that served as an incentive for a limited process of decolonization, mainly in India and Palestine.

The problem of Palestine was entrusted to the United Nations in February 1947. By then the Arab League had already committed the Arab world at large to an independent Arab Palestine. The Hashemites in Transjordan began secret negotiations with the Jewish Agency on the division of Palestine between themselves and the Jewish leadership, which had declared in a convention held in America in 1942 that it would not be satisfied with less than the whole of Mandate Palestine as a Jewish state. The scene was set for a final showdown.

# CHAPTER 4

# Between Nakbah and Independence: The 1948 War

## THE UNSCOP DAYS

Bernard Newman, a British tourist, could still enjoy a normal day in Jerusalem towards the end of the Mandate, strolling in the Kedron Valley, on the way up to the city. He chose an hour of the day that a few weeks later would be particularly dangerous for foreigners, the time of the evening prayer. His is almost the last account we have of the situation before violence broke out. His report is full of sounds: snatches of the muezzin's from the minarets drowned by the many-toned bells of the Orthodox churches, or the more solemn boom from the bells of the Catholic churches. Nearby, goat-bells tinkled, and the shrill voices of children playing could be heard from the south. But he also noted the harsh sound of klaxons and the rattle of armoured cars.[1]

This picture, which gives a background to daily life in Palestine at the time, was to change radically. The script for this drama was written outside Palestine. Previous attempts on the part of the Mandate to end the conflict gave way to dependence on the new international policeman, the United Nations. Palestine was the first serious regional conflict to be dealt with by the organization. From its foundation, the UN was paralysed by Cold War politics. On the basic outline for Palestine, however, Russia and the USA, the two superpowers concurred: Palestine was to be divided between the Zionist movement and the Palestinians.

The eleven members of the official UN body appointed to decide the fate of Palestine, UNSCOP, the United Nations Special Committee on Palestine, also arrived at this conclusion. These officials had no experience in the Middle East or any knowledge of the Palestine situation, and had visited the area very briefly. They seemed to be more impressed by their gloomy visit to the camps of the Jewish Holocaust survivors in Europe than by what they saw in Palestine. In Europe, however, the tragedy had already occurred; in Palestine it was about to happen.[2] It took UNSCOP nine months, between February and November 1947, to make a decision on the country's fate. They had been given a ready-made partition programme by the able and well-prepared Zionist representatives, while the Palestinian and Arab side failed to propose any coherent alternative. Despite this, the Palestinians' consensual rejection of partition was fully known to UNSCOP. For the Palestinians, leaders and common people alike, partition was totally unacceptable, the equivalent in their eyes of the division of Algeria between the French settlers and the indigenous population. The strong Palestinian objection prevented a unanimous decision on partition, but it was not strong enough to avert a majority one, achieved to a certain extent by American and Russian pressure.[3] In their infrequent tours of Palestine, the committee members were welcomed by the Zionist leadership, but boycotted by the Palestinian politicians, an imbalance that also contributed to their decision to back the Zionist demand for partition as a logical solution to the conflict. The last British attempt to limit illegal Jewish immigration, the return of the *Exodus*, full of Holocaust survivors, to Germany, which coincided with one of UNSCOP's visits, accentuated even further the nexus between the Holocaust and the establishment of a Jewish state in Palestine.

In the months of the UNSCOP deliberations, life in Palestine continued much in the same pattern as it had since the end of the Second World War. The rural areas were now more stable, as the number of people leaving them decreased. They were also less affected by Zionist settlement. The Jewish effort was directed to uncultivated land in the northern tip of Palestine's desert, the Negev, and to other areas allowed by the restrictions of the White Paper of 1939, and thus was experienced less in the heart of the region. The towns continued to be sites of bi-national cohabitation and economic interaction opposed strongly by the political leaderships on both sides. The number of people involved in politics did not grow dramatically, and the fate of the majority was still decided by the few.

Such ordinariness was an illusion. Those who were most aware of the abnormality of the situation produced by the British insistence on leaving Palestine without any proper arrangements for a transitional period or any substitute regime were best prepared to fill the vacuum to their advantage. Since May 1946, the Zionist leadership had been preparing itself for what it saw as a final showdown with the local population. There was no clear blueprint until 1948, but there was a clear mind-set that went back to the 1930s, when Zionist leaders had, as one of many options for a solution, begun toying with the idea of an enforced eviction of the local Palestinian population.[4] The difference now was that the Palestinian refusal to accept a UN solution provided a pretext for implementing a systematic expulsion of the local population within the areas allocated for a Jewish state, areas already demarcated in the UNSCOP report. In fact, the Yishuv's leaders felt confident enough to contemplate a take-over of fertile areas within the designated Arab state. This could be achieved in the event of an overall war without losing the international legitimacy of their new state.

While Palestinian peasants and Jewish settlers continued at that time to cultivate their land, and in some cases to maintain agricultural ties and other forms of interaction, active Zionist officials began assessing the wealth of Palestinian villages within the territory allocated to the Jews in the UNSCOP report. They accumulated vital information about these places and put it into a kind of intelligence almanac, or register of Palestinian villages. This register included information on the villages catalogued according to parameters such as population, agricultural production and their history in relation to the Zionist movement. A brief account of this register was provided later to commanders of units attacking these villages during the civil war before the end of the Mandate, and also during the more 'official' war with the Arab armies between May 1948 and January 1949. It transpires from these summaries that the strategic location of villages was also an important factor in their fate, apart from their wealth or previous relationship with the Zionist community. Villages that were near vital routes or in proximity to Jewish settlements had very little chance of remaining intact after being occupied by the Jewish forces.[5]

These confident preparations did not mean, however, that the majority of the Jewish community was not living in fear at the prospect of the end of the British Mandate. Many of its members anxiously awaited war with a large Arab army. This distress was very efficiently exploited by the leadership to recruit the community for winning the battle over post-mandatory Palestine. Intensified enlistment, coercive taxes, the prevention of emigration from the land and increased attempts to bring in new immigrants were all part of a well-orchestrated mobilization. At the highest political level, the gaps between the different ideological movements were narrowed and the military command centralized. Although there were cracks in this united front, compared to the situation on the other side, the Zionists' readiness was impressive.[6]

The Palestinian nationalist notables, although more alert than ever to the Zionist mobilization, were helpless, even when the will to act was there. Once they had surrendered diplomacy to the Arab League, the diplomatic battle was no longer in their hands. They still boycotted the UN, joining in with the Arab League's general handling of the crisis, which consisted of a policy of brinkmanship between warlike rhetoric and secret negotiations aimed at postponing any international resolution. This policy was complicated by the independent approach taken by King Abdullah in Jordan (Transjordan became Jordan in March 1948), who, with British blessing, began serious negotiations with the Jewish Agency over his partition plan of dividing Palestine between his kingdom and the Jewish state. The plan was accepted in principle by the Jewish side and implemented during the war itself, ensuring a safe annexation of eastern Palestine to Jordan in return for limited participation by the Hashemite Legion in the overall Arab war effort.[7]

The nationalist notables were unaware of both these diplomatic manoeuvres and the intensive preparations activated by the Jewish political elite. They sensed the tension in the Arab world between the high level of military rhetoric and the low level of military preparedness, but continued to hope it would be enough to deter the UN from implementing the partition resolution. They probably underestimated how the absence of any serious groundwork on the Arab side, compared with the vigorous military build-up on the Jewish side, affected the final balance of power in the region. They put their effort into recruiting a few thousand soldiers and collecting money in those UNSCOP days; they even resurrected the national committees, but failed to put them under one unified command. As I mentioned in the previous chapter, each committee was loyal to a different faction in the political make-up of Palestine, torn between parties loyal to the Husayni family or to their rivals, the Nashashibis.

On 29 November 1947, UNSCOP presented its recommendations to the UN General Assembly. Three of its members were allowed to put forward an alternative recommendation. The majority report advocated the partition of Palestine into two states, with an economic union. The designated Jewish state was to have most of the coastal area, western Galilee, and the Negev, and the rest was to become the Palestinian state. The minority report proposed a unitary state in Palestine based on the principle of democracy. It took considerable American Jewish lobbying and American diplomatic pressure, as well as a powerful speech by the Russian ambassador to the UN, to gain the necessary two-thirds majority in the Assembly for partition. Even though hardly any Palestinian or Arab diplomat made an effort to promote the alternative scheme, it won an equal number of supporters and detractors, showing that a considerable number of member states realized that imposing partition amounted to supporting one side and opposing the other.

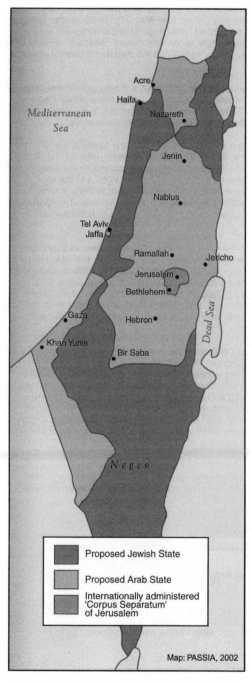

Map 3. The UNGA Partition Plan, 1947

The next day brought the first outburst of intra-communal violence, activated by hot-headed youth on both sides. It was less spontaneous than it seemed to outside observers. A month earlier, Israel Galilli, the chief of staff of the military force, had ordered the concentration of troops in the north and south of Palestine. These forces were ready to respond by force to angry and violent demonstrations, and were attacked by the *shabab*, the local Arab youth.[8]

A slow deterioration into a widespread civil war in the next few months generated second thoughts in the UN, and in Washington, about the desirability, indeed, the feasibility, of the partition plan. But it was too late for a large number of Palestinians, evicted from their houses after their leaders lost the early battles with the Jewish forces. Twelve days after the adoption of the UN resolution the expulsion of Palestinians began. A month later, the first Palestinian village was wiped out by Jewish retaliation to a Palestinian attack on convoys and Jewish settlements. This action was transformed into an ethnic cleansing operation in March, which resulted in the loss to Palestine of much of its indigenous population.[9]

The UN reassessment was also too late for those Jewish settlers and Palestinians who lost their lives in the more organized confrontations that ended in mutual slaughter. It was also too late to prevent the surge of warlike rhetoric in the Arab world, where more serious preparations for a military campaign were begun. In short, the Mandate disintegrated before the UN could make up its mind how best to replace it. The British government did not help by prohibiting the arrival in Palestine of UN officials who wanted to supervise the transition according to the partition resolution. It is doubtful whether their arrival would have prevented the Palestinian catastrophe or the war. At best, we would have had an additional source for what took place in those months leading to the actual Arab–Israeli war. These developments extended from December 1947 to 15 May 1948, when the last British soldier left Palestine.

The deteriorating situation meant that, from January 1948, increasing numbers of Palestinians were drawn into the political and military drama in which Palestine had been embroiled since the British decided to evacuate in February 1947. At the beginning of 1948, the first units of Arab volunteers entered Palestine, organized within the Arab Salvation Army, a paramilitary organization sponsored by the Arab League and commanded by Fawzi al-Qawuqji, a veteran Syrian soldier who had fought in Palestine as a volunteer in 1937. The official mission of this force was to counter the upper hand initially seized by the Jews via their swift possession of army bases and civilian posts evacuated by the British. There was another force in the country, the Arab Legion, the units of which were an integral part of the Mandate's police force. These units did not withdraw with the rest of the British forces, and were stationed in the west bank of the River Jordan.

Al-Qawuqji's forces were not very effective in defending the local civilians; they also introduced a foreign, at times alien, element into the lives of local Palestinians. They were reported as being condescending and acting as military rulers in the areas in which they stayed.[10] Their presence was also strongly felt due to the hasty departure of many members of the local Palestinian elite, who left in fear of the oncoming conflict and in the hope of returning to a calmer Palestine (70,000 left between September 1947 and March 1948). This exodus produced a collective sense of insecurity and terror among many segments of the Palestinian urban population. On the other hand Arab Legion forces were somewhat more effective in protecting Palestinians, but were used mainly in strengthening pro-Hashemite elements within local politics at the expense of persons known to be loyal to the Arab Higher Committee. The legionaries were preparing the ground for the future annexation to Transjordan of as much of eastern Palestine as they could seize.

## THE ETHNIC CLEANSING OF PALESTINE (MARCH–MAY 1948)

In March 1948, the military campaign began in earnest. It was driven by Plan D, a military blueprint prepared by the Hagana in anticipation of combating the Arab forces in Palestine and facing the Arab armies after 14 May 1948. Until March 1948, clashes between the two communities, beginning the day after the UN partition plan was accepted by the General Assembly, were scattered, random and uncontrolled. Plan D was prepared as an attempt to organize the Jewish effort; an attempt not mirrored in any way by the Palestinian leadership. The latter made some effort at uniting paramilitary groups under one command, and fusing the various national funds into one budget. They also tried to create an overall apparatus that would run the 'national committees', and would be responsible for defending villages and neighbourhoods as well as for sustaining law and order once the British forces were evacuated. Compared with the systematic Jewish preparations, these efforts were ineffectual and risible. There was enough military will to try to capture vital road junctions and attack isolated Jewish settlements, but not the resilience to sustain those achievements. For a while, the paramilitary forces led by Abd al-Qader al-Husayni and Hasan Salameh succeeded in cutting the road between Tel-Aviv and Jerusalem, the designated capital of the Jewish state, but all these actions collapsed once Plan D was put into operation in April and May 1948.

The Jewish leadership felt the need to be more systematic, less because of possible Palestinian successes, than because it apprehended a change in the international, in particular the American, mood and approach to the Palestine question. In March 1948, the American administration developed second thoughts about the practicability of the partition plan. The American delegation to the UN offered an alternative solution: an international trusteeship over Palestine for five years, followed by a review aimed at a permanent settlement. Strong lobbying by the Jewish community in the United States averted this change of policy, but it indicated the feebleness of the UN's commitment to the creation of a Jewish state in Palestine.

Plan D was put into full operation in April and May. It had two very clear objectives, the first being to take swiftly and systematically any installation, military or civilian, evacuated by the British. The success of this goal depended on the sympathies of the British officers or officials in charge. Those with pro-Zionist affinities provided the necessary prior information to enable the Hagana to occupy headquarters of essential services and key military bases. The pro-Palestinian Britons, on the other hand, could not always locate those they wished to help.

The second, and far more important, objective of the plan was to cleanse the future Jewish state of as many Palestinians as possible. The main military force was the Hagana, which had several brigades. Each brigade received a list of villages it was to occupy. Most of the villages were destined to be destroyed, and only in very exceptional cases were the soldiers ordered to leave them intact.

In addition, some of the brigades were to engage in the take-over of the mixed Arab–Jewish towns of Palestine and their environs. This meant occupation and the expulsion of the Palestinian population. This was the fate of Jaffa, Haifa, Safad and Tiberias. (In some Israeli, and even critical Israeli, historiography, Haifa is singled out as a place where there was a genuine attempt by the Zionist leadership to persuade the local population to stay.) The campaign for Haifa began on 20 April 1948. A few days earlier in Haifa, the Jewish forces had committed the Dir Yassin massacre, a well-publicized bloodbath. The local people were terrorized, and further intimidated by explosions set off by Jewish forces in Arab neighbourhoods and harassed by sniper fire all around. Very few Palestinians stayed in the city, and their leaders considered the Jewish offer to stay deceitful and hypocritical. Their fear for their lives was accentuated by massacres committed in Balad al-Shaykh, where in January 1948 scores of Palestinians were slaughtered in retaliation for a terrorist attack on Jewish workers in the nearby refinery.[11]

Several massacres were committed near the mixed towns, sometimes in retaliation for Palestinian attacks on Jewish convoys, but quite often they were unmitigated acts of brutality. They may have been meant to, as they eventually did, force Palestinians living in areas falling into Jewish hands to flee under the threat of death or eviction. These atrocities were not randomly committed; they were part of a master plan to rid the future Jewish state of as many Palestinians as possible.[12]

Like many master plans throughout history, Plan D was general, and in parts vague. No less important than the plan was the atmosphere created, which paved the way for the ethnic cleansing operation in Palestine. Thus, while the actions of the Hagana were part of a master plan, it had no clear and specific local directives. The plan was executed because the soldiers in the battlefield were oriented by a general attitude from above and motivated by remarks made by the Yishuv's leaders on the need to 'clean' the country. These remarks were translated into acts of depopulation by enthusiastic commanders on the ground, who knew that their actions would be justified in retrospect by the political leadership.

By the time the British left in the middle of May, one-third of the Palestinian population had already been evicted. The British were officially responsible for law and order during the early phases of the removal of the indigenous population, a depopulation that was assisted by a first wave of about 70,000 Palestinians belonging to the social and economic elite of the country, who had fled Palestine by January 1948. This departure of the urban elite explains in part why the expulsion policy was so effective in that first phase of the war in and around the mixed Arab–Jewish towns as well as in western Jerusalem. The end of the Mandate also signalled the end of the first phase in the 1948 war, which was akin to a civil war situation, and lasted for six months from December 1947 to May 1948. In the second phase, established participants, such as the British army, disappeared, and new ones, such as regular Arab armies, appeared for the first time.

### THE PALESTINE WAR (MAY 1948–JANUARY 1949)

The second phase consisted in part of trench warfare and the occupation of military positions. It had features of a modern war, with random air bombardment of civilian targets and heavy shelling of neighbourhoods in mixed towns. It was a long war, punctuated by considerable lulls. Two truces were signed during the second phase, and from January 1949 onwards almost all the Arab armies concluded an armistice agreement with the new Jewish state.

That the Arab states succeeded in fielding any soldiers at all is remarkable. Only at the end of April 1948 did the politicians in the Arab world prepare a plan to save Palestine, which in practice was a scheme to annex as much of it as possible to the Arab countries participating in the war. Most of these armies had very little war experience, and were barely trained by the end of the Mandate. The co-ordination between them was poor, as were the morale and motivation of the soldiers, apart from a large group of volunteers, whose enthusiasm could not compensate for their lack of military skills. The Arab world, its leaders and societies, vowed to save Palestine. The politicians were hardly sincere; the soldiers and their commanders were probably more genuine in their commitment to salvage Palestine.

The poor level of performance on the battlefield was not just an Arab phenomenon; it was evident on the Jewish side too, which was at first handicapped by lack of firepower. This was amended during the first truce in the war, in June 1948, when the Zionist leaders managed to purchase arms from the Eastern bloc, while Britain, obeying a UN decree, imposed an embargo on three armies that used only British-made ammunition: Egypt, Iraq and Jordan.[13] Among the Jewish troops was a large number of fresh immigrants with no war experience; but the core of the army was better prepared and more experienced. The number of fighting men on both sides, including those from neighbouring Arab countries, was equal almost throughout the war.

The Arab governments fielded about 25,000 troops, and as the war went on raised the number to 100,000. Similar numbers were deployed by the Jewish community, including both the Hagana and the Irgun.

Before May 1948, the crucial elements in the two camps were the Hagana's special forces, the Palmach, and the paramilitary units of the Palestinian side. The Palmach had 7,000 men at its disposal in 1948. These were well-trained soldiers, facing an equal number of Palestinians with poor arms and hardly any military discipline or experience and divided into factional units owing their allegiance to clans, or at best to ideological parties.

On 14 May 1948, the state of Israel was declared. At 1 a.m. the next day, the American president, Harry Truman, announced his country's *de facto* recognition of the new state. An hour earlier, Sir Alan Cunningham, the last British high commissioner, had left the country. Two days later, the Soviet Union added its recognition, but went further than its rival superpower and granted a *de jure* recognition. One after the other in the following days, other states recognized Israel. No one seemed to consider or dwell on the possible implications of this act on the fate of the majority of Palestine's people, the Palestinian Arabs.

At midnight on 15 May, while Cunningham was leaving, an Egyptian force of about 10,000 troops (half of which were trained soldiers) crossed the border between the Sinai and the Negev. On the same day, this contingent proceeded quickly to the coast, attacking isolated Jewish settlements along the way and capturing some of them. Egyptian aircraft bombarded Tel-Aviv from the air. Syrian and Lebanese troops crossed their respective borders with ex-Mandate Palestine, but were halted by the fierce resistance of Jewish settlements near the borders. The Arab Legion forces only faced resistance near four isolated Jewish settlements in the Gush Etzion area near Jerusalem; every major town they entered in the West Bank, or what would be called the West Bank, offered no Jewish resistance. The Legion paused near the city of Jerusalem, the fate of which remained undecided despite the tacit understanding before the war between the Hashemites and the Jews on the partitioning of post-Mandate Palestine between them.

On 19 May, the Legion attacked the city of Jerusalem. Its troops succeeded in capturing the Jewish quarter in the Old City, but otherwise had put little effort into defending Arab neighbourhoods on the western side of the city, which enabled the Jewish forces to create their own enclave in that part of Jerusalem. They also found a way of opening the road to Tel-Aviv, the designated capital of the Jewish state. The Iraqis, the Jordanians' main partners, recorded one victory: they averted an Israeli attempt to occupy the city of Jenin. Apart from this they were used by the Jordanians to maintain law and order in Samaria, now practically under Jordan's control.

Five days into the fighting, the UN did what it should have done long before: it reassessed its policy on Palestine. On 20 May, the General Secretary appointed a mediator. Count Folke Bernadotte was given the task of recommending an alternative solution to partition. The Security Council called for a cease-fire, which was answered only two weeks later.

A week of fighting passed. The only Arab successes were against isolated Jewish settlements, but the attackers were unable to hold onto the areas they occupied, and were retreating by the time the first week of fighting ended. The basic Egyptian achievement was in joining forces with the Arab Legion around Bethlehem and southern Jerusalem, but this was short-lived. The two Arab contingents lost this vantage point, and the Jewish forces drove a wedge between the Egyptian troops there and those stranded in the Negev in an area known as the Faluja pocket (where incidentally Gamal Abd al-Nasser served as a young officer). The Syrians and the Lebanese began losing ground as soon as they started their operations. On 18 May, the Jewish forces occupied Acre. Those Palestinians who had arrived from Haifa in the middle of April as refugees were driven out once more, this time making their way to Lebanon.

By 24 May, the situation on the northern front was clearer. The Syrian, Iraqi and Lebanese forces, which had entered northern Palestine, began a hasty withdrawal. A Syrian counter-attack on 6 June failed, and the Arab forces were left within a small zone of Palestine adjacent to the Sea of Galilee. After the 1948 war, this area became the main bone of contention between Syria and Israel, the struggle for which ignited the tensions leading to the 1967 war. In other fronts the situation was similar. The lack of ammunition, long supply lines and an absence of military experience left the Arab side unable to withstand the Jewish forces, which, although consisting of a similar number of troops, were more experienced and better equipped.

On 10 June, the first truce was signed. Parts of southern Palestine were still in the hands of the Egyptians, and the West Bank and East Jerusalem were in Jordanian hands. In at least two places there was a readiness to accept this situation as positive and a basis for a post-war settlement: Amman, where King Abdullah was happy to have such a large portion of Palestine in his hands, and London, where the foreign secretary, Ernest Bevin, and his Middle Eastern experts saw such a division of Palestine as fair and functional. For the British policy makers, this formula was a plausible solution to the conflict, as well as an arrangement that served the British interests in the area quite well.

But in Tel-Aviv, Cairo, Damascus and Baghdad, there was a will to continue the bloodshed, with each party hoping to make more territorial gains. For some of the Arab politicians, this was a case of political survival, as stopping the military operations might have signalled an admission of defeat to the growing nationalist opposition at home. They should have known better, as on the eve of the lull Israel flaunted its military power and superiority by bombarding all the nearby Arab capitals.

During the lull in the fighting, the Arab armies failed to replenish their arms supplies, since Britain was resolved to observe the UN arms embargo on the warring parties. The Jewish forces, on the other hand, continued to circumvent the sanction by importing considerable quantities of heavy arms from the Eastern bloc countries that were disobeying the UN policy. The parity of the first week was replaced by a Jewish superiority once fighting was resumed in the middle of June 1948.

The flow of arms to the Jewish forces was to have a grave effect on political stability. In the middle of the truce, the Jewish side was slipping dangerously towards civil war. The attempt to unite all the underground factions into a single military unit had proved very difficult. In particular, the Irgun, with its fanaticism and nationalism, refused to accept a central authority. On 22 June, it tried to smuggle a shipload of arms to strengthen its own military power. The ship was discovered by the Hagana and destroyed. Two persons directly involved in the incident would carry the consequences of this clash into Israeli politics. One was Menachem Begin, who was on the ship and would make a political career out of his attempt to vindicate those on board the ship. The other was Yitzhak Rabin, one of the Hagana commanders on the ground, whom veteran Irgun supporters would regard as a traitor. Many years later they brought up the incident again after Rabin signed the Oslo accords, fuelling the campaign of hatred that culminated in his assassination.

On 8 July, fighting recommenced for ten days before a second truce was imposed. The initiative was now firmly on the Jewish side. Israel's leaders, furnished with new weapons but apprehensive lest the international community impose an unfavourable solution on them, made an effort to complete a take-over of most of Palestine. In August the successful Israeli campaigns continued, leading to their complete control of Palestine, apart from the West Bank and the Gaza Strip. Both sides lost many troops in the battles, but the Arab armies in particular suffered high casualties. The Israeli government lost no time in capitalizing on its military successes in order to radically transform the political situation in Palestine. In August, the Israeli coin, the lira, replaced the existing currency. In the same month, the Israeli government began to lay claim to the spoils left behind by the British. They took over many bank accounts, both public and private. Some of the governmental accounts were of course kept in London, and it was the British government that completed the total dispossession of the Palestinians from any share in the ex-Mandate's wealth by handing over those remaining accounts to the Jewish state in the early 1950s. The Palestinians, to this day, have failed to gain access to any of the money accumulated during thirty years of British taxation in Palestine.[14]

August also saw a huge wave of Jewish immigration. This placed an economic burden on the Zionist community, which was already fighting for its life. In particular, the people of Jerusalem were living in harsh conditions under military rule, and could hardly absorb newcomers. Fortunately for them, however, the Hashemites were withdrawing from the battlefield by August, and a weak limb in the Zionist body was saved.

Another symbol of change was the arrival of American and Russian diplomatic representatives in Tel-Aviv, although this diplomatic prestige was endangered when Jewish extremists assassinated Count Bernadotte in

September 1948, thereby clashing for the first time with the UN, which until then had been openly pro-Zionist. For the Jewish leader David Ben-Gurion, the least acceptable part of Bernadotte's plan had been to cede the Negev and annex it to Jordan, a plan fully supported and encouraged by the British government. With Bernadotte's demise, the way was clear for a complete military take-over of that part of Palestine. The Israelis occupied Beersheba in October 1948 and the Israeli army even threatened to enter Sinai and the West Bank; i.e. to enter Egypt proper and ignore the tacit understanding with Jordan. The UN tried to deter the Israelis with sanctions, the USA sent a sharp warning, and the British gave an ultimatum that the Israeli operations were a *casus belli* in London's view. These moves succeeded in keeping the Israelis within the cease-fire lines.

There was little the Arab states involved in the war could do in the face of such a military conquest. They consented to enter, under UN supervision, a series of dialogues between Israel and the Arab countries involved (apart from Iraq, which did not have a border with Israel). The negotiations produced armistice lines that held in the case of Syria, Jordan and Egypt until 1967, and in the case of Lebanon until 1978. However, these arrangements did not permanently prevent another war, and were a source of frequent border skirmishes. In a way, it appears that the Nobel Prize granted to their architect, Ralph Bunch (Bernadotte's deputy when the mediator was murdered), was unwarranted. At the time, at least, they stopped the fighting.

### THE ETHNIC CLEANSING OF PALESTINE
### (MAY 1948–JANUARY 1949)

While a conventional war raged in several parts of Palestine, in others it took a very different form. The conventional war occurred on the edges of what was to be the Jewish state and within areas the Jews coveted in the proposed Palestinian state. Within the Jewish state proper, a strange and chilling situation developed around three hundred or so Palestinian villages. In order to convey to readers what happened, I will focus briefly on the chronicles of 64 villages out of the 370 wiped out by Israel, in order to highlight a situation within the heart of rural Palestine that led to its almost complete disappearance.

These villages lay in the area between the coastal towns of Tel-Aviv and Haifa. One of the Hagana's brigades, the Alexandroni, was entrusted with the mission of Judaizing this part of Palestine. From the end of April until the end of July 1948, a grim scene was repeated in almost every village.

Armed Israeli soldiers surrounded each village on three sides, and put the villagers to flight through the fourth side. In many cases, if the people refused to leave, they were forced onto lorries, and driven away to the West Bank. In some villages, there were Arab volunteers who resisted by force, and when these villages were conquered they were immediately blown up and destroyed.

By 14 May, the day the Jewish state was declared, 58 villages had already been wiped out. Six remained. Three, Jaba', Ijzim and Ein Ghazal, would be obliterated in July. Two, Fureidis and Jisr al-Zarqa, about 35 kilometres north of Haifa, are still there today. These two villages provided cheap labour to the veteran Jewish settlements of Zichron Yaacov and Binyamina, and thus were spared.[15]

Tantura, the largest of the six remaining villages, was caught in the middle of Jewish territory like 'a bone in the throat', according to the Alexandroni official history of the war.[16] On 23 May, its day came too. Tantura was an old Palestinian village, large by the standards of that period, with around 1,500 inhabitants, and dependent on agriculture and fishing. Two or three notables, including the mukhtar, the head of the village, were offered terms of surrender by the Jewish intelligence officers. They rejected them, suspecting, quite rightly it seems, that surrender would lead to expulsion. At first, the Jewish commander contemplated sending a van with a loudspeaker calling on people to surrender, but this did not happen. On the night of 22 May, the village was attacked from four sides. This was uncommon, as we have seen. Lack of coordination led to a complete encirclement of the village, a situation that left a large number of villagers in the hands of the occupying force.

The captives were moved to the beach. There, the men were separated from the women and children, who were expelled to nearby Fureidis. (Some families were reunited eighteen months later.) Two hundred men between the ages of thirteen and thirty were massacred by the Alexandroni and other Jewish forces. Both revenge and a calculated wish to kill men of fighting age motivated this bloodshed. There were similar incidents in many other locations, the details of which still await the research of future scholars.[17]

In Galilee and the Negev, as on the coastal plain, other Israeli brigades used similar strategies for Judaizing the new state. The Israeli operations in Galilee were based on a systematic plan of expulsion, but one that depended heavily on local circumstances, which created a pattern that in hindsight seems illogical, to say the least. For example, the city of Nazareth and the town of Shafamru, not on particularly good terms with the Jewish settlement, were left intact, while a village near Mount Tabor that wished

Figure 5. The women and children of Tantura shortly after the occupation in May 1948

to conclude a non-aggression pact with the Yishuv was destroyed and its inhabitants expelled. The systematic aspect was in the methods employed, of first terrorizing the population, executing a few to induce others to leave, and then inviting an official committee to assess the value of land and property in the deserted villages or neighbourhoods.

By the winter of 1949, the guns were silent. The second phase of the war had ended, and with it the second, but not the last, stage of the 'cleansing' of Palestine was over. The third phase was to extend beyond the war, until 1954, and will be dealt with in the next chapter. While in the first phase it was urban Palestine that was subjected to expulsions and massacres, the bulk of the population living in the rural areas became victims of this policy after May 1948. Out of about 850,000 Palestinians living in the territories designated by the UN as a Jewish state, only 160,000 remained on or nearby their land and homes. Those who remained became the Palestinian minority in Israel. The rest were expelled or fled under the threat of expulsion, and a few thousand died in massacres.

Thus, when winter was over and the spring of 1949 warmed a particularly frozen Palestine, the land as we have described it in this book – reconstructing a period stretching over 250 years – had changed beyond recognition. The countryside, the rural heart of Palestine, with its colourful and picturesque villages, was ruined. Half of the villages had been destroyed, flattened by Israeli bulldozers which had been at work since August 1948 when the government had decided either to turn them into cultivated land or to build new Jewish settlements on their remains. A naming committee granted the new settlements Hebraized versions of the original Arab names: Lubya became Lavi, and Safuria Zipori, although Iteit retained its original name. David Ben-Gurion explained that this was done as part of an attempt to prevent future claim to the villages. It was also supported by the Israeli archaeologists, who had authorized the names as returning the map to something resembling 'ancient Israel'.[18]

Urban Palestine was similarly crushed. The Palestinian neighbourhoods in mixed towns were destroyed, apart from a few quarters that were left empty, to be populated later by Jewish immigrants from Arab countries. The non-mixed towns experienced two very different fates. The people of Lydda, Ramleh and Majdal were evicted by force, suffering massacres and humiliation in the process. Shafamru and Nazareth, on the other hand, remained intact, but were hopelessly overpopulated by streams of refugees fleeing from nearby villages.

Three-quarters of a million Palestinians became refugees. This was almost 90 per cent of those living in what was designated as the Jewish state. By the winter of 1948, they were already in tents provided by international charity organizations, warmed only by the UN resolution promising them a quick return to their homes. Those living in the Gaza Strip became acquainted with Egyptian military rule, harsh at the time, but mostly indifferent, in a packed area that included the largest segment of the refugee community. Those in the West Bank who were still in their own homes and had retained their connection to the Hashemites carved out a new political and economic future for themselves. Those who found themselves as refugees there were crammed into tented camps, living off charity and solidarity. Those who still hoped for an independent Palestine soon encountered the rough treatment of the Hashemite secret service and police, but later succeeded in creating a national political infrastructure for independent action.

Palestine was lost to the Palestinians in the 1948 war, as much on the diplomatic front as on the battlefield. The tacit understanding reached between Israel and Jordan on the eve of the war over the partitioning of post-Mandate Palestine neutralized the Arab Legion, Jordan's efficient, British-led army, which confined its activity to the area around Jerusalem. This was a strategic decision that determined the balance of power in the 1948 war. In all, apart from a short period of parity, the Jewish side had more, but not significantly more, soldiers and ammunition as the war continued.

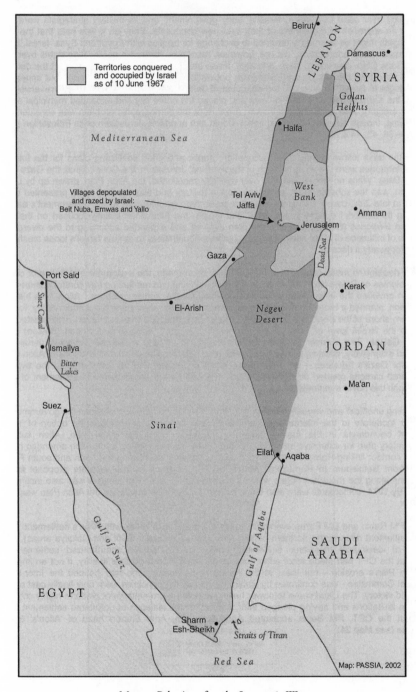

Map 4. Palestine after the June 1967 War

It was highly mobilized compared to its opponents, and far better organized. The Hagana could draw from a reserve of Western-trained and homegrown officers with military experience. It had an effective centralized system of command and control and fought over a relatively small area, enabling it to operate swiftly and more efficiently than the Egyptian or Iraqi armies, fighting a long way from home.

The settlement policy of the Jewish Agency left many settlements in isolated positions, and the general balance of power was not reflected around these spots. There were, according to the official Israeli foundational mythology, a few Jews against many Arabs in several battles, and Jewish acts of heroism were indeed performed on these killing fields, but this was not universal. Nonetheless, the 660,000-strong Jewish community suffered 6,000 deaths, of which 2,000 were civilians: in all, 1 per cent of the population.

Palestine now became a new geo-political entity, or rather three entities. Two, the West Bank and the Gaza Strip, were ill-defined, the first fully annexed to Jordan, but without the population's consent or enthusiasm; the second in limbo under military rule, its inhabitants prevented from entering Egypt proper. The third entity was Israel, bent on Judaizing every part of Palestine, and building a new living organism, the Jewish community of Israel.

The catastrophe that befell the Palestinians would be remembered in the collective national memory as the Nakbah, the catastrophe, kindling the fire that would unite the Palestinians in a national movement. Its self-image would be that of an indigenous population led by a guerrilla movement wishing without success to turn the clock back. The Israelis' collective memory would depict the war as the act of a national liberation movement fighting both British colonialism and Arab hostility, and winning against all odds. Their loss of 1 per cent of the population would cloud the joy of achieving independence, but not the will and determination to Judaize Palestine and turn it into a future haven for world Jewry in the aftermath of the Holocaust.

# CHAPTER 5

# The Age of Partition (1948–1967)

## DISLOCATION AND DISPOSSESSION

About two-and-a-half million people now lived within the borders of what had been Mandate Palestine. In the newly created state of Israel, these included newcomers, the majority of them Jewish immigrants from Eastern Europe and Arab countries, but also the 160,000 Palestinians who somehow had been able to stay on the land. Nearly one million of Palestine's indigenous population had been made refugees; many of these had been expelled to the West Bank and the Gaza Strip, others to nearby Lebanon, Syria and Jordan.

The refugees came from all walks of life, but those who found themselves thrown together in the camps shared a similar socio-economic background. Whether camp dwellers or not, rich or poor, they had all experienced the collective and personal trauma that would consolidate their future ties as a national community, their sense of identity centred on their lost homeland. This allows us, indeed obliges us, to include the history of the refugees within that of the land itself. The majority were farmers, who began to prosper after the Second World War but found that this little changed their standard of living as much of their profits were spent in their villages on the construction of a social and welfare infrastructure that the Mandate had failed to provide. Now, in 1948, expelled by force from their homeland, they were beggars who depended on United Nations hand-outs, and living in the hope of soon returning to their homes. Putting it differently, about one million Palestinians were still living in Palestine itself, where they were now outnumbered by a million-and-a-half Jews, while another million Palestinians lived near the borders of Palestine, mostly in refugee camps.[1]

The 'society' of what had been Mandate Palestine included others apart from the indigenous people who had been expelled and the newcomers who had settled on their land. These were the veteran Zionists, some from as early as the 1880s. The first half of the 1950s were years in which both newcomers and established residents had to find ways of adapting to the new geo-political situation around them. In political terms, those times were marked by indecision, lost opportunities and irreversible resolutions. It proved a precarious transition in Palestine, in which some fared better than others.

The main victims, however, were the refugees in the camps. Their quality of life was determined by the regimes under which they were now living, as it was the host countries' official policies and economic resources that determined how big the camps would be, how close together the mud huts would be built, and what basic infrastructure there would be.

No less important in the life of the refugees was the UN. The organization defined a refugee as 'a needy person and his direct descendants, who as a result of the war in Palestine has lost his home and his means of livelihood'.[2] The winter of 1948–49 was particularly cold and bitter, and the 750,000 persons who qualified as refugees would hardly have survived were it not for American welfare organizations and international aid agencies.[3]

In January 1949, after the money from such charitable organizations ran out, the UN established a single body to deal with the Palestinian refugee problem, the United Nations Relief and Works Agency (UNRWA). This was the brainchild of American entrepreneurs who were not interested directly in the political dimensions of the refugee problem, but believed they could link the refugees' settlement in Arab countries with a kind of Marshall Plan for the Middle East. As in Europe, the idea was to promote better standards of living as the best means for containing Soviet expansion.

That the American involvement centred on the welfare aspect of the problem explains why UNRWA proved unable to change the refugees' status or well-being significantly. Although it promised to support them in their transition to repatriation, UNRWA never succeeded in turning this into reality. It also vowed to protect the refugees and the rights they had under international law, another promise that remained unfulfilled. Instead, its main achievement consisted of moving them from tents into mud huts built within low-walled camps, with a few narrow lanes running through these new shanty-towns of the Middle East. The now familiar sight of these refugee camps was a constant reminder to the world of what one author called the 'bitter harvest' of the 1948 war.[4] The original huts and the new additions were all built from temporary materials, mainly clay, instead of the traditional stone, which encapsulated the refugees' transitional status and highlighted their anticipation of soon being repatriated, as laid down in UN Resolution 194, or, in the case of the more romantic among them, of the liberation of Palestine as promised by the guerrilla organizations vowing to defeat Zionism and Israel.

Within a year, by May 1949, the refugee problem had disappeared from the international agenda. At first, it had featured as one of three outstanding problems marking the Palestine question, the other two being the future of Jerusalem and the partitioning of the land. It was this triangular perception of the conflict that formed the basis for the UN peace efforts throughout 1948–49. The solution to these three problems was also clear to the UN: the unconditional repatriation of the refugees, the internationalization of Jerusalem, and the partitioning of the land according to the distribution of the two populations. All three points formed the core of the proposals put forward by Count Bernadotte, the UN mediator sent to the region. After his assassination by Jewish extremists in September 1948, his proposals were taken up by the body replacing him, the UN Conciliation Commission.

Bernadotte's proposals became the principal guidelines for a peace conference convened in April 1949 in Lausanne, Switzerland. There, under American pressure, Israel consented for one day, 11 May to be exact, to negotiate over the three proposals, only to renege within twenty-four hours. During that period, the Jewish state was accepted as a member of the UN. Once accepted, it felt secure and confident enough to adopt an officially inflexible position towards a UN-sponsored solution that it did not like. For a while, the US administration exerted pressure on Israel to keep to its consent to discuss the three issues, but to no avail, and the process petered out.[5]

While the international deliberation over the refugees' future bore no fruit, some Arab countries had to take swift decisions and formulate their own policies towards the refugees in their countries, since their presence dramatically changed delicate religious balances, as in Lebanon, or ethnic ones, as in Jordan, where there was a strong possibility that the refugees' arrival and the annexation of the West Bank would lead to the country's Palestinization. Abdullah of Jordan was keenly aware of this danger and set out to assimilate the Palestinians. From the beginning, refugees in Jordan were allowed occupational freedom, and were also entitled to leave the camps, provided they showed loyalty to the regime. This was coupled with a ruthless elimination of any real or imagined manifestations of an alternative Palestinian identity in the newly enlarged kingdom.

The Jordanian policy in the 1950s was highly ambivalent. While it invited Palestinian refugees in, Jordan still regarded all Palestinians, whether refugees or permanent inhabitants of the West Bank, as a potentially subversive community that had to be supervised and controlled. The material and financial superiority of the West Bank *vis-à-vis* the rest of Jordan led to further fears of possible secession, or a future Palestinian take-over. The tension between the West Bank residents and their new ruler did not ease with time, nor did the relationship improve under the reign of Abdullah's grandson, King Hussein, who came to power in 1953. The same can be said about the relationship between the camp dwellers on the eastern bank and the authorities. Only those Palestinians who settled in the East Bank, outside the camps, were able to normalize their existence over time, which may explain why some integrated willingly into their new society.

At the same time, Jordan was a much more welcoming 'host state' than Lebanon or Syria, for instance. From the beginning, the Lebanese government employed an uncompromising policy of oppression and exclusion towards the refugees. Palestinians arriving in Lebanon were mostly self-sufficient peasants or farmers from Galilee, or expellees from Haifa and Acre. They all faced exceptional hardships, and were treated as foreigners in terms of housing and employment. The government, apprehensive lest the refugees disturb Lebanon's delicate ethno-religious balance, confined them to miserable camps. The same applied to civil rights. At least forty occupational categories were closed to them.[6] Those who did find work remained in the lower ranks, often the fate of immigrant communities, but in the case of the Palestinians the result of a deliberate ethnic policy.[7]

The Syrian government was more relaxed in its attitude towards the refugees, allowing free enterprise to flourish in terms of the small businesses they could open, but it was as harsh as the Lebanese about unskilled work. There were too many poor and unemployed Syrians who needed the underpaid jobs and who quite naturally displayed animosity towards competitors.

The most favourable conditions awaited refugees in the Persian Gulf states, which became a coveted, but rarely reached, destination. The adventures of the three desperate fictional heroes, or rather anti-heroes, of Ghasan Kanafani's story *Men in the Sun* poignantly reflect this situation.[8] But even in that relative paradise, conditions were attached to survival. One had to be employed in order to be able to stay, or risk being treated as a 'guest worker', deprived of basic rights. The surest way of gaining permanent residence was to marry a local citizen. Refugees who fulfilled these conditions had the opportunity to use their skills and exploit their qualifications.

From Israel's point of view, the varying conditions meant that the refugees remained a 'problem'. The government in Jerusalem was constantly on the alert lest the international community insist on implementing the commitment it had made to the refugees in Resolution 194. To avert this, the Israeli government began, in August 1948, to execute an anti-repatriation policy, which resulted in either the total destruction or full Jewish take-over of every deserted Palestinian house and dwelling, both in the villages and the urban neighbourhoods. In fact, once the UN and the international community lost interest in promoting repatriation, the Israeli government was able to proceed with the take-over of more villages, unhindered by world public opinion. It first created the legal foundations for its anti-repatriation policy, passing legislation in the Knesset in 1950 that allowed the government to go on confiscating Palestinian property and use it for Jewish public purposes. In 1953, the army too was authorized to make use of Palestinian villages and fields. This legislative campaign provided the constitutional basis for the continued depopulation of Palestinian villages in the name of security. In those early years after the 1948 war, the army occupied dozens of Arab villages in the north and coastal plain, and expelled their populations. In the south, the Bedouins were settled by force in a process of dispossession that robbed them of the vast tracts of land they had owned during the late Ottoman period, and in some cases even earlier, and of their nomadic culture.[9]

The continued depopulation was closely connected to Israel's official absorption and settlement policy. The government wished to settle Jewish immigrants on deserted Palestinian land and property as quickly as possible, and as close as possible to the disputed borders. But despite these efforts, the population in some areas adjacent to the borders remained Palestinian, and Israeli security experts feared that this geographical proximity would encourage cross-border cooperation among Palestinians. Though such alliances never materialized, this proximity served as one of the principal justifications, or rather pretexts, for the imposition of harsh military rule on these areas.

Many of the Jewish immigrants sent by the central government in the 1950s to new settlements on the border came from Arab countries. Locating them on the border, often on the ruins of deserted Palestinian villages, served several purposes. It provided an easy solution for problems of accommodation and land. It also stretched the Judaization of Palestine into geographical areas it had been unable to reach during the Mandate. The Israeli Foreign Ministry argued that this provided 'natural justice': the Jewish immigrants had been expelled by the Arab world (only true of Iraq), and could now be given homes vacated by Palestinians. By explaining the settlement policy in this way, Foreign Ministry officials sought to persuade the international community that a population exchange of a kind had taken place, and that there was no need to search any longer for a solution to the refugee problem.[10]

This campaign of land and village confiscation continued intermittently from 1949 to 1954. The prey were helpless, the predators tenacious. In an interesting twist, the main beneficiary proved to be none other than the socialist kibbutz movement, Hashomer Hazair, which officially carried the slogan of bi-national coexistence high on its banner. It was the most leftist, but at the same time proved to be the greediest, of the three major kibbutz movements in the young state of Israel.[11]

This dissonance between ideology and reality produced some fine (and admittedly agonizing) deliberations among its members, but none of these stopped the process of ethnic cleansing. Hashomer Hazair had a party, Mapam, which came second in the first-ever Israeli general election in 1949 to Mapai, the dominant Labour Zionist movement headed by David Ben-Gurion. Mapam had had its own paramilitary group during the Mandate, the Palmach, whose commanders regarded the 1948 war as a missed opportunity, as they believed Israel could have seized all of western Palestine. Whenever the circumstances again seemed favourable, for example in 1951, 1956, 1958 and of course 1967, they pressed for the occupation of the West Bank.[12] When it came to acquiring more land in Israel itself for the movement's kibbutzim, they had no scruples, even if it meant forcibly removing their immediate Palestinian neighbours from the villages in which they had lived for centuries.

Forty Palestinian villages were depopulated between 1949 and 1952, their inhabitants either moved *en bloc* to other villages, driven across the border, or dispersed within the country. The people who lost their homes but remained inside Israel joined the large community of internal refugees, today numbering about 200,000 and constituting the most politicized element in the Israeli Palestinian community.[13]

The tragedy of the loss of more villages was further highlighted by the hasty erection of new Jewish settlements on top of the 370 Palestinian villages destroyed in the 1948 war and on the land of those evicted after the war. In July 1949, Ben-Gurion personally supervised a large project to give 'Hebrew names to all the places, mountains, valleys, springs and roads, etc.' in the country. This act of 'memoricide' was completed in 1951.[14]

### PATTERNS OF RESPONSE: GUERRILLA FIGHTERS, ISOLATION AND CO-OPTATION

Over time, the Palestinian refugee camps everywhere acquired more permanent features, and came to resemble small Middle Eastern towns, each with its own market place in the centre, coffee-houses and shops. And yet, as mini-cities, they were very small and severely overcrowded. Their most conspicuous feature was the flag or blue board of UNRWA, which was attached to every building that had a public function, such as schools, food shops, and health clinics. UNRWA became the principal employer in the camps themselves. Teachers, doctors and social workers were all on its payroll. They worked under impossible conditions. The camps lacked basic infrastructure in water, sewerage, housing, electricity or roads, and were the poorest dwellings in the entire Arab world. By the late 1950s, violence and despair were channelled into guerrilla activity, which recruited boys, and some girls, from an early age.

This process was part of the re-emergence of the Palestinian national movement. Two aspects need to be highlighted: one was highly political and active, in fact hyperactive; the other was social and cultural, a less visible but more measured process of at first disintegration and then cohesion. Main participants in the first were the members of the various Palestinian national organizations who, from sunrise to sunset, were busy inventing a new 'tradition' – the Palestinian guerrilla movement. A sign of the lifestyle they adopted was the array of ceremonies, rallies, days of celebration and commemoration, and their accompanying insignia and customs, all presented in the most up-to-date discourse of decolonization and Third World nationalism.

This trend within the Palestinian national movement was nurtured in Gaza by Palestinian members of the Muslim Brotherhood, the pan-Islamist movement founded in Egypt in 1928 by Hasan al-Banna. Active both in the Gaza Strip and the West Bank, this form of political Islam was the only organization with a significant following in the camps in the 1950s, where it built a network on the traditional orientations of the peasant and lower-middle-class camp dwellers. For the latter, there was little in the secular field of politics to attract them, given the resounding failure of the national leaderships in Palestine and the Arab world in 1948. They did not become religious activists but rather nationalist fighters, who keenly used the Brotherhood's organization as a model for their own activism against Israel.[15]

The refugee community soon became politicized to an extent that ideology or politics had never succeeded in achieving. Political activity took time to crystallize, and was at first leaderless and individualistic. It centred around the mythical figure of the Palestinian fighter (*fida'i* pl. *fida'iyyun*), who was willing to sacrifice his life for the cause of Palestine, however ill-defined at the time. If he survived, his bravery gave him a commanding position within his own society.

The area of operation of the *fida'iyyun* was the guarded border between Israel and the rest of Palestine, and activities initially consisted of attempts to retrieve lost property. As their camps were near the borders, Palestinian refugees watched their lands and assets being taken over by Jewish immigrants, now citizens of the state of Israel. Encouraged, to some extent, by the Egyptians and Jordanians to salvage as much as they could of their lost property, the bolder ones began conducting armed raids on isolated Jewish settlements close to the Gaza Strip and the West Bank, at times killing the new Jewish 'owners' of their property, sometimes striking randomly at any Jew they encountered, but most often returning empty-handed to their camps. Gradually, Palestinians with a clearer sense of politics and nationalism began to organize these incursions into a more systematic form of combat against the Jewish state. The result was the *fida'i* units, the beginnings of Palestinian resistance. Initially, these units were supervised and controlled by the Jordanians and the Egyptians, who did not want the new 'army' to act too independently and drag them into a war proper with Israel. The Palestinians themselves were also hesitant about such an escalation, given the Israeli tendency to retaliate with a shoot-to-kill policy, which, throughout the 1950s, resulted in the death of thousands of Palestinians.[16] The Israelis reacted harshly even to the early, limited *fida'i* actions, attacking and killing civilians. The special elite units on the Israeli side that carried out these reprisals became the backbone of the commando units of the Israeli Defence Force (IDF), whose feats helped create, both inside and outside Israel, the mystique of the Israeli invincibility.

From the cadre of young *fida'iyyun* sprang the most significant Palestinian organization, Fatah, which had at its centre figures such as Yasser Arafat and Khalil al-Wazir (Abu Jihad). The former was a distant relation of the Husayni family, his origins still blurred today by his self-invented biography or by the memoirs of those around him; the latter was a young refugee from Ramleh. With their friends, these two operated in the refugee camps in Gaza, where they set up a national group for the liberation of Palestine; the Arabic initials of its name 'the Movement for the Liberation of Palestine', spelled *fatah* 'victory' when read in reverse. By 1954, Fatah had begun a series of mini sabotage attacks on Israel, using the Muslim Brotherhood structures to recruit the *fida'iyyun* to their side and away from the Egyptian army.[17] Before long, political activism thrived not only in the camps, but also in the urban centres of the West Bank, the Gaza Strip, Amman and Damascus.

Politics was now totally divorced from the world of the old nationalist notables, who were not able to exert influence beyond the mid-1950s, except in one instance. This was the assassination of King Abdullah in July 1951, by someone probably connected to Amin al-Husayni. The nationalist notables directed their wrath towards Abdullah for his attempt to conclude a peace treaty with Israel, beyond the armistice agreement he had signed with the Jewish state in April 1949. In the later agreement, Abdullah ceded even more Palestinian territory to Israel. The agreement encountered an obstacle when the newly acquired territory, Wadi Ara', with 12 villages and 15,000 inhabitants (later called 'the Little Triangle'), was found to include a Palestinian population. However, the territory was strategically vital for Israel, as it connected the coastal town of Hadera with the eastern town of Afula, and was coveted despite its Arab character. It became the second-largest concentration of Palestinian citizens within the state of Israel, after Galilee.[18]

Although not directly blamed for letting the Nakbah happen, the notables lost credibility and were no longer trusted to carry on the political struggle. Nor, for the middle class at least, was political Islam an alternative. Urban Palestinians were more attracted by leftist and Marxist ideologies. As more well-to-do activists, they were particularly enterprising in the West Bank around the Communist Party there, and in the Gaza Strip, where they recruited for a new party, the Arab nationalist movement called al-Qawmiyyun al-Arab, the precursor of the leftist fronts such as the PFLP and PDFLP in the late 1960s.[19] A closer look reveals that these activists were middle-class professionals, educators and students, whose career or financial success was blocked. In Jordan, they were joined by other alienated groups wishing to make the movement a more Arab and radical entity. Nor were they inventing the wheel in terms of Arab ideology. The Free Officers of Egypt and the Ba'ath Party in Syria had already devised a convenient, albeit vague, vision of an Arab world liberated from its predicaments of the 1950s. This was a mixture inspired by the ideologies of pan-Arabism, socialism and anti-imperialism, which presented all three as the best weapons with which to fight European military presence, Zionism, and the ills of local capitalism.

The Palestinian contribution to the history of post-colonial ideas was to link the liberation of Palestine with a wider effort to solve the pan-Arab imbroglio. At first, Palestinian leftist ideology was a fellow-traveller in the general movement, but with time it became the driving force towards a more radical revolution in several Arab locations. Palestinian leftists were instrumental in bringing about changes in regimes and in installing leftist politicians as heads of state, as in South Yemen and Lebanon, although these changes were short-lived. Leftist politicians were eventually ousted by more nationalist and authoritarian military regimes, which proved less committed to socialist and Marxist ideologies and, equally, less interested in the fate of Palestine (the notable exception being the Republic of South Yemen).[20]

The majority of the Palestinian middle class, wherever they lived, was, pragmatic enough to play according to the rules of the main political game. The urban middle class within what had been the Mandate (Israel, the West Bank and the Gaza Strip) strived to exploit the educational opportunities at their disposal. While political space was limited, basic education was affordable and accessible, whether in Jordan, the Gaza Strip or Israel. In all three locations, as in most of the other countries in the Arab world where Palestinians were living in urban centres, education was free. It was also available in UNRWA's schools in the refugee camps. Today the Palestinians are one of the most highly educated groups in the Arab world.

Educational infrastructure was essential for refugees anxious to escape from economic and social hardship, but opportunities were not always available. In Lebanon, employment was limited by government policy, while in the Gaza Strip there were no real opportunities for work. In Israel and Jordan, the problem was different. In both countries, due to discriminatory laws and conduct, Palestinians could never hope to work in jobs that matched their qualifications or answered their reasonable expectations. This discrepancy between education and opportunity rekindled the fire of radicalism that had been lit by the trauma of the Nakbah.

At the end of the 1950s, urbanite political activity converging with the efforts of organizations such as Fatah produced a clearer sense of national orientation. In less than a decade, Palestinian activists in their different locations had succeeded in formulating through their parties' platforms and discourse the two clear Palestinian goals that would guide them in the post-Nakbah era: the creation of a Palestinian state, and the return of Palestinian refugees. As the state they envisioned was to replace Israel, the second goal would have been achieved by the success of the first.[21] Later, in the 1970s, when the Palestine Liberation Organization (PLO) was willing to accept a state in the West Bank and the Gaza Strip, it was hard to see this as compatible with the implementation of the right of return to historical Palestine.

The activist core of radicals, the old nationalist notables, and the Islamist activists in the camps, all appeared to share an approach: the need for an armed struggle to recapture Palestine. The notables had very little to offer in this respect. It was the less fortunate refugees who more eagerly joined the armed struggle and became its heroes and leaders, thereby revolutionizing the social structure of Palestinian society. This radical approach began to attract regional and global attention after 1956.

For the majority of Palestinians, economic survival remained the priority. This could be seen in the daily routine of many of the refugee camp dwellers. Of the approximately two million Palestinian refugees, only a few thousand took up arms, or attempted to effect Palestinian liberation through writing or diplomacy. For the majority, politics became a constant, intrusive element in their lives. The rhetoric, the hyper-national activity, and the recruitment (usually voluntary but sometimes coerced) to the cause disrupted both hierarchy and tradition. The younger generation now took precedence over the older, patriarchal one; women began playing a more central role on the public stage; and the clans lost their dominance almost totally and were gradually replaced by the nuclear family. As happened throughout the twentieth century to immigrant communities in the West, families needed the young and educated to communicate with the new world around them, which resulted in a further reduction in the status granted to seniority and age.[22] A similar revolution occurred in the communities of Jews immigrating to Israel from Arab countries and among the Palestinian minority in Israel.[23]

Individual ways of adapting to new conditions, as distinct from the collective one, took place in the business sector, the workplace and the labour market in general. This can be illustrated by the economic history of the West Bank from 1948 to 1967. There was no economic leadership in the annexed West Bank, let alone a social or political elite that could determine economic policies. The capital of both East and West banks was Amman, and every aspect of life was dealt with from there. Nonetheless, the capacity for business and economic success of Palestinians in the West Bank affected the Jordanian economy as a whole. In other circumstances, this will and energy could have been deployed collectively for the benefit of an emerging independent Palestinian state; instead, it was diverted into creating prosperity for the host country alone. In Jordan, the Palestinian community of businessmen, industrialists and agricultural producers had turned a non-existent Jordanian economy into a thriving market. After years of ruling an almost uninhabited arid area, the Hashemites now had something more akin to a modern state.

There are always those who benefit from economic growth and those who suffer or at best gain little from it. Land was scarce in the post-1948 West Bank. It was also a part of Palestine where urbanization suddenly soared to an unprecedented level. The result was conflicting demands which complicated economic development. In the 1950s, many West Bank landowners had prospered by buying land during the Mandate and using it mainly for citrus groves. Some now profited by selling the land for urban purposes. However, with their long background of nomadism and desert economics, the policy makers in Amman visualized their new Jordan as an agricultural country, not an urban society. Hence, the politicians in Amman exempted from taxes anyone who persisted in agricultural production, but were less helpful towards urban entrepreneurs. As a result, land remained in the hands of the few, rather than being sold for urban expansion, and land owners were encouraged to intensify agricultural production. As they had to pay even less to tenants and agricultural workers than before, they had a clear commercial incentive to preserve most of the West Bank as an agricultural area. Government and notable families alike profited from this policy; the refugees and farmers much less so.

There was also a ready-made market for their produce. In the 1950s, several Arab countries, in particular the emerging rich kingdom of Saudi Arabia, began demanding food and agricultural products in higher quantities than ever. Agricultural land expanded faster, almost doubling between 1948 and 1957.[24] The very few crops that had survived the commercialization of agriculture in the previous 250 years, such as wheat and barley, now disappeared in favour of more marketable crops such as citrus fruit, vegetables, olives, figs, and even dairy products. The West Bank became the source of high-quality food for the rest of Jordan and the Arab world. There was one difference, however; a relatively higher number of land owners benefited from this process than in the days of the Mandate. Their standard of living improved dramatically, notwithstanding the Nakbah. This is a paradox, admittedly, but one that painfully illuminates the polarization within West Bank society, given the low standard of living in the refugee camps.

A small group of refugees was among the few who benefited from the direction taken by the West Bank economy. They left the camps, purchased arable land and cultivated it. For example, refugees in al-Khalil (Hebron) utilized previous connections with the Bedouins of al-Karak on the eastern bank, buying land from them and creating a livelihood outside the camps. Another success story was that of the refugees in camps in the Jordan Valley, who used UNRWA and Jordanian funds to establish their own agricultural settlement in Karameh, a place that plays an altogether different role in the next chapter. But most refugees were unable to realize their potential in such a way, and those working in agriculture were exploited as a cheap labour force.[25]

The Hashemite kingdom of Jordan used laws and tax exemptions to bolster the large land owners, who prospered under its rule. These land-owning families also controlled the trade routes and businesses. First, in the traditional way, families such as the Nimrs in Nablus used their old connections with the Bedouin tribes to dominate trade, and then worked their way up to the higher administrative echelons of the relevant Jordanian ministries. Christians and Muslims alike benefited greatly from the monopoly they were establishing over production and distribution. Yet the largest share of merchandizing remained in the hands of East Bank families. As we saw in the previous chapter, the transfer of the interests of notable families from politics to economics was a pattern that started after the Second World War, when the Nashashibis opted for business rather than national leadership.

Other families with a rich political past were now deeply involved in the business of making money. Such was the case with the Abd al-Hadis, who began cultivating seedlings successfully in the 1960s. They were represented in the local cadres of mayors, members of parliament, and others who helped prop up Hashemite rule in the West Bank. They were, however, no longer involved in Palestinian political life, which was centred on the refugee camps, and were more active on the eastern than on the western bank of the Jordan. They would be brought back into politics by the Israeli occupation in 1967 but, in a democratic vote in 1976, would lose to the PLO.

The new economic interests of the old nationalist notables left little room for smaller traders, land owners and manufacturers, who had no comparable access to the supervisory bodies established by the Hashemites to control exports and imports in the West Bank. The interests of small land owners were theoretically represented by the minister of agriculture, a position which the Hashemites sensibly reserved for a West Bank resident. However, this post was always given to members of leading families that had proved their allegiance to the Hashemites during the Mandate.

While the traditional notables controlled economic life more firmly than ever, they were hampered politically by the Hashemite dynasty. Although they had access to civil service and secondary government posts, they were not allowed to act collectively in pursuit of nationalism. The vacuum this created was filled when the *fida'iyyun* shifted their locus of activity from the Gaza Strip to Jordan. Soon younger members of the leading families joined this new form of politics, weakening the authority of notable families in Palestinian politics still further.

Among the majority of the Palestinians in the West Bank who did not think that they had benefited from being 'saved' by the Hashemites in

1948, there was a growing realization that they too were under occupation. This collective sense would ebb and flow throughout the nineteen years of Hashemite rule in the West Bank. At its peak it was the driving force behind large demonstrations that culminated in an uprising in 1956 which was brutally quelled by the Jordanian army. General tensions with Egypt and Syria led the opposition to try to exploit the uprising as part of their overall attempt to radicalize Jordanian politics. In 1957, a coup attempted by Jordan's general chief-of-staff, Abu Nawar, failed. (In 1958 the king was saved by the arrival of British forces.)[26]

These were confusing times for West Bank Palestinians who sought a stake in politics. On the one hand was the pull of nationalism and on the other the rewards of co-optation. The ruling dynasty was even willing to offer military governorships to people from notable families previously not allied to the Hashemite national leadership. The famous Palestinian historian Arif al-Arif was awarded a governorship in East Jerusalem, as was Ahmad Khalil, the former mayor of Haifa. East Jerusalemites in particular were elevated to some of the highest ranking posts in the West Bank administration. Appointment by the king presupposed loyalty, but also meant further division among the notable families. Periods of democratization and free elections, such as occurred in the early 1950s in the West Bank, also eroded the notables' position even further.

The twin processes of radicalism and isolation were also found at work within the Palestinian minority in Israel. While other Palestinians were confined in camps, or became citizens of Jordan or non-citizens in the Gaza Strip, 160,000 Palestinians within the new Jewish state were put under military rule in October 1948. This was to last eighteen years; and the memory of those dark times has played a formative role in the construction of Palestinian identity in Israel to today, and strained to breaking point the relationship between the minority and the majority. The leaders of the Jewish community were unprepared for the bi-national situation as it surfaced in post-Mandate Palestine; they had counted on creating a pure Jewish state. Although they had supported the partition resolution in 1947 which implied a Jewish state with an almost equal number of Jews and Palestinians, it is possible that even in 1947 they assumed that war as well as their own expulsion plans would eliminate any Palestinian presence.[27] Thus, while every other aspect of political life was widely debated, we see no systematic debate, on the eve of Israel's foundation, about the status of the Palestinians in the new Jewish state.

The legal status of the military rule that was imposed on the Palestinian minority in October 1948 was grounded in the mandatory emergency regulations the British had issued in 1945 against the Jewish underground, which gave military governors extended authority over the people under their rule. These same regulations now became a pernicious tool in the hands of callous and sometimes sadistic military rulers, who generally were drawn from non-combatant units just before their retirement. Their cruel behaviour consisted mainly of harassing the population with a range of abuses not unlike those to which new army recruits were subjected. There were other aspects to Israeli military rule. Under its umbrella, the official land confiscation policy was able to continue in the name of 'security' and 'public interest'. Political activists even vaguely suspected of identifying with Palestinian nationalism were expelled or imprisoned.

With the stick came the carrot. The prime minister's advisers on Arab affairs devised an elaborate web of inducement and control. In return for wealth and prestige for themselves and better living conditions for their own communities, notables in the Palestinian community were easily tempted to mute their identification with nationalism. They were further meant to show their society what benefits could accrue to anyone willing to comply with Israel's policy of co-optation. This was a strategy that worked well through the patriarchal and hierarchical structures still in place in rural as well as nomad areas. However, heads of villages (mukhtars) and heads of tribes (sheikhs) who agreed to become agents of government policy soon found themselves largely ostracized by their communities, who called them *adhnab al-hukuma*, 'the government's tails'. In the long run, this method of co-optation proved ineffective and counter-productive as it strengthened processes the Israeli government wished to stop. When the military regime was abolished in 1966, most of these notables lost their positions.

Ben-Gurion was particularly inventive in creating ways of co-optation. Verging on the absurd was his idea of turning the Palestinians into an Arab *millet* in Israel. Another more realistic idea was to drive a wedge between Christians and Muslims by presenting and treating the Christians as more loyal to the Jewish state.

Interestingly, the Israeli authorities' intense interest in and manipulation of the religious affiliation of the country's Arab citizens continues to this day. Like the British, the Israelis thought it would prove easier to control different religious communities than face a national minority. But contrary to their plans and predictions, religious identity never became an influential factor in the pro- or anti-Israeli attitudes of the Palestinians.

There was, however, a difference between being Muslim or Christian. Being a Christian Palestinian in Israel involved a balancing act between several spheres of identity. For others, a more pronounced Christian identity co-existed easily with the crystallization of a national identity; in fact Christians often played leading roles in the nascent Palestinian national movement.[28] The Christian ascendancy within Palestinian politics in Israel was also facilitated by the total collapse of the Muslim structure and hierarchy in Palestine in the 1948 war. The senior *ulama* left the country, and it was many years before political Islam would reappear as a significant force. Meanwhile the Israeli government replaced the former Muslim structure with one better suited to helping it impose its authority on the Palestinian minority.

With the Muslim structure also went its financial capabilities. The public endowments which had been run by the Supreme Muslim Council until the Mandate decided to expropriate them during the Arab revolt, became 'absentee property' in 1948, as did private endowments, whose supervisors were 'absentees'. In 1965, the Knesset instructed the custodians of absentee property to release the non-absentee endowments to their lawful benefactors and ordered the transfer of the public endowments to an Islamic committee – loyal to the government, of course. Not surprisingly, the former thrived while the latter stagnated.[29]

The destruction of Islamic structures and financial infrastructures opened the way for Christians to play a more central role in the Palestinian community in Israel. Christian politicians took on leading positions in the Communist Party, the only organized group expressing the national aspirations of the Palestinian minority, and were also strong in the collaborationist Arab sections of the Zionist parties. The Greek Catholic Church, under the guidance of its charismatic Mutran Hakim, was conspicuously active on both sides of the political spectrum.

Communism was important for the Orthodox Church because it was Russian; for some Orthodox it facilitated replacing their past loyalty to the tsar with a new allegiance to the USSR. But more than anything else, the Communist Party was a forum where urban Christian intelligentsia could meet Muslim workers (the lower socio-economic stratum was predominantly Muslim), and together try to shape an agenda for action and combat their common social and economic hardships. Significantly, despite its allegiance to an a-national ideology, the Communist Party emerged as the only national party; that is, it enabled people to express their national aspirations without risking arrest, as long as they did so in the form of Marxist discourse. There was still a huge Jewish community in the Soviet Union, and this, together with the obvious importance of the USSR in world politics, explained the pragmatic and tolerant attitude of the Israeli government towards Israel's Communist Party.

The politics of the Palestinian community in Israel was still elitist and largely male-dominated. Even the debates between collaborationists and communists took place within elite politics, while the rank and file had to survive the brutality of the military regime and the growing economic hardship. The Palestinian minority had the highest level of unemployment and underemployment caused by the accelerated proletarianization of a society that was traditionally mostly agrarian. Peasants employed in unskilled and poorly paid jobs had to return home every day to the families they were struggling to support, as they were not allowed to stay overnight in Jewish areas. For only one group, women, this meant a relative improvement. As they too were now needed to work outside the home, women could in return demand more education and a larger say in the community's affairs. However it would be wrong to describe this as a feminist revolution among the Palestinians in Israel.[30]

Among the cultural elite, one group stands out as united, and aloof from the tension between collaboration with the Jewish state and opposition to it. These were the poets. Poetry was the one area in which national identity survived the Nakbah unscathed. What political activists did not dare express, poets sang out with force. Poetry was the one medium through which the daily events of love and hate, birth and death, marriage and family could be intertwined with the political issues of land confiscation and state oppression and aired in public at special poetry festivals, such as the one that took place periodically in Kafr Yassif in Galilee. The Israeli secret service was powerless to decide whether this phenomenon was a subversive act or a cultural event. The security apparatus would be similarly puzzled in the early 1980s, when it began monitoring festivals organized by the Islamic movement.[31]

Meanwhile, Jewish counterparts of these Palestinian poets were among those Israelis who worked hardest to have the military regime abolished. They were backed by some of the more pragmatic politicians who realized that the regime was complicating Israel's relations with the region and the world at large. Given their self-image as liberals, some of these politicians wished to grant the Palestinians full citizenship. But as long as Ben-Gurion was prime minister, or at least held the strings behind the scenes until 1967, the policy towards the Palestinian minority was determined by a security-minded group of decision makers. Unfailingly harsh, this policy was executed by Ben-Gurion's advisers for Arab affairs, who were in favour of expelling as many Palestinians as possible and confining the rest within well-guarded enclaves. This sounds uncannily familiar in 2003, with Israel having re-occupied most of the West Bank and confined the population in numerous small 'bantustans'.

The expulsionists marked the 'present absentees', Palestinian refugees who were wandering within the state of Israel, homeless and stateless, as the first group to be deported. Communist Party activists, supported by Moshe Sharett, the foreign minister, came to their rescue and in the end only a small number was actually expelled.[32] Sharett was a key figure in the movement for the abolition of the military regime; but it took more than fifteen years for the Zionist liberals (among them Menachem Begin, who was appalled by the use of British emergency regulations against the Palestinian minority as he remembered too well how they had been used against himself and his friends) and socialists (such as Mapam) to achieve this.

Furthermore, in the debate on this question, 'public opinion' was on the side of the prime minister. The local Hebrew press was unanimous in its support for the government's policy. Yet, given all the repression, one basic right was never taken away, although Ben-Gurion contemplated even this. This was the right to vote and to be elected. On these two rights the inner debates of Mapai make interesting reading. Also, it is impossible to miss the irony in the fact that the raw instinct for vote gathering was allowed to overshadow the principal issue of full apartheid. In particular, the Histadrut could not resist the treasure the Arab electorate might supply, and fought, as though they were genuine humanitarians, for the right of Palestinians to vote. Even Ben-Gurion, who wrongly predicted that all Palestinians would vote *en bloc* for the Communist Party, reluctantly recognized that they could be a useful tool for keeping Mapai in power.

The immorality of the military regime was highlighted by the Kfar Qassem massacre. On 29 October 1956, the day the IDF invaded the Sinai Peninsula as part of its joint campaign with Britain and France to topple Nasser, the Israelis imposed a curfew on all Palestinian villages. This was inflicted on the population without notice. Kfar Qassem was not the only village where people returned to their homes later than the prescribed time of sunset, but for some reason the Israeli border guards decided to punish this particular breach of the curfew by massacring forty-eight civilians: women, children and young men. This failure of the state to protect its own citizens incurred little or no public indignation, and was further compounded by the light sentences meted out to the perpetrators.

In the long run, however, the Kfar Qassem massacre sent shock waves across the country, and led the government to change its position. Criticism was not aimed at the decision-making apparatus itself as much as at the leniency shown to the murderers. Moreover, the 'good behaviour' of the Palestinians in Israel during the Sinai operation convinced many that the military regime was useless and even harmful. Even the head of the Israeli secret service, Isar Harel, tried to convince Ben-Gurion that from a security point of view abolishing military rule would be much more constructive than retaining it. In this he was fully supported by the director-general of the Defence Ministry, Shimon Peres. However, nothing was to happen until Ben-Gurion lost the premiership.

There was also division among the Palestinians on military rule, but typically this was not appreciated by the Israeli political system. In the early 1950s, the government was divided on the question of Palestinian conscription to the IDF. The secret service predicted that the Palestinian minority in Israel would reject conscription, and suggested that all that was needed was to call up the intake for one year. When they refused, the government would be able to declare that the Palestinian community as a whole refused to serve in the army. When the experiment took place in 1954, to the surprise and bewilderment of the secret service, every conscript responded to the call-up. In addition, the Communist Party supported the potential recruits and the call-up day was turned into a festive event. No one was actually conscripted; the policy makers simply ignored these people's readiness to serve. What is more, the government's interpretation of the events gave it another tool in its discriminatory policy against the Palestinian minority, which still is being applied today: only people who have served in the army are eligible for state benefits such as loans, mortgages, and reduced university fees. There is also a close link between industry and security in the Jewish state, which means that significant sections (almost 70 per cent) of industry are closed to Palestinian citizens because they have not served in the army.

The military regime with all its horrors was a closed chapter by 1966. It left deep residues of bitterness and mistrust, though it did not ruin the chances of coexistence altogether. But it is undeniable that the basic laws passed by the Knesset in the early 1950s served to reinforce a discriminatory situation that persists today. Three such laws immediately affected, and continue to affect, the Palestinian citizens of Israel: the law of return, the naturalization law, and the law of Keren Hakayemet (the Jewish National Fund).

These citizenship laws gave precedence to Jewish immigrants, even Jews who were only potential immigrants, over indigenous Palestinian citizens in almost every sphere. In property, they created an apartheid-style system of land transactions. They were used to legalize retrospectively the expropriation of land, and the prohibition of selling to Palestinians state land (still most of the land available in Israel) or even absentee land. Most importantly, the laws defined most of the land for sale in Israel as the exclusive and perpetual property of the Jewish people. The result was that almost all Palestinian-owned land was taken by the government and turned into state land, to be sold or leased only to Jews. By the end of the confiscation frenzy and the formulation of the policy legalizing it, 92 per cent of the country's land had fallen into Jewish hands. Palestinian land, which on the eve of the war amounted to about 4.6 million dunams within the territory that became Israel, was reduced by 1950 to half a million dunams.[33] By 2000, even though the Palestinian population had grown tenfold, the amount of land available to them remained almost unchanged.

### THE SUEZ CAMPAIGN

The Suez war of 1956, unlike the 1948 war, did not encompass large sections of the population living between the River Jordan and the Mediterranean or in the refugee camps scattered within an area of 150 square miles around ex-Mandate Palestine. Therefore, the following concentrates not on the war itself, but rather on the processes that led to its outbreak, as these did affect society as a whole.

On the Israeli side, the November 1956 campaign was the outcome of an increasing politicization of the society, while a growing level of militarization made it subject to the whims of its power-hungry leaders. Consequently, the marginalization of moderate, dovish Israeli statesmen such as Moshe Sharett by the more hawkish and uncompromising David Ben-Gurion activated an aggressive Israeli policy against the neighbouring Arab states.[34] Two images underpinned Ben-Gurion's perception of the Arab world in general, and of the Palestinians in particular. One was the vision of the 'ancient kingdom' of the Israelites resurrected as a modern bastion of Western interests in the Middle East. This outlook, in various permutations, was shared by many of the generals in the army, particularly by the general chief of staff, Moshe Dayan. They all dreamed of a Greater Israel expanding to the north, east and south, which they thought to achieve by exploiting the overall instability in Arab politics at the time: a weak Lebanese regime, repeated coups in Syria, a young, inexperienced king in Jordan, and revolutionary rulers in Egypt, uncertain as yet of their regional and Arab policies. This was a transitional phase in Arab politics but Ben-Gurion felt emboldened to insist on a more active retaliation policy against *fida'i* activities, greater intervention in the politics of Lebanon, where he wanted to establish a new pro-Israeli Christian entity, and the pursuit of an uncompromising policy against Syria. For example, he wished to occupy the demilitarized zone between Israel and Syria, in dispute since 1948 and a cause of constant border skirmishes. He also held onto his dream of occupying the West Bank or extending Israel by annexing the Sinai Peninsula.

The second image that guided Ben-Gurion had more to do with negative emotions. For him, the Arab world was intrinsically hostile. He refused to accept Martin Buber's assertion – sounding a voice of reason and openly challenging the views of the prime minister at the time – that some of the intransigence was in direct response to Israeli aggressiveness. Some of the Arab rhetoric and actions after the 1948 war had worked to convince large sections of the Jewish community that the prime minister's harshness was justified, as many of them were equally far removed from reconciliation or peace. Also by now, the institutionalization of the Palestinian guerrilla movement had begun in earnest, replacing individual and civilian incursions into Jewish territory with systematic acts of sabotage, against which the Israeli army retaliated with growing ferocity and brutality.

However, the Arab leaders themselves were sending ambiguous messages of both peace and war to the Israeli leadership, of which Ben-Gurion chose to see only the more hostile approaches. Many of the Arab leaders immediately after the 1948 war were much more committed to the peace process the UN had started and was nurturing, than was Ben-Gurion. What explains Ben-Gurion's intransigence was the emphasis the UN was still putting on the refugee question, more specifically on the need to repatriate them unconditionally. But the Arab world also presented another, more hostile, front, which was broadcast in fiery public speeches and publicized through inflammatory articles in the local press, all employing warlike rhetoric and promising revenge for the 1948 defeat. The Egyptian and Syrian leaders went beyond words and struck large arms deals with the Eastern bloc, modernizing their armies and preparing them for war. When they partly translated words into action by engaging in guerrilla warfare on the Jewish state's borders, the inevitable Israeli retaliation, often out of all proportion, sowed insecurity in the Arab regimes bordering Israel, and contributed much to creating an 'eve of war' atmosphere.

For a while, during Sharett's short term as prime minister (1954–55), it seemed as if history would take a different turn. But operating a shadow cabinet from his retreat in Sdeh Boker, a kibbutz in the northern Negev, Ben-Gurion devised a clandestine terror attack on Egyptian soil in 1954, aimed at prompting the British to take a tougher attitude towards Nasser following their decision to evacuate their forces from the Suez Canal. (The British forces had been pushed into the Canal Zone after the July 1952

Free Officers' revolution in Egypt.) The operation was the brainchild of the Israeli military intelligence, but went astray because of the amateurish performance of the Egyptian Jews recruited for the mission. In the Israeli collective memory, this stands out simply as Ha-Parasha ('the affair').

Ironically, Ha-Parasha marginalized the only person who could not possibly have been involved, Moshe Sharett. The public sense was that the military–political system was in total disarray, and Ben-Gurion was entreated to return to politics. He did so in February 1955, first as minister of defence, and later again as prime minister. Within a few days of his return to the centre of political life, he succeeded at one stroke – a large-scale retaliation operation in Gaza – in destroying the delicate edifice of trust that Sharett and Nasser had begun building in a series of secret negotiations exploring the chances for peace between Israel and Egypt.[35] But Ha-Parasha was not over, and would bring Ben-Gurion down eight years later, in 1963. Until then, however, he was in control, with no one to oppose him in his next move, the Sinai campaign.

Ben-Gurion was looking for a war, as was his chief of staff, Moshe Dayan. They found one by aligning Israel to the Anglo-French plot to overthrow Nasser. The ex-colonial powers had their own agenda. The Egyptian president had become their *bête noire* the moment he nationalized the Suez Canal in January that year in response to the USA withdrawing its support for Egypt's Aswan Dam project, and then openly refused to join the Western bloc in the Cold War. The French had their own quarrel with Nasser because he supported the liberation movement fighting the French in Algeria. Thus, alongside his wish to enlarge the state of Israel, destroy hostile Arab leaders, and quash the emerging Palestinian resistance movement, Ben-Gurion found another incentive to join this colonialist scheme, this time offered by the French. They proposed to supply arms to the IDF and provide Israel with the initial materials necessary to achieve nuclear capability.[36]

It would be wrong to depict Nasser as totally innocent or passive in this war game. He had blockaded Israel by closing the Straits of Tiran, the only gateway to the southern Israeli port of Eilat, and confiscating goods destined for Israel in the Suez Canal. As he would again in 1967, he provided the Israelis with a welcome pretext for their expansionist and aggressive policy. Precisely when Nasser was deliberating how to respond to the Alpha Plan, an Anglo-American peace proposal put forward in February 1955, Ben-Gurion sent his army on a large-scale retaliation operation against Palestinians in the Gaza Strip, pushing Nasser into an overall confrontation with Israel.[37]

Israel's military victory was swift, but the political consequences were less impressive. Within a few days, the Israeli army had penetrated into the Gaza Strip and most of the Sinai Peninsula, while the Anglo-French air force protected them, bombarded Egypt, and sent paratroopers into the Canal Zone. But Israel could not keep its forces there for too long. A concentrated effort by both the USA and the USSR led to an Israeli withdrawal from the parts of the Sinai Peninsula it had succeeded in occupying, and freed Egypt from the presence of the British and French soldiers on its soil.

One obvious result of the 1956 war was that it deepened the involvement of the army in Israeli life to unprecedented levels. As I see it, the militarization of Israeli society that had begun with the victory of 1948 was completed by the 1956 Sinai victory (the forced withdrawal did not affect the gains of the 1948 war). On the Palestinian side, it opened the way for a revolution in strategy, tactics and structure in the political movement emerging in the refugee camps.

## REVOLUTIONIZING POLITICS: THE RESISTANCE MOVEMENT INSTITUTIONALIZED

The *fida'i* infrastructure suffered a major set-back when Israel occupied the Gaza Strip for a short while during the Suez war and arrested and expelled all those listed as *fida'iyyun* in the captured Egyptian files. This may explain the relative calm that descended for a while on the Palestinian political arena after the 1956 Suez war but was rekindled by the 'Arab Cold War', the fierce political struggle for hegemony that raged between 1958 and 1964. This took the form of a two-fold confrontation: on the one hand Nasser and his allies were pitted against traditional pro-Western Arab monarchies, and on the other Nasser confronted other radical leaders such as Abd al-Karim Qasim, who overthrew the Hashemite dynasty in Iraq in 1958. The ultimate manifestation of radicalism was a well-publicized commitment to liberate Palestine. In this, the Iraqis had the upper hand. By the end of 1959, Qasim was employing a pro-Palestinian rhetoric, declaring he wanted to create a Palestinian entity in the West Bank and the Gaza Strip with the help of a new Palestinian army.[38]

Nasser could not respond effectively, as his interests and troubles lay in Syria. In 1958, he united Syria and Egypt and formed the United Arab Republic (UAR). Military units, including those of the Palestinians, were now watched closely, not as means of fighting Israel, but as part of a network to sustain the fragile union. Within this new geo-political situation, the role of Fatah was formalized.

Fatah was not a significant political factor before 1958, when its founders decided to construct a national infrastructure that would be able not only to carry out an armed struggle but also to sustain independent Palestinian life and politics. The organization succeeded in widening its circle of supporters by publishing a journal, *Filastininuna* ('Our Palestine'), between 1959 and 1964, and in retaining its military capability by allying itself closely to Syria. The most striking phenomenon of Fatah in those early years was its young membership, made up of both students and workers, some of whom quickly made their way to the top. This made Fatah significantly different in composition and orientation from the traditional political parties of the Mandate period. No less unusual was the absence of an articulated ideology: Palestine had to be liberated, Israel destroyed, and there was no room for the Jews who had come after the First World War. Beyond that, however, this programme could not be easily located on the political spectrum between left and right, or included in any dictionary of post-colonial ideologies.

The UAR collapsed after three years, when a group of Syrian officers allied to the Ba'ath Party took over. Nasser was then able to focus more closely on the question of Palestine, even more so after his rival, Abd al-Karim Qasim, was overthrown in a coup in 1963. In the same year, Syria was once more briefly thrown into turmoil when another group of officers, again in the name of the Ba'ath but with closer ties to Egypt and to the Soviet Union, ousted their predecessors. Before long, the new rulers of Damascus and Baghdad on the one hand, and Nasser on the other were using the Palestinian armed struggle as a pawn in their own political games.

A clearer Palestinian ideology was to be found in the philosophy of another Palestinian organization, mentioned briefly above: the Arab nationalist al-Qawmiyyun al-Arab. This was a leftist refugee movement founded in 1951 at the American University of Beirut and led by a medical student, George Habash. It expanded into a significant force after 1956, when it declared open support for Nasser's policies during the UAR period and wisely retained cordial ties with the Syrian regime after the UAR had collapsed. The group's military capability was enhanced because they were ready to be coached by the Syrian military intelligence. However, by orientation and declared aim, the movement focussed less on liberating Palestine than on revolutionizing the Arab world at large. Only in the mid-1960s would the graduates of al-Qawmiyyun al-Arab become a proper guerrilla organization, under the name of the Popular Front for the Liberation of Palestine (PFLP), and direct their energy exclusively toward the armed struggle against Israel.[39]

However, the political histrionics described here meant very little on the ground. The Palestinians living within the borders of ex-Mandate Palestine in particular felt detached from pan-Arabism. Their lives were affected much more by their geo-political location than by ecstatic vows by Arab or Palestinian leaders to liberate their homeland.

If we look at the story of one Palestinian village, Barta', we find that, as a result of the Israeli–Jordanian armistice agreement of April 1949, it was divided into two, a not unusual outcome. Barta' west was annexed to Israel, while Barta' east was included in the Jordanian West Bank. Economically, the western part fared better, although its inhabitants were incorporated into an alien, at times hostile, political regime. They became non-citizens like the rest of the Palestinians in Israel, deprived of basic human and civil rights. Culturally, they were marooned within a state that portrayed them as primitive and backward. Barta' east was spared such social and cultural difficulties, but suffered from the loss of land, most of which had been confiscated by Israel.

The border, which between 1948 and 1967 ran through the centre of the village, was sealed, and no family meetings, let alone reunions, were possible. As a result, two Palestinian collective identities developed under two very different political systems. Much ingenuity and creativity was needed in the face of Hashemite pressure to assimilate on the eastern side, and of repressive Israeli military rule on the western side. When the two parts were united after the war in June 1967, the communities continued to operate as two distinct villages, and still do today. Not only were they now speaking different Palestinian dialects but, until at least the 1990s, they were also following different political orientations.

The absence of refugee camps within Israel contributed more than anything else to the distinct difference between the Palestinians living on either side of what was called the 'green line'. This was the border between Israel and the West Bank, and its green colour on official maps indicated its inconclusive nature in the eyes at least of the UN (on whose maps final borders appeared either in black or sometimes in purple). When refugees streamed into the West Bank and the Gaza Strip, their presence undermined the traditional structures of society there, threatening to revolutionize the Palestinian political milieu altogether.[40] As this revolutionary zeal was lacking in Israel, the politics of Palestinians there would remain far less radicalized than those of other segments of Palestinian society.

By the end of the 1950s, radicalization directly affected the nationalist notables, who made one last effort to seize the reins of power and, with the help of radical Arab regimes, tried to resurrect Palestinian nationalism through the creation of a new body, the PLO. The idea was laudable, but its execution faulty. At first it appeared to be nothing more than another political act divorced from the interests and agenda of most Palestinians.

## THE BOGUS PLO (1964–1968)

In their last political stand, and still headed by Amin al-Husayni, the remaining nationalist notables utilized the Arab cold war to carve a niche for Palestinian activity within the Arab League in Cairo. Characteristically, this was done to secure individual positions for themselves as much as from a genuine wish to struggle for Palestine. The Arab League was no longer a bastion of traditional Arab politics. Radical regimes now determined the tone and agenda of this regional association, and it was much easier to persuade its leaders to embrace a Palestinian organization. Nevertheless, the League's patrons felt much more comfortable with the old nationalist notables. As Amin al-Husayni was too controversial to be selected as the head of the new all-Palestine organization, they opted for Ahmad al-Shuqairi, a subaltern member of the Arab Higher Committee, who after 1948 had begun a career within the Saudi Foreign Ministry.

Although the radical Arab regimes and the traditional monarchy of Saudi Arabia had very little in common, they shared one political ambition: to embarrass the Hashemite regime in Jordan. Even after the ousting of Glubb Pasha, they regarded Jordan as a British outpost in the area. John Bagot Glubb was the commander in chief of the Arab Legion from 1938 and led the army in the 1948 war. He was blamed after the war for the loss of Lydda and Ramleh, an accusation ignored by the young King Hussein, until he himself felt threatened by Glubb and decided to expel him to Britain. There was no better issue than the Palestinian question with which to test Jordan's pan-Arab patriotism. Hence, the architects of the new structure, the PLO, chose Jerusalem as the venue for its inauguration. The ceremony took place in the Intercontinental Hotel in January 1964. The gloomy expression on the face of young King Hussein in photographs of the occasion shows how unpalatable the new organization was to him.

At first, Ahmad al-Shuqairi seemed dynamic. He had been refused entry in November 1963 to the UN annual conference on the Palestinian refugees, and was now directing all his attention to the Arab world. Immediately after the Jerusalem ceremony, he established PLO representative bodies throughout the Arab world, in order to impress on these communities that the refugees had another representative apart from UNRWA. The PLO also had an organized army affiliated with it, the Palestinian Liberation Army (PLA). Crucially, however, neither the branches of the PLO nor the PLA units succeeded in winning the trust of the refugees. They became clubs and career posts for the urban middle class. While the PLO's reliance on Nasser impressed no one, it should be said that by now Nasser had become more genuinely interested in the cause of Palestine and worked hard and intensively to unite the Arab world and prepare it for a future confrontation with Israel. However, like his predecessors in 1948, he did not include the Palestinians in the well-publicized, frenetic path towards the next battle with the Jewish state. It was the continuing exclusion of Palestinians from real power and decision-making that left many doubtful of the sincerity of Nasser's plans and ambitions.

The demise of the short-lived League-sponsored PLO was at the hands of the *fida'i* movements, none of whom joined it. Instead, they created an informal association of their own, known as al-Muqawwama ('resistance'), a fraternity of fighters modelled on the Viet Cong (one of its most often used metaphors was that of 'Arab Hanoi'), and the FLN (Front de Libération Nationale) of Algeria. It was hoped to make the Arab countries adjacent to Israel a launching pad for guerrilla attacks on behalf of the liberation of Palestine. In addition to metaphors, they also acquired weapons and skills from revolutionary movements in the Third World. Fatah remained central, but by the mid-1960s George Habash had formed his own guerrilla movement (PFLP).[41]

Guerrilla activity intensified after a long lull for organization and re-cruitment, and with it Israeli retaliation. In 1966, the Israelis carried out a large-scale operation against the village of Samua' in the West Bank, further damaging relations with Jordan. The growing tension along this border was one of the factors pushing a reluctant King Hussein into a military alliance with Syria and Egypt, an alliance that, among other signs of hos-tility, was regarded as a *casus belli* by the more militant section of the Israeli government.

It was Syria, not Jordan or Egypt, that bore the brunt of the struggle against Israel. Since the early 1960s, a war of attrition had been going on along the Israeli–Syrian border, triggered by Israel's construction of a na-tional aquifer to transfer water from the north to the south of the country. Both sides lost many soldiers in this bloody dispute. The skirmishes es-calated into a small-scale war in 1962, after which the exchanges of fire across the border threatened to spill over into a full confrontation. Condi-tions were ripe for the growth of Palestinian *fida'iyyun* groups and for the spreading of (obviously false) claims that Palestine's liberation was near at hand.

Al-Muqawwama's inability to achieve much towards liberating Palestine was partly due to its failure to remain united. It was plagued by internal dissension from its inception. The PFLP had clear revolutionary goals, such as helping to transform traditional Arab regimes and establishing a Marxist state in liberated Palestine, while Fatah, as mentioned before, was vague about the nature of the future state. But the resistance movement was united in waiting for a convenient moment to take over the PLO, and the moment came after the 1967 war.

### SUBDUING ISRAELI POLITICS: INSTITUTIONALIZING A STATE

While the radicalism of Palestinian politics would be institutionalized after 1956 in the form of guerrilla movements and clandestine organizations in the West Bank and Gaza as well as within party politics in Israel, Jewish society in Israel was going through very different changes. It had been politically and economically centralized as part of a conscious effort from above to homogenize a multi-ethnic society. The fusion process was a showcase for experts on crude modernization. The Jewish community consisted of a modern Western society, the veteran Zionists from Europe, and many non-Western (Eastern or Oriental) groups that were waiting to be modernized. These were Palestinians, Jews from Arab countries, and ultra-orthodox Jews. Israeli scholars in the new sociology department at the Hebrew University were able to teach theories of modernization and at the same time advise the government on how to implement them.

The method had a 'catchy' name – 'melting-pot process'. The model community consisted of the veteran European Jews, who had already become modern Israelis under the influence of the Hebrew revival, the militarism of Israeli society, and the settlement ethos, all coloured by Marxist, socialist and nationalist narratives. Hebrew courses for new immigrants were the most important means of indoctrination. In November 1948, an academy for the Hebrew language was founded in Jerusalem, and policed the different potential dialects, keeping them within the fold of Zionist idioms and ideals. No less relentless was the fight against the use by Arab Jews of Arabic. When, as a way of earning a living, an Egyptian Jew, Abraham Israel, wanted to show an Egyptian film he had brought with him, the Israeli censor allowed him to only at the cinema in the then still purely Palestinian town of Nazareth.[42] Thus the claim of homogeneity was made against a background of actual heterogeneity and discrimination, a tension that would surface only at the end of the 1980s.

The revival of Hebrew also brought one of the most impressive achieve-ments of Zionism: with the renewal of language came the invention of a new Israeli-Hebraic culture. The old biblical language proved to be modern, adaptable and inspiring. After a shaky beginning, which produced language not unlike what modern English prose would look if it were interspersed with Shakespearean phrases, Israeli writers, novelists and journalists began to excel in articulating daily worries and hopes in a liberated and easy-flowing new language. Very soon it also had its own slang, another sign of its vitality.

With this new linguistic freedom of expression came an urge for freedom of expression in political terms. The 1950s were a decade in which satirical writing flourished, although the political establishment kept a close watch on this emerging cultural phenomenon. This era also produced thriving political cabarets, which Ben-Gurion did not hesitate to censor if they contained material embarrassing to the government.

In contrast to these linguistic successes, attempts to re-invent Judaism along secular lines proved more difficult. The early representatives of this new Hebrew culture openly expressed their distaste for religion and pinned their hopes on secularism. However, the politics of the early state pushed the secular element in Zionism into compromises with religious circles. In 1953, after realizing the importance of religious parties for sustaining stable coalitions, Ben-Gurion authorized his government to initiate all-encompassing religious laws which applied to every Jew in Israel whether secular or religious. In August that year, the rabbinical courts were given absolute authority over matters of marriage and divorce. The move would prove crucial. Until then it had been difficult to identify Judaism with nationalism, but the new arrangement was a first step on the way to blurring the distinction between religion and nation. In June 1956, a new party was formed, the national religious party, Mafdal. It possessed an impressive educational network, and was dedicated to safeguarding the religious nature of Jewish nationalism in Israel. It was also fertile ground for the development of Gush Emunim, the Jewish settlers' movement in the West Bank after 1967.

There had been regular clashes between secular and ultra-orthodox Jews in the streets of Jerusalem, often with injuries on both sides. In September 1956, an ultra-orthodox boy was killed in one of these riots. The cultural divide was openly exposed when another young boy, Yossef Schumacher, was kidnapped from his secular mother by his ultra-orthodox grandfa-ther. It took the Israeli secret service two-and-a-half years to locate the boy in America and repatriate him, closing a case that had agonised the

Jewish community in Israel. The appearance of Mafdal on the cultural political scene further highlighted the isolationist nature of non-Zionist ultra-orthodox Judaism in Israel, which from now on became ever more secluded and confined within its own self-imposed ghettoes.

The national memory of contemporary Israel is fragmented by the tension outlined above between 'reality as lived' and 'reality as recollected'. For those who make up the country's social and cultural elite, mainly Ashkenazi Jews, the 1950s have remained the 'golden days' of *Israel haktanah* ('little Israel'), fondly recollected as the halcyon times before Israel became racked by the rebellions of deprived groups of Palestinian and Mizrahi citizens, and when a sense of solidarity prevailed, and a well-defined canon of books, poetry, plays, popular songs and, above all, national ceremonies commemorating heroic chapters in Zionist history determined the country's culture.

The imagined 'little Israel' was not without problems, however. These were also the uneasy days of the official *Zena* ('scarcity' in Hebrew, also translated as 'modesty'), an economic regime declared, in April 1949, by Dov Yoseff, a minister specially appointed to monitor the population's consumption habits. People were given coupons with which to buy food and clothing, all subject to quotas. The economic crisis and the accompanying shortages in employment and housing occasionally produced violent clashes between Mizrahi Jews and the police. These seldom led to social revolution, apart from isolated cases such as the Wadi Salib uprising of 1959. Wadi Salib was a previously Palestinian neighbourhood of old Muslim Haifa that had been ethnically cleansed in 1948 and repopulated by unskilled Jewish workers, mostly from Morocco. Violence erupted when a minor incident between a policeman and a worker exposed the gap between rich and poor. A surprised Labour government sent in the police in an effort to quell the outburst of frustration by the Jewish workers, the ones in whose name it claimed to govern. The unrest then spread to other places where unemployment prompted more Jews from Arab countries to demonstrate, only to be brutally dispersed by the police too.[43]

Those were indeed difficult times and affluence was enjoyed by only a few. But for many today the 1950s stand out in the national memory as the belle époque. One reason for this is that the dire years were soon over (by 1954 to be exact), and were replaced by an economic resurgence for many Jews, though not for those living in Wadi Salib. In a curious way, the regime of austerity temporarily benefited the Jews who came from Arab countries by creating shared want in all sections of society and thus a sense of solidarity that had not been there before. When this dissolved due to an unholy alliance between veteran Ashkenazi consumers and traders, its main victims were the Mizrahi Jews. They became a permanent cheap workforce, easily isolated and used to displace the Palestinian labour force. Competition for unskilled jobs between Arab Jews and Palestinians was exploited cynically for political purposes on Israel's borders. The Palestinians had been expelled from their villages near the borders, and Arab Jews were being settled on their land; now the latter also began taking jobs previously done by those Palestinians. To this should be added the cycle of Palestinian infiltration and Israeli retaliation, all occurring on the borders and further heightening the tension and animosity between these two victim groups of the veteran Ashkenazi Jewish community and Zionism.[44]

Economic growth from that year onward was facilitated by three main factors: mass immigration, intensive activity within the military industry, and territorial expansion. For more than a decade these elements propelled Israel towards prosperity and stability. Around 1964, however, a recession set in, brought about by a decrease in immigration and a decline in military industrial production. Recessions, however, are rarely the product of hidden 'market forces' alone. In 1960s Israel, there was an orchestrated policy of opposing militant groups of workers who had begun realizing that their main trade union, the Histadrut, was letting them down. Already a mammoth enterprise, the Histadrut failed to mobilize most of Israel's workers. In addition, it had its own factories and business complexes, and was Israel's main employer. Militant workers became angry when they discovered that the Histadrut was actively working against over-employment by maintaining a level of unemployment. Because of the recession, however, jobs were limited, which prevented workers from acting independently.[45] By February 1966, the recession had deepened, and the government began paying unprecedented sums in unemployment benefits. Riots broke out in slums such as the Tikva neighbourhood of southern Tel-Aviv, inhabited by mostly Moroccan Jews, whereby the police killed two demonstrators. Economic crises, moreover, are useful in the hands of ruthless politicians.

The recession produced a public mood that enabled the Israeli government to be more aggressive and adventurous in its reaction to Nasser's brinkmanship in the spring of 1967. Political adventurism needed a powerful military machine, and this was achieved through a special relationship with France (a second-best option for Ben-Gurion, as he would have preferred the Americans). A sophisticated air force and the beginnings of nuclear capability were conveniently developed with the help of German reparations which had begun flowing into Israel from 1952 onwards.

In 1958, Ben-Gurion requested and received permission to assist American and British efforts to curb Nasser's influence in the Arab world. British marines flew over Israel on their way to Jordan to help King Hussein ward off a possible pro-Nasserite coup. A civil war had been instigated in Lebanon by the Maronite President Camile Chamoun, who sought a second term in office in violation of the Lebanese constitution. His plans were abetted by the CIA. The Western powers, however, attributed the war to pro-Nasserite Muslims. Western interests in general were seen to be at risk in the area. Hashemite Jordan looked frail as well.[46] Ben-Gurion informed the Americans that should the Hashemite regime collapse his army would occupy the West Bank. However, all ended well for the Hashemites in Jordan. Two years later, Ben-Gurion reaped the benefits when he was able to establish a better relationship with the American administration, empowering Israel even more.

Ben-Gurion admired the USA, and did all he could to ally the Jewish state to the superpower. He also showed extra zeal in combating communism in Israel, and from the beginning tried to gear Israeli culture towards a pro-American orientation. In 1949, the Israeli censor had forbidden the staging of Konstantine Simonov's play *Mr Smith Goes to America* because of its anti-American propaganda.[47] In the heyday of McCarthyism this was a welcome show of solidarity.

Ben-Gurion's pro-American orientation in politics or culture met no serious opposition in Israel. On the other hand, the financial connection with Germany shook the political establishment and beyond. Seven years after the end of the Second World War, Ben-Gurion had advocated recognition of the 'new Germany' in return for huge reparation payments. This policy was not consensual, and aroused robust, and at times violent, objections by Holocaust survivors, whose cause was adopted by Menachem Begin, the leader of the opposition's largest party, Herut (formerly the Irgun).[48]

The complex relationship with the Holocaust, and indirectly with Germany, was dealt with on two levels: in the commercial sector, where ties with the 'new Germany' were formalized and cemented without much ado, and in the psychological sphere, through two public and highly emotional trials. The first was the Kastner trial. Israel Kastner was a Zionist activist who in the Second World War had run the Zionist operation to rescue the Jews of Hungary from extermination. He conducted negotiations with Adolf Eichmann, the senior Nazi official responsible for extermination in Europe, and offered 10,000 trucks in return for 1 million Jews. A mishandling of the negotiations brought about their failure, but Kastner continued to save Jews wherever he could. He acted on direct orders from the Zionist leadership in Palestine.

After immigrating to Palestine he entered the leading party, Mapai, and upon the creation of the state became a senior official in the Israeli Ministry of Trade and Industry. Some survivors, however, regarded him as a Nazi collaborator. When one of them, Malciel Greenwald, put these accusations in writing in 1952, Kastner sued him for libel. This was against the background of a general hysteria in Israel, where a witch-hunt was underway for suspected Nazi collaborators. Among the immigrants were indeed several hundred *kapos*, Jews who had been appointed as guards in the concentration camps by the Nazis, and who often abused and tormented their fellow Jews to save their own lives. Some of these were brought to trial by people who themselves had played an ambivalent role in the concentration camps. (The Holocaust is referred to in Israel as the 'other planet', where incomprehensible acts were committed by human beings against other human beings. Any attempt to judge others morally and logically with hindsight seems futile, even inhuman, in that context.)[49]

Kastner's libel case began. A shrewd lawyer for the defence, Shmuel Tamir, twisted the evidence and exploited the public mood to turn Kastner from a plaintiff into a defendant. The judge, Benjamin Halevy, was strongly affiliated to Herut, the opposition party leading the campaign against normalizing Israel's relationship with Germany. The trial provided him with an opportunity to show the world at large that normalization was not yet possible. More importantly, he hoped to include the Labour leadership in implicit accusations of collaborating with the Nazis. Kastner could have been vindicated had the leaders of the former Yishuv, on whose behalf he had negotiated with the Nazis, testified in his favour. But they repudiated their association with him, and in the verdict Kastner was accused of collaboration with the Nazis for personal gain and prestige. The prime minister at the time, Moshe Sharett, who too should have testified on Kastner's behalf, concluded in his diary: 'A nightmare, horror.'[50] The daily *Haaretz* criticized the verdict sharply, but it was Menachem Begin, the leader of Herut, who made the most out of the affair, as this was the eve of general elections in Israel. He found strange allies in the communist members of the Knesset, who with Herut demanded that Kastner be tried according to the Israeli law of 1949 for the prosecution and trial of Nazis and their associates. Mapai did not lose the 1955 elections, but Kastner was nevertheless left isolated. This episode, together with Ha-Parasha, ended Ben-Gurion's short political exile, and he was reinstated as Israel's prime minister. The law against the Nazis was never used against Kastner, since the trial had little to do with the Holocaust, but more to do with the 1950s political agenda. The Israeli government used the law to kidnap Eichmann in 1962 and bring him to trial in Israel. Angry Holocaust survivors later assassinated Kastner.

Ben-Gurion wanted a well-publicized trial to teach Israeli youth the difference between Jewish communities that had gone 'like lambs to the slaughter' and the Jewish state, which was now taking revenge in the name of the slaughtered.[51] Ben-Gurion was also still living with the aftermath of the Wadi Salib riots. He claimed that the Moroccan Jews knew very little about the Holocaust, and that if taught about it would more easily tolerate their hardships. When Martin Buber and others suggested an international court for Eichmann, Ben-Gurion became furious, accusing them of undermining Israel's sovereignty. The trial, which resulted in Eichmann's execution, became a model for the future manipulation of Holocaust commemoration in Israel. Images of the Holocaust would thereafter be exploited to justify Israeli discrimination against Palestinians or the second-class North African Jews. Until today, whenever the state is criticized on moral grounds, including internationally, Israel is quick to silence such criticism by presenting itself as the sole legitimate community of Holocaust survivors.[52]

## THE MARGINALIZATION OF 'ARABISM' IN ISRAELI SOCIETY

In the makeshift hut camps for newly arrived immigrants, in the slums of the big towns, and in the newly isolated settlements near the borders, Mizrahi (Arab) Jews did not have time or leisure to deal with past horrors, being preoccupied with their current hardships. The past was even less relevant to the Palestinian citizens confined within the military-ruled areas in Galilee and Wadi Ara'. These Arabs, Jews, Muslims and Christians made up almost half of the overall population of Israel.

The new alliance with Germany, however, spawned new financial realities, increasing the sense of deprivation and dismay. German reparations, while justifiably allowing many European Jews in Israel to prosper, widened the gap between Ashkenazi and Mizrahi Jews even further. The sense of inferiority attached to anyone Arab, whether Jewish or Palestinian, was reinforced by the state's cultural policy. A monolithic culture of memory developed that repressed the experiences of marginalized groups within society. The economic policy, their exclusion from the cultural canon and their entrenchment on the social and geographical margins of society alienated the Mizrahi Jews, particularly from Morocco, as well as the Israeli Palestinians. Unlike the Palestinian citizens, the Jews from Arab countries had at least the hope of better things to come, of being coached into becoming 'new Jews'.

The Israeli army spearheaded the effort to Westernize the Arab Jews. However, the general socio-economic divisions also applied inside the army, and Mizrahi Jews, often reluctant conscripts, were given logistical posts, a lasting stain on their prestige and later civilian careers in a society that revered commando fighters and air force pilots. Thus the army promoted militarization instead of acting as an agent of modernization or socialization, and became a significant factor in shaping Israel's foreign relations within the Middle East. To a large extent it determined the nature of relationships that developed with the few allies Israel could buy, such as Iran and Turkey, who were impressed by its commando units, secret service and developing military industry. Militarist nationalism was thus in constant need of achievement but also required, and was given, enthusiastic feedback from many young Israelis, whose indoctrination was underway from infancy. The hostility of the Arab world around them, revealed everywhere on public stages, radio stations and in the press, was invoked to reinforce the belief that their cause was a just one and to deepen the conviction that no other options were available.

Their common social and economic marginalization did not produce any camaraderie between Moroccan Jews and Palestinians, no doubt due to their differing national aspirations. Arab Jews hoped that emphasizing their Jewish origins would help them to be accepted as 'authentic' Zionists, a hope as yet unfulfilled. These Jews wished to be de-Arabized in order to be Israelized; when these hopes failed, they began searching for their Arab roots. This complex relationship between Jews who are ethnically Arabs and the other Jewish groups goes back to the pre-state era. It is best understood if we remember that Jews in the Arab countries were not initially attracted to Zionism in great numbers. Nor were the leaders of the Jewish community in Palestine interested in winning them over. A few individuals, mainly from Iraq and Syria, were caught by the Zionist spell and made their way to Palestine. Their knowledge of Arabic and of the Arab world made them ideal candidates for the Yishuv's intelligence service. They were rewarded later by being among the very few Mizrahi Jews to reach high positions in the intelligence community and the foreign ministry.

Two processes, converging in 1948, generated the mass Jewish immigration from the Arab world. One was the growing identification in the minds of Arab governments and rulers, as well as of the general public, of Jewish life in the Arab world with Zionism and the Palestine conflict. The other was the Zionist drive to import the Arab Jews to Israel. In other words, in the aftermath of the 1948 war, both Israel and the Arab regimes identified the Arab Jews as potential Zionists. They found themselves between a rock and a hard place: they could either bow to the Arab regimes' demands to show particular zeal in fighting Zionism, or accept the Zionist offer to immigrate at the price of losing everything they had owned in the Arab countries. The Zionist leaders saw the demographic potential of the million or so Jews living in the Arab world for consolidating the Jewish state. Significantly, this demographic consideration had played no role in Zionist thought before the Holocaust, when the envisaged Jewish state had been depicted as a European entity. After the loss of six million Jews, the Zionist project needed numbers to survive, even if they came from 'underdeveloped and primitive' areas of the world. A campaign was begun to convince Jews to come to Israel.[53]

The Arab Jewish communities differed from one another in several respects. The Iraqi community was an ancient one and was concentrated in Baghdad, where it was well established and felt no urge to leave. With the 1948 war, it was encouraged to leave by Prime Minister Nuri al-Said of Iraq, who promised that this would be part of an exchange programme in which Iraq would take in Palestinian refugees. When this did not materialize, the Iraqi government passed legislation that made affiliation with Zionism a felony. In 1951, it ordered the expulsion of Jews who refused to sign a statement of anti-Zionism. Almost all the Iraqi Jews were forced to leave without their property, which the Iraqi government appropriated. The Jewish Agency, for its part, sought ways to contribute to the instability of the Jewish community, and sent agents who planted bombs near synagogues in Baghdad, in order to create additional terror and insecurity. This did much to bring this ancient community of Babylon back to Zion.[54]

The Jewish community in Egypt had fared quite well since the reign of Muhammad Ali at the beginning of the nineteenth century. Like the Copts, the Jews provided services to the court and the country as a whole. This changed around 1948, particularly as the Egyptian king, Farouq, wished to play a leading role in the Palestine question, as did the Muslim Brotherhood. When hostilities erupted in Palestine at the end of 1947, the Jews in Egypt were in a similar situation to that of their co-religionists in Iraq, with the Egyptian government demanding similar guarantees of anti-Zionism and issuing similar penalties. The Egyptian treatment did not amount to expulsion, but life was transformed, and eventually most of Egypt's Jews would leave the country, either for Israel or other destinations.[55]

The largest group of Arab Jewish immigrants came from Morocco. They lived in poorer conditions than any of the other communities in the Arab world, but had their own economic and social elite. This community had been endangered by the Nazi invasion of North Africa in the Second World War, but was safeguarded by Morocco's king Muhammad V, who even managed to protect them from the Vichy government, a fortuitous policy followed loyally by his heir and successor, King Hassan II. The Zionists therefore had to work hard to persuade Moroccan Jews to leave such a safe haven for the insecurity of Palestine. It was in fact only the struggle for liberation from France that motivated the largely Francophile elite to move to Europe and Canada, abandoning the less well-to-do sections of the community to their lot. Those left behind were more easily tempted by Zionist agents to leave now independent Morocco for a new future in the land of Israel, of which until then they had thought of only in religious terms.

When Arab Jewish immigrants arrived in Israel, they were greeted in a manner devised to show them that they had left a primitive traditional existence for the sake of a modern one, and ought to be grateful. 'Modern' was a distorted description of the economic reality of Israel in the early 1950s. In fact, in order to modernize the economy, Israel needed the labour of Jews from the Arab countries, especially as the government was expanding its hold over as much land as possible and maximizing its colonization effort. Land and modern industry were deemed the dual factors that would allow the local economy to take off, and for that the government needed a massive workforce. The Mizrahi Jews served that purpose.[56]

Even after many years, most Mizrahi Jews have not escaped the lower occupational stratum their new state assigned to them. This failure and the frustration it engendered would cost the Labour Party, in control between 1948 and 1977, its political hold over the country. Later, a form of neo-Zionist fundamentalism emerged among Mizrahi Jews that aimed at turning Israel into a theocracy.

It was difficult for the Mizrahi Jews to resist their relocation as a cheap labour force. They lacked financial means, which made them hostages to the power of the state absorption apparatus, which was run by Eastern European Jews harbouring racist and condescending views about Arabs in general, and Arab Jews in particular. They were dependent on those officials for education, housing, employment and every other aspect of their welfare and well-being.

Nor were they the only ones subjected to such treatment. Survivors of the Holocaust who arrived in Israel after 1948 were similarly received by absorption officials. Holocaust survivors were particularly loathed by native Israelis, who regarded them and their whole experience as the antithesis of Zionism and its heroic struggle in Palestine. Like the Arab Jews, these European Jews were callously put in camps that must have reminded many of them of concentration camps, even though physically there was no resemblance whatsoever. They were also put through a humiliating process of decontamination and medical treatment, which included mass spraying with detergents such as DDT. Their lives improved once in Israel, due to the compensation they received from the Germans. Iraqi Jews fared better than other Arab Jews owing to their economic skills, and refused to be moved around and coerced into settling where it did not suit them or working in jobs that did not fit their qualifications.

North African Jews were mainly unskilled workers who were pushed into the development towns the government had erected on the borders with the hostile Arab countries. The intention was to expand the Jewish community, which tended to prefer the urban centres on the coast, and provide a human buffer against the infiltration of Palestinian refugees after the 1948 war. Some of the North African Jews were asked to repopulate the deserted and abandoned Arab neighbourhoods in what had been the mixed towns of Palestine, thus making a mockery of the Israeli commitment to look after this property through the office of the state's custodian of absentee property. The choicest part of the absentee spoils had already been taken by public bodies and then by the kibbutz movements, and what was left was turned into crowded slums for North African Jews.

The Arab Jews were the main recipients of the poor-quality public housing in Israel. Furthermore, it was not even free; tenants had to pay for it with loans, mortgages and guarantees. Some of the buildings had impossibly small apartments and were at first designated as temporary (as were the caravans for the Ethiopian Jews who were brought to Israel in the 1980s, and are still living there under the most unpleasant conditions). These flats were an unwelcome change from the open courtyards they had known in the Arab world and which had provided a valued private outside space. Now large families were crammed into claustrophobic cubes, which aggravated an already tense atmosphere that had its origin in the general breakdown of the traditional family structure and hierarchy. The older generation could not communicate with the surrounding society, while the young had neither the means nor the education to do so adequately. This also explains the high proportion of North African Jews that drifted into petty crime in Israel.

The situation of the North African Jews deteriorated, especially during the first decade, due to the high rate of unemployment. As the Histadrut was not immune from Ashkenazi racist attitudes, Arab Jews did not receive the same service and benefits as other unemployed, nor did they enjoy the union's help in their demand for equal pay for equal work. For the Histadrut, as for the clerks in the absorption apparatus, the Arab Jews remained part of a primitive culture, who stood very little chance of ever achieving the desired degree of progress towards modernity.

The education system also expected the young generation to ignore everything even indirectly connected to their past and origins. Ellah Habib Shohat, now a renowned scholar in the United States, tells how, as a young immigrant from Iraq to central Israel, she would stand in front of the mirror practising speaking Hebrew in an accent that would not betray her Arab origins. The speaking of Arabic was forbidden, as were its customs and costumes. Instead, immigrants were offered a second-rate education, full of Zionist indoctrination but inadequate in preparing them for social mobility and progress.

The Mizrahi Jews were also needed in order to expand agricultural production. They were not invited to join the Ashkenazi kibbutzim, except for young children, called *yaldei huz* ('external children'), who were admitted without their parents. These children gained the privilege of an exceptional mobility and integration uncommon among Mizrahi, and especially Moroccan, Jews. In general, Mizrahi Jews were thrust into collective cultivation of the land in areas not desired by the kibbutz movement, where they worked in citrus groves and on other agricultural projects.[57]

A few individuals in the construction industry succeeded in escaping destitution by becoming managers or owners of building companies, but most remained in their dismal situation. The vicious circle was maintained by a wide social welfare system, as social workers perpetuated the inequalities with false theories of modernization. This served the capitalist interests of the Ashkenazis. The large profits resulting from the low wages paid to North African Jews were an incentive, to put it mildly, to ignore the situation. Managerial positions were in effect closed to Mizrahi Jews in the early 1970s, when there was only one in management in the public construction business (out of thirty-three companies).[58]

The doors of higher officialdom were as firmly closed as those of management, proving that it was not, as the leading Israeli mainstream sociologists would have it, an ontological problem of primitivism, but the result of a policy of discrimination. In those days, the Yemeni Jews suffered more than the others in terms of negative perceptions. Amos Elon, the leading columnist in *Haaretz*, wrote of them: 'They are the troublemakers among the immigrants.' He wished to shatter the myth of their industrious approach to work.[59] He was equally hostile to other immigrants from Arab countries. Two years later, in April 1953, Elon questioned the wisdom of bringing the Jews of Tunisia to Israel.[60]

The affected communities tried to organize an all-Arab Jewish party, but this soon broke down along more distinct ethnic lines, the Yemeni Jews for instance establishing their own parties in the Knesset.[61] It was the Herut opposition party of Menachem Begin, from Poland, that finally provided a political channel for their social and economic frustration.

The same patterns of discrimination remained in operation against the Palestinian minority in Israel after 1956. The co-optation policy, the military regime, and the basic predicament of being a Palestinian citizen within the Jewish state generated several political responses, all of which pointed to a strong wish to remain part of the Palestinian people while at the same time becoming citizens of Israel with equal rights. Some believed that communism would lead to a social revolution, rendering nationalism secondary and bringing equality to all. Others joined the Communist Party for less altruistic reasons. They used the internationalist discourse to disguise their more authentic national aspirations, the expression of which would have indubitably led them into trouble with the Israeli authorities. Affiliation to communism ensured career support via the party or, even better, a ticket to higher education in the Eastern bloc, which could open the door to professions such as law and medicine, which the Palestinians in Israel were practically, though always unofficially, barred from pursuing.[62] Others tied their political future to Zionist parties, creating their own satellite parties or joining as members. This may have furthered their own interests, but did very little, compared with the communists, to improve the collective lot. Thus, by 1967, the Communist Party had become the most significant political force within the Palestinian minority.

Very few opted for a direct confrontation with the Israelis by openly declaring allegiance to Palestinian nationalism as represented by the *fida'i* movement. After 1959, the popularity of al-Muqawwama soared among Palestinians in Israel. The radical leaders of the Israeli Communist Party, such as Tawfiq Zayad and Emil Habibi, were periodically jailed, interrogated or tortured for their support for the right of return of the refugees or for their open call to abolish the military regime. This kind of activity peaked in 1961 after the government expropriated more than 5,000 dunams from several Arab villages for the construction of Carmiel, a new Jewish town in Galilee.

From this milieu sprang the al-Ard ('the land') group, in 1959. Its members echoed Nasser's anti-Western rhetoric, and vowed to join him in a struggle against 'reactionary regimes'. In a way they strove to open a diplomatic outlet for these ideas in what for them was occupied Palestine, although admittedly they supported the UN partition Resolution 181 of November 1947 as a basis for a new geo-political solution. They were banned from activity, while some were arrested, and others exiled.[63]

Political Islam was still in its infancy in pre-1967. The reasons for its emergence mirror the emergence of political Islam in general: a combination of socio-economic hardship, lack of state welfare policies and the weakening of secular alternatives for action. Each Islamist movement in the Middle East was unique, with a particular agenda, whether national or social, that overshadowed the religious one. In the case of Israel and Palestine, the national agenda was at least as powerful as, if not more so than, the religious one, particularly in the 1980s.

Curiously, the rise of Islamism was triggered mainly by the visit of Pope Pius VI to Israel and Palestine in 1964. Young Christians enthusiastically embarked on preparations for the visit, and opened clubs and activity centres, especially in Galilee. Their ardour was catching, and young Muslims responded with similar zeal, becoming involved in community work. Their main achievement was in occupying the days of the unemployed and underemployed in Palestinian Galilee and Little Triangle. The growing of beards, the wearing of traditional garments, and a more eager participation and interest in Islamic politics in the Arab world (voicing discontent with the way Nasser treated the Muslim Brotherhood in Egypt, for instance) were all part of this new phenomenon. An unofficial successor to the Grand Mufti, Shaykh Ahmad Abdallah, was the prime mover behind the scenes. He also collected funds for building more mosques.

IN LIMBO: THE BEDOUIN AND THE DRUZES

Between the Oriental Jews and the Palestinians stood two groups that scholars would in due course include in the Palestinian community, but that were then, and perhaps still are, regarded as distinct ethnic minorities. These were the Bedouin and the Druzes. In the period discussed here, they defined themselves and were officially defined as distinct groups.

For them, politicization meant navigating safely between the temptations of co-optation and the perils of resistance. The Bedouin life and culture changed little between 1831 and 1948. In the previous century their numbers had increased once they were allowed by the Egyptian rulers (1831–40) to frequent Palestine from bases in the Sinai Peninsula, and they continued to make their presence felt, particularly after the Ottoman restoration. They maintained their nomadic way of life in the eastern and northern parts of the country during the late Ottoman period, but after 1900 it was primarily in the south, al-Naqab, or the Negev, that the main concentration of nomadic and semi-nomadic Bedouin persisted.

At the turn of the twentieth century, eighty tribes were registered in seven different locations, marked as bases. This elementary structure remained intact until 1948. In 1947, there were 80,000 Bedouin in the south of Palestine, but the Israeli expulsion policy did not spare them, and when the winds of war subsided, only 13,000 were left. They regrouped into twenty tribes in three locations, spread throughout the Negev. They were promised a better status than other Arabs, once the tribal heads agreed to send the young men to the Israeli army. However, this promise has remained unfulfilled for most. (Some were resettled in the 1960s in the north of Israel with a better standard of living than those in the south, but not better than the average Palestinian citizen).

Because of the Bedouin, the Negev was the only geographical area in Israel relatively untouched by modernization fervour. Camels and herds of sheep and goats were still an important part of Bedouin life. However, agriculture and semi-proletarianization, similar to what affected the rest of the Palestinian community in Israel, were beginning to influence Bedouin life at the end of the 1950s, leading to the abandonment of nomadic life. The second half of the decade was particularly dry, and five successive years of drought drove many of the Bedouins north, where the government eventually allowed them to settle in a few villages. Those in the south forsook pastoral life for unskilled work in agriculture, construction and maintenance.

The Druzes represent a more successful example of co-optation. They are a religious sect, an offshoot of Shiite Islam. In Israel, this is considered to be a separate religion, and its communal conduct differs somewhat from similar communities in other Middle Eastern countries (there are Druzes in Lebanon, Syria and Jordan, apart from Israel). During the 1948 war, the elders of the community, sensing the way the balance of power was moving, signed a pact of allegiance with the Jewish state. This should have made them first-class citizens as far as full rights and state privileges were concerned. However, they were confined to special units in the army and were not socio-economically equal to most Jewish citizens. Nevertheless, most of their leaders wished to continue co-optation and cooperation with Israel.[64] Like many other, indeed almost all, of the groups living between the River Jordan and the Mediterranean, they would rethink the past only after the 1967 watershed.

# CHAPTER 6

# Greater Israel and Occupied Palestine: The Rise and Fall of High Politics (1967–1987)

Between the 1948 and 1967 wars, politics savagely invaded the lives of every-one living between the River Jordan in the east and the Mediterranean in the west. Elite politics, more militarized and nationalized than ever before, now demanded the full attention, daily participation and unconditional loyalty of Palestinians and Jews alike. There were very few islands of peace where people felt immune from the intrusion. Political elites on both sides had a hold over their societies that they had never had before and would not have again for a long time. Dissenting voices were stifled, and any remain-ing impulses towards cohabitation disappeared almost entirely. But we also find elite politics beginning to lose its importance in people's lives. This was particularly true after the 1973 war. For many groups not occupying centre stage, politics was only one of the media through which they inter-acted with the state or the national elites. As most marginalized groups also suffered from economic deprivation, their main concern was daily survival. Tradition and culture continued to act as anchors or defence mechanisms in the face of a harsh reality.

Nowhere was this distance more evident than in the Palestinian society. The best example is the case of the Palestinians living in the West Bank and the Gaza Strip, for whom existence also meant surviving the political reality of the occupation. For this community, military rule was a traumatic experience that united poor and rich alike. The withdrawal from politics was more evident in the refugee camps, although not those within the occupied territories. The camp dwellers in the Arab countries seemed to lose hope in the political leadership's ability to change their fortunes, and, like the Palestinian community in Israel, allowed a minority to be radical in their name.

This period began with the war of June 1967. The hysteria accompanying this war, apocalyptic and elated in the case of the Jews in Israel, traumatized and fearful in the case of the Arab world, has diminished with the years.

A more sober and realistic appraisal has taken its place. As time passed, larger segments of the Jewish community in Israel came to appreciate the negative impact this war of six days had on their lives. On the other hand, Arab societies in general, and the Palestinians in particular, succeeded in putting the event in a perspective that left the catastrophe of 1948 as the most formative event in their lives.

## THE WAR OF JUNE 1967

No sooner had the Sinai campaign ended than war rhetoric on both sides of the divide heralded the imminence of another violent round of fighting between Israel and the Arab world. Unlike during the previous phase in the conflict, 1948 to 1956, the rhetoric was not balanced by peace efforts. On the contrary, it was accompanied by an arms race that for Israel included the acquisition of nuclear capability. On the Arab side it was high-lighted by a massive build-up of modern armies with new weapons and inflated security budgets. On both sides, investment in weapons of mass destruction took priority over social and economic needs. Governments on both sides abandoned their welfare responsibilities, and some of them would pay dearly for this prioritization. The absence of sound social and economic policies created a vacuum that was eagerly filled by political Islam on the Palestinian side, and Jewish fundamentalism on the Israeli side. As the hysteria of the war faded, its transparently ambivalent and disappointing political achievements helped the resurgence of political fundamentalism even more. Charismatic leaders with radical interpretations of their religions could easily offer themselves as the bearers of new solutions, inspiring and guiding their societies in troubled times. Not surprisingly, these leaders became central figures on the political stage.

Rhetoric changed to action in the middle of May 1967. On 14 May, Israel entered a period of painful anxiety after it was revealed that Egyptian forces already in the Sinai Peninsula had violated previous agreements and moved towards the border. The Egyptian leader, Gamal Abd al-Nasser, was drawn into this aggressive policy by the unprecedented deterioration of the situation on the Israeli–Syrian border. Long-standing tension over who should control an area that the armistice agreement of 1949 had defined as no man's land had heightened in January 1967. As mentioned before, this was caused by the Israeli construction of an aquifer to channel water belonging to both countries into Israel and Syrian retaliation in the form of diversion projects, aimed at minimizing the flow of water down the river. In April 1967, a kind of mini-war raged, with both sides using tanks and aircraft, which culminated in a devastating show of the Israeli air force's superiority in the skies over Damascus.[1]

The Egyptian entry into the Sinai came in response to a desperate call by the then Syrian defence minister, Hafiz al-Asad, to help ease the pressure on his country. Asad's Soviet advisers fed him with inaccurate reports of an Israeli build-up in preparation for an overall attack on Syria. There was panic in Damascus, which prompted high-level political negotiations that ended in a military alliance between Egypt, Syria and Jordan.

The Israeli government, under Levi Eshkol, responded by mobilizing reserve soldiers and fortifying its presence on the Israeli–Egyptian border. Nasser reacted by closing the Tiran Straits, blocking maritime traffic to the southern port of Eilat. A hesitant Eshkol promised retaliation on Israeli radio, creating more panic with his poor performance, which was eagerly exploited by David Ben-Gurion. Ben-Gurion probably wished to take advantage of Eshkol's flagging image to regain political power for himself, although by then he was too weak and marginalized to be effective. Nevertheless, his criticism of Eshkol provoked public demand for a government of national unity. On 1 June 1967, Menachem Begin and Moshe Dayan were brought into the cabinet. Dayan was put in charge of orchestrating Israel's strike on the Arab world four days later, on 5 June 1967.

One group in Israel did not share in the general panic: the Palestinian minority. Some of them were elated by the idea of a new war, believing that a concerted Arab effort would effect their liberation. Their leaders, however, were realistic enough to recognize that the disaster of 1948 was about to be repeated. Like the leaders of the *fida'i* movement, they had very little trust in a pan-Arab campaign to save Palestine.

Nasser's motives for embarking on a policy that was to lead to his defeat remain uncertain. However, it is clear that he provided significant sections of the Israeli political elite with a perfect opportunity to realize their dream of a Greater Israel.

Since the 1950s, the Israeli army had been developing plans for a swift occupation of the West Bank. These plans were now put into action, and within several days this goal had been achieved.[2] Behind it lay a mixture of strategic and nationalist thinking that had emerged within the heart of the Labour movement among a group that scholarly Israeli circles refer to as the 'redeemers', those who regarded the West Bank – Judea and Samaria in their vocabulary – as a vital part of the Jewish state, which had to be retrieved. The redeemers were mostly veteran kibbutzniks who enjoyed almost mythical status. They strongly believed that, in 1948, Israel had missed its opportunity to create more defensible borders. At the same time, they were romantic nationalists who regarded the West Bank as the heart of ancient Israel, without which the realization of the Zionist dream would remain incomplete. However, apprehension about Western reaction, and Ben-Gurion's realization of the potential demographic problems for Israel should it annex such a large number of Palestinians, meant that, until June 1967, they had not acted to realize their aspirations.

Now, however, Israel did not occupy just the West Bank. At the end of a six-day campaign, it controlled the Gaza Strip, the Sinai Peninsula and the Golan Heights. In a classical example of blitzkrieg, a highly motivated and professional Israeli army exploited the element of surprise and used its superior Western arms to great advantage, exposing the inferiority of the Arab countries' Eastern bloc military equipment.

Israel now stretched from the Suez Canal to the northern tip of the Golan Heights. Large areas of new territory were now in the hands of an ideological movement obsessed with space and land. Dynamic construction efforts that provided many with jobs and new affluence characterized these early years of the building boom. Fortified walls were erected throughout the new territories, the most famous of which was the Bar Lev line (named after the then general chief of staff), which ran parallel to the Suez Canal as a kind of a Maginot line, and which, in the 1973 war, functioned much like its Second World War model. New roads were added that led to new settlements being built in the occupied territories, in contradiction of international law. It also extended the opportunities for entrepreneurs to prosper through investment in construction. These thriving enterprises, as always in the modern history of Israel and Palestine, stood in direct contrast to the continued deprivation of the Palestinians in general, and the refugees in particular.

### STRUGGLE FOR SURVIVAL: PALESTINIAN REFUGEES AFTER THE 1967 WAR

When it was over, the June 1967 war, also known as the Six Day War, found the Palestinians, like most of the Arab world, in shock and almost completely paralyzed. The Palestinian people were once more divided into categories stemming from a new geo-political situation. Although the dichotomy between refugees and non-refugees remained intact, other communities of people in the West Bank, the Gaza Strip and Israel were united by the sheer fact of being under the control of Israel.

The camps and other Palestinian refugee communities were swollen by a new wave of displaced people, fleeing or expelled by force from the territories newly occupied by Israel. This was a smaller demographic shift than in 1948, but nonetheless added to the burden of an already oppressed community. In 1972, 1.5 million refugees were registered, of whom 650,000 lived in thirteen large camps in Palestine, Jordan, Syria and Lebanon. The number of refugees would increase to about 2 million by 1982.[3]

At the start of 1967–68, the refugees were still located within UNRWA's domain, but gradually many of them gravitated towards the *fida'iyyun* sphere of influence. There was very little UNRWA could offer the refugees once it had almost completely given up its original commitments (repatriation and resettlement) laid down in UN resolutions. After the UN and the United States stopped insisting that Israel agree to repatriation, UNRWA might have had the chance to promote assimilation had its resettlement schemes been connected to long-term development projects in areas inhabited by refugees. However, the UN lost interest in such projects and became content to be simply a relief agency.

It should be stressed that, in any case, resettlement was an unsatisfactory solution for the refugee problem, as most refugees clung to the hope of being unconditionally repatriated, as the UN had promised them in Resolution 194. So in a way UNRWA's failure to assist assimilation did not alienate the refugees; the agency had always been expected to help them survive while they were waiting to return to their homeland. Many refugees joined UNRWA itself as employees, making it almost a Palestinian outfit.[4]

After the 1967 war, UNRWA's policy changed little; as did the attitudes of the host countries. As a result, the dismal economic and social conditions did not improve. As statistics are available for the post-1967 period, we can translate adjectives such as 'dismal' into more concrete terms. One way is to look at UNRWA's budget. The organization was spending 13 dollars a year on each refugee. In practice this meant life without meat, fruit or vegetables. People had to exist on 1,500 calories a day, supplied by flour, sugar, rice, pulses and oil. The UN spent less than 4 dollars per person a year on health, and less than 12 dollars per person on education. After 1967, these amounts were reduced, for lack of donations. 'We provided the bare minimum,' reported the head of UNRWA in 1966. This 'bare minimum' was bestowed on a population 'living in dwellings which are unfit for human habitation: some in dark cellars, others in crumbling tenements, others in grossly overcrowded barracks and shacks . . . nearly all the . . . camps are extremely overcrowded with five or more persons living in one room. They lack adequate roads and pathways and many camps are deep in mud in winter and dust in summer'.[5]

Life was difficult due to economic deprivation, but it was also marred by hostility from the local host societies. Fawaz Turki, a refugee, described in his memoirs the taunts, degradation and abuse directed at the refugees from every quarter; from the official who handled the processing of work permits to the police officer 'who felt he possessed a carte blanche to mistreat you'.[6] Despite this, there were individual success stories. A few hundred refugees were able to use past skills or occupational opportunities to improve their standard of living and find personal betterment outside the camps, while others were able to acquire the skills needed by the growing middle classes of the host countries in order to become tilers, plasterers and electricians. They excelled in artisanship in the construction industry.

Finding a job did not always mean an immediate improvement in one's standard of living, however. In Syria and Lebanon refugees were not allowed to purchase arable land, and it was almost impossible for a refugee to own a house or a flat. Jordan was different; there was no prohibition on land purchase and real estate transactions, and money earned could be well spent.[7] But even in places such as Jordan, where conditions were more congenial, the majority of refugees, originally an agricultural community, lived in humiliating conditions. These former peasants, however, did not lose the ability to sustain themselves. Many became self-sufficient as sharecroppers, also working in service industries wherever they could. Even in Lebanon, refugees tried to make the most of the very short annual period in which they were allowed to work as seasonal labourers during the harvest.[8]

The Syrian government, while prohibiting land purchase, at least allowed refugees to seek jobs in the construction business. After the 1967 war, construction became a profitable business in Syria, but there was a shortage of local workers. The refugees had little choice but to accept this opportunity, although for some it meant giving up aspirations for more varied and profitable jobs. Like so many immigrant societies, they used the money they earned in this line of employment for the education of their children, hoping to provide them with a different future. Thus construction and building were the main sources of employment for Palestinians not only in different parts of Palestine and Israel but throughout the Middle East, regardless of the changing circumstances in which each community of refugees found itself.

In Jordan and Israel, other areas of employment were also open, such as light and heavy industry. The scope of opportunities was more impressive in Jordan than in Israel. The close link that exists in the Jewish state between industry and the military limited the access of Palestinians to employment in industry. In Jordan unlimited access to employment did not mean unlimited availability, however. Although offering a varied spectrum of job opportunities, the Jordanian local urban market was not large enough to sustain the numbers of hopeful Palestinians arriving in its small towns. They often tended to stay around the cities even when disappointed, building shanty towns barely suitable for human habitation, often worse than the conditions in the refugee camps they had left behind. This mass urbanization significantly lowered local wages, and employment became underemployment. The jobs were hardly sufficient for survival, and the temptation to return to the camps and be on UNRWA's payroll was strong.[9]

Not all the Palestinian refugees suffered the same level of deprivation. Those in Jordan who were employed by rich Palestinians in the construction business, and there were quite a few, did much better. Discussing the Palestinians in Jordan as a separate community is to stumble in the dark, however, as official Jordanian statistics do not distinguish between Palestinians and Jordanians.[10]

Outside the realm of Palestine's neighbouring states, there were often impressive individual success stories. Newspapers reported that peasants exploited vocational expertise gained in the camps as a springboard to the opportunities of Arabia and the Persian Gulf. As mentioned in the previous chapter, immigration to the oil-rich countries had begun in the 1950s. At first the atmosphere was not congenial, as the Palestinians had a well-developed sense of workers' rights and organized the first strikes at ARAMCO (Arabian American Oil Company) and other leading oil companies. However, the outstanding growth in revenues in the late 1960s improved work conditions and calmed industrial relations in these areas. The new wealth created even more demand for the skilled hands of Palestinian workers. In the national Palestinian narrative, these refugees are disparagingly presented as having chosen personal wealth rather than political participation in the national effort. Some would redeem themselves during the intifada by offering their wealth for the cause.[11] Still, their success was not generally shared with others. Those who left the camps were mostly young people, who in some cases did not return, although they continued to support their immediate, and even their extended, families.

The refugees became the landless proletariat of Palestinian society. Life was governed by finding work, perhaps in the fields of a local landlord during harvest, or in the workshops and offices of relief organizations in the camps. Some worked as street vendors. Survival depended on the economies of the host countries or on temporary labour, with earnings usually insufficient to keep an average family.

The PLO, meanwhile, regarded the refugees in the camps as potential recruits for its liberation struggle. Hopeful candidates went through a course

of military training and elementary, nationalist, education. Successful graduates of this preparatory course were rewarded with positions of influence
within the community. In some refugee camps, they were able to build
up autonomous welfare, health and education systems better than those
provided by UNRWA or the host countries.

Al-Muqawwama emerged from the 1967 war much stronger, and won
legitimacy throughout the Palestinian world. The movement's leaders
achieved this by adapting concepts such as those of Frantz Fanon, who
advocated the primacy of the struggle itself over its objectives. Hence, the
eighth clause of the PLO's charter declared that 'the armed struggle for the
liberation of Palestine is a strategy, not tactics'. The struggle itself was seen
as the way to maintain the national identity; there was no need for achievements beyond that. As it happened, there were no achievements to report in
the realm of 'liberation': the PLO was leading one of the few Third World
liberation movements that had yet to free one inch of its homeland.[12]

The movement's area of operation moved from an urban, bourgeois
milieu into the camps, particularly in Lebanon and Jordan. Geographically
this meant moving its headquarters closer to the refugee community, and
so nearer to the borders with Israel. The *fida'iyyun* were now able both to
commence guerrilla warfare against Israel, and to compete with UNRWA
as a regulator of life in the camps, where they began to provide social
and economic services. They promoted themselves among the refugees
as a legitimate authority, able to govern and protect them. The fact that
they were also fighters, crossing into Israel, gave them an added aura of
heroism. However, their authority was mostly illusory, especially in Jordan
and Syria. Ironically, due to the total isolation imposed on the refugee areas
there, it was only in Lebanon that the *fida'iyyun* achieved real authority.
Al-Muqawwama's effective assumption of authority was completed in 1968,
when, spearheaded by Fatah, it revolted against the PLO's leadership and
installed Yasser Arafat as its leader instead of Ahmad al-Shuqairi.

The coup had two contradictory effects on the PLO. It allowed Fatah to
tighten its control over the organization, although at the same time victory
highlighted the dissension within Fatah's own ranks. Fatah tightened its grip
on the whole organization by restructuring the PLO along Leninist lines.
Power emanated from above; a classic case of centralized democracy. At the
top was the executive committee, the cabinet, which selected the central
committee, the government, which then supervised the Palestine National
Council (PNC), the parliament. Only half of the Council members were
selected from the *fida'i* organizations; the other half consisted of representatives of professional organizations. To this legislative skeleton were added

pre-state departments: a political department, which was the PLO's foreign ministry, and an army, the Palestine Liberation Army (originally founded by the Arab League). The organization also had its own welfare service, Samed, and its own Red Crescent society. This structure resembled that of the Zionist organization during the Mandate (see chapter 3).

The establishment of Samed by the PLO in 1970 weakened UNRWA's role as the principal employer. Samed was a welfare organization originally intended to assist bereaved families of fighters who had been killed in action, but was soon expanded to deal with unemployment, particularly in Lebanon, the West Bank and the Gaza Strip. This nationalization of the welfare system did much to help the PLO enhance its standing among the refugees, a status lost only in the 1990s, when it seemed to sideline the issue of return during the peace negotiations with Israel.

Similarly, the Red Crescent was more than an ambulance and hospital service. It took over another function of UNRWA: the workshops producing household commodities. This was both a source of employment and a response to such basic daily needs as furniture, kitchen utensils and clothing.

## POPULAR UPRISING, GUERRILLA WARFARE
## AND TERRORISM (1968–1972)

After the 1967 war, al-Muqawwama's natural focus became the struggle for the liberation of the occupied West Bank and Gaza Strip. The initial strategy was to wage a popular guerrilla war from within the occupied territories. For that purpose, even Arafat himself travelled the countryside, trying to construct a rural base for such a revolt, inspired by Maoist practices and ideologies. He was hunted by the Israelis but was not caught, nor did he achieve his goal. After a few months it was clear that a Maoist model would not fit a population that, by and large, was not ready to provide an active base for such a confrontation.

An old notion was revived of turning Jordan into Israel's North Vietnam, in other words a foreign launching pad for guerrilla attacks, and executed quite successfully. It began in 1967, with about 100 attacks on military installations and bases, which rose to more than 2,000 in 1970. Fatah led the way with systematic attacks on military installations and targets across the Jordan. Israeli retaliation was prompt, although not always successful. In March 1968, for example, near the Palestinian settlement Karameh in the Jordan Valley (one of UNRWA's few successes in settling refugees), Palestinian fighters, along with Jordanian soldiers, defeated a large Israeli contingent.[13] After Karameh, young people in their thousands joined the *fida'iyyun*.[14] The PNC was subsequently taken over by al-Muqawwama. Al-Shuqairi was deposed, and soon afterwards Arafat was installed as his successor. Fatah people were appointed to all key positions. The PLO's charter, composed originally in 1964 under Nasser's influence, was altered to reflect its changing ideology. Three clauses (eight, nine and ten) were added, stressing the need for a people's war of liberation and emphasizing the PLO's independence from pan-Arab control.

The coup was followed by disagreement between Arafat and two former associates, Naif Hawatmeh and George Habash. This was a conventional power struggle, but was also motivated by tactical disagreement about methods of attaining the liberation of Palestine and an ideological dispute concerning Palestine's future image and form. Hawatmeh wished to see the whole Arab East becoming a paradigm of Trotskyite socialism, while Habash more modestly advocated close ties with Moscow and its brand of Marxism–Leninism. The two at first cooperated, in an organization called the Popular Front for the Liberation of Palestine (PFLP), but Hawatmeh later left and created his own movement, the Popular Democratic Front for the Liberation of Palestine (PDFLP).[15] These two movements have remained key players in the Palestinian polity.

After 1968 the PFLP became inspired by Latin American revolutionary ideology, especially the writings and deeds of Che Guevara, adapting his views to the Middle East situation. This led the group to broaden its revolutionary goals to include the toppling of 'reactionary' Arab regimes. Thus, while Fatah was seeking the support of Arab governments, the PFLP operated within grassroots opposition movements in the Arab countries.

Both the PFLP and PDFLP opted for bolder guerrilla activities, from Jordan and Lebanon, and began a terrorist campaign outside Israel (followed a few years later by Fatah). The PFLP was the first to hijack aeroplanes, while Fatah waged a guerrilla war on the border of the occupied West Bank and Jordan. In 1969 the PFLP hijacked three aircraft, landing them in the Jordanian desert and blowing them up, without their passengers, when their demands for the release of Palestinian prisoners in Israel and for a change in Western policy towards the Arab–Israeli conflict were not met.

In Jordan, the PLO became overconfident. Exploiting to the full the inexperienced King Hussein, and a demographic balance of power that made Jordan almost a Palestinian state, Fatah built an infrastructure in the refugee camps there as a base for the war against Israel. It was also used as a framework for organizing the refugees' lives. Unlike the nationalist notables, this national elite put education and welfare on its list of priorities, and therefore had much more popular support, even given its failures, which were many.

The radical Arab regimes, such as the FLN (Front de Libération Nationale) in Algeria, preferred Fatah's tactics to terror in the air, perhaps partly because the PFLP chose Algiers as the venue for its first operation, the hijacking of an El-Al airliner in July 1968. The Israeli government agreed to release Palestinian political prisoners in return for the hostages in that infamous first hijacking. Until 1976, when the Israeli army raided Entebbe in Uganda and released Jewish and Israeli hostages from a hijacked Air France aeroplane, deals were usually struck. In December 1968, however, when the PDFLP attacked an El-Al aeroplane in Athens, the IDF retaliated with a raid on Beirut's international airport, destroying planes belonging to Arab airlines.[16]

The first two years of the revolution were exhilarating as far as the leaders of Fatah and the two other organizations were concerned. Fully armed PLO fighters openly roamed Amman and other towns. This was too much for King Hussein, whose intelligence services were feeding him with (probably exaggerated) warnings of an imminent PLO take-over of Jordan. His attempt to disarm the PLO in the refugee camps in September 1970 ended in a bloodbath. The episode almost turned into a regional war, when Syrian units invaded northern Jordan as a show of solidarity with the Palestinians, but were deterred by an Israeli ultimatum, which saved King Hussein. The person who stopped the bloodbath was Nasser. He obtained a cease-fire and, just before he died, fashioned the agreement that transferred the PLO to Lebanon. The move from Jordan and the consequent shift of guerrilla activity to Lebanon and Israel's northern border weakened the ties of the PLO with the Palestinian community living under Israeli occupation in the West Bank and the Gaza Strip.

The PLO's high profile among the refugees and, to a certain extent in the occupied territories and Israel as well, did not stem from its political commitment to liberate Palestine, nor did it offer most Palestinians practical help in their daily struggle for survival. Its vitality lay elsewhere. It was a magnet to which social and professional organizations were drawn, filling a vacuum created by the lack of a state apparatus. Thus unions representing teachers, women and lawyers supported the idea of a larger political movement that could represent their particular and national interests. This sentiment corresponded well with that of the guerrilla movements, and in some respects also seemed justified in the eyes of Arab politicians ostensibly committed to the Palestinians' cause.[17]

This high profile enabled al-Muqawwama to transform the PLO, but a price was paid for its close association with the refugee camps, which distanced it, for a while, from Palestine's heartland. There, in the West Bank and the Gaza Strip, the 1967 war and the occupation had changed the lives of the community, mostly for the worse. The inability of the PLO to remain in constant touch with those Palestinians under the yoke of occupation undermined its standing in this community. Without the PLO, the different Palestinian groups in the occupied territories, the refugee camps and Israel failed to find common ground. This situation lasted until the outbreak of the first intifada in the late 1980s.

## THE OCCUPATION (1967–1982)

For years Israeli leaders tended to talk about 'an enlightened occupation' when assessing the first decade of Israeli rule in the West Bank and the Gaza Strip. From its beginning, however, when 590,000 Palestinians in the West Bank and 380,000 in the Gaza Strip fell under Israeli hegemony, there was little that could be described as 'enlightened' about the harsh and brutal occupation. The first blow inflicted on the population was the Israeli expulsion policy. The pragmatic leadership of the Jewish state, although exhilarated by its sudden acquisition of the whole of ex-Mandate Palestine, was nonetheless nervous about absorbing such a large number of Palestinians. Expulsion was neither an alien concept nor an unfamiliar practice to the Zionist movement. Immediately after the war, the former head of military intelligence, Haim Herzog, was appointed as governor-general, so to speak, first of Jerusalem and then of the whole West Bank. Under his administration, on 17 June 1967 Palestinian citizens living within the Jewish quarter of the Old City of Jerusalem were either evicted or offered money to leave. All were asked to sign a document relinquishing their right of return. The residents of three refugee camps north of Jericho were expelled too. A number also fled during the war and after the expulsions.[18] In Palestinian discourse they are referred to as *nazihun* ('uprooted'), to distinguish them from the *laji'un*, the 1948 refugees. Only one expulsion attempt by Israel failed: a 1971 plan to transfer refugees from the Gaza Strip to the West Bank. A few hundred inhabitants of the Jabaliyya camp were transferred to the West Bank, but local resistance dissuaded the Israelis from further expulsions.[19]

Jerusalem not only saw the beginning of the Israeli expulsion policy, it was also the site of the first 'pilot project' of Jewish settlement on occupied territory. In early 1968, the Israeli authorities appropriated vast areas of

East Jerusalem, a third of which were private property, and re-zoned them as new Jewish neighbourhoods. Alarmed architects and ecologists warned the municipality in vain that the hasty decision, motivated by ideology and taken without any serious environmental planning, would be disastrous.[20] Jerusalem was thereafter encircled by several ugly suburbs, which crouched menacingly on the hills overlooking the Arab city below.

The Israeli government was still formulating its policy towards the most recent refugees. In August, it announced that it was willing to allow the repatriation of refugees who had left after 1967, but understandably these overtures were met with suspicion, and only 150 people returned. After that, the unofficial Israeli policy was not to allow refugees to return to the occupied territories. This policy became official in 1977, when Likud came to power with Menachem Begin as the prime minister. His government adhered to a Greater Israel ideology: any decrease in the number of Palestinians, or increase in the number of Jewish settlers, in the occupied territories was seen as likely to help make the dream a reality. (Many in the Labour Party also supported this stance.) Thus, the threat of expulsion and relocation was one of the many burdens imposed by the occupation on the local population. It is difficult to describe its worst aspects. While mass expulsions took place at long intervals, passive bystanders and activists alike were subjected to military harassment in the form of house searches, curfews and abusive interrogation at checkpoints on a daily basis.[21]

'Resistance' was, in the eyes of the Israelis, very liberally defined. Any show of opposition to the occupation, such as a rally, a strike, distribution of petitions or the waving of the Palestinian flag, was met with severe brutality. The Israeli campaign against political activity began in July 1967 with the expulsion from East Jerusalem of four notables who called on the population to adopt Mahatma Gandhi's tactic of civil disobedience. (Many years later, when an American Palestinian, Mubarak Awad, tried to introduce a more sophisticated version of non-violent resistance he was treated by the Israelis as an arch-terrorist.) Worse was to come. Moshe Dayan, the Israeli minister of defence, was told in July 1967 of armed resistance in the West Bank town of Qalqilya, and immediately ordered, as the first act of collective punishment in a long series of such acts, the destruction of the town. Half of Qalqilya's houses were demolished in this operation.[22]

Ariel Sharon, the commander in charge of the Gaza Strip, was particularly zealous in the quelling of resistance, individual or collective. Since presiding over a massacre in Qibyya in 1953, his career had been punctuated by bloody clashes with Palestinians everywhere. At first, Sharon was content to leave in charge the local notables who had run the municipal and legal systems during the Egyptian era. Thus for instance, as in the West Bank, the education system was restored to the status quo ante, which meant Jordanian supervision in the West Bank and Egyptian supervision in the Gaza Strip. However, Sharon soon realized that he was dealing with a highly politicized refugee community, which could not easily be co-opted to this pattern of continuity. They tested his authority by questioning Israel's or Egypt's authority in the camps. Time after time, the youth, and some middle-aged men and women, took up arms, and used stones, Molotov cocktails and whatever they could find in a show of resistance against the Israeli occupation. These early attempts at revolution were soon quashed under the fire-power of tanks and heavy guns employed indiscriminately against the local civilian population. It was not until the 1987 intifada, and then the al-Aqsa intifada (*Intifadat al-Aqsa*) in the autumn of 2000, that the Israeli army resorted again to such destructive retaliation against a popular uprising.

The ability of the army to deal so harshly with any form of political resistance, armed or peaceful, was underwritten by the legal status Israel granted to the West Bank and the Gaza Strip. The Israeli government declared from the very onset of its occupation that these areas were 'territories under custody' in which military rule would apply. This somewhat anaemic phrase meant that in practice the people living in the territories were robbed of all basic human or civic rights. At the same time, the government did all it could to avoid being limited by international law guidelines on the administration of occupied areas; guidelines that were systematically violated by the Israelis. For that purpose, in January 1968 the Israeli minister of the interior declared that the West Bank, the Gaza Strip and the Golan Heights were not 'enemy areas'. This allowed Israel to alternate between the application of Israeli law, as in the Golan Heights, where it granted civil rights to a small community of Druzes, and the deprivation of such rights in all the other areas. The international community was not oblivious of these practices and there were objections, but the uproar subsided before it made any impact on Israeli conduct.

The legal basis for this regime was the notorious mandatory emergency regulations of 1945, which were mentioned in the previous chapter as the legal basis for the military regime imposed on the Palestinians in Israel until 1966. The Israelis now added a new regulation allowing the army to expel from anywhere in Israel and Palestine anyone suspected of being a security risk. It was used extensively, against Palestinian activists within the state of Israel as well those living in the occupied territories.[23]

The Israeli government claimed that all it did was to continue Jordanian adherence to these regulations. This was unfounded. The Jordanians had never used these regulations, nor had the Egyptians in the Gaza Strip. This is not to say that the Jordanians and the Egyptians had respected civic and human rights, they had not, but the Israelis must take sole responsibility for imposing a regime devoid of any democratic rights.

The Israeli military authorities used this military regime excessively in the first decade after the 1967 war. By 'excessively' I mean frequent acts of collective punishment for any gesture that was regarded as subversive or resistant to Israeli occupation. The destruction of houses, expulsion, and arrest without trial were the most common uses of the regulations.[24] As under military rule in Israel, the formal right to vote and be elected remained, but was meaningless as it did not include the right to form independent parties. In 1972 and 1976, the Israelis allowed the population to vote in municipal elections. However, after a sweeping victory for PLO candidates in 1976, the Likud government, coming to power in 1977, banned elections and with it deprived the local population of their remaining rights.

From the beginning of the occupation, international jurists commented on the illegitimacy of the Israeli resolution to maintain the territories as an occupied area without adhering to the requirements sanctioned by the Geneva Convention for the treatment of such areas. Israel violated almost every clause in that convention by settling Jews there, expelling Palestinians and imposing collective punishment. The Israeli Supreme Court took upon itself the task of monitoring the legitimacy of the regime very early in the occupation. In the history of modern warfare, there is no case, apart from this one, in which a civilian judicial authority supervised military rule. This extraordinary resolution was taken in 1967 when Meir Shamgar, who went from being the military attorney-general to the government's legal adviser, allowed Palestinians in the occupied territories to appeal to the Supreme Court. By 1988, almost 40 per cent of appeals to the Supreme Court were from Palestinians there. In practice, this allowance achieved little. Hardly any of the appeals could stand if the army asked the courts to authorize and legitimize its acts retrospectively against individuals or collectives in the name of security.[25]

The only respite from this predicament was, ironically, to move to East Jerusalem. In 1976, Israel, on the one hand, had annexed East Jerusalem, a part of Palestine that enjoyed a relatively open environment. On the other hand, the annexation robbed the city of its Palestinian identity, and was accompanied by the construction of illegal settlements. Many Palestinian newspapers and journals, however, moved their editorial offices to Jerusalem, hoping to be able to publish more freely, a hope not always fulfilled.

Moving to Jerusalem, or between any destinations in the occupied territories, has remained the exclusive right of Jewish settlers and those locals with special permission to do so. The restrictions imposed on freedom of movement were, and still are, harsher on those seeking to leave the West Bank and the Gaza Strip. This hardship was particularly acute in the case of Palestinian workers who were invited to join, as unskilled labourers, the booming Israeli economy around 1968. As early as November 1967, workers were reported as creeping illegally into Israel to find jobs in the orange groves. They were paid a quarter of the average Jewish salary at the time.[26] The workers were allowed to enter Israel at dawn, but had to leave by dusk. A year later, in September 1968, the Israeli government legalized what the minister of interior called the 'import of workers, since we lack "ordinary" workers'.

THE SETTLEMENTS AND INTERNAL DEBATE IN ISRAEL
(1967–1973)

Towards the end of the 1960s, harassment of the local population came to the West Bank in the new form of Jewish settlement. The settlement movement was motivated by party politics in Israel. From within this political hotbed both secular and religious groups advanced the cause of the 'redemption', the idea that Israel had returned forever to the heart of its ancient homeland. At the core of the secular movement was the right wing of the Labour Party. The name Labour Party (Mapai) was an invention of the post-1967 period. After the 1967 war, it united with other parties both to its left and to its right, thus ending the pluralist nature of socialist Zionism. In the 1980s, it absorbed the left-most socialist Zionist party, Mapam, and was re-named Ma'arach ('alignment'), which remained its official name until the 1980s. When in the mid-1980s Mapam left this alliance, the Ma'arach reverted to Labour (Ha-Avoda).[27]

After the 1967 war, debate within this so-called socialist party focused on the question of the occupied territories. One particular branch within the united party, the former members of Ahdut Ha-Avoda, insisted that the Sinai and the Golan Heights were an integral part of Eretz Israel. This wing of the Labour Party consisted of veteran Zionists, usually from kibbutzim. On 15 June 1967, the kibbutz movement of the Labour Party had called for immediate Jewish resettlement of western Eretz Israel, thus taking the leading role in the redeemer movement. Its principal ideologue was an old Zionist colonizer called Yizhak Tabenkin, who had been active since the Mandate and wielded respect and authority in the movement.

Ahdut Ha-Avoda was led by the 1948 war hero Yigal Alon. Alon was not a full-fledged redeemer. He tried to balance pragmatic approaches with the redeemers' cause. In 1967 he proposed a scheme, adopted by his government, based on a geographical division of the West Bank into Jewish and Hashemite–Palestinian areas. He pushed fervently for the construction of as many settlements as possible within the Jewish area. His basic notion was that Israel, even after withdrawal, had to be in full military control of the areas stretching from the River Jordan to the Mediterranean. He published his views in a book which inspired his followers to claim the whole of Palestine in the name of security considerations. Alon was behind the construction of a settlement town near Hebron in 1974 under the biblical name of Qiryat Arba.

Nevertheless, those demanding land for 'security' reasons made less progress than their religious counterparts in Mafdal, the religious national party. They began their settlement projects in the early 1970s, establishing new communities that were approved retrospectively by the Labour government.[28]

Before this, Mafdal had had a very different history, characterized by political pragmatism and moderation. In 1970, it split after the death of its charismatic leader, Haim Moshe Shapira, and a rebellion by members of the party's youth movement, Bnei Akiva. The leader of the young faction was Zevulun Hammer. He was supported by Israel's chief rabbi, Shlomo Goren. Goren was the military chief rabbi of the 1967 war, and was famous for blowing the *shofar* – the traditional Jewish horn – on the Wailing Wall, declaring his intention to accelerate the coming of the Jewish Messiah to Jerusalem. His enthusiasm was curbed by the Israeli defence minister at the time, Moshe Dayan, who feared a global confrontation with the Muslim world. This cautious attitude was lacking in September 2000, when Ariel Sharon, then an opposition leader, entered the Haram uninvited, igniting the al-Aqsa intifada.

A more influential figure was Rabbi Zvi Yehuda Kook. This distinguished rabbi ruled that the West Bank and the Gaza Strip were holy parts of the land of Israel, not to be handed over to non-Jewish sovereignty in any circumstances. Kook would become the spiritual inspiration for the Jewish settlement movement in the occupied territories. Kook was Goren's mentor, and Goren rewarded him by frequently issuing halachic injunctions sanctifying Israeli rule all over Palestine. The Mizrahi chief rabbi, Yaacov

Nissim, had already defined the occupied areas as sacred holy lands and forbidden, on religious grounds, any future withdrawal from these areas.[29] Like the settlers he supported, Goren's religious outlook was a mixture of flexibility towards the social practices of a modern Jewish community and a fundamentalist, chauvinist interpretation of Judaism in matters of foreign and security policies.

Goren and others began employing a messianic discourse about Judea, Samaria and 'Aza, areas presented as not only vital for Israel's survival but also for the advent of the Messiah. This eccentricity took centre stage with the ascendance of Likud to power. Indeed, one of Menachem Begin's first acts was to instruct government personnel, including members of the media, to use the biblical terms for the occupied territories.[30]

Once the 'young Gorenites' began settling in the areas they found a new leader, Rabbi Moshe Levinger. He turned this messianic zeal into an institutionalized movement, Gush Emunim ('community of believers'). They settled illegally near supposedly biblical sites, resisting government attempts to evict them, and then negotiating the terms of settlement. They began in the midst of the old city of al-Halil (Hebron), in April 1968, and succeeded in eliciting recognition from a hesitant prime minister, Levi Eshkol (1963–69). The same pattern repeated itself elsewhere in the West Bank and Gaza Strip. In northern and southern Sinai, as well as in the Golan Heights, the settlement movement was encouraged by the government, and thus was more organized and structured, attracting people who had little to do with 'redemption ideology'. They were lured to these places by cheaper housing and the beautiful surroundings.

The settlement enterprise was accompanied by a mass confiscation of land. This was begun by the army, seeking land for its camps and installations, but afterwards most of the coveted land was allocated to the settlers. By 1972, Israel had confiscated over 1.5 million dunams of land, almost 28 per cent of the West Bank, and by 2000 this had risen to almost 42 per cent.[31]

The Labour government included some who opposed the settlements. These were the 'custodians', who believed that Israel should keep the territories in custody in return for peace.[32] Prime Minister Levi Eshkol represented this position, and had even urged his government to adopt it as official policy just after the war ended. He had very little support within the government, however, and it was not until after the 1973 war that the custodians contributed significantly to the public debate over the territories' future. On one subject, however, custodians and redeemers concurred:

Greater Jerusalem, almost a third of the West Bank, was to remain Israeli territory.

In September 1967, an Arab summit at Khartoum published its famous three noes: to negotiation, to recognition of Israel, and to peace. Behind a façade of rejectionism, however, Nasser himself allowed more room for possible future negotiations.[33] But in the 1969 election, the moderate Eshkol could not prevail against the more inflexible Golda Meir.

Likud, after coming to power in 1977, openly supported the settlement movement. While Labour's settlements were decided on security grounds, Likud was in favour of settling near allegedly historical sites. This was greatly assisted by Israeli archaeologists, whose 'scientific' rulings helped buttress the legal process of settlement. The judicial authority in Israel enabled the confiscation of Palestinian land and registration in the *tapu* (land register) of the new settlements as state land. In a rare decision, the Israeli Supreme Court ruled in October 1979 against this procedure in the case of the 1975 settlement Elon Moreh, near Nablus. Both the government and the settlers ignored the ruling.

As mentioned above, the custodians regrouped after the 1973 war, and succeeded in provoking a debate among the politicians at least about the settlements' future. They rarely put forward moral considerations. Their main line of argument was demographic, and it failed to impress the Israeli public. The incorporation of such a large number of Palestinians would undermine previous efforts at Judaization and the depopulation of 1948. A small group from among the political elite and the custodians, and from academic and cultural circles, advocated negotiating with either King Hussein or a local Palestinian leadership for a quick Israeli withdrawal in return for peace.

On the margin of the custodian camp, a new radical movement emerged. As yet insignificant as a political force, it put forward a peace plan which many years later would affect a larger group of artists, academics, playwrights, film makers and other figures in the arts. It would also open the way for a dialogue with the PLO that would lead to official contact between the two sides. Their reasons were moral and ideological. Its first members struggled to sustain their freedom of speech in a hostile environment. The famous Orientalist, Aharon Cohen, who called for an unconditional Israeli withdrawal from the territories, was forced by his kibbutz to retract publicly, while a colleague of his, who refused to do so, was ousted from his kibbutz. In the months after the 1967 war, a more Trotskyite orientation would shape these views into a group called Mazpen ('compass'), which raised a small, but constant, voice of clear objection to Zionism in general and the occupation in particular.[34]

A far more significant political voice on the left was the Communist Party, which clearly stated its adherence to the two-states solution, long before anyone in the more official custodians camp accepted it as reasonable. (Note that by 'custodians' I mean the pragmatic doves within the Labour Party, but not beyond it.)

The debate inside Israel was focused on the West Bank, and little thought was given to the future of the Gaza Strip. It was clear to policy makers and grassroots activists that the Egyptian regime had no wish to re-annex the latter. Some Palestinian leaders tried to contact Israeli leaders to negotiate the establishment of an autonomous Palestinian entity both in the Strip and in the West Bank, or even a state, under Israeli auspices. But most efforts were concentrated at government level. Most Palestinians understood that daily survival now had to be coupled with a growing uncertainty about the political future of their homeland.

## SURVIVAL UNDER OCCUPATION

There was a third way.[35] Life under occupation was not the simple dichotomy of a brutal occupier and an oppressed occupied. The impulse to rebel was mitigated by individual expectations of improvement and hopes of profiting from the new socio-economic conditions developing under the occupation. This is probably why Fatah failed immediately after the war to lead a popular guerrilla uprising against the Israeli occupiers. The West Bankers were more positive towards the new occupiers than Arafat wished. Traders and businessmen strengthened their ties with the Israeli economy, lured by hopes of a higher standard of living.

The less fortunate members of the society, poor, unemployed farmers and peasants living in cramped conditions, were sucked into the pool of labour needed by the Israeli economy. They were sought by construction companies obsessed with what the Israeli poet Nathan Alterman so aptly described as 'covering the land with a gown of cement'. People were employed not only in construction. Together with the Palestinian citizens of Israel, they provided nearly a quarter of the labour in Israeli industry in the mid-1970s,[36] and made up 50 per cent of the workforce in construction and agriculture. By 1974, about 45 per cent of the employed Palestinians in the West Bank and 50 per cent in Gaza worked in Israel. Half were in construction, the rest in agriculture and industry. In the Gaza

Strip, the ever-growing population added to the sense of suffocation and oppression.

These Palestinian workers were badly paid and treated, and had no social security, but nonetheless earned more money than they would within their own territory. After the PLO left for Beirut, political pressure on the Palestinian workers eased, and they even found jobs on the first Jewish settlements in the West Bank, beginning with housing projects for settlers near Nablus and Hebron.

The refugees crossing the 1967 borders into Israel made up half of the Palestinian workers in Israel proper.[37] They returned home as underpaid, almost enslaved labourers, aliens in their own homeland. As if this was not enough, the daily routine of such workers was as humiliating as the national significance of this 'act of return'. It consisted of daily commuting, beginning at sunrise at an Israeli checkpoint, where they were quite often subjected to maltreatment and harassment. From there they moved to areas referred to as 'the slave markets', where prospective Israeli employers would choose the lucky ones as workers for the day. The 'slave markets' sprang up on the outskirts of every major city, where Palestinian workers could be seen crammed together in 'human pens', and allowed to run wildly to jeeps and trucks that might take them to factories, restaurants, farms or anywhere they could be hired as unskilled workers. At the end of the day they would be paid wages that were pittances by Israeli standards, but better than Jordanian or Egyptian wages.[38] By the beginning of the 1980s, about 150,000 Palestinians were living in this way.

People coped with their situation in various ways. In the late 1980s, there was an unusual reaction to the conditions under which people were existing in the West Bank. Workers started to attack their employers with knives or to run amok in Jewish crowds. They were usually motivated by a combination of religious zealotry and anger at recent Israeli maltreatment at the borders, or brutal interrogation or arrest. Despite the frustration of the population, the number of workers involved in violence such as this was small.[39]

Religion also resumed a more important role in the way individuals responded to a harsh reality from which there seemed to be no escape. People were at first attracted to the Muslim Brotherhood, but the organization was too vague politically to provide a concrete solution to their predicament, and they turned instead to Palestinian organizations such as Hamas and Islamic Jihad, which had emerged with a clear national-religious agenda. A few managed to stay in Israel itself. Many had relatives in Israel, and some also wished to marry into Palestinian Israeli families, although this usually meant that the Palestinian Israeli bride or groom had to move into the occupied territories.

The Israeli economy's role as a supplier of jobs was not its only impact on the occupied territories. Small industry in the occupied territories exported commodities to Israel, and the consequent increase in production created new jobs too. However, unemployment remained a severe and constant problem. Moreover, the Israeli economy itself fluctuated between prosperity and recession. When it thrived, employers in the West Bank had to pay their workers more, which most of them could hardly afford. When it was in recession, as between 1974 and 1988, the soaring inflation in Israel devastated the Palestinian economy in the territories.[40]

The Israeli confiscation of land created land hunger among the Palestinians, which also affected their economic situation. The scarcity of land, however, did not produce an immediate shortage in agricultural work due to the mass emigration of West Bankers to the Gulf states in the first decade of Israel's occupation. There was also temporary relief for uprooted villagers at harvest time and during the fruit-picking season, when big orchard owners needed labour for their citrus, almond and olive plantations. Demand was so high that women and children were also recruited.

Israeli agricultural advisers, who were part of the administrative body running the occupied territories, introduced modern cultivation technology. For some this meant further job losses, but for others, especially those living on the more arid eastern side of the West Bank, the greenhouse technology imported from Israel enabled small land owners to offer their products all year round.

By the 1970s, many farmers were struggling to remain on the land. The confiscation of land, among other factors, intensified the urbanization process. This led to the emergence of profiteers who speculated in real estate without alleviating the housing problem. The fluidity in real estate benefited some refugees, who could for short periods rent flats at relatively low prices. However, most refugees could afford only short leases before landlords raised rents.[41]

In the Gaza Strip, refugees were not as fortunate. There was no land available, even for refugees who were willing to leave and start a different life there. The Strip's main predicament, apart from the occupation, was population explosion. Although the Israeli demand for unskilled workers did produce jobs for many, it by no means served as a solution to unemployment and to one of the highest poverty levels in the world.[42]

Thus the picture everywhere seemed to be a mixture of resistance, daily survival and adaptation. The thread that ran between these options was woven by the Palestinian politicians, some of whom were self-appointed while others were elected, as was the case in 1976. The politicians in the occupied territories were at first passive pawns in the high drama around them. They represented a society whose land was coveted by powerful neighbours in the east, the Jordanians, and in the west, the Israelis. This made formulating a political agenda almost impossible. They were influenced by, but not influential on, the PLO's point of view. More than anything else, however, knowledge of American politics was essential to influence their society's future.

In the first twenty years of the occupation, the local population, leaders and ordinary folk alike, were excluded from the negotiations over the future status of the areas in which they lived. While the people of the West Bank and the Gaza Strip were caught between harassment and economic survival, Israel, Jordan, the United States and, later on, Egypt conducted a series of diplomatic engagements aimed at determining the sovereignty of these parts of Palestine.

### PAX AMERICANA, WAR AND PEACE (1973–1977)

As we have seen, the occupation led to constant violations of human and civil rights, on the one hand, and an incremental process of Judaization of the West Bank and the Gaza Strip on the other. These dismal twin realities were possible because the West Bank and the Gaza Strip were, although higher than the refugee question, low on the peace agenda. This was determined to a large extent by American foreign policy and, of course, by Israel.

The role of the United States as a facilitator of Israel's intransigence in the conflict was partly due to the improvement in the military relationship between the two countries. After years of repeated rejection of requests for heavy arms, the Israelis found a more receptive American administration in that of Lyndon B. Johnson. The change in American policy has often been attributed to the president's hawkish view of the Cold War and the effectiveness of the Jewish lobby. In September 1969, the first sophisticated Phantom aircraft arrived from the USA. The Israeli public was asked to donate money for its purchase. This was not just propaganda, as it was several years before arms supplies were financed by American taxpayers as part of an annual grant to Israel.

The USA, however, wished to be more than Israel's protector. It broadcast itself as the conflict's peace broker as well. This task was entrusted to the American foreign secretary, William Rogers. His peace efforts were based on

UN Resolution 242, adopted by the organization in November 1967, and calling for an Israeli withdrawal from all the territories it had occupied in the 1967 war in return for peace with its Arab neighbours. Rogers added an edge. Arab countries willing to participate in negotiations on this basis were expected to join the American camp in the Cold War. Washington wished to exclude, and eventually did, the Soviet Union from any significant influence in the Middle East. This drive gradually deepened American involvement in the peace process. Before the American assumption of the peace process, the UN had tried to persuade both sides to adopt Resolution 242 as a basis for peace, with the help of yet another Swedish mediator, Gunar Yaring. Like that of his predecessor, his mission ended in failure.[43] Israel eventually accepted the principle of resolution 242, but only as a basis for a solution to the situation in the Sinai Peninsula. It refused to apply it to the Golan Heights, the West Bank, or the Gaza Strip. The Israeli Foreign Office even translated the resolution into Hebrew in a way that implied that it did not have to withdraw from all the territories it had occupied.

The American peace effort, after almost twenty years of isolation from such diplomatic activity, was accompanied by a new diplomatic jargon, borrowed from the world of business, built on cost–benefit principles and devoid of any reference to moral values. Its 'buzzword' was 'peace process'. The Palestinians searched this new vocabulary in vain for terms such as 'decolonization', 'an end to the occupation' and 'moral justice'. They were instead confronted with a language that regarded the balance of power as one between two partners equal in all aspects of the conflict: blame, guilt and justice. There was in reality no peace process. But, as Noam Chomsky rightly remarked, this jargon very conveniently allowed American involvement as coaches of the so-called 'process'. It also meant that there was no comprehensive attempt to solve the conflict, but that progress in negotiations, or even the negotiations themselves, became more important than results.

The Americans played a more neutral role in the case of the bilateral Israeli–Egyptian negotiations, realizing that even Nasser in his last days was willing to implement the Resolution 242 principle fully. But, like the Israelis, they were only fully convinced after two successive Egyptian presidents, Gamal Abd al-Nasser and Anwar Sadat, engaged Israel in two wars to regain the Sinai Peninsula. In March 1969 Nasser began a fruitless war of attrition over the Suez Canal, which lasted until August 1970. A peace initiative, proposed by William Rogers, failed to elicit an agreement to withdraw in return for peace from the intransigent Golda Meir, prime minister from 1969 to 1974. Sadat's surprise attack of October 1973, which had been prearranged with the Syrian president Hafiz al-Asad, succeeded in activating a peace dialogue, which led to a partial Israeli evacuation of the peninsula, to be completed when President Sadat made his historic trip to Jerusalem in November 1977, pledging a full diplomatic peace with Israel in return for a total Israeli withdrawal from Egyptian soil.

The 1973 joint Syrian–Egyptian attack caught Israeli intelligence unprepared, and the near defeat on the battlefield sent shock-waves through the political system as a whole, contributing to the demise of Labour as the leading political power in the state. Its arch-rival, the Likud leader Begin, had left the coalition government in 1969 in protest against Israeli agreement to enter negotiations. He would return to power in 1977, only to hand over the whole of the Sinai to the Egyptian president.

This third round of fighting, in 1973, between Israel and the Arab world did not affect, nor was it focused on, the Palestine question. It is one of the more curious twists in this narrative of conflict that the bloodiest of all the Arab–Israeli confrontations was fought over issues that did not concern most of the people living between the River Jordan and the Mediterranean. The only relevance of the war for these people was that it weakened the hegemony of the Israeli political elite, and shattered the illusion of unity of purpose within Israeli society. While it affected Palestinian society outside Israel, it was of no importance to those living in the occupied territories or in the refugee camps.

The 1973 war might have ended with an even more devastating Israeli defeat had it not been for Sadat and Asad's hesitancy, as military commanders, as to how to proceed after an unanticipated victory, and for an intensive American support operation for Israel, which tipped the military balance after the early days of the war. The two leaders had wanted a limited war, and achieved their major objective: the resumption of the peace process.

The Soviet Union backed Egypt until 1972, and would probably have been willing to continue, had Anwar Sadat not expelled Soviet military advisers from Egypt in July 1972. The Soviets, nonetheless, shipped significant supplies to Egypt, although not to the extent that the US assisted Israel.

THE QUESTION OF BORDERS: THE JORDANIAN OPTION
AND GREATER ISRAEL

The 1973 war was a traumatic event that promoted the disintegration of Israeli politics and culture. The myth of Israeli invincibility was shattered, and while some saw this as a good reason to become more insistent in the search for peace, others turned to God, toughening their positions on peace and territorial compromise. What added to the confusion and the erosion of self-confidence was the high number of deaths, about 3,000, compared with the few hundred in the 1967 war. A general sense of grief fell on the country and affected the government's prestige.[44]

The basic failure was believed to be the malfunction of the intelligence apparatus. The scope of the failure was revealed to the public in April 1974, with the publication of a report prepared by a committee chaired by the then president of the Supreme Court, Shimon Agranat. The report blamed the IDF and its chief for the intelligence failure, while exonerating political leaders from responsibility for the surprise attack on Israel. But it seems that quite a few members of the Jewish community in Israel reached a different verdict, and regarded both Prime Minister Golda Meir and her defence minister, Moshe Dayan, as the principal culprits. A protest movement, both popular and spontaneous, sprang up in the wake of Agranat's report. It consisted of several groups, which pressurized the Labour Party to remove Meir and Dayan from office, even after the party won the national 1974 election, the last one for many years.

A new Labour leader was now needed, and there was no better candidate than the 1948 hero, Yitzhak Rabin. Rabin was serving as ambassador to Washington, and was therefore not involved in the army's failure. Before becoming prime minister, he had to overcome, in the first ever democratic elections within the Labour Party, his arch-rival Shimon Peres. Until then, party leaders had been chosen by a selection committee, not elected by the ordinary members. The two met repeatedly as competitors for party leadership, dragging the Labour Party as a whole into instability with their petty personal rivalry. Rabin was the first Israeli-born prime minister, personifying the dream of the nationalist and militarist society that had been in the making since 1936.

Rabin was the leader of a movement whose power was waning. The pre-eminence of the party had already been eroded, and during his first year in office there was a breach in the alliance between his party and the religious national party, Mafdal. This alliance had been formed when, despite the protests of the redeemers and settlers, the veteran leader of Mafdal, Yosef Burg, led his party into Rabin's coalition.

The delivery of American F-15s to Israel created a coalition crisis when the gifts arrived on a Saturday, when, according to an agreement with the religious parties, all traffic was to cease. The crisis led to Mafdal's departure from the government and a call for new elections. One calamity followed another. Rabin was prevented from re-seeking his party's candidature after it was revealed that his wife held an illegal bank account in Washington. This petty offence was insignificant in comparison to an array of corrupt deeds committed by other Labour leaders, but nevertheless he had no choice but to resign.

During his three years in office he had been occupied mainly in diplomacy. The peace accord was underlined, as before the war, by a UN Security Council resolution, this time number 338. It was similar to Resolution 242, although indicating a concern (but no more) for the future of the Palestinian refugees. After 1975, with the legitimization of the PLO in the UN, the organization's Middle Eastern resolutions all focused on the refugee question and were much more pro-Palestinian. This was mainly the result of the increase in the number of Asian and African countries in the organization, although progress in this regard was hampered by repeated American vetoes in the Security Council.

William Rogers was replaced by Henry Kissinger as the prime mover behind the 'process'. A genuine pro-Zionist, he generally echoed the basic Israeli perceptions of Palestinian nationalism. In a crude manner this had been already expressed by Golda Meir, who had declared that there was no such thing as the Palestinian people, and that therefore there could only be one possible partner for negotiations over the occupied areas – the Hashemite kingdom of Jordan.

This was the 'Jordanian option' of the Labour Party, which was aimed at dividing the former Mandate between Israel and the Hashemites in Jordan, at the expense of the Palestinians. It underpinned both their tactics and their strategy *vis-à-vis* occupation and peace. In the past it had prompted Ben-Gurion to collude with King Abdullah in the 1948 war. This time, the Israelis offered the Jordanians a smaller portion, only part of the West Bank (between 10 and 15 per cent of Palestine).[45]

If the Jordanians and the Israelis differed it was on the role accorded the Palestinians. While the Labour vision was of a de-Palestinized Palestine, Hussein was more cognizant of the Palestinian identity of the West Bank. In 1972, he countered the Israeli plans with a scheme of his own, suggesting a federation between Palestine (i.e. the West Bank) and Jordan on a bi-national model. The Rabin government failed to show generosity even towards the Jordanians, and Henry Kissinger shuttled in vain between Amman and Tel-Aviv, trying to convince King Hussein to accept part of the West Bank in return for a bilateral peace. Hussein did not go to war in 1973, but neither did he make peace on the basis of the stringent Israeli offer (nor was the PLO ready to accept the Jordanian idea of a federation). He then sought to negotiate with the PLO as well as Israel for a future settlement in the West Bank, but failed on both counts. Kissinger introduced interim agreements for both the Sinai Peninsula and the Golan Heights, shrinking the Israeli empire slightly.

The decline in the fortunes of the 'Jordanian option' increased the popularity of the 'Greater Israel' option after 1977, an ideology that worsened life for many Palestinians, and destroyed the dreams of peace of many Israelis. Its end also affected the Palestinian community in Lebanon in 1982.

The intensive diplomatic whirl generated by Kissinger and others had hardly affected, or for that matter benefited, the society as a whole. While the American secretary of state was shuttling from one capital to the other, deeper forces were at work below the surface. Kissinger did not bring peace to Palestine and Israel, but the Israelis felt more 'secure', or became less concerned with 'security', which allowed social and economic problems, suppressed for years, to reappear and trouble the state and its institutions.

## THE MIZRAHI REVOLUTION

The most significant of these internal problems was the growing tension between Mizrahi Jews, especially those from North Africa, and the political establishment of the Labour Party. The relative prosperity of the Jewish community as a whole after the 1967 war reinforced the sense of stagnation and neglect among the Mizrahi Jews. The leaders of the local economy lauded the recovery of Israel from its pre-1967 recession, but there were few signs of this prosperity in the slums of Jerusalem and Tel-Aviv, mostly inhabited by Moroccan Jews. Nor was it apparent among the Mizrahi communities in the small towns encircling Tel-Aviv, such as the once prosperous Palestinian towns of Lydda and Ramleh. Nor did the thriving economy benefit Jews from Iraq, Kurdistan, Buhkara, Yemen and Tunisia, who had settled as farmers in agricultural communities (*moshavim*) near tense borders and away from city centres. Prosperity was also absent from the dozen or so new and ugly development towns erected for the Arab Jews everywhere in the country. The economy of these towns was tied closely to one or, at best two, factories, usually producing textiles or food, and totally dependent on the local and global fortunes of these traditional industries. In the post-1960s industrial world, there was little hope for communities reliant entirely on such factories. At the end of the 1980s, their owners, both the Histadrut and private industrialists, sold these assets for a good profit, which was not shared with their loyal workers, who by that time found themselves unemployed in numbers equalled only among the Palestinians in Israel.

In the years just after the 1973 war, unemployment was less of a problem than was the visible lack of proper human, social and educational infrastructure in the deprived areas. The sense of discrimination was reinforced by the realization of many young people that they would be stuck on the same unskilled, underpaid and low-status rungs of the socio-economic ladder as their parents. This socio-economic marginalization was echoed in the patronizing cultural attitude adopted towards anything Mizrahi (apart from food), resulting in an underground music movement, first in the form of illegal radio cassettes with Mizrahi, Arabic and Mediterranean music, which later became a powerful tool for social protest and a vehicle for the careers of Mizrahi pop stars. Strangely, it was a Greek singer by the stage name of Aris Sun, who had opened a nightclub in Jaffa in October 1967, who pioneered the introduction of Mediterranean and then Arab music into the local pop culture.

Music not only symbolized an attempt to construct a particularistic ethnic identity; it also satisfied the craving of a new generation of Jewish youth for a more global popular culture. After the 1967 war, the government had used the police to combat the mushrooming of discotheques and nightclubs in Tel-Aviv, and the national theatre was alarmed by the rebellion of playwrights such as Hanoch Levin against 'recruited culture'. Tel-Aviv as a geo-cultural centre proved more resistant than other parts to the national engineering of culture from above. Its Palestinian parallel, by the way, would prove to be Ramallah, with its islands of universal and popular culture. Both became havens of more universal values, styles and tastes, although they isolated themselves from the rest of the Jewish and Palestinian societies in the process.

The further marginalization of the Mizrahim eventually produced more than a clandestine cassette market. Their exclusion from the prosperity enjoyed by the Ashkenazim and a growing awareness of similar protest movements abroad generated a new, more focused discontent. It began with a movement called the 'Black Panthers', modelled on the African American organization. This was the most radical manifestation of Mizrahi frustration, particularly among Moroccan Jews. The movement sprang up in the slums of Jerusalem and Tel-Aviv, but had little popularity in the development towns, where Moroccan Jews lived in similarly poor conditions. The Labour government under Golda Meir responded with indifference. When told that Black Panther activists were refusing to leave her private lawns on which they were demonstrating, she uttered a sentence that became part of the Israeli political lexicon and political satire: 'Hem Yeladim lo nehmadim' (They are not nice children). Not content with words, her government always arrested activists the night before a planned demonstration, on the grounds that 'these are criminals who will not be able to demonstrate in a civil way'.[46]

The militarization of Israeli society continued vigorously after the 1967 war, and with it indifference towards social and economic deprivation. Service in the army became the principal criterion for patriotism. Rabin's election as prime minister reinforced this mood. In 1974, his government introduced severe sanctions against Israelis living abroad and refusing to return annually for reserve duty in the IDF.

In the development towns, young politicians who had become disillusioned with the Labour Party were attracted by Menachem Begin and his new party, Likud, formed with the help of Ariel Sharon. This right-wing party showed no desire to act on poverty or social discrimination, and its Greater Israel ideology interested very few in the troubled areas of Israel. Its sole attraction was that it was anti-Labour. This lured enough Mizrahi Jews, frustrated by years of discrimination and impoverishment, to bring Begin to power in 1977.

THE BEGIN REVOLUTION

Menachem Begin's journey to power had been long. He had had to break through the dominance of the Labour movement in every sphere of Israeli life, a dominance dating from the very early stages of the Zionist project in Palestine. Before the 1967 war, neither he nor his colleagues who advocated the establishment of a Jewish Zionist state in all of mandatory Palestine were considered legitimate political partners. The 1967 war won Begin his first ministerial portfolio and, although he resigned in 1970, he remained popular and did not lose sight of opportunities. At first he formed Gahal, a bloc between his own party Herut (the right-wing revisionists and the Irgun of the Mandate era) and the Liberal Party. He took on two generals to compensate for his own lack of military background: Ezer Weizmann, a legendary air force commander and the nephew of the first Israeli president, Haim Weizmann; and Ariel Sharon. In the 1970s they formed Likud ('cohesion' in Hebrew).

A coalition of dissatisfied Israelis brought Begin to power: Mizrahi Jews suffering from years of discrimination, religious Jews feeling marginalized in the Jewish state, Labourites shocked by the 1973 Arab surprise attack, and expansionist Jews (both secular and religious) hoping Begin would impose Israeli rule over the occupied territories. The Mizrahi Jews brought Begin to power, but the disappointed Ashkenazi Jews toppled Labour. They did

Figure 6. Demonstration of the Black Panthers in Jerusalem, 1972

not vote for Begin, but did not support Labour. Many abstained or voted for a different party. They even formed their own party, the Democratic Movement for Change headed by the 1948 war hero, Yigal Yadin.

Not surprisingly, once in government Likud had little to offer those who had brought it to power. Social and economic policies were the portfolio of the Liberal Party, whose leaders made it a priority to eliminate Labour's meagre socialist legacy. It seems with hindsight that Labour policies were a far cry from a conventional socialist or social democratic policy, despite the Labour Party's decision in January 1968 to adopt the *Internationale* along with the national anthem, *Hatikvah*.[47] In any case, the Liberal ministers in Begin's first (1977–81) and second (1981–4) governments adopted a free-market policy. Their economic guru was Milton Friedman. Under his influence, as happened in several Third World countries, the Israeli economy was torn by hyperinflation and an unbridgeable gap between rich and poor, before being restored to a softer version of an open-market economy by a Labour–Likud coalition government. This was established in 1984, and ended a seven-year term by Likud alone.

Likud's initial foreign-policy gambit surprised the world at large, as it responded favourably to another peace effort by Anwar Sadat. Begin's first Likud government included some veterans from the old administration, such as Moshe Dayan. He and Ezer Weizmann, now a dove, pushed Begin into signing a bilateral peace agreement with Egypt in 1979. This agreement had won the support of the Israeli public after a dramatic surprise visit by Anwar Sadat to Israel in November 1977, a psychological ploy that weakened their siege mentality and intransigence. Sadat came to Jerusalem, disappointed with previous international efforts to solve the conflict, such as an attempt to convene an international peace conference, which had ended in failure. Incidentally, this last peace initiative could have helped the PLO, as the Soviet Union had insisted that its status, the problem of refugees and the occupied parts of Palestine, were to be central aspects of the negotiations. Jimmy Carter, the first American president to locate the Palestine question at the centre of the 'peace process', had fully endorsed this prioritization. It was forestalled by the Sadat initiative, which had been prearranged by senior Israeli and Egyptian politicians long before Sadat's historic visit. The Egyptian president knew he would receive the whole of the Sinai Peninsula in return for normalization of his country's relations with Israel.

Politicians who had previously vowed never to concede an inch of the Sinai now became enthusiastic supporters of the 'peace camp'. An extra-parliamentary movement called Peace Now, consisting of veteran soldiers serving in combat units, produced a public atmosphere supportive of Begin in his negotiations with Sadat. While not always smooth, the negotiations ended with a formal peace treaty and the normalization of diplomatic relations between the two countries. The reservist officers of Peace Now had implied that they would not participate in an unwarranted war in the future. This was an unfulfilled threat, as many of them did not hesitate to join the 1982 invasion of Lebanon.[48]

It was two years before the peace treaty was finalized on the White House lawn, imprinted on the public mind with the famous photograph of the intertwined handshake of Carter, Sadat and Begin. Israeli television broadcast live every aspect of the negotiations, from Sadat's appearance on the steps of his aircraft in Jerusalem in November 1977, until the ceremony in which the two leaders received the Nobel peace prize at the end of 1978. The blanket media coverage had a great effect on public opinion and helped Begin overcome hardliners, such as his future successor Yitzhak Shamir. Such a public relations blitz was needed because the treaty involved the withdrawal from and destruction of several Jewish settlements in the Sinai, including two thriving towns, Ofira and Yamit. However, the previous siege mentality and psychology of isolation quickly disappeared. Israeli tourists swarmed to Egypt, eager to enjoy again the experience of visiting a neighbouring country by bus and in peace.

Much of this euphoria subsided. The Egyptian president had promised the Palestinians that he would link the bilateral agreement to a settlement of the Palestine question, but never succeeded in doing so. Likud returned the Sinai so that the West Bank and the Gaza Strip would be sidelined in the peace agenda. Both sides concurred on a new term, 'autonomy', as a strategic goal for settling the problem of the occupied territories, which in essence meant the status quo in those areas. For Egyptian civil society, left and right, secularists and Islamists alike, it was tantamount to betraying the Palestinian cause. They had the power to turn the peace with Israel into a 'cold' state of affairs, where much of the past hostility and enmity remained intact.

Israel's relations with Egypt were never truly normalized. The number of Israeli tourists declined, and hardly any Egyptians visited Israel. Nonetheless, the cycle of war was over, considerably undermining any pan-Arab military option against the Jewish state. The business communities on both sides gradually strengthened their ties, a trend that has continued.[49]

The 'autonomy' concept enabled Begin on his return to power in 1981 for a second term to solidify the Jewish settlement movement in the occupied territories. It was Ariel Sharon, first as housing minister and then defence minister, who masterminded the scheme. The only disappointment for the advocates of Greater Eretz Israel was that Sharon wished to Judaize the areas rather than annex them. This pragmatism enabled Likud and Labour finally to end a long public debate about the occupied territories. When both lost interest in social and economic affairs they were able to form two coalition governments, between 1984 and 1988. The bad blood between them, the manipulation of Mizrahi hostility towards Labour by Likud, and a conventional political struggle for power prolonged an internal Israeli affair. Palestinian political life continued with increasing indifference to Israeli politics. As far as most Palestinians were concerned, little changed, whoever was in power.

### NAVIGATING BETWEEN AGENDAS: THE POLITICS OF PALESTINE (1967–1987)

Palestinian politicians, both inside and outside Palestine, lacked the power to determine the occupied areas' future, let alone that of the rest of Palestine or to decide the fate of the refugees. They were successful in other things however. For instance, the political activists in the occupied areas developed their own political agenda. They saw the areas as occupied Palestine, or what was left of Palestine. Second, their priority was to end the occupation. Towards this they demanded a total Israeli withdrawal, the dismantling of Jewish settlements, and the establishment of independent Palestinian rule.

The few politicians who remained faithful to the Hashemites in Jordan slowly lost their power and disappeared altogether from the political map. The pro-PLO leadership that replaced them was tolerated by the Labour government, but when Likud came to power in 1977 it designated the PLO as a subversive element.

The situation of Palestinians in the occupied territories worsened under Sharon's term as defence minister, during which the weight of occupation was felt more heavily than ever. The local political bodies did not wait for a PLO response. In 1981, they created their own infrastructure to face the new conditions, headed by a new institution, Lajnat al-Tawjih (Committee of Guidance). The establishment of a national leadership was a *casus belli* for Sharon. He responded by arresting many of its members, and eventually combined his struggle against them with an overall plan to destroy the PLO in Lebanon. He also tried to arrange, with the help of a reputable Israeli Orientalist, Menachem Milson, a puppet leadership, called the Village Leagues, which however disappeared as suddenly as they had appeared.

Among the various political bodies facing the brutality of the occupation during Sharon's era was the Palestinian Communist Party, which called for the partitioning of Palestine with the Jewish state, although for most Palestinian politicians this notion was still a heresy (the Palestinian charter vehemently rejects the idea). Far more important in my eyes, however, the Communist Party stressed the need to build a civil society inside the occupied territories. Similar positions were taken by the Popular Democratic Front for the Liberation of Palestine, which was the first body within the PLO to suggest the two-state solution as a new strategy (it dropped 'Popular' from its name shortly after the split with the Palestine Front for the Liberation of Palestine in 1969).[50] This proved impossible in the Sharon era, but after his fall from grace in the wake of the 1982 Lebanon war the communist agenda of recognizing the possibility of dividing Palestine into two states and of building up civil institutions despite the occupation began to gain currency in the occupied territories.

The PLO moved closer to this agenda in 1974, when Fatah published its 'Programme of Stages'. This was a policy document stating that the liberation of the occupied territories had priority over the dream of redeeming Palestine as a whole. It did not specify a timetable for the latter, or indeed say whether it was a firm objective, but it was a pragmatic shift that affected the PLO as a whole and led to a gradual abandonment of the armed struggle in favour of diplomacy. This had also been facilitated by the Arab summit decision to recognize the PLO as 'the sole and legitimate representative of the Palestinian people'. This dictum was adopted later by the UN in 1975, by the European Community in 1981, and *de facto* by the USA in 1988 and Israel in 1993.

The move to pragmatism was feasible only for Fatah, which, unlike the PFLP and PDFLP, had distanced itself from revolutionary discourse or practice. It avoided intervention in the politics of Arab states, limited its domestic indoctrination policy to national goals of liberation, and was willing to change tactics and strategy. Indeed, the two other organizations rejected Fatah's decision to limit the goal of the liberation movement to the establishment of an independent state in the West Bank and the Gaza Strip. Fatah was in control, however, and through its leadership a web of contacts was woven between the PLO in Lebanon and the Committee of Guidance in the occupied territories. The other factions strengthened their ties with the occupied areas, establishing shadow offices matching those in Beirut in the major Palestinian towns. Although Lebanon was the hub of Palestinian politics, the Palestinian national movement was a transnational body, acting according to pressures from more than one place.[51]

Thus, in just over a decade (1970–81), the politics of nationalism in the diaspora had recombined with those in the occupied territories. During that decade, the PLO established itself in Lebanon after most of its offices and fighters were moved there. It was located in two areas. The political leadership bought houses in Beirut, the site of the organization's established departments and of its new ones, such as an archive, publication house and international departments. The other location was in southern Lebanon, in the tough terrain around the Palestinian refugee camps. The military operations against Israel were conducted from the al-Arqub area in south-eastern Lebanon, where Fatah guerrillas had carved out for themselves an autonomous territory in the 1960s.

The differential structure of left and right within the PLO was fragmented further during its time in Lebanon by the deeper involvement of the Arab states in the movement. As before, the balance of power between the various groups within the PLO was determined by the ability to show boldness and inventiveness in the fight against Israel. Southern Lebanon became a launching pad for attacks on Israel, some carried out by Katyusha missiles on Jewish settlements, others through the taking of hostages to obtain the release of Palestinians already imprisoned in Israel. Many of these actions failed, although they succeeded in terrorizing the population of northern Israel and engendered insecurity, which led the various Israeli governments to launch large-scale retaliations.

In some cases, the Israeli victims of Palestinian guerrilla warfare were children, as in the case of the Ma'alot operation in 1972, when the high school of this northern Israeli development town was attacked by the PDFLP. Most of the children killed in the attack died when special Israeli units tried to storm the school, a cycle of violence that repeated itself in other operations where the Israelis refused to negotiate. Also in 1972, eleven Israeli athletes were murdered by the Fatah group Black September after being taken hostage at the Olympic Games in Munich in an operation that ended in bloodshed during a clumsy German rescue attempt. Most Black September members were later assassinated by the Israeli Mossad, which conducted a war of revenge against those involved in the Munich massacre. The guerrilla warfare also continued along familiar lines, with the planting of bombs in Israel, the hijacking of aeroplanes, and attacks on military installations. Southern Lebanon became a battlefield, depopulated in some parts at least during periods of unrest.

This activity required a sizeable arsenal. The USSR became the PLO's main arms supplier, but training was offered by more than one source. Several leading revolutionary regimes assisted the movement: China, North Korea, Algeria and Cuba. The PLO was also entangled in an international web encompassing anarchist, terrorist, guerrilla and liberation movements all around the world, including the IRA, the Red Brigades in Italy, the Baader-Meinhof gang in Germany, the Red Army from Japan, and the Viet Cong. Some of these movements sent their people to train in the PLO's enclave in southern Lebanon.

In the midst of this, Fatah formulated its most pragmatic policy yet, encapsulated in the Programme of Stages. This was an interesting, and for a while successful, mixture of guerrilla warfare and diplomatic initiatives. However, while Arafat was received as a head of state in many Arab capitals, he could not be recognized as such by anyone outside the Middle East, not even by his most ardent supporter, the Soviet Union. Nor was his legitimacy secure in the Arab world. His arch-rival was President Asad of Syria, who monitored Palestinian political life more closely than any other Arab leader and demanded unconditional loyalty to his policies. Fatah resisted, and an unbridgeable abyss opened between Damascus and the PLO.

In many ways, Arafat was his own worst enemy. His greatest failure was his inability to keep the PLO out of the Lebanese civil war, which erupted in 1975. An exaggerated sense of self-esteem and a false appreciation of his importance and that of his organization within Lebanon led him to try to play a leading role there. Against the advice of some of his closest associates, he involved the PLO in the Muslim–Christian strife, openly taking the Muslim side. In 1970, the Lebanese government had not wanted the PLO on its soil, but had been too weak to reject Egyptian and Jordanian pressure, but resented the interference in its internal affairs. The PLO could have remained neutral, but felt that its position in Lebanon depended on a Muslim victory.[52]

The fluctuating fortunes of the war and the opportunistic policies of Syria, whose army invaded Lebanon in 1976, exposed the refugee community there to repeated attacks by anyone who felt the PLO was serving the 'enemy'. The Syrians slaughtered Palestinians in Tel-Zaatar in 1976, when they were allied to the Christians, and later, when they decided to back the Muslims, they encouraged a faction of the PLO headed by a colonel, Abu Musa, to attempt to depose Arafat.

When the Muslims fared better, as a result of a shift in Syrian policy, the PLO improved its position in the country, enabling it to focus once more on the armed struggle against Israel. A series of bold and imaginative operations was carried out, the most famous being an attack on a vital junction on the Haifa–Tel-Aviv highway in 1978. More than twenty Israeli civilians died, and the Israeli government retaliated by occupying southern Lebanon. The Israeli intimidation of the population there prompted the Shiites to move to Beirut. This event led to both the Islamization of Lebanon and the militarization of the struggle against the Israeli occupation.

In 1982, the state of Israel, the Shiites of Lebanon, the PLO, the Christian Phalangists and the Syrians all found themselves involved in a war that, while limited in conventional terms, would have a far-reaching impact on Israel and Palestine, politically and socially.

## THE WAR IN LEBANON AND ITS AFTERMATH (1982–1987)

Several of the processes described so far converged in the Lebanon war of June 1982. The first was the rise in Palestinian consciousness in the occupied territories. The second was the increase in Palestinian resistance operations from southern Lebanon. The third was the desire of the Likud government to eliminate the Palestinian question altogether by force. The first two led Sharon to push Begin to invade Lebanon.

Sharon was assisted by a nationalist chief of the general staff, Refael Eytan, and together they promoted an aggressive Israeli policy in southern Lebanon. Their actions strained even further the tensions in the triangular situation that had developed there over previous years. The three players were the Syrian forces in the Baqa Valley, the PLO units relocated from the Mediterranean coast to Jabal al-Shaykh (the Hermon mountains near the Syrian–Lebanese border), and the Israeli army in the south, aided by its own Maronite militia called the South Lebanon Army.

After particularly heated clashes in 1981, both the PLO and Syria tried to reach a *modus vivendi* with the Israelis, assisted by Philip Habib, a special envoy sent by the Americans. An unwritten cease-fire was concluded at the end of the year but was abandoned when, in June 1982, the renegade from the PLO, Abu Nidal, sent assassins to kill the Israeli ambassador in London, Shlomo Argov (he was only badly wounded). This gave Sharon and Eytan an excuse to commence a war against the PLO in an operation euphemistically called 'Peace for the Galilee'. Sharon misled his prime minister into believing that the operation would be limited to the occupation of more of southern Lebanon. From the start he had intended to occupy Beirut, chase out the Syrians, install a Maronite pro-Israeli government in Lebanon and destroy the PLO.

In the event, Lebanon was destroyed in carpet bombing from the air and shelling from the ground. Other results of this invasion were the evacuation of the PLO headquarters to Tunis in September 1982, tighter Syrian control over the country, and the appearance on Lebanon's political scene of the Hezbollah, a new radical political Islamist Shiite movement backed by the Humayni regime in Iran.

Israel, in addition, found its Vietnam. It had, for the first time in its history, initiated a war that was controversial among its citizens. Such wars inevitably produce protest movements, and the one that emerged after the Lebanon war focused less on the misery of Lebanon than on the growing number of Israeli casualties, both in the war and in subsequent combat with the local resistance movement led by the Hezbollah. Each day a group holding a vigil outside Begin's official residence in Jerusalem announced the number of soldiers killed.

Begin's previous ploys, such as fomenting Ashkenazi–Mizrahi tensions, which had worked well in the 1981 elections, did not save him now; they also resulted in a rare political assassination. A disgruntled Moroccan Jew from Jerusalem's poor neighbourhoods joined a group of extreme right-wing Israelis connected to the American Jewish rabbi Meir Kahana, and threw a hand-grenade into a crowded Peace Now demonstration, killing one person and wounding several others.

That the war did not prove a landmark in the perceptions and attitudes of political leaders in Israel towards the Palestine question can be explained by the introverted nature of the Israeli protest movement. Like the custodians in the case of the West Bank and the Gaza Strip, those joining the political stage were only concerned with their self-image and the number of Israeli deaths in the war – 'the occupation corrupt' as Amos Oz, a young kibbutz teacher, wrote in 1967 – and failed to mention that war also oppresses and destroys.

Had they looked beyond their own concerns they would have realized how callous yet another Israeli attack on Palestinian refugees was. As in the 1948 and 1967 wars, refugees in the Lebanon war again became the principal victims of the Israeli drive for territory, security and dominance. Their suffering had begun even before the invasion. They had been uprooted several times from 1976 during the civil war and the early Israeli invasions. By 1979, 1.8 million refugees were registered in Lebanon. At the height of the 1982 Israeli invasion of Lebanon, the number was well beyond 2 million. As several researchers visiting the camps in those days remarked, refugees had developed a survival routine, however poor and unsatisfying. This 'normal life' was disrupted first for those in Beirut affected by the Lebanese civil war, then for those in the southern refugee camps during the Israeli invasion of 1978, and for the rest after the Lebanon war.[53] After 1982, the Palestinian refugees in Lebanon were, and still are, ghetto-ized in eleven camps run by UNRWA, and since the PLO's departure from the camps have suffered from malnutrition, high levels of unemployment and the absence of a decent sanitary and medical infrastructure.

The low point of the invasion was the massacre in September 1982, by Christian Phalangists, of the inhabitants of two refugee camps, Sabra and Shatilla, in southern Beirut. Hundreds of Palestinians, men, women and children, were slaughtered by a Maronite militia, encouraged and incited by Israeli military officers of the highest rank. The connection with the IDF was clear enough to convince 400,000 Israelis to protest against the massacre, and led to the establishment of a commission of inquiry headed by a former Supreme Court judge. This commission dismissed several senior officers involved and ruled that Sharon, the minister of defence, was unfit to serve in such a high position. He became Israel's prime minister in February 2001.

Yasser Arafat was now removed from Palestine and in a serious rift with the other PLO groups. The latter chose Damascus as their base, and formed the 'rejectionist front', opposing Arafat's policy of seeking a diplomatic solution to the question and his later shift towards the United States as the peace broker in the Arab–Israeli conflict.

Arafat's isolation increased when two colleagues who had run Fatah and the PLO most efficiently and charismatically were killed in the late 1980s. Abu Jihad (Khalil al-Wazir) was murdered by the Israelis in his home in Hamamat, near Tunis. Abu Iyad (Salah Khalaf) was assassinated in the same area by Abu Nidal's organization. The latter was an obscure group which had declared allegiance to radical and extremist Arab regimes, such as Saddam Husayn's Iraq and Mu'amar Qadafi's Libya, but was apparently also in the service of other states and secret services around the Middle East.[54]

Arafat was now paying the price for chronic problems within the PLO that had begun at the movement's inception. It housed a proliferation of small groups, all clients of one Arab country or another. Before the Lebanon war, this fragmentation had been disguised. However, once in Tunis, the PLO was more restricted in its ability to formulate a consensual policy, and spent more time dealing with internal rifts.

In the years after the Israeli invasion of Lebanon, therefore, the Palestinian political hub moved even further away from Palestine itself, and was even less able to attract the attention or interest of the Jewish body politic in Israel. Among the Jews in Israel, nonetheless, the internal debate, ever inward-looking, intensified after the war. At the centre of this debate stood two extra-parliamentary movements, Peace Now and Gush Emunim. Their revitalization in the 1980s was part of a more general polarization of hegemonic politics in the Jewish state.

### BREACHES IN THE WALL: THE POLARIZATION
### OF ISRAELI SOCIETY

The Peace Now–Gush Emunim debate about the future of the occupied territories, the former wishing to leave them but the latter to retain them, should be put into a historical perspective. Peace Now was the close successor of the Zionist pragmatism preached by Moshe Sharett in the 1950s, but it had little in common with Brit Shalom, which had advocated a binational state during the Mandate. Peace Now was firmly within the Zionist consensus, and provided no alternative paradigm or discourse. In the 1990s, a new group of 'pragmatic doves' formed their own party, Meretz, which was to the left of the Labour Party. *Meretz* means 'stamina' in Hebrew, but it was also an acronym of the names of the three minor parties from which it was formed: Shulamit Aloni's civil rights movement, a hard-core liberal party called Shinui ('change'), and the socialist party Mapam.

Pragmatism in this case meant a typical Israeli worship of security and deterrence, not a value judgement on peace as a preferred concept, or sympathy with the predicament of the other side in the conflict, or recognition of one's own role in the making of the predicament. These were 'security doves' who, during the Oslo process (1993–99) included people from the centre and right wings of the Labour Party, the left wing of Likud, and a number of small centre parties built around charismatic ex-generals who generally disappeared after one election campaign. This military connection explains why Peace Now found it hard to oppose the invasion of Lebanon in 1982. The movement had initially supported the invasion, but by the time it began to have doubts most of its reservist officers were already involved in the fighting. To the left of Peace Now, a new movement, Yesh Gvul ('there is a limit'), openly preached conscientious objection, a call later extended to soldiers serving in the West Bank and the Gaza Strip. Although quite a significant voice in the public debate over the Lebanon war and the continued Israeli presence in southern Lebanon, it was less impressive as an influence on the occupied territories' future.

In local Israeli jargon and in the political discourse employed by the media and academia, the 'peace camp' in Israel is the 'left'. Elsewhere in the world this would necessarily mean a social democratic or socialist platform, or at least an accentuated concern for socially and economically deprived groups within a given society. The peace camp in Israel has focused entirely on the diplomatic manoeuvres since the 1973 war, a game of little relevance for a growing number of groups in post-1973 Israeli society. The failure of this 'left' to identify with the problems of these groups has alienated them and led some of these groups to move to the 'right', that is, the 'anti-peace' camp. In general there were two particular groups that moved in this direction: the Mizrahi Jews and the ultra-orthodox Jews. Although the peace camp had contact with the Palestinian minority in Israel, which fully supported any Israeli effort to compromise, Palestinian hopes for positive, practical results of this contact were disappointed.

The 'right' in Israel evolved around the settlers' movement in the occupied territories. It contained both soft- and hardliners. Although not giving up the idea of Greater Israel, the softer pole made strenuous efforts towards institutionalizing itself within the body politic. Yitzhak Shamir, who succeeded Begin as prime minister after the latter's withdrawal from politics in 1983, was very close to Gush Emunim's goals. On the 'hard' line stood Meir Kahana and his supporters. This American Jew concentrated on recruiting Mizrahi Jews in deprived areas as grassroots supporters for himself and his henchmen, mostly fanatical immigrants from the USA and the USSR, to a movement called Kach ('so be it'). They were numerous enough to win Kahana a seat in the Knesset in the 1984 elections, but alarming enough in their Nazi-like ideology to be banned from the next election in 1988.[55]

'Right' and 'left' were categories too vague to cater for particular cultural groups in the emerging multicultural fabric of 1980s Israeli society. The Black Panthers movement disintegrated, but three new Mizrahi-based movements appeared. Ohalim ('tents'), a group of activists in slums and poor neighbourhoods, argued that deprivation was partly a result of excessive investment in Jewish settlements in the occupied territories. A second group, Tenuat Mizrahim Israelis (TAMI), a Mizrahi movement, was started by a prominent family from Morocco, but was short-lived. The third, and most successful, group based on the politics of identity was Shas, an ultra-orthodox Mizrahi movement, which began in 1984 as part of a revolt by Mizrahi Jews against the Ashkenazi-dominated ultra-orthodox side, and became the most popular social and political Mizrahi movement in the history of Israel. It was, and still is at the time of writing, led by the charismatic rabbi Ovadia Yossef, a former chief rabbi of Israel. Since 1988, Shas has held the balance of power after every election in Israel, and therefore has been part of every government. Other parties representing the politics of identity emerged. Some old ones, like those of the Ashkenazi ultra-orthodox, also gained some power within Israel's coalition politics.

Three old campaigners dominated politics after the Lebanon invasion: Yitzhak Shamir, leading Likud; Shimon Peres, sharing power with Shamir in several coalition governments between 1984 and 1988; and Yitzhak Rabin, Peres' second-in-command and arch-rival in the Labour Party. This trio's inability to agree on essential questions of policy is one of the main reasons for the very slow and unproductive pace of the diplomatic effort in the Middle East after the Lebanon war. Their era was marked by the exclusion from the political agenda of any issue not connected to the question of borders. They appeased the various groups on the 'right', refusing any territorial compromise or inclusion of the 'peace camp', which was willing to go back to the June 1967 borders.

While the politicians found common ground, their supporters continued the struggle over public opinion. Both blocs took to the streets for mass demonstrations whenever they wished to react to a political event. However, the right wing had its own militia, the settlers, which gave it added power to terrorize the peace activists. This militia also deterred Israeli governments from taking a bold decision on dismantling the settlements. Such a decision might have caused a civil war. The possession of weapons made politics dangerous; the arming of civil society had begun in earnest immediately after the 1967 war. In the autumn of that year, the Israeli Interior Ministry reported that it could not cope with the demand for firearm licences.[56]

The right and left camps polarized Israeli society to the point of paralysis in a way reminiscent of the Italian political system, where it is impossible for one side to win an election decisively, but each is strong enough to deny the other victory. What could have tipped the balance in the peace camp's favour was a political alliance with the Palestinian minority in Israel.

## PALESTINIANS IN ISRAEL (1967–1987)

The Palestinians in Israel went through significant transformations in the 1970s. The reunion under abnormal conditions with the Palestinians in the West Bank and the Gaza Strip highlighted their unity of purpose, but it also exposed the conflicting agendas on both sides of the green line. The political movement in the West Bank and the Gaza Strip focused on liberation from Israeli occupation. The Palestinians in Israel, while supporting this cause, stressed as their priority the struggle for equality within the Jewish state.

The most pressing issue after 1967 was land. After the Six Day War, the Israeli governments of Eshkol, Meir and Rabin had given energetic Judaizing officials a free hand to wage another campaign of land expropriation in Galilee. *Yehud hagalil* ('Judaizing the Galilee') was a clandestine programme until 1976, when it became an open slogan of the Housing Ministry. In 1975, Israel Koning, the head of the interior ministry's Galilee division, systemized this wave of Judaization. In a report to Prime Minister Rabin (leaked a year later to the press), he defined the Arabs of Israel as 'a cancer in the Jewish body that had to be curbed and contained' by increasing the number of Jews in Galilee.

The report was soon translated into a brutal policy of land confiscation.[57] Jews were asked to settle in Galilee in every possible way: new towns, new kibbutzim, new community centres. For this purpose, the emergency regulations from the British Mandate were used again to expropriate land without compensation or the right of protest. The land was used for new Jewish towns (no new Arab town has ever been built in Israel) and community centres in order to attract upwardly mobile people from Tel-Aviv. Land was also expropriated for the Israeli army, which seemed to be in constant need of more training grounds.

Palestinian members of the Communist Party decided, after years of internationalizing their politics, to formulate a particular national agenda. They, with others, established the committee for the defence of the land. The charismatic Communist leader, Tawfiq Zayad, a national poet as well as a politician, took advantage of this new initiative to win the local election in Nazareth, the only Palestinian town in Israel. The Communist Party, now expanded to incorporate non-communist Palestinian and non-Zionist Jewish bodies, declared itself the new Democratic Front for Peace and Equality (Jabha in Arabic). This transformation enabled the party to enlarge its membership and become more active within Palestinian national politics in Israel, probably at the expense of traditional communist goals such as activity among the more deprived socio-economic layers of society. In Israel, ethnic origin corresponded so closely to socio-economic position that Jews who advocated social equality and economic justice were doing so mainly for the sake of the Palestinians in Israel. At the time the Front was formed, and for long afterwards, the poorest Jewish town, Yeruham, still had a much higher standard of living, by any known criteria, than Me'ilya, the richest Arab community in Israel.

Jabha channelled the dismay and wrath felt by thousands of Galileans whose land and houses had been taken from them by force. The emotion erupted on the last day of March 1976, in a protest remembered ever since as the 'Day of the Land'. Six Palestinians lost their lives in clashes with trigger-happy Israeli police. The sight of the state's security forces killing it own citizens was one even the more hawkish Israeli politicians did not wish to see. The incident led to a brief *rapprochement*, and a halt to the land confiscation. Galilee was not Judaized; but Arab–Jewish tension remained.

There could be no real reconciliation while the economic gap between the two communities, the limited options for social mobilization in the Palestinian minority, and above all the growing sense of alienation from the state continued. The state excluded them as full citizens, occupied their nation-state, and refused to recognize the Nakbah and its own share in it. For example, official Israeli statistics showed that only 1 per cent of Palestinians in Israel were enrolled in the official education system beyond the age of sixteen, and only 4 per cent between the ages of thirteen and fifteen.[58] The low percentage of Palestinian acceptance at Israeli universities did not meet their drive for higher education; hence many young people found their way to Europe, and those connected to the Communist Party to Eastern Europe, in pursuit of academic careers.

The Lebanon war produced new dilemmas in the relationship between Palestinians and Jews in Israel itself. As the late poet and novelist Emil Habibi put it, 'My country was at war with my people'. Perhaps surprisingly, identification with the PLO in a war that the Israelis claimed was meant to protect the people of Galilee (mostly Palestinians who did not wish for such protection) did not change the approach of the Palestinian minority in Israel, which was centred on democratic action and generated a process of democratization that matured after the 1982 war.[59] The community leaders and intellectuals became more aware of their community's unique position as a group that had been subjected to an external system in their own country. As such they were not like immigrants who willingly accepted the code of a host country, nor were they individuals torn from their families; they were an indigenous community, and yet were excluded from nationhood in their own homeland.

Palestinians in Israel and in the occupied territories, although struggling for what at least until the 1990s seemed like different agendas, were carrying out their collective political struggle in similar ways. Intellectuals, students and workers, and women (highly visible on the ground, though not in the leadership) were the main agencies to continue the struggle. Similarly, political identity and the land question were the two main issues at the heart of political life both in the occupied territories and in Israel itself. The difference in the nature of Israeli control over the life of Palestinians in the two localities determined the particular experience of each community, as either second-class citizens of the state of Israel or inhabitants of occupied territories ruled by a military regime.

Citizenship allowed more freedom to express political goals, whereas occupation necessitated a more subtle and convoluted approach through political poetry, the attribution of heroism to remaining in Palestine and not emigrating, and through a strong belief that powers such as the PLO, the Arab world and the international community would rescue the occupied society. When these methods proved futile, large sections of the younger generation opted for open resistance, leading their society to the uprising of 1987.

The social and political intricacy can be partly explained by the relationship between the Palestinians in Israel and other groups in the society. The Palestinians were part of the emerging multicultural politics of Israel, in which the politics of identity fragmented the political scene into parties representing particularistic ethnic, religious and cultural agendas. Each in its own way conveyed a sense of being victimized by the state in the past or in the present. They did not form alliances, however. Even the political co-operation between the 'peace camp' and the Palestinian minority was limited. By the 1980s, with the emergence of national Palestinian parties in Israel, first led by Muhammad Mi'ari and Abd al-Wahab al-Darawshe, and then much more successfully and impressively by Azmi Beshara, the issue of peace was closely associated with the future of the Palestinian minority in Israel. This was too much for the Zionist left to accept, as it opened up the whole question of Israel's identity, democratic conduct, and its future between Europe and the Middle East.

For an alliance to work, either the left had to abandon Zionism or the Palestinian minority ignore its national affiliation. In relative terms, it was to be a pact between what I have elsewhere called 'post-Zionists,' Jews willing to forsake all or part of the Zionist interpretation of reality, and Palestinians prepared to put the civic agenda above the national one. While the former process was late in starting and weak, the latter was quite forceful. The

Figure 7. Palestinians at a West Bank checkpoint in December 2002

gap in intensity and conviction dismantled the potential alliance, however, before it had properly materialized.

The Palestinians in Israel employed the two strategies Cornell West recognized in the struggle of African Americans: the wish to be fully integrated even at the price of co-optation, on the one hand, and the homogenization of the collective identity as part of a struggle for autonomy and even independence, on the other. The two strategies could be fully employed only after the end of the military regime imposed on the Israeli Palestinians in 1966.

On an individual level, co-optation persisted even after the political agenda condemned it. As long as economic benefits could be associated with such a mode of behaviour, it had some success. But the overall stagnation and lack of growth among the Palestinians in Israel, coupled with a continued policy of discrimination in all aspects of life and topped by the open hostility in the occupied territories, brought the political agenda of nationalization closer to the private experience and conduct of the society as a whole.

### THE ROAD TO INTIFADA

While the Palestinians in Israel were living in an almost impossible situation, the rest of the Palestinians, following the Lebanon war, were developing their own agendas. Before the war, two groups had drawn closer in a process already described: the Palestinians within the occupied territories and the PLO now based in Tunis. The danger of this process was that the common agenda was a struggle to end the Israeli occupation at the price of sidelining the issue of refugees. Although not irreversible, this marginalization sowed dissent in a community hardly in a position to afford discord.

The fusion of the agendas eventually resulted in the intifada of December 1987. The causes of the uprising lay in yet another futile chapter in the regional politics of peace, orchestrated by the Americans, who supported a Labour Party wish to give most of the West Bank to Jordan. The failure of this attempt created a vacuum yet again, which was welcomed by the political elites who did not wish to take dramatic decisions but proved unbearable for those under occupation.

The new effort in the so-called peace process, begun after the Lebanon war, moved in three directions. The first was an attempt to settle the impossible Lebanese imbroglio. It ended in 1985 in an unsatisfying division of power between Israel, Syria, Shiite militias and the Lebanese government, each carving out for itself a piece of land in southern Lebanon, where the PLO still had power over the impoverished Palestinian refugee camps. After 1985, the Shiite militia Hezbollah began a campaign of guerrilla resistance, causing hundreds of Israeli casualties in bold suicide attacks, ambushes and direct confrontation with the occupying Israeli army. The second direction was a strange *rapprochement* between Yasser Arafat and King Hussein, ending in a limited mandate given by the PLO to the Hashemite king to negotiate the fate of the West Bank on its behalf with Israel. The third direction was an open dialogue between Israelis and Palestinians in the occupied territories on a professional and intellectual level as much as on a political one.

Of the three, the second seemed at first to be the most fruitful. Armed with a PLO mandate, King Hussein tried to reach an agreement with Israel in a series of private and secret negotiations with both Peres and Rabin, culminating in a draft agreement in February 1987. But the two Labourites were members of a coalition government with the hawkish Yitzhak Shamir, who refused to ratify the draft, dooming to failure another peace effort. King Hussein later claimed that it was Peres' tendency to leak his every achievement that destroyed this chance of an agreement.

The failure of the agreement closed a long chapter in Israel's 'Jordanian option' but opened the way for more direct local Israeli–Palestinian dialogue, which intensified and became for a while the only remaining axis of negotiation over the fate of Palestine. It only became a valid option, however, after the Palestinian uprising of late 1987 broke out.

# CHAPTER 7

# The Uprising and its Political Consequences
## (1987–1996)

After twenty years of occupation, life in the occupied territories consisted of a familiar, but almost intolerable, routine for most of the Palestinians there. By the beginning of 1987, it was clear that no outside factors would help extricate the people from their harsh situation. The Palestinian issue was the last on the list of priorities at Arab summits. Palestinians could not fail to notice that, even when these leaders treated Palestine as a priority, they had very little to offer in the way of solutions or deliverance to the people living either under occupation or in the refugee camps. The PLO political strategy, conducted from Tunis and based on the construction of a Cairo–Amman diplomatic safety net for Arafat, produced no solutions, either to the occupation or the refugee problem. The PLO appeared resigned to the loss of its homeland and to the Palestinians' failure to achieve self-determination. The Israeli political situation remained mired in inflexibility and intransigence, as it had been since 1967.

The only vibrant political arena was that of local politics in the occupied territories. It had a young national leadership, consisting of professionals and middle-class urbanites, each affiliated loosely to one of the many PLO groups in Tunis. But this leadership also lacked any clear strategy for ending the occupation, a frustrating failing that was accentuated in the 1980s by the liberation of oppressed people in East Asia, Eastern Europe and South Africa.

Against this background, the historian can only wonder why a local uprising was so late in coming. It did finally occur, and its leaders chose a term already in use by grassroots movements in the Arab world, *intifada* ('shaking off'), to describe their attempt to end the Israeli presence in the West Bank and the Gaza Strip. When it happened, in December 1987, it was all-encompassing. The limited size of the occupied areas and the nature of the military rule imposed on them made opting out impossible. The various Israeli governments had never relaxed their grip, and continuously interfered in every aspect of the lives of the occupied population.

The uprising forced the Israelis to cease temporarily what sociologists called a 'creeping annexation'. From 1987, there was a traceable process of gradual incorporation of Palestinian territory into Israel (either Greater Jerusalem or through settlements), as well as the establishment of docile autonomous rule in other areas in a pattern akin to the tribal fiefdoms in Lesotho and the South African bantustans.

'Creeping annexation' also had economic dimensions, the most important of which was the absorption of the surplus Palestinian workforce into the Israeli economy. By 1987, Israel had transformed its economy into a Reaganite or Thatcherite free-market capitalist system. Such an economy needed a cheap, compliant workforce from the occupied territories. This was facilitated via a kind of neo-colonialist relationship, with the delegation of municipal, welfare and economic power to co-operative local mayors and council heads, a power structure that enabled Israel to exploit to the full whatever the occupied territories had to offer to an economy that in many ways could not have survived without it.[1]

The attempt to govern by proxy, at least in parts of the territories, was defeated by the diminutive size of this part of Palestine. The drive for Jewish settlement, for instance, was obvious everywhere, to those in annexed and in theoretically autonomous areas alike. Jews were settled in areas earmarked by all Israeli governments as vital for Israel's 'existence'. These areas were thus annexed to Israel, and were to be excluded from any future deal or territorial compromise in the West Bank and the Gaza Strip.

The uprising had all the makings of an anti-colonialist movement. The creeping annexation had led to the integration of the local economy into the Israeli economy. It had created a relationship of dependence that had become by far the most important aspect of life under occupation. Apart from 1975, when the Israeli economy slipped into recession, the economic boom of this market affected some economic activities in the occupied territories. In general it meant a rise in consumption levels and a decline in unemployment. These two factors led Israeli academics to boast of a successful process of modernization in the occupied areas.[2] But the paradigm of neo-colonialist dependence meant that there was no investment in the Palestinian areas, and no infrastructure for depositing and accumulating superfluous capital and profits. In fact, these two indicators of economic activity, saving and investment, declined under the creeping annexation. Worse in economic terms was the effect on local industry. The Israelis dumped their products on the territories, undercutting local factories and producers. This was accompanied by an aggressive marketing campaign of Hebraizing signposts, public spaces and individual consciousness.

Economics is a matter of balance. The creeping annexation had produced a two-way economic flow. From the occupied territories came cheap labour and pre-capitalist commodities mainly valued according to the labour involved in their production. In the other direction flowed commodities resulting from capital investment rather than intensive labour. According to one estimate, this meant that surplus profits of around 2 billion dollars generated in the occupied territories were swallowed up by the Israeli economy.[3] Workers commuting to Tel-Aviv, housewives buying Israeli milk in the grocery shops and farmers bringing vegetables to market were not aware of this imbalance, but were nevertheless experiencing this form of neo-colonialism through their daily budgets, and the amount of surplus money to which they had access.

The realization of the economic price paid by dependence on the occupiers' market was visible in additional ways. It was seen by the Palestinian workers comparing their wages with those of their Jewish colleagues (they were paid half as much). It was also painfully evident to independent professionals who had to pay taxes at a rate bureaucrats are free to impose on an occupied population. It was obvious to entrepreneurs who had to go through a humiliating and degrading process of pleading for concessions and subcontracts. Finally, it was driven home to thousands of villagers who were forced to leave their farms. This micro-economic understanding explains best why revolutionary discourse on the need to rebel, to protest, to say 'enough is enough' was so compelling.

In sociological terms, therefore, the direct victims of the occupation were those who produced and saw no return on their investment. Their situation was reinforced by the victims of the Nakbah, the refugees, within the occupied territories. The nature of these groups precluded any systematic planning or direction of an uprising; a groundswell of protest was bound to carry them with it, but nobody could know how, or where, their anger would take them. The uprising was a universal outburst of suppressed dismay, frustration and anger against economic exploitation, land expropriation, daily harassment, Jewish settlements and the sense of no escape from a long-endured occupation. It added to the dormant hostility deep in the minds and hearts of the refugees.

The intifada began in December 1987 in Gaza's refugee camps, which, like those in the West Bank, housed 850,000 refugees out of the 1.5 million altogether in the occupied territories at that time. A third of this population were children under fifteen, and according to UNRWA's report the average age in the camps was twenty-seven.[4] Those men who could find work made a living as hired labourers, mainly in Israel. However, on the eve of the intifada, more than 35 per cent were unemployed. The average family of five persons made do with a room and a half, usually with an outside toilet and nothing comparable to a *madafa*, a living room, an important space for Middle Eastern families and for their relations with their neighbours.

The refugees were also the most politicized sector of the society, which probably explains why they had borne the brunt of Israel's collective punishment policy in the two years preceding the uprising. The worst of these punitive acts was the sealing off of houses, or rather of refugee huts. Considering the limited space such 'houses' offered at the best of times, one can only imagine the effect of such punishment on the population.

Although economic deprivation inevitably produced the motivation for political action, it also gave rise to the bitterest harvest of the Israeli occupation, collaboration. The harsh conditions made it easy for Israel's secret service, the Shabak, to recruit collaborators. In due course the political activists retaliated, and many of these collaborators were killed, some brutally. Israel tried later to resettle some of the informers in Palestinian villages and neighbourhoods in Galilee and Wadi Ara', angering the population there who considered them traitors. The Israelis were eventually forced to find other refuges for them.

In the first year of the intifada, 400 refugees were killed in clashes with the Israeli army. Tens of thousands were wounded, according to most sources, although the Israelis claimed it was only a few thousand. All agree, however, that most of those wounded were children and women. The wounded were not only victims of live ammunition or rubber bullets, but also of systematic beatings by Israeli soldiers and border police.[5] Although the Israelis did not resort to mass expulsion during the intifada – they would do so in 1993 – most of the sixty or so Palestinians expelled were refugees. Even though this number was relatively low, the act sowed further seeds of hatred and animosity.

While the refugees started the uprising, the burden of keeping it alive rested on the shoulders of rural Palestine, as was the case in the 1936 revolt. The farmers proved to be the most significant factor: demonstrating, directing the riots, stoning the occupiers. The first villager to be killed by the Israelis in the uprising exemplified the rural participation in the overall effort to terminate the occupation. Seventeen-year-old Talal Hawihi came from Beit Hanun in the Gaza Strip, a village located near a refugee camp, where many men worked as hired labourers in Israel. He was killed while participating in a series of actions near his village, a kind repeated everywhere in the West Bank and the Gaza Strip in the first four months of the intifada. These included stoning soldiers, preventing workers from getting to the crossing points and declaring the villages liberated areas, at least for a few days, before the soldiers returned. They proclaimed their short-lived liberation by flying the Palestinian flag from electricity poles, covering the walls of the villages with graffiti, and erecting sand or garbage barricades around the village. The IDF reacted to each protest by bombarding the villages with tear-gas and then charging in large numbers. Later on, the 'softening' included the shooting of steel bullets wrapped in rubber in preparation for the Israeli reoccupation of these villages.[6]

The courage to face, almost unarmed, a highly sophisticated army was drawn from several sources. A crucial role was played by the frequent pamphlets issued by the National Unified Command, which served both as a newspaper and a manual for the intifada. The Command was a body hastily established at the beginning of the uprising, and was later appropriated by the PLO. Its leaflets provided a general analysis of the occupation, in economic and social terms, and, more importantly, specifed very distinctly the exact targets to be attacked, such as buses carrying workers to Israel or to work in the settlements, and goals to be attained, such as the liberation of villages and dismantling of the Jewish settlements.

Another source of inspiration, quite unexpected from a historical perspective, was the Palestinians in Israel. They reacted even more swiftly than the PLO in Tunis to the events in occupied Palestine. A few weeks after the uprising started, they began organizing strikes and demonstrations on a special day called the 'Day of Peace', in which for the first time political action was co-ordinated between Palestinians on both sides of the green line. The Palestinians in Israel preceded the Jewish left in pointing to the particularly brutal and callous manner in which the IDF and the Shabak were reacting to the intifada. This included mass arrests without trial, torture during interrogation, assembling all the men in reoccupied villages and in some cases subjecting them to merciless beatings, and above all, a new measure, cordoning off villages as 'secure military areas', preventing entry and exit for days on end. This last method was used more frequently after it became clear that the international media, and particularly the television networks, conveyed images that for the first time since 1948 presented the Palestine problem in a way that reflected the Palestinian narrative.[7]

The contribution from the Palestinians in Israel, later supported by some sections in the Jewish left, was enhanced by Palestinians in the occupied territories who had decided, despite their own struggle, to commemorate the Day of the Land in 1988 as a significant juncture in the rural uprising. This act of solidarity formed an association in the public mind, on both sides of the green line, between the land confiscation and killing in Galilee in 1976 and similar acts, on a wider scale, in the occupied territories in 1987. It also brought home the nature of neo-colonialist economic dependence, so strikingly similar in the relationship of Israel with both Palestinian communities.

This solidarity led to bolder, extended acts of resistance. In turn, the intensification of the uprising brutalized the Israeli soldiers and commanders even further. They added to their inventory of collective punishment acts such as house demolition, the erection of high fences around refugee camps, and the assembling of men in the centres of villages, refugee camps and neighbourhoods, and abusing and torturing them. The Israeli military managed to compress into a few months the same amount of brutality they had previously inflicted over a period of almost twenty years. The Israeli novelist David Grossman won national acclaim by predicting the intifada in one of his books, *The Yellow Wind*.[8] A sensitive novelist, he had observed the growing hatred in the eyes of refugee children under the shadow of Israeli callousness. The *Haaretz* journalists Gideon Levy and Amria Hass also underlined how this heritage of cruelty undermined the chances of peace in the 1990s.

The resemblance of the intifada to the 1936 revolt was striking. The major involvement of rural Palestine ensured its widespread effectiveness: half of the intifada's deaths came from the villages, most of the houses demolished in the uprising were located in the rural areas, and the worst acts of retaliation were committed in the villages. Towards the end of the intifada in 1991, the Israeli army resorted to an economic clampdown on villages as a last resort, cutting off electricity and water, and preventing olive-picking during the height of the season.

GENDER AND CLASS

A significant difference between the two uprisings was that, in the 1987 intifada, rural women took a central role, boldly confronting the army. Their commitment to the cause can be gauged from the death toll: one-third of the overall casualties were women.[9] The participation of urban women was even higher, as the patriarchal structure in the villages kept some women at home, who were in principle willing to go out and challenge the occupiers.

The role of urban women in the intifada was crucial to its early success in more than one way. It was both a spontaneous initiative and a response to a call from men in leading national positions. This marked a significant break from past modes of political behaviour. Until 1965, women's participation in national politics had been limited mainly to the wives of leading activists. In 1965, as part of the overall structure of the PLO, a general union of Palestinian women was established. However, it was meant to supervise only 'women's' issues such as welfare and health.

The intifada proved a catharsis for women's politics of identity in every walk of life. It provided a release for their frustration in the face of the double burden of a patriarchal society and the Israeli occupation. Like their menfolk, women in refugee camps, city neighbourhoods and villages had to work in Palestine and Israel. They were paid less and treated more badly than men in the labour market, while their incorporation in the outside world did not relieve them of any traditional domestic chores.[10]

Long before the intifada, therefore, there was an incentive for women to choose politicization as a means of gender mobilization. This is demonstrated by the increase in the number of women arrested or detained without trial, from a few hundred in the early 1970s to several thousand in the early 1980s. Their growing contribution and sacrifice was appreciated by the various bodies functioning as the national leadership. Lajnat al-Tawjih allocated women one seat in its ranks, while other bodies, particularly parties and factions on the left, gave them more.

In the 1970s, women had entered politics through student organizations, themselves a new phenomenon on the local scene. Outside the territories, young women were already spearheading some of the bolder acts of guerrilla warfare and terrorism. In one respect the occupiers added a positive contribution to women's advancement: the Israelis cancelled a 1955 Jordanian regulation prohibiting the participation of women in elections. When the Israeli authorities allowed municipal elections to take place in 1976, they included women in the process. There was no feminist agenda behind this act, personally decided upon by the then minister of defence, Shimon Peres. His advisers had told him that women were a conservative electorate, and so would vote for pro-Jordanian politicians. In practice, they voted for national and 'radical' candidates. Women were not only voters; they were also elected as representatives to the twenty-four municipalities formed in these elections.

Their level of participation increased in direct proportion to the deterioration of the national condition. Thus, the rise of Likud to power and its unprecedented oppressive occupation drove even more women into the national resistance movement. This meant more than conventional political activities; it included the fine arts, theatre and more subtle activity within welfare and educational NGOs.

In the years before the intifada, women's committees declared an interest in both national and gender issues. The beginning of this phase of activity was the UN-sponsored International Women's Day in 1978, and interest intensified throughout the 1980s. One can therefore see why women were present in all phases and aspects of the uprising: throwing stones, organizing strikes, and formulating diplomatic policies in the overall attempt to translate the intifada into a political gain.

Yet, in terms of occupational distribution, the uprising did not revolutionize women's lives. An important reason was the importance that both women and men placed on domestic economics; the need for self-sufficiency in response to Israeli sanctions highlighted the crucial role housewives had to play in supporting the uprising. This occurred with the full support of the National Unified Command. Women founded cooperatives, both outside and inside the home, providing whatever they could manufacture to counteract the growing Israeli sanctions.

The gender issues in the intifada were also clouded by the prominent role political Islam played in the uprising. As its impact on life all over Palestine and Israel transcends the uprising, it will be dealt with extensively in the conclusion to this book.

Another group of Palestinians involved for the first time in nationalist activity was children and youths, who paid dearly for their bold participation in the uprising. Ironically, and tragically, the high number of children killed helped to convey the Palestinian version of events forcefully to the international community through the electronic media, providing visual proof of the brutal nature of the Israeli response.

As in the 1930s, the workplace turned into a battlefield. Palestinian workers eagerly took part in this mass attempt to transform the nature of the occupation, seeing in their employers the personification of the occupiers. However, in the long run, the workers proved less resilient than the farmers. Their total dependence on their employers prevented them from opting, as farmers could, for alternative modes of existence. By the third year of the intifada, their energy seemed to dwindle.[11] Their power of resistance was further eroded by the devaluation of the Jordanian dinar in the autumn of 1988. Their salaries were paid in dinars, and the devaluation halved their wages. The National Unified Command asked Palestinian employers not to cut wages, and later even asked them to raise salaries, but this did not work for long. The community was too poor to provide such altruistic help, and the situation was aggravated by the Israelis' use of economic sanctions as part of the war against the intifada. Yet, while half of the casualties came from the rural areas, the workers, mostly refugees, both men and women, constituted the other half. Hardly any middle-class Palestinians fell in the war against the occupation.[12]

The role of the bourgeoisie was more concerned with sustaining long commercial strikes. This was achieved after some months of hesitation by the trading community. The patriotic image of this part of the middle class was further enhanced by its initiation of a tax revolt against the Israelis. Each locality had a traders' committee, which would decide on boycotts of the web of levies that had been imposed on productive professionals since the start of the occupation.

The uprising, in both cities and villages, was organized through a network of popular committees. These were modelled on the national committees of the 1936 revolt, but unlike their predecessors were democratic rather than elitist in nature, being appointed ad hoc by local villagers or neighbourhood residents. Their fluid character prevented Israeli military intelligence from analysing or infiltrating the sources of authority or the hierarchical struc-ture. From the early 1980s, an organization called the 'popular framework' had existed in rural areas, especially in the West Bank. The framework consisted of several committees, such as the committee for voluntary work (*lajnat al-aa'mal al-tatawai'*) or the youth committee (*lajnat al-shabab*), which organized social activities and a welfare system under the nose of the Israeli civil administration that claimed responsibility for such services, but in practice did very little in this regard.[13]

In the urban areas, the crisis of the intifada revived the trade unions as a regulating and organizing force. Unlike the popular committees, the unions attempted to maintain regular contact with the National Unified Command (NUC), which became the unofficial authority during the up-rising. At first the NUC consisted of the more enthusiastic layer of local political activists, but was later remodelled along the lines of the PLO ex-ecutive committee. The unions' power of influence can be deduced from the high number of arrests, without trial, of union leaders by the Israelis during the Intifada.

All over the occupied territories the uprising succeeded as long as the decentralized structure of the committees was left intact. While that was the case, roughly until the end of 1988, the National Unified Command moderated, rather than determined, the activity. However, the routinization of the uprising led to a decline in local initiative and an increase in the centralizing aspirations and self-accredited authority of the Command. By the middle of the uprising this body consisted mainly of radical students, lecturers and ex-politicians.

Before the uprising was a year old, the PLO leadership, taking advantage of its success, produced one of the most important Palestinian documents since the PLO charter of the 1960s. This was the Declaration of Independence, announced publicly on 15 November 1988 at the PNC meeting in Tunis. It was first and foremost an attempt to redirect the uprising towards Palestinian agendas not necessarily represented in the political action taken against the Israeli occupiers in the West Bank and the Gaza Strip. The document clearly stated old and new Palestinian concerns such as the fate of the refugees, the future of Jerusalem, and the nature and borders of the future Palestinian state. It was the first document that referred openly to a commitment to adhere to the principle of equality between men and women in the future state, a tribute to the leading role played by the women in the uprising.[14]

This document had other features. It was drafted in response to the organization's new strategic requirements, namely the need to improve the PLO's relationship with the USA. The PNC meeting in Tunis was preceded by intensive negotiations between the PLO and the USA, which opened a new chapter in USA–PLO relations. These led to the inclusion of USA-based Palestinians of high international repute in the diplomatic corps that was helping to shape the PLO's policy. As a result, the Declaration of Independence recognized the partitioning of Palestine both as a crime against the Palestinian people and as a necessity for ending the conflict. This was later followed by public declarations by the PLO about the end of the armed struggle and the recognition of the state of Israel in principle. But before the PLO took centre stage, the leadership on the ground in the occupied territories initiated their own diplomatic campaign. They chose Jerusalem as their base, and used a hotel, the Orient House, once owned by the leading family in the city, the Husaynis, as a kind of government headquarters. There from 1989 onwards, they maintained contact with foreign diplomats, State Department officials, Israeli MKs (Members of the Knesset) from both right and left, and, above all, tried to appear to the population at large like a government. They had to wait until after the Gulf war of 1990–91, however, for their moment of glory.

When Saddam Hussein invaded Kuwait in the summer of 1990 and the USA responded by waging a war against him in early 1991, the PLO openly took the Iraqi ruler's side. This cooled the PLO's relationship with the USA, but also highlighted the accessibility and attractiveness of the Orient House leadership in the eyes of the Americans and the Israeli peace camp.

At the end of the Gulf War, a peace conference in Madrid in 1991 dealt with the Palestine question. This twist in events originated with an

American refusal to deal with Iraq diplomatically as well as an American commitment to the Syrian ruler, Hafiz al-Asad, to include the Golan Heights in a discussion in an international forum. This American pledge was made in return for the symbolic but very significant Syrian participation in the anti-Saddam coalition in the Gulf War.

Nothing came of this lavish event. Progress in an agreement over each of the disputed areas in the Palestine question depended on Israeli good-will, which could not be elicited from the government of Yitzhak Shamir, who believed that the status quo was Israel's best strategy. But it did trigger a trilateral diplomatic process between Israel, Jordan and the Palestinian Orient House group, which took place mainly in Washington throughout 1992, until Rabin replaced Shamir as prime minister in the summer of that year. Fruitless Israeli–Syrian negotiations over the Golan Heights also began at this time, and lasted until the death of Hafiz al-Asad in 2000.

Alongside the high politics, which as always produced unfulfilled hopes for change, there was an impressive local attempt in the West Bank to use the political drama to build the infrastructure for a state. This was initiated by the *tawaqim* ('teams'), who had spent years at the Orient House professionally planning every aspect of life and government in their future state. Their efforts were ignored and, like so many other crucial achievements of the Palestinians under the occupation, were eclipsed by the Oslo accord and its aftermath.

### THE OSLO PROCESS AND AFTER

The Oslo plan was devised by Israelis of the Zionist left. They were members of the Labour movement who had a mandate to go beyond that movement's traditional positions and seek an agreement with the PLO based on a solution acceptable to the Zionist parties left of Labour. The negotiators met a group of pragmatic members from the PLO's second echelon, based in Tunis. The Palestinian negotiators came to Oslo on the basis of the resolutions adopted by the PNC accepting the principle of partition as the basis for a solution to the conflict. This shift in the PLO's position reflected Arafat's recognition of his organization's inability to force an agreement based on the establishment of a secular Arab state in the whole of ex-Mandate Palestine. Nonetheless, Arafat's PLO retained its insistence on the Palestinian refugees' right of return and remained committed to the establishment of a fully independent Palestinian state, free of Jewish settlements, with Jerusalem as its capital. However, these points were, for the first time in the PLO's history, negotiable rather than precepts of a national ideology.

This new pragmatism was born of a matrix of discrete developments, each in its turn weakening the PLO: the disappearance of the Soviet Union as the PLO's supporting superpower; the decrease in Saudi financial assistance in the wake of the PLO's position in the Gulf war; and the overall decline in the PLO's fortunes in the Arab world at large and in Palestine in particular following its evacuation from Lebanon in 1982. As with the Declaration of Independence of November 1988, this move was prompted by the intifada's success at attracting public support, both inside and outside Palestine, to an extent never previously attained by the PLO's guerrilla movement. Above all, it was part of a long process, beginning in 1974, which turned the PLO into a pragmatic force in the Middle East, using a mixture of force and diplomacy. Finally, the 1992 Israeli elections also played an important role. Jewish society was now willing to give a chance to a government openly declaring its readiness to vacate occupied land. Thus, the Oslo document represented the meeting point between an Israeli wish to compromise territorially and a PLO willingness to begin peace negotiations with such a compromise – but by no means to conclude them.

Despite the unfavourable background against which the PLO conducted these negotiations, and notwithstanding the superior position of Israel in the balance of power between the two sides, Oslo appeared at the time to open a significant window of opportunity for the leaders of the Palestinian national movement. The agreement came into being in the form of a document called the Declaration of Principles (DoP), which was proclaimed on 13 September 1993 and signed on the White House lawn in a ceremony that included the typical American pageantry of 'peace'.

A shrewd observer reading the principles carefully would soon have noticed the precarious nature of the new agreement. Article 5 clause 3, for example, showed clearly why the document did not so much end the conflict as expose its real nature. This clause enumerated three subjects to be dealt with in future negotiations, after the successful implementation of an interim agreement between the two sides: the question of Jerusalem, the fate of the Palestinian refugees, and the problem of the Jewish settlements in the occupied territories. Additionally, the clause allowed each party to bring forward for discussion, pending agreement by the other, any other topic of its choice.

The main PLO concession was to link the successful implementation of the interim period with negotiations on the final status of the territories and these three topics. The document specified the processes for the interim period: an Israeli withdrawal from Gaza and Jericho, to be followed by a gradual transfer of certain civil functions from Israel to the PLO, and an eventual Israeli withdrawal from all Palestinian towns and population centres. At the end of the period, talks on the final settlement were to commence. This interim agreement was dictated by the Israelis, and tailored according to their perception of security. Moreover, it represented the Israeli conception of the conflict's nature and substance. The agreement dealt only with problems emanating from the 1967 war, as if that was the basis of the situation, and everything preceding it was irrelevant to a peaceful resolution of the conflict. While the agreed interim phase contributed to ending Israeli control over the lives of a large number of Palestinians, it did not take the Palestinian perception of the conflict into account, or advance any solutions for the uprooted Palestinians who had lost their homeland in 1948. The Palestinian concession of accepting the Israeli demand to make 1967 the centre of the Oslo accord was buttressed by symbols of Palestinian sovereignty in every evacuated area, most importantly – and this went beyond symbolism – the recognition of the PLO's authority in these areas.

Most importantly, however, the framework of the interim phase was tolerated by the Palestinians because of the promise given in article 5, clause 3 of the document. The refugee problem and the Jerusalem question were important, but the PLO hoped especially that it could also raise the issue of full statehood in future negotiations. All three issues were related to the consequences of the 1948 war, a war that in many ways had constructed the new national identity of the Palestinians and dictated their national agenda.[15] The PLO owed its existence to the 1948 refugee community, and its *raison d'être* has never been to bring an end to the Israeli occupation of 1967, a secondary task, but to rectify the evils of 1948.

Although hidden in a clause, these promises included in the Oslo document represented a PLO achievement. Apart from being recognized by Israel for the first time in its history, the PLO received an Israeli agreement to negotiate on three issues that it regarded as being at the heart of the conflict. The Israelis very skilfully added to these a 1967 issue, that of the settlements. This was a contentious and delicate matter for the Israeli electorate, and they wished to postpone negotiations over it for as long as possible. The document stressed, however, that Israel's participation in such negotiations was conditional on a 'successful and peaceful' implementation of the interim agreement, effectively an Israeli veto. 'Peaceful' meant in a way that would satisfy the Israeli concept of security, so the implementation of that phase was to be monitored and executed by Israeli generals.[16]

The agreement in practice, then, was a far cry from the document. This reflects the tension between the situation as envisaged by political elites and the experience of the population on the ground. In a series of agreements,[17] dictated by the Israeli generals faced with a Palestinian team that lacked any professional expertise in legal and strategic matters,[18] interim objectives of the Oslo document seemed to become the basis for the final and permanent settlement of the conflict. A series of Israeli acts, or Palestinian concessions, rendered impractical and useless any future negotiations relating to the final status of the territories or to the questions of refugees and Jerusalem.

The process annulled some of the principal promises made in the Oslo document. Article 31, clause 7 declared: 'Neither side shall initiate or take any step that will change the status of the West Bank and the Gaza Strip pending the outcome of the permanent status negotiations.' From 1994 onwards, Israel began a construction effort, including building new settlements and expanding old ones, and erecting border fences that delineated the partition of the West Bank prior to negotiations. Massive land confiscation and settlement expansion marked the four years (1992–6) of the Labour premiership. The Labour government invested 46 million dollars in the Jewish settler population of about 144,000 in the occupied Palestinian territories, much more than its Likud predecessors, and by 1996 the settler population had increased by 48 per cent in the West Bank and 62 per cent in the Gaza Strip.[19] All this made the settlers' eviction less realistic than ever.

In each of the agreements signed after Oslo, the balance of power and Israeli superiority were translated into reality on the ground. This was manifested in all spheres of life, which enabled the Israelis to gain influence through the employment of violent means such as arrest, detention, and house demolition.

Apart from making final talks impossible, there was an additional violation of the Oslo document. Article 31, clause 8 declared that 'the two parties view the West Bank and the Gaza Strip as a single territorial unit, the integrity and status of which will be preserved during the interim report'. However, a series of bypasses and tunnels divided up the territories, creating an imagined map of a Jewish West Bank above, in more than one sense, the Palestinian one. Jews were not just living next to Palestinians, but above them, or were digging tunnels below them. The small Jewish settlements were connected to larger ones and to Israel proper by highways; the Palestinians living in the area encircled by settlements could only move through a series of military barriers with great difficulty, if at all.

The paving of highways, the digging of tunnels and the cantonization of the West Bank (more will be said later of Gaza and Oslo) were 'the Oslo process'. These arrangements derived their legitimacy not from the DoP, but from the various agreements signed by Israel and Oslo's new creation, the Palestinian Authority (PA).

Palestinians travelling from one part of the West Bank to another or from the areas under the PA's authority to work in Israel could see better than anyone the patterns of continuity between the pre- and post-Oslo realities. The brutality and callousness of Israeli soldiers and policemen on the crossing points and roadblocks within Israeli territory confirmed that the West Bank had simply turned into a bantustan. The occupiers stayed on the checkpoints, able to inflict any kind of mental and physical abuse on those using the borders between Israel and Palestine. This too was a violation of the Oslo document, apart from being a continued occupation. Article 10, clause 1, sub-clause A stated: 'There shall be a safe passage connecting the West Bank with the Gaza Strip for movement of persons, vehicles and goods'. Clause B declares: 'Israel will ensure safe passage for persons and transportation during daylight hours (from sunrise to sunset) . . . but in any event not less than 10 hours a day'. This was violated not only in the case of the passage between Gaza and the West Bank but also within the West Bank itself.

The tension between the pledges made in the document and the situation evolving on the ground was reflected in the gap between parameters and functions. The Israelis controlled the parameters while Palestinians were allowed some limited functions. But even in the field of functions, the Oslo process did not go far. The Palestinian functions were limited to the running of daily life in the PA areas. They were decorated with symbolism substituting for real sovereignty, such as flags, units, names and titles such as 'Palestine's post'. It is what the Palestinians call a lot of *salata* (honours) without *sulta* (authority).

The new situation produced new patterns of life, which explains why, despite the obvious disadvantages, a significant number of Palestinians in the West Bank and Gaza were for a long time willing partners in the process. The various mechanisms erected to regulate life in the PA's areas provided jobs for the PLO people from Tunis and for an additional large number of local Palestinians. These employed people formed the main body of Palestinian support for the agreement, as they now had a vested interest in maintaining the status quo.

The advantages promised in the accord could be seen more vividly in Gaza, which was less fragmented by the accord than the West Bank. Its separation from the West Bank had been accepted as an arrangement that would exist for a long time, whether the Oslo document were implemented verbatim or according to a pro-PLO interpretation. Thus, in Gaza, the relative territorial integrity at first produced a sense of relief at the removal of the direct Israeli occupation in the form of no more curfews, no more break-ins at night, and no more harassment on the roads. It took more than a year for the repeated border closures[20] and the arbitrary restrictions on movement outside the Strip to drive home the message that the Oslo process had turned Gaza into a huge prison, with a Palestinian flag inside and Israeli soldiers guarding the fences. The border closures resumed as an Israeli reaction to the bombings by the Islamic resistance movements Hamas and Islamic Jihad as part of their campaign against the accord. Most of these acts violated not only the provisions of the Oslo document but also several articles, notably article 33, of the Fourth Geneva Convention 'Relative to the Protection of Civilian Persons in Time of War of 1949'.

The Oslo process lingered until 1999, mainly due to its appeal to the Israeli public and the international community. To the Israelis, Oslo was presented in the public discourse and electronic media, at least until the election of Benjamin Netanyahu in 1996, as a peace process. Much effort was invested in conveying this message of progress, and the violent hostility of the Zionist right to Oslo strengthened the conviction of many Israelis on the left that they were defending a genuine peace process against its enemies. Finally, in the international, and particularly the American, discourse the Oslo accord, or 'Oslo' for short, was peace.

Around 1996, reality overtook the images the political leaders had created of the Oslo process. After that, the question was no longer whether Oslo had brought peace to the torn land of Israel and Palestine, but rather what price its people had paid for illusions sold to them by shortsighted politicians.

## IN THE SHADOW OF POLITICS: RELIGION, NATIONALISM AND MULTICULTURALISM

In the late 1980s, a new political actor appeared on the local scene in Israel and Palestine: the Islamic movements. These were Hamas, Islamic Jihad in the occupied territories (and in southern Lebanon), and the Islamic movement in Israel itself. 'Political Islam' is a fairly new term, replacing 'Islamic fundamentalism', but it seeks to explain the same phenomenon. In general, the term is a scholarly attempt to assess the impact of religion on politics in the Arab world and beyond. It is by no means definitive, and each religious movement needs to be understood in its own context.

Like other Islamists in the late twentieth century, those in Palestine and Israel were anti-American and hence opposed to peace deals brokered by the USA. The close association between Israel and the USA, and its impact on the fate of the Palestinians, was an easy agenda to pursue. But this interest in politics was only one aspect of the political Islamic groups in Israel and Palestine.

The introduction of Islamic concepts into the political scene was based on a genuine return to religion and tradition in Israel and Palestine. The wish to reconnect with past codes of conduct was not limited to Muslims, but was evident in the Jewish community as well. Religion in Palestine and Israel proved, as I predicted in my preface, a resilient and adaptive force, rather than a dwindling relic of traditionalism so easily dismissed by the gurus of modernization theories.

Religion proved to be an effective response to the pressures of endless uprooting, deprivation and discrimination experienced by many Palestinians throughout the second half of the twentieth century. It also offered a redemptive outlook on life for Jews in Israel, who were living under less harsh conditions but were nonetheless experiencing dismay and frustration born out of economic hardship and lack of orientation. The political aspect of the religious revival only made it more attractive as an alternative; not only as a daily praxis but also as a plan that promised change, in a situation where the worst had already been experienced.

Religion also began to provide justification for the most extreme forms of political activity. In its name and for its sake violence could be inflicted on enemies of all kinds, both the other side in a conflict and the 'traitors' within. It inspired Palestinian youth to become human bombs, blowing themselves up in Israeli towns and public spaces, and it motivated zealot settlers to murder indiscriminately their Palestinian neighbours. One such settler assassinated Israel's prime minister, Yitzhak Rabin, in November 1995. While there were other explanations of why Israelis and Palestinians resorted to such forms of violence, such as old grudges, the violence tended to be represented as part of a divine mission. Not that a return to religion always ended in violence. For many of those from less deprived sections of society, it was a guide in an individual search for salvation and piety that increased the number of recruits to both Islam and orthodox Judaism.

As a social force, this new version of religion fitted well into the making of a civil society both in Israel and Palestine. Interpreting the world in a religious manner was reinforced by the state's, or the political elite's, neglect of large areas of life in their communities. This failure by the state or the nation to encompass the lives or the identities of its subjects allowed other ideologies to claim to fulfil that role. In the 1980s, these new groupings coloured the map of Israel and Palestine with a rainbow of different identities, all smaller than that of the 'nation', and all asking either to control the state or at least to be autonomous within it in the name of an identity transcending the limitations of a state. The religious politics of identity differed from the other groupings in that it also aspired to be a substitute for nationalism, or at least an improved version of it, but one inevitably leading to a more extremist, uncompromising confrontation with the 'Other', whatever that might be.

As far as the Palestinians were concerned, whether in the occupied territories or in Israel itself, the PLO or national leaderships had since 1967 lost some of their hold over their communities. This meant that there was more space and motivation for individual and collective adaptations of more pious modes of behaviour. This was evident in two areas. In the rural areas, traditional concepts and beliefs had remained steadfast for centuries and could easily be given a more political orientation – especially given the encroachment of the Israelis into the lives of locals. It was also apparent in the poor urban neighbourhoods, such as in Nazareth, Hebron and Nablus. The fact that many of the more fortunate city dwellers were highly secularized in style and outlook only made those in more deprived areas more antagonistic towards wealth and intellectualism.

In the early 1980s, individual return to Islam in the occupied territories became collective and nationalist.[21] The failure of the PLO to provide protection against harassment and military control propelled many people into the arms of political Islam. This movement also originally received Israeli support. The government's Orientalist advisers recommended that it solidify political Islam as a counter-move against the national politics preached by the PLO. When their 'protégé' turned against them, with even more force and determination, it was too late.[22]

In Israel itself, despite the overall deprivation of the Palestinian community, there were still striking socio-economic imbalances between the two geographical centres of Arab life in the Jewish state. In the north, Galilee was generally better off than the Little Triangle, where the population was crammed into a small space and allowed only a limited occupational spectrum. Not surprisingly, petty crime and unemployment soared. It was in Wadi Ara' that political Islam sprang up, where life was lived in even more miserable conditions than in the refugee camps, inner cities and pauperized villages of the West Bank and the Gaza Strip.

Contrary to the conventional modernization models, the more secular and affluent section of the Palestinian people, those inside Israel, gravitated towards, and sought inspiration from, their more traditional, much worse off compatriots in the West Bank and the Gaza Strip. It was the Strip also that guided the relatively better off West Bank in terms of political religious radicalization. In many ways, national politics also flowed the same way.

The young people and a relatively high portion of women, sections within society who were not given a decisive role in the political struggle, were the ones attracted to the path of personal salvation offered by various interpretations of Islam. These ranged from the mystic Sufis to the fundamentalist vision offered by offshoots of the Muslim Brotherhood. One was Abdullah Nimr Darwish, who dominated the politics of Islam in Israel in the 1980s before losing power to more charismatic young leaders emerging in the deprived and densely populated area of Wadi Ara'. Like many leaders, he received a formal Islamic education in Nablus and Hebron in the early 1970s, where he was introduced not only to the world of learning but, more importantly, to the varied activities on offer for a militant politician in the Islamic mode. These ranged from the *risalat*, epistles originally sent by the Prophet to the community of believers but now turned into modern-day political messages, to clandestine cell organization and sabotage and violence. Preaching in the mosques was, however, the most visible part of that activity. The sermons called for the restoration of the golden Islamic age in Palestine; that is, the revival of Muslim control of the country in strict adherence to the quranic code. The basic message could be peppered with references to the Jews, imperialism and, more significantly, with commentary on current politics, usually reflecting the PLO's position on the Palestine question. Any combination of these ingredients was enough to get someone such as Abdullah Nimr Darwish into trouble, and indeed he spent long periods during the 1980s in Israeli prisons after he had formalized his activity in an organization called Usrat al-Jihad ('the Jihad Family'). After being released, he watered down his criticisms, and was a founder member of al-Haraka al-Islamiyya ('the Islamic Movement'), a legally registered NGO. In the late 1980s and early 1990s, the movement participated successfully in municipal elections, defeating both veteran communist politicians and agents of Zionist parties. In some cases, the newly elected mayors and heads of local councils excelled in running their municipalities, solving long-standing problems. They were eventually hampered by government animosity and, more decisively, by internal schisms and corruption.

The return to religion in the Jewish community was part of the cultural rift tearing that society apart after 1967. It was not new. In the 1950s there had been clashes between religious and secular Jews. The attempt by ultra-orthodox Judaism, anti-Zionist at heart, to isolate and ghettoize their lives failed. For some ultra-orthodox groups, anti-Zionism even included

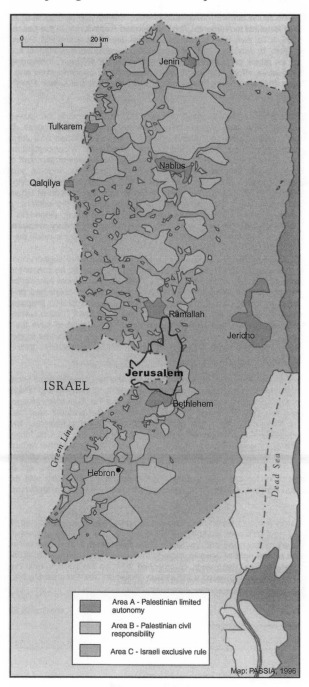

Map 5.  Interim Oslo Agreement, 28 September 1995

Figure 8.  Haifa 2002, a view from the Carmel

the readiness to live under foreign or Palestinian rule. For most, however, it meant an unrealistic wish to live within a state without being part of it. They were in practice unable to cut their communities off from the lure of the more hedonistic and promiscuous secular society in which they lived.

In the *Kulturkampf* that ensued in Israel after 1967, the national balance of achievement and loss tilted in the secularists' favour. Capitalization, globalization and privatization added more secular facets to public life in Israel. An example was the advent of television, and the decision of the Supreme Court, against fierce opposition from religious groups, to allow it to be broadcast on Friday nights. For an outside reader this may seem trivial, but it was part of the struggle over what in Israel is called the status quo. This is like a photograph, taken in 1948, on the day of Israel's creation, of religious and secular life in the public sphere. If, for example, buses were allowed to operate on the Sabbath in Haifa, or if entertainment centres of all kinds were closed on Friday nights, this was how things should be. In practice, however, the status quo did change, and secularism increased in public life. The Supreme Court played the most crucial part in this process. Its most important decision in this respect was in early 1970, when it allowed a Jewish citizen married to a non-Jewish woman to register his children as Jews (according to the Halacha one can only be a Jew if born to a Jewish mother). Typically however, the Supreme Court did not express an opinion on what constitutes being a Jew; this was left to the politicians. In about 1972 there was legislation to the effect that Jews are those that local rabbinates consider to be Jews, an open-ended issue that was never solved.

Ever since, the question of Jewishness in Israel has been determined by the political balance of power in the government and the Knesset coalition. It became an important issue during the massive immigration of Jews from the dismantled Soviet Union in 1989. Those who were welcomed, but not recognized as Jews, could not benefit from the generous range of benefits awaiting every immigrant, although all it took to qualify was the falsification of genealogical documents to invent a Jewish mother. Many did this and, years later, I have seen some of these Jews praying piously in the Russian and Greek Orthodox churches in my neighbourhood.

Looked at from another angle, the rift that always surfaces in Israel at times of relative calm is that of the politics of identity. Until 1993, the year of the Oslo accord, while elite politics centred on whether or not to keep the territories or to reach a compromise with either the Jordanians or the Palestinians, the society at large was focused on the question of identity rather than on issues of borders and peace.

# Conclusion: Post-Oslo Palestine and Israel

## THE DEATH OF OSLO

By the time this book was written, the Oslo process had been declared dead and irrelevant. Instead of bringing healing to a torn country, the peace efforts led it into yet another wave of bloodshed at the beginning of the twenty-first century. Political Palestine, the West Bank and the Gaza Strip, was at war with Israel, as a result of which much of it came under occupation. This meant that historical Palestine, apart from chunks of the Gaza Strip, were under the full control of the Jewish state. Even before the eruption of this last wave of violence, it became painfully clear that the peace accord of the 1990s was doomed to fail. As early as 1995, most Palestinians had labelled the Oslo process as yet another form of occupation, and most Israelis felt that it had failed to safeguard their personal security. For both communities, it seemed useless to ponder whether this unfortunate state of affairs had been anticipated by their leaders, or whether this was a genuine peace process that had gone astray despite the good intentions of the politicians.

A decade later, it seems to me that the major problem was that the practical consequences of the Declaration of Principles agreed upon by Yasser Arafat, Bill Clinton and Yitzhak Rabin on 13 September 1993 on the White House lawn bore little relation to those principles. It was the balance of power, tilting dramatically in Israel's favour, which determined how the principles would be translated into reality. This was achieved with very little generosity or sensitivity on the part of the Israeli negotiators. It could not be resisted by the weakened Palestinian delegation, bereft of any meaningful standing *vis-à-vis* the Israelis or the Americans after a series of setbacks that affected the PLO's position in the world: the collapse of the Soviet Union, their ill-fated support for Saddam Hussein in the Gulf War and the financial crisis that had emptied the PLO's treasury.

Israel therefore was able to impose its own version of a settlement in Palestine: a strong Jewish state dominating a small Palestinian protectorate, without a solution to the refugee problem or a significant Palestinian presence or sovereignty in Jerusalem. This 'settlement' was maintained by the Rabin, Netanyahu, Peres and Barak governments between 1993 and 2000. Their strategy was very popular among the Jewish population; as the 1996 Israeli elections have shown, the majority of Jewish voters were willing to enforce the Israeli version of the Oslo accord even more harshly, as advocated by Likud. But Oslo's greatest attraction for the Israelis was that this minimalist interpretation could be accepted without endangering the Zionist consensus within the ruling political elite. Immediately after the 1996 Israeli elections, Yossi Beilin, a leading dove in the Labour Party, commented that he believed Labour and Likud could find common ground for peace making.[1]

Tragically, this narrowing of the ideological discord within the Zionist polity resulted in the Rabin assassination. The assassin represented the far right of the settler movement, fearing, unfoundedly, that Rabin was ready to compromise with the Palestinians for the sake of peace. Rabin was willing to dismantle isolated settlements, but not to risk an overall confrontation with the settlement movement, and hoped to coerce the Palestinians into accepting a mini-state in return for full peace. Interesting, even telling, were the reasons given by the assassin for his act. He claimed that Rabin had been elected on the basis of the support of the Palestinian minority in Israel, thereby legitimizing them, and had to be stopped at all costs. The breakdown of the Oslo process in the summer of 2000 accelerated the process of de-legitimizing the Palestinian minority in a way that showed that the assassin was, in a macabre way, successful in his principal objective.

A common platform for peace was the best way for the larger political parties, such as Likud and Labour, to avoid relying too heavily on fringe ideological parties which had become stronger at the expense of the two main parties due to a new election system in which the prime minister was elected directly.[2] The smaller parties represented the politics of identity: communities such as Mizrahi Jews, Russian Jews, orthodox Jews, secular Palestinians and political Islamists. Looking at the two parties' platforms from the 1996 election shows a considerable overlap on the question of Oslo. Labour proposed that in the final peace agreement none of the 144 Jewish settlements in the occupied territories should be dismantled, and that most should come under Israeli sovereignty. This was also Likud's position. The two parties concurred with Labour's reference to Jerusalem as 'the eternal, united capital of the state of Israel'. Both sides also seemed reconciled to the idea of some sort of Palestinian state on whatever territory would be left over; a state with very little actual sovereignty or independence.

In 1996, elections also took place in the occupied territories. Fatah won most of the important seats for the newly formed council and cabinet. It was a pragmatic leadership, willing to compromise with Israel, provided the latter would withdraw to the 5 June 1967 borders, share sovereignty in Jerusalem and agree on a reasonable solution to the refugee problem. The chief negotiator on behalf of the Palestinians was Mahmoud Abas, known as Abu Mazin, who reached a tentative agreement with several Labour leaders in February 1996, a basis for future negotiations that was totally rejected by Netanyahu's government (1996–99).

Economic discussions on the future were conducted in parallel with these abortive attempts to further an agreement on the future of the occupied territories. Both political leaderships seemed to consider a capitalist and free-market economy the best response to the economic calamities that years of occupation had brought upon the Palestinians, and to a certain extent on the poorer sections of Israeli society. Under the Paris agreement, which were the economic component of Oslo signed in 1994, Israel and Palestine were to be one economic unit, with interconnected customs systems and a joint taxation policy.[3] The Palestinians demanded their own currency, but this issue was never resolved.

The economic vision of Oslo, like the rest of the accord, was determined by the balance of power, to the Palestinians' detriment. The Paris agreement granted Israel the right of veto on any development scheme put forward by the PA. This meant that the monetary and developmental policies of Israel and its currency exchanges were to play a dominant role in the Palestinian economy. Other aspects of the economy, such as foreign trade and industry, were also totally dominated by the Israelis according to the interim agreement.

The introduction of the Israeli version of a capitalist society into the Palestinian areas could only be a disaster. With the absence of a democratic structure and a very low GNP, the measures offered by Oslo would have turned the areas under the PA into the slums of Israel. This situation was already developing without the overall failure to bring the Oslo accord to a successful completion. In 1995, an industrial park, called the Eretz Plant, was built on the buffer zone between Israel and the Gaza Strip. Despite the name, it was a production line where all the workers were Palestinians, and the employers Israelis who were able to pay their workers very low wages without committing themselves to any social security or union obligations. This was why industrialists in Israel saw themselves as belonging to the peace camp. This was only one aspect of the capitalization of the peace process. Another was the support given to it by a limited number of Palestinians, who benefited from such economic transactions. As before Oslo, the Palestinians in the occupied territories remained underpaid, underemployed and exploited by the neighbouring economy in ways that hardly improved their impoverished situation.

While this double burden of economic misery and a lack of genuine progress on the national front eventually led to a Palestinian attempt to revolt against the post-Oslo situation, the Israeli political leadership seemed to be content with slow, almost unseen, progress towards peace and reconciliation. The terror campaign by militant Islamists began in earnest in 1994 with suicide bombings, which had been first employed by the Hezbollah in Lebanon in its successful war to liberate the southern part of the country from the IDF's control. The campaign produced insecurity and unrest in the Jewish community as a whole, but seemed not to rattle the political system.

The terror attacks prevented Shimon Peres from capitalizing on Rabin's assassination, and he lost the 1996 election to Benjamin Netanyahu, who did not change significantly the policy towards the Oslo accord. In fact, he continued to fulfil some of its previous obligations, such as withdrawing from part of Hebron. There was now full Palestinian control of areas defined as areas A, which included all the Palestinian towns and their environs. In areas B, between these Palestinian enclaves and the blocs of Jewish settlement, Israel and the PA shared security responsibility, while Israel had full control of areas C, where the Jewish settlers lived.

On both sides, the dissociation between the political elites and their societies continued. In Israel, most members of the Jewish community failed to comprehend or show interest in the various interim agreements as the terror campaign in Israeli cities continued. Worse was the situation on the Palestinian side, where the hopes aroused by the Oslo accord were shattered, and pent-up indignation and frustration turned into open rebellion when the Israeli government decided in September 1996 to open a tunnel for (mainly Jewish) tourists under Haram al-Sharif. This was a limited uprising, but was followed by a full-scale intifada after a stalemate in the negotiations over a permanent settlement in the summer of 2000 at Camp David between Clinton, Arafat and Barak. The immediate provocation for the uprising was a violation of the sacredness of the Haram, in the form of an uninvited visit by Ariel Sharon.

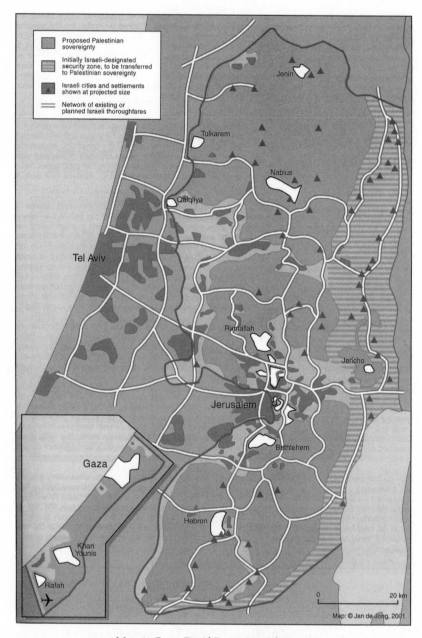

Map 6.  Camp David Protection, July 2000

THE ROAD TO SUICIDE: ISRAEL AND PALESTINE IN 2001

At this time, traditional leaders, both political and spiritual, on both sides were taking advantage of the situation to re-enter the public consciousness. In the occupied territories they had emerged from the 1987 intifada with increased prestige, and even made an impressive performance in the 1996 elections.

On the Jewish side, the ultra-orthodox party Shas won 17 seats out of 120 in the 1999 elections. Their popularity stemmed from years of ethnic discrimination. They claimed to be able to break a chain of injustice stretching back to Wadi Salib in 1959, and did not hesitate to employ political opportunism to avoid alienating more secular Mizrahi Jews from their extreme religious fundamentalism.

However, once in the Knesset and part of the government, the newly elected members of parliament began to neglect the interests of those in the derelict development towns and impoverished city slums who had voted for them. The Israeli legislature continued incrementally cutting subsidies and benefits for the poor and cushioning the already comfortable life of the rich.

Their Palestinian counterpart within Israel, the Islamic movement, was less successful on its own account, but probably more beneficial for those it represented. They were far less corrupt and power seeking, but were hampered by an internal rift dating from 1993, which had split the Islamic movement into two branches, the northern and southern parts of the Wadi 'Ara area. The southern branch was more pragmatic, and was prepared to play the Israeli political game according to the rules. It also accepted the legitimacy of the PA and its president, Yasser Arafat. The northern branch was more militant, and rejected the Oslo agreements. Both branches, like Hamas, saw the whole of Palestine as a holy endowment, a *waqf*, and thus the rightful property of the Muslim people of Palestine. But they could not agree on a joint strategy regarding elections. In 1996, this led to a decision not to run. But in 1999, the southern branch joined other more secular and national groups in a united list, which became the largest Israeli Palestinian party, replacing the Front (which included the Communist Party).

Both branches, however, helped to unite Palestinians on both sides of the 1967 borders. This uniformity of identity was revealed in the joint struggle for the sanctity of Jerusalem. It was this urge to defend Haram al-Sharif that ignited the second intifada in October 2000, called *Intifadat al-Aqsa* both in the occupied territories and in Israel itself. At the time of writing, all the factions of Palestinian political Islam are united behind the PA in this intifada, support that could dwindle if a 'peace' process were reactivated. They, like the Jewish fundamentalists, are a fixture in individual as well as collective politics, the fortunes of which depend on two factors. The first is the ability of national elites to remain dominant, by any means possible, and the second is the will of these groups, Jewish or Muslim, to develop reasonable co-existential relationships with the more secular sections of their communities.

The Oslo process presented the Islamic bloc with the same dilemma that faced by the Islamic movement within Israel. Like any dogmatic political body, it had to adhere to its declared positions, usually phrased in a way that precluded compromise. This excluded it from participation in the peace process of which the January 1996 election was an important part, as it felt obliged to boycott the elections. But the election was conducted against a background of growing public disappointment in the Oslo process, and what seemed the division of the West Bank into cantons, controlled economically and militarily by Israel with the help of byroads and blocs of settlements. There was also frustration at the non-democratic conduct of the Palestinian security forces, which terrorized the inhabitants much as the Israeli secret service had done. Such an atmosphere could have helped the Islamic bloc, as its representatives told the electorate which candidates for the new Palestinian parliament were acceptable to it, even though it did not participate in the elections. Ultimately, however, Arafat's decisions excluded even those elected with the Islamic bloc's blessing from any say in local politics.

At times when the peace process seemed to be succeeding (1996), or when the PA was taking the military initiative against Israel (2000), the Islamic paramilitary wing resorted to suicide bombings. This phenomenon attracted considerable international scholarly attention. The common view was that this was an inherently Islamic phenomenon, and so scholars were advised to study the early Muslim scriptures and writings. While this was a useful general recommendation for students of the Middle East, it is useless in helping us understand the particular kind of terror sown by the Islamists of Palestine in the wake of the Oslo accord. Islamic law in fact condemns suicide, and Sunni Islam, to which all the Palestinian Islamists belong, encourages toleration and peace rather than jihad. Moreover, Israel and Zionism, not the political forces opposing them, have justified their acts on the basis of religious precepts. Finally, Judaism, like Christianity, is legitimate in the eyes of even the extreme Islamists, despite the occasional use of anti-Semitic rhetoric during inflammatory speeches by fanatical leaders or leaders under pressure. This rhetoric relies on a reservoir of images first used in the polemics between Christianity, Islam and Judaism in the early medieval period, but is now mainly used by politicians, not religious thinkers. So there is no religious support, either legal or textual, for the act of suicide. The Western media in their desperate effort to classify it have depicted it as a mystical or metaphysical phenomenon, but there is very little evidence to support this interpretation.

Terrorism in the form of suicide is actually connected to the emergence and development of political Islam in Palestine. This began with the setting up of a branch of the Egyptian Muslim Brotherhood in Palestine. The Brotherhood retained its hold over Palestinian politics in the West Bank and the Gaza Strip between 1948 and 1967, until it was overshadowed by the rise of the PLO. It re-emerged as a formidable political force after the hardships of occupation led to the revival of personal religion and the Iranian revolution in 1979 raised the public popularity of politics in the name of religion rather than of nation.

The focus of the Brotherhood's activity in the 1970s was the mosque. By 1979, there were 750 mosques in the occupied territories, twice as many as there had been in 1967. The mosques attracted the lower socio-economic strata of society: workers, the unemployed, refugees, teachers and students, peasants and city dwellers. They provided economic aid, social contact and religious preaching. The more the national leadership failed to ease the burden of the occupation, the more the mosque became the refuge for those suffering from it the most.

The political senses of the Brotherhood were sharp enough to link the mosques into a single network, enhancing and legitimizing the movement's status *vis-à-vis* the PLO. This alertness was vindicated on the first day of the intifada. On that day the leaders of the movement founded the Islamic resistance movement Hamas. The new organization immediately formed a military wing whose main objective was a strategy for fighting the occupation, thus wrong-footing and overshadowing the PLO.

Shortly after 1967, a splinter group of the Brotherhood had come into existence, trying to distinguish itself by extreme tactics while adhering to the same brand of political Islam as other, similar Palestinian movements. This group became an organized movement, calling itself Islamic Jihad. At first it was easy to prove their extremism in the struggle against occupation, compared to the cautious Brotherhood. But it was more difficult to compete with the new Brotherhood, the Hamas movement.

This is the context in which the suicide bombers should be viewed. It is partly a tactical choice to highlight the originality and commitment of a given political Islamist group to the struggle against the occupation. The Hezbollah in Lebanon had demonstrated the most daring method: young people willing to destroy themselves as human bombs. Islamic Jihad was the first to regard such actions as martyrdom, and Hamas followed suit. By the time of the second intifada, in October 2000, it was the preferred method of those wishing to oppose the occupation by force. Israel employed F-16s, Merkava tanks and Apache gunships; the Palestinians responded with suicide bombing, with the participation of Fatah's secular offshoot Shuhada al-Aqsa ('al-Aqsa martyrs') and the Marxist PFLP alongside the original bombers. Intellectuals and politicians doubted the wisdom of committing these acts in Israeli civilian areas, but were more inclined to condone those employed against the army and the settlers. The youth made heroes of the martyrs, with many of them wishing to follow suit.

At first, the Hamas military wing, the Izz al-Din al-Qassam brigades, had found it difficult to recruit potential martyrs. But indoctrinating young people trapped in a harsh world of military occupation, poverty and deprivation was by no means impossible. The willingness to participate was not the fruit of a particular political culture, but rather the result of a successful combination of charismatic leadership and certain existential conditions. (We know that not every young recruit ultimately agreed to complete the deed, so there must be a psychological factor involved.) By 2000, all this had changed. With 50 per cent unemployment, constant Israeli blockading of the West Bank cities, an electric fence around the Gaza Strip, and no hope for a political solution, there was no longer any need for preachers and 'senders', only for a constant supply of explosives and hand grenades.

When and if the wave of violence that began in 2000 subsides, the society between the Mediterranean and the Jordan will have many other pressing issues to deal with. It is, like many other societies in this part of the world, caught between forces of localization and globalization. This is not just a clash between secularism, representing universal values, and political national religions, representing local values. The power of local economics as opposed to the domination of a supranational economy is also a factor. Israel and Palestine are, on the face of it, in two very different categories. Israel has an expanding economy, while the Palestinians are in danger of being swallowed by the global economy. But the situation is not that clear cut. Israel's fragile economy has not reached the level of those in the West. A lack of natural resources, coupled with inefficiency, high investment in the army, and local isolation (including the Arab boycott) have all contributed. Large sections of its economy are thus vulnerable, and totally dependent on monetary, industrial and financial policies formulated elsewhere.

What will in future stabilize this intricate matrix of identity, politics and economics is a lasting correlation between national identity and socio-economic realities. In this respect very little has changed in comparison to the end of the nineteenth century. Land is still the most valuable resource for survival in Palestine, and the process that began with the first wave of Zionist immigration, the expropriation by purchase or eviction of Palestinian land, is continuing. Since 1882, while many new Jewish villages, settlements and towns have been erected, not one new Palestinian town or village has been built. The obsession with land acquisition continues to threaten the livelihood of Palestinians, who increasingly respond with violence. Villagers in Galilee lose their land to Judaization programmes, Bedouins in the Negev are driven out of their traditional territories, and the settlement project in the West Bank has not ceased since 1967.

In the 1990s, agreements on land, and on other pressing issues, seemed for a while to enable the society to deal with other outstanding items such as education, health and ecology. Civil society of a sort, especially in the more well-to-do Jewish community, sprang up. Alternative medicine, education and ways of life were the fads of a society disappointed by tradition, religion and modernity. But this lull is now over, and it seems that 'the conflict' has won again, destroying even a chance for the two communities to concentrate on welfare and well-being rather than survival.

The re-emergence of the national and ethnic conflict as a major facet of life sidelined the politics of identity, any civil society activity, and all interest in social and economic reforms. The violence is gathering momentum as this book concludes, sweeping up those who have been in limbo since 1948: non-repatriated refugees, occupied Palestinians, unemployed Mizrahi Jews, and Palestinian second-class citizens in Israel.

# Epilogue

The end of the twentieth century saw the barometer of peace swing franti-
cally between hope and despair in a land torn apart by conflict. In the
early 1990s, the pointer had tilted towards the positive pole. The historic mutual recognition between Israel and the PLO in September 1993
raised many hopes. It allowed the Palestinians to experiment with self-rule,
admittedly only in 22 per cent of mandatory Palestine, as a step on the
road to a more comprehensive nation-building programme. Almost every
aspect of life was covered by this experiment in which the three classical
authorities – executive, legislative and judicial – were established with, in
principle, a system of checks and balances. This was supposed to be augmented by a more democratic financial framework to be supervised by the
European Union, a new educational system and a national broadcasting
authority. This initial phase was expected to culminate in the 1996 elections
for a parliament and for government.

In practice, none of the programmes turned into a chapter in nation-
building. Israeli commentators were quick to note that the political culture
of the Palestinian leadership under Yasser Arafat – a culture of corruption
and dictatorship in their eyes – was the principal cause of the failure. But
it seems that the 'nation-building' exercise was a sham because the Oslo
process was not, after all, the coveted step towards peace and independence.

The Oslo process, if examined from a twenty-first century perspective,
seems to be yet another tragic chapter in the history of peace-making in
Palestine and Israel. The peace attempts in the past, beginning with the first
Camp David accords in 1978 and 1979, had something in common: they
avoided some of the real issues at the heart of the matter, such as the refugee
problem, although they were driven by genuine concerns about the conflict
and its victims. These efforts were orchestrated by American mediators who
usually adopted the Israeli, not the Palestinian, point of view. According
to the former view, the conflict in Palestine began in 1967 with the occupation of the West Bank and the Gaza Strip; hence peace meant an Israeli

withdrawal from these areas. The Camp David accords, and then the Oslo process, tried to persuade the Palestinian leadership that the best they could expect would be limited sovereignty in the West Bank and the Gaza Strip with neither territorial integrity nor a capital. Additionally, the Palestinian leaders were asked to forsake the only reason for their struggle since 1948: the right of return of the refugees expelled by Israel in 1948, a right recognized by the United Nations in December 1948. Arafat, Palestinian leader then president, refused to sanction such a deal as a final settlement when asked to do so at Camp David in the summer of 2000. The people under occupation rose once more in reaction to what they considered the humiliating offer made by President Clinton and Prime Minister Barak that summer.

The second intifada has raged since October 2000. It spilled over into Israel itself, where the old frustration of the Palestinian minority burst out in solidarity with the Palestinians killed in the confrontations that followed the visit of the then opposition leader, Ariel Sharon, to Haram al-Sharif in Jerusalem. Unarmed Palestinians went out to protest against the Sharon visit and the humiliating offer made by Barak at Camp David and were met by fully-equipped Israeli border police. Thirteen Israeli Palestinian citizens were shot dead by the police and, despite an honest inquiry by an official commission headed by the Supreme Court Judge Theodore Or, the fences between the two communities were not mended. In the twenty-first century, a new assertive young generation of Palestinians, redefining their community as a national one and demanding that Israel be made into a state for all its citizens, faced an ever more ethnocentric, sometimes racist, Jewish majority, for whom removing the Palestinian minority if things got out of hand was a serious possibility.

After the deaths after Sharon's visit, the Palestinian resentment took another form: old and new Palestinian militias, representing every known group or faction in Palestinian politics, began to operate with a dangerous unity of purpose and action. Whether they were called the Martyrs of al-Aqsa or the Izz al-Din Battalions, whether they were communists or Islamists, they took up suicide bombing as the sole way of ending the occupation. The Israeli retaliation was even more severe than in the past, culminating in the destruction of the Jenin refugee camp, with the deaths of scores of Palestinians, in April 2002. This followed the indiscriminate killing of 30 Jews at a Passover meal in Netanya a few days earlier. The social and economic fabric of Palestinian society was destroyed in the process, while the personal security of Israelis and their relatively high standard of living was eroded in an unprecedented way.

Two years into the carnage, and especially after the horrific events in Jenin became public knowledge, the American administration resumed its peace efforts. In the winter of 2002–03, these culminated in a plan called the 'Road Map'. This had taken two years because the American president, George W. Bush, had shown no interest in involving the US administration in the mess left behind by his predecessor, Clinton. However, on 11 September 2001, Washington was alerted to the need to take a renewed interest in world affairs in general, and Middle Eastern ones in particular. Osama Ibn Laden, a son of one of Saudi Arabia's richest families, had developed his own interpretation of political Islam, and had built an organization called al-Qaeda that would enable him to confront US power wherever he chose. He began his war in the late 1990s with the bombing of American embassies in East Africa. In September 2001, members of al-Qaeda hijacked four airliners, crashing two into the World Trade Center and one into the Pentagon.

The American response gave expression to the neo-conservative agenda of cultural supremacy and economic hegemony. Afghanistan's Taliban regime was toppled, and in 2003 it was Iraq's turn. Unsettled accounts between the president's father and the Iraqi ruler, Saddam Husayn, a wish to control Iraq's oilfields, a desire to signal to Islamic Iran and anti-American Syria that they could be next, as well as strong Israeli lobbying for action led to an American invasion of Iraq in March 2003.

Great Britain, as one of America's few major allies in the war, had insisted that a peace plan for Palestine should be presented as one of the prime objectives of the imposition of a new world order in the Middle East. In May 2003, with the overthrow of Saddam Husayn's regime in Iraq and the main military campaign at an end, the 'Road Map' for peace in the Palestinian–Israeli conflict was endorsed by the quartet of the US, the EU, Russia and the UN. It set out a series of steps for leading to the establishment of an independent Palestinian state in the occupied territories by 2005 (without defining where its borders would be) in return for a Palestinian promise to end the terrorist attacks against Israel. Although it was a thick dossier it had very little to offer that would change the reality on the ground and it also suffered from all the deficiencies of previous attempts to solve the conflict.

While the discourse of peace was revived at the level of governments and foreign ministries, suicide bombs continued to explode in Israeli shopping malls, on buses, and near military installations. The Israelis reoccupied most of the areas from which they had recently withdrawn and maintained their isolation of Arafat in his compound in Ramallah, declaring him irrelevant. The American and Israeli attempt to impose a new leader, Mahmoud Abbas (Abu Mazin), one of Arafat's old associates, also totally failed. After a few weeks as the first ever prime minister of Palestine, Abu Mazin resigned. He admitted that he could not wield authority without Arafat's support, nor could he control the Palestinian struggle to end the occupation. Meanwhile the Israeli authorities kept up their domination of every aspect of Palestinian life: border closures, abuse at checkpoints, house demolitions, the assassination of military and political activists, mass arrests and the start of the construction of a wall separating the territories of the West Bank from Israeli territory.

This was not the first wall to be built. In the mid-1990s, the Israelis had encircled the Gaza Strip with a huge wall, electric fences and guard towers, which had effectively sealed off the Strip and turned it into a kind of huge prison camp. A similar wall, with the same purpose, was now planned to divide the West Bank from Israel, with large inroads to ensure that some of the major Jewish settlements would be on the Israeli side of the divide. For many Palestinians, the territories left to them under the projected 'Palestinian state' seemed to be yet another prison camp.

After Abu Mazin's resignation, Arafat offered someone closer to him, Ahmad Qari' (Abu Ala) as Prime Minister. However, in some respects, neither name nor person is relevant. No Palestinian leader, including Arafat, is willing to act the part of what seems to the people to be the chief warden of two huge prison camps, where unemployment is nearly 75 per cent, half of the houses are in ruins, lawlessness reigns, and most people cannot even visit nearby villages or safely reach hospitals, schools, universities or their businesses.

The tragedy of Palestine is that the next peace plan, whenever it appears, will also be based on the false assumption that peace means an Israeli withdrawal to its 1967 borders and the establishment of a Palestinian state next to it. The presence of so many Palestinians in Israel itself and the significant presence of Jewish settlers in what is supposed to be the future Palestine both cast doubt on the feasibility of this idea, which failed to persuade the indigenous population of Palestine in 1947.

But far more importantly, this model has very little to offer the main victims of the Palestine conflict and the people whom the peace process should serve most – the refugees. As this book hopefully has succeeded in conveying, the history of Palestine is first of all the story of an indigenous people who were joined by newcomers. The non-elite among them looked for ways of adapting to the new reality of immigration and settlement, while the political elites preferred conflict and sought military means to impose their interpretation on the course of events.

The political leaderships failed and the civil societies tried, albeit in a very limited and unimpressive way, to save what was left of their lives and their security. For any political peace iniative to succeed, the chapter of Palestine's dispossession needs to be closed. Recognizing the very act of dispossession – by accepting in principle the Palestinian refugees' right of return – could be the crucial act that opens the gate to the road out of conflict. A direct dialogue between the dispossessed and the state that expelled them can refresh the discourse of peace and may lead people and leaderships alike to acknowledge the need to seek a united political structure which, at different historical junctures in this story, has seemed possible.

# Notes

INTRODUCTION: A NEW LOOK AT MODERN PALESTINE AND ISRAEL

1 Antonious 1938 pp. 21–35.
2 Patati 1957 pp. 173–200.
3 Bhabha (ed.) 1970, p. 1.
4 Anderson 1991 pp. 204–206.
5 Levi, 1966.
6 Gerber 1998 pp. 563–572.
7 Foucault, 1972 in Colin Gordon (ed.)

I FIN DE SIÈCLE (1856–1900): SOCIAL TRANQUILLITY AND
POLITICAL DRAMA

1 McCarthy 1988, p. 6.
2 Farsoun and Zacharia 1997 pp. 24–25; Doumani 1995, pp. 1–20.
3 Firestone 1990 pp. 91–130.
4 On the nature of this feudal system see Scholch 1986 pp. 123–9.
5 Masterman 1918 pp. 56–71.
6 Cannan 1920 p. 4.
7 This is the theory explored in Geertz 1986.
8 One of the best sources is Kahle 1912 pp. 139–178.
9 This is explored fully in the research on women appearing in court. See Agmon
1994 pp. 36–59.
10 Cohen et al. 1993 (Hebrew).
11 A good example is Yazbak 1998 pp. 163–188.
12 See description from the 1930s referring to earlier period, in Mogannam 1937
pp. 35–49.
13 See introduction and collection in Mabro (ed.) 1991. For a full account see
Archer and Fleming 1986.
14 Doumani 1999 pp. 27–28.
15 See example in Maoz and Pappe (eds) 1997 pp. 163–208.
16 Hourani 1981 pp. 36–66.
17 Mardin 1993 pp. 347–374.
18 Darwazeh 1986 p. 66 (Arabic).

269

19 Douwes 1999.
20 Abu Izz al-Din 1929 (Arabic) is the first to mention it. It is further explored in Kimmerling and Migdal 1993 pp. 3–35.
21 Scholch 1993 pp. 77–118.
22 Al-Tamimi and al-Bahjat 1987 Vol. 2 pp. 104–122.
23 Tsimchoni in G. Ben-Dor (ed.) 1979 pp. 73–100.
24 See McCarthy for near estimates pp. 10–24.
25 Butrus Abu Maneh, 'The Rise and Fall of the Sanjack of Jerusalem in the Late 19th Century' in G. Ben-Dor (ed.), The Palestinians and the Middle East Conflict, *ibid*, pp. 21–34.
26 See Butrus Abu Maneh 1990 pp. 1–44. For a more general view on Palestine, see relevant entries in Manna 1995.
27 Szyliowicz 1973 pp. 1–22.
28 Baer 1979 p. 114.
29 Smelser and Lipset 1966.
30 Khalidi 1997 pp. 35–63.
31 One such school was opened by Samuel Gobat in 1853. See Kober 1968 (German).
32 Russell 1985 pp. 17–18.
33 Haymson 1918 pp. 126–164; also Tibawi 1986.
34 This unity ended in 1886 in the wake of Germany's unification. See Hechler 1883.
35 Colbi 1969 pp. 85–90 (Hebrew).
36 Klausner 1960 p. 11 (Hebrew).
37 Nordau 1941 p. 218.
38 Ibid.
39 Schama 1978.
40 Spafford-Vester 1950 pp. 192–194.
41 Immanuel Wallerstein acknowledged the layers of cultural globalization. See Wallerstein 1990 pp. 63–67.

2 BETWEEN TYRANNY AND WAR (1900–1918)

1 Deringil 1999.
2 Palmer 1993 pp. 164–174.
3 'The Women's Movement' in the *Palestinian Encyclopedia*, Vol. 2, Damascus: PLO Publication, 1984, pp. 212–213.
4 Frumkin 1954 (Hebrew).
5 Blyth 1927 p. 158.
6 On the new land regime within the context of the reforms see Quataert in H. Inalcik and D. Quataert (eds) 1994 pp. 843–893.
7 Scholch 1993 pp. 267–283.
8 Public Record Office FO 78/5353, three letters July 1904.
9 Quoted in *Korot* 3(21), (March 1972) p. 17 (Hebrew).
10 Rupin 1968 pp. 164–5 (Hebrew).
11 Sternhell 1998.

12 Shafir 1989 pp. 54–61.
13 Halpern and Reinharz 1998 pp. 46–58.
14 Naor and Levinson 1984 pp. 5–31 (Hebrew); Katz 1994 pp. 287–291.
15 See IDAN 1999 'The Sacred Scrolls of Tel-Aviv' pp. 32–42.
16 I wish to thank Rahel Hazanov Alexander who showed me her family letter collection, which included letters of Yacov Hazanov from June 1905 on these and other matters.
17 See Nini 2000 (Hebrew). Whole book devoted to this episode.
18 Al-Husayni 1930 pp. 93–98.
19 *Al-Quds* no. 42, 30 March 1909.
20 *Al-Muandi*, 23, 9 July 1914. This paper appeared for only one year and is quoted by Yehosuha 1974 p. 50 (Arabic).
21 Issue 334, 7 February 1913.
22 Bernstein 1987 (Hebrew).
23 Abu Ghazzalah n.d. p. 115 (Arabic); Tibawi 1956 p. 193.
24 Al-Khalidi 1925 p. 2 (Arabic).
25 Government of Palestine, *Report of Palestine Administration*, July 1920–December 1921, p. 50.
26 Makover 1984 p. 26 (Hebrew).
27 *Filastin* 8 August 1914.
28 *Filastin* 14 October, 1914.
29 Ram 1996 p. 273 (Hebrew).
30 Yehoshua 1981 p. 43 (Hebrew); Khalil al-Skakini, Diary, 28 September, 1914.
31 McCarthy 1988 p. 5.
32 Ben Zvi 1936 pp. 156–161 (Hebrew).
33 Sluzki 1954 Vol. 1 pp. 324–344 (Hebrew).

### 3 THE MANDATORY STATE: COLONIALISM, NATIONALIZATION AND COHABITATION

1 McCarthy 1988 p. 26.
2 Asaf 1970 p. 201 (Hebrew).
3 Department of Education, Government of Palestine, *Note on Education in Palestine, 1920–1929*, p. 4 (microfilm report in the library of Haifa University).
4 Tibawi 1956 pp. 24–25.
5 Bowman 1947.
6 Gurney 1920 pp. 1–20.
7 Pirie-Gordon 1919 p. 79.
8 Biger 1994 pp. 118–131.
9 Asaf 1970 p. 276.
10 Mezer and Kaplan 1990 pp. 165–66 (Hebrew). See also Mezer 1998 pp. 26–29.
11 Porath 1974. First volume follows chronicles of this group of politicians.
12 Khalidi 1997 pp 94–126.
13 See Pappe 1997.
14 On the rifts within the families see Khalaf 1991.

15 Horowitz and Lissak 1978 pp. 250–272.
16 This particular achievement is stressed in Shepherd 2000.
17 Government of Palestine, *Report of the High Commissioner on the Administration of Palestine, 1920–1925* (22 April 1925), pp. 13–14; see also Haymson 1950 pp. 47–48.
18 Nardi 1945; Segev 2000 317–319.
19 Anglo-American Committee of Inquiry 1991 Vol. 2 p. 611.
20 Ronen Shamir 2000.
21 Al-Budairi 1980 (Arabic).
22 Al-Hut 1981 (Arabic).
23 See Owen in Abed (ed.) 1988 pp. 13–35.
24 Barbara Smith 1993.
25 Shapiro 1976.
26 Lewis French, Reports on Agricultural Development and Land Settlement in Palestine, Jerusalem, December 1931.
27 Qanu 1983 p. 16 note 8.
28 Meredith 1975 pp. 485–487.
29 Public Record Office CO 733/230/17249/2, no date, Secretary of State for the Colonies' Reaction to the French Report.
30 Swedenburg 1995.
31 Firestone January 1975 pp. 3–23 and April 1975 pp. 173–194; Washitz 1947, p. 22 (Hebrew); Stein 1984.
32 Baer, in Migdal (ed.) 1980; and Zureik, in Nakhleh and Zureik (eds) 1980 pp. 47–63.
33 Adler 1988 pp. 97–120; Miller, in Migdal (ed.) 1980 p. 127; al-Safari 1937 p. 174 (Arabic).
34 Hala 1974 pp. 540–541 (Arabic).
35 According to Avi Shlaim, Ben-Gurion also saw the report as heralding the end of British rule in Palestine. See Shlaim, 1999 p. 19.
36 Mattar 1988 pp. 86–107.
37 The Labour Archive, Protocols of the Executive Committee of the Histadrut, Jaffa, 30 December 1920, pp. 1–2.
38 Three books deal with cohabitation in Haifa in particular and also mention other cases. See Bernstein 2000; de Vries 1999 (Hebrew); Lockman 1996.
39 Reported in Baruch Katinka, *Then and Now*, Jerusalem, 1961 (Hebrew).
40 Greenberg, in Pappe (ed.) 1995a, pp. 157–178 (Hebrew).
41 Lockman 1996, pp. 332–335.
42 *Ba-Machaneh*, 8 March 1946.
43 Al-Budairi 1979.
44 Kaufman (ed.) 1998.
45 This is the conclusion of Nir Yehudai 1997 p. 105 (MA Thesis Haifa University).
46 A Survey of Palestine Vol. 2 p. 555.
47 Ibid p. 863.
48 Naval Intelligence Division 1943 p. 162.
49 Kazanelson-Shazar 1930 (Hebrew).

4 BETWEEN NAKBAH AND INDEPENDENCE: THE 1948 WAR

1 Newman 1947 p. 143.
2 Gracia-Granados 1948.
3 Pappe 1994 pp. 16–46.
4 See three different views on this: Benny Morris, 'The Causes and Character of the Arab Exodus from Palestine: the Israeli Defense Forces Intelligence Service Analysis of June 1948' in Pappe, 1999b pp. 193–210; Nur Masalha, in Pappe, ibid, pp. 211–220; and see Ilan Pappe, 'Were They Expelled?: The History, Historiography and Relevance of the Refugee Problem' in Ghada Karmi and Eugene Cortran (eds), *The Palestinian Exodus, 1948–1988*, London: Ithaca, 1999, pp. 37–62.
5 Morris 1988; Palumbo 1987.
6 Pappe 1994b pp. 102–134.
7 Shalim 1988.
8 Gilad (ed.) 1957 p. 15 (Hebrew).
9 Khalidi 1992.
10 Qasmiya (ed.) 1975 (Arabic).
11 See different approaches to Haifa in Morris, 1998; Masalha 1999; Palumbo 1987 pp. 58–81.
12 Abu Sita 1999 pp. 171–196.
13 Amitzur 1996.
14 Bialer 1990.
15 Morris 1990, pp. 191–222.
16 IDF Publications, *The Book of the Alexandroni Brigade* (Tel-Aviv 1964), p. 96 (Hebrew).
17 Pappe 2001 pp. 19–39.
18 Benvenisti 2000.


5 THE AGE OF PARTITION (1948–1967)

1 For statistics for this period see Gilbar 1997.
2 UNRWA Annual Report 1951, A/905, supplement 16, p. 67.
3 Pappe 1988, pp. 124–161.
4 Hadawi 1967.
5 Pappe, 1994b, pp. 203–243.
6 Farsoun and Zacharia 1997 pp. 154–155.
7 Peretz 1993 p. 415.
8 Ilan Pappe 1995b pp. 157–174.
9 For a detailed account of these expulsions and transfers see Masalha 1997, pp. 7–14.
10 Shenhav 1999 pp. 605–630.
11 Amitai 1988 (Hebrew). See also Beinin 1990. pp. 77–99.
12 Pappe (due for publication 2003).
13 On domestic refugees see Zureik 1997 pp. 61–74.

14 Bevenisti 2001.
15 Sayigh 1997 p. 48.
16 Morris 1993.
17 Sayigh 1997 pp. 35–112.
18 Shlaim 1988.
19 Sayigh p. 49.
20 Abidi 1965 pp. 201–202.
21 Sayigh, pp. 51–54.
22 Farsoun and Zacharia 1997 p. 149.
23 Pamela Ann Smith 1984, pp. 90–92.
24 Ibid p. 92.
25 Baron 1977 pp. 163–4.
26 Pappe, in Nevo and Pappe (eds) 1994a pp. 61–94.
27 Flapan 1987.
28 Cragg, 1992 pp. 240–241
29 Reiter 1989 pp. 21–45 (Hebrew).
30 Al-Haj 1987.
31 Nakhleh 1975b pp. 497–516.
32 Pappe, in Troen and Lucas (eds) 1995 pp. 617–658.
33 On land confiscation see Lustick 1980.
34 Shlaim 1999 pp. 143–185.
35 Ibid.
36 Golani 1998.
37 Shamir, in Louis and Owen (eds) 1989 pp. 81–90.
38 Shemesh 1988.
39 Sakakini 1975 (Arabic).
40 Pamela Ann Smith 1984, p. 77.
41 Danziger, in Gabriel Ben-Dor (ed) 1979 pp. 347–376.
42 *Haaretz*, 2 March, 1950.
43 Kalev, in Offir (ed.) 1999 pp. 149–158 (Hebrew).
44 Levy 1997.
45 Shalev 1984.
46 Gednizier 1997.
47 *Haaretz*, 11 September, 1949.
48 Segev 1991 pp. 173–6 (Hebrew).
49 Shaked 2000 pp. 36–80 (Hebrew).
50 22 June, 1955.
51 Segev p. 311.
52 Aredent 1994.
53 Shohat 1988 pp. 1–27.
54 Gat 1987 p. 186, says it will never be known how much Israel was behind the bombings, but it seems that he himself has enough evidence to substantiate the claim.
55 Beinin 1998.
56 Sivirsky and Bernstein, in Ram (ed) 1993 pp. 120–147 (Hebrew).

57 Sivirsky 1981 (Hebrew); Smooha 1981.
58 Sivirsky and Bernstein 1993 p. 132.
59 *Haaretz*, 28 December, 1951.
60 *Haaretz*, 29 April, 1953.
61 *Haartez*, 28 December, 1951.
62 Kaufman 1997.
63 Zureik 1979.
64 Firo 1999.

## 6 GREATER ISRAEL AND OCCUPIED PALESTINE: THE RISE AND FALL OF HIGH POLITICS (1967–1987)

1 Morris 1999, pp. 302–345.
2 Pappe (for publication in 2003).
3 The most updated number for 2001 is 4,942,121 quoted by the Joint Parliamentary Middle East Councils Commission of Enquiry – Palestinian Refugees, *Right of Return*, p. 22.
4 UNRWA 1984.
5 Quoted in Pamela Ann Smith 1984 p. 150 note 27.
6 Turki 1972 p. 53.
7 Plascov 1981.
8 Sayigh 1979.
9 Tamari 1981.
10 Pamela Ann Smith, p. 169.
11 This comes out very clearly in Riad Massarwa's play, *A Station Called Beirut* (published in Acre: Al-Mussawar 1983), an adaptation to the 1982 Lebanon War of Kanafani's *Men in the Sun*.
12 For an example see Sirhan 1975 pp. 91–107.
13 Farsoun and Zacharia 1997 p. 182
14 Hudson 1969.
15 Cobban 1984.
16 Sayigh 1997 p. 516.
17 Brand 1988 pp. 3–4.
18 Masalha 1997 pp. 80–90.
19 Ibid.
20 *Haaretz*, 10 January 1968.
21 Aruri (ed.) 1989.
22 Lifshitz 1987 p. 77 (Hebrew).
23 *Haaretz*, 3 January 1968.
24 Hofnung 1996.
25 Shehadeh 1988.
26 According to Uri Avineri's *Haolam Hazeh Weekly*, 1 July 1968.
27 *Haaretz*, 21 January 1968.
28 Sprinzak 1986.
29 *Haaretz*, 31 October 1967.

30 Sofer 1988.
31 For figures in between see for instance Benvenisti 1986.
32 Sella 1986.
33 Meital 1997.
34 S. Wigoder and M Wigoder 1999, in Adi Offir (ed.) pp. 195–204 (Hebrew).
35 See Shehadeh 1984 (Hebrew).
36 Don Peretz 1993, p. 414, note 10.
37 Pamela Ann Smith p. 171.
38 For an in depth study of the economic situation in the Gaza Strip see Roy 2001.
39 Pappe 1989 (Hebrew).
40 Abu Shokar, Abu Jaber, Buhbe and Smadi 1990, pp. 93–109.
41 Pamela Ann Smith pp. 161–162.
42 Kishk 1981.
43 Shlaim 1999 pp. 298–318.
44 *Haaretz*, March 7, 1974.
45 Shlaim, pp. 329–334.
46 *Haaretz*, 1 March 1971.
47 *Maariv*, 7 January 1968.
48 Bar-On 1996.
49 Meital 1997.
50 Alain Gresh 1980 pp. 1–30.
51 Khalidi 1986.
52 Said 1994 pp. 69–77.
53 Farsoun and Zacharia 1997 p. 165.
54 Seale 1992.
55 Ravitzky 1986.
56 *Haaretz*, 24 November 1967.
57 Yiftachel 1997 pp. 505–519.
58 Nakhleh 1975 pp. 29–35.
59 Rouhana and Ghanem, in Ilan Pappe (ed.), 1999b pp. 223–46.

7 THE UPRISING AND ITS POLITICAL CONSEQUENCES (1987–1996)

1 Tamari 1992 pp. 7–28 (Hebrew).
2 See Israeli (ed.) 1988 (Hebrew).
3 According to Jamil Hilal it was 500 million after seven years of occupation. See Hilal 1976 pp. 207–210.
4 UNRWA, Situation of Palestine Civilians under Israeli Occupation: Gaza Strip, March–May 1991.
5 Al-Haq Law in the Service of Man 1988.
6 Masalha 1997 pp. 122–123.
7 Barghouti 1990.
8 Grossman 1988.
9 Kutab, in Sivirski and Pappe, 1992 p. 135.
10 Jad, in Nassar and Heacock (eds), 1990.

11 Hilterman, ibid.
12 Tamari 1990.
13 Hunter 1991, pp. 136–141.
14 Palestinian National Council 1989 pp. 213–222.
15 These issues had been recognized as the basis for peace by the UN General Assembly in Resolution 194 (IV) adopted on December 11, 1949. See Pappe 1992, pp. 195–202.
16 Pappe 1999a pp. 95–112.
17 These were in chronological order: the Agreement on the Gaza Strip and the Jericho area signed on May 4, 1994. This was followed by the Agreement on the Preparatory Transfer of Powers and Responsibilities (Israel–PLO) signed on August 29, 1994. Then came Oslo B: Interim Agreement between Israel and the Palestinians, signed on September 28, 1995. This agreement has 7 annexes dealing with among other things redeployment, Palestinian elections, economic relations and cooperation on security matters. It has 9 maps attached to it dividing the areas of the West Bank into A, B and C according to the level of Israeli presence under the redeployment. The last map defines the Israeli withdrawal from Hebron. This agreement was signed only on January 17, 1997 under the title 'Protocol Concurring the Re-deployment in Hebron'.
18 Said 2001.
19 Settlement Watch Report no. 8 (Peace Now Jerusalem, 31 July 1996).
20 Usher 1996 pp. 33–37.
21 Ziyad Abu Amr, *Islamic Fundamentalism in the West Bank and Gaza*, Bloomington: Indiana University Press 1994.
22 Ziyad 1993 pp. 5–19.

CONCLUSION

1 *Haaretz*, 4 June 1996.
2 Arian and Shamir 1999.
3 Economic Agreement between Israel and the PLO (The Israel Chamber of Commerce, Tel-Aviv 1994).

# Bibliography

## SOURCES IN ENGLISH

Abidi, A. 1965 *Jordan: A Political Study 1948–1957*, London: Asia Publishing House

Abu Maneh, B. 1979 'The Rise and Fall of the Sanjack of Jerusalem in the Late 19th Century', in G. Ben-Dor (ed.), *The Palestinians and the Middle East Conflict: Studies in their History, Sociology and Politics*, Haifa: University of Haifa

1990 'Jerusalem in the Tanzimat Period', *Die Welt des Islams*, 30

Abu Sita, S. 1999 'The Feasibility of the Right of Return', in Ghada Karmi and Eugene Cortran (eds), *The Palestinian Exodus, 1948–1988*, London: Ithaca Press

Abu Shokar, A., K. Abu Jaber, M. Buhbe, and M. Smadi 1990 'Income distribution and its Social Impact in the Occupied Territories', in K. Abu Jaber, M. Buhbe and M. Smadi, *Income Distribution in Jordan*, Boulder: Westview Press

Adler, R. 1988 'The Tenants of Wadi Hawarith: Another View of the Land Question in Palestine', *International Journal of Middle Eastern Studies* 20

Amitzur, I. 1996 *The Origin of the Arab-Israeli Arms Race: Arms, Embargo, Military Power and Decisions in the 1948 Palestine War*, New York: New York University Press

Anderson, B. 1991 *Imagined Communities*, London: Verso

Anglo-American Committee of Inquiry 1991 *A Survey of Palestine*, Vol. 2, Washington: Reprint by the Institute of Palestine Studies

Antonious, G. 1938 *The Arab Awakening*, London: Hamish Hamilton

Archer, R. and J. Fleming 1986 *Lady Ann Blunt; Journals and Correspondence, 1878–1917*, Cheltenham: Alexander Heriot

Aredent, H. 1994 *Eichmann in Jerusalem: A Report on the Banality of Evil*, New York: Penguin

Arian, A. and M. Shamir 1999 *The Elections of Israel, 1996*, Albany: State University of New York Press

Aruri, N. (ed.) 1989 *Occupation: Israel over Palestine*, Belmont MA: Association of Arab American University Graduates

Baer, G. 1979 'Jerusalem's Families of Notables and the Waqf in the East in the 19th Century', in D. Kushner (ed.), *Palestine in the Late Ottoman Period*, Leiden: E. J. Brill

1980 'The Office and Functions of the Village Mukhtar' in Joel Migdal (ed.), *Palestinian Society and Politics*, Princeton: Princeton University Press

Barghouti, M. 1990 'Jeep Versus Bare Feet: The Villages in the Intifada', in Jamal R. Nassar and Roger Heacock (eds), *Intifada: Palestine at the Crossroads*, New York: Prager

Bar-On, M. 1996 *In Pursuit of Peace: A History of the Israeli Peace Movement*, Washington: United States Institute of Peace Press

Beinin, J. 1998 *The Dispersion of Egyptian Jewry: Culture, Politics, and the Formation of a Modern Diaspora*, Berkeley: University of California Press

1990 *Was the Red Flag Flying There?*, Berkeley: University of California Press

Benvenisti, M. 1986 *1986 Report: Demographic, Economic, Legal, Social, and Political Developments in the West Bank*, Boulder: Westview

2000 *Sacred Landscape: The Buried History of the Holy Land since 1948*, Berkeley: University of California Press

Bernstein, D. S. 2000 *Constructing Boundaries: Jewish and Arab Workers in Mandatory Palestine – A Case Study of Haifa*, New York: State University of New York Press

Bhabha, H. K. (ed.) 1970 *The Nation and Narration*, London and New York: Routledge

Bialer, U. 1990 *Between East and West: Israel's Foreign Policy Orientation, 1948–1956*, New York: Cambridge University Press

Biger, G. 1994 *An Empire in the Holy Land: Historical Geography of the British Administration in Palestine, 1917–1929*, Jerusalem: Yehuda Magness Press

Blyth, E. 1927 *When We Lived in Jerusalem*, London: J. Murray

Bowman, H. 1947 *A Middle East Window*, London: Longman, Green and Co

Brand, L. A. 1988 *Palestinians in the Arab World*, New York: Columbia University Press

Al-Budairi, M. 1979 *The Palestine Communist Party: Arab and Jew in the Struggle for Internationalism*, London: Ithaca Press

Cannan, T. 1920 *Mohammedan Saints and Sanctuaries in Palestine*, London: Luzac and Co

Cobban, H. 1984 *The Palestinian Liberation Organization: People, Power and Politics*, Cambridge: Cambridge University Press

Cragg, K. 1992 *The Arab Christian: A History in the Middle East*, London: Mowbray

Danziger, R. 1979 'Algeria and the Palestinian Organizations' in G. Ben-Dor (ed.), *The Palestinians and the Middle East Conflict: Studies in their History, Sociology and Politics*, Haifa: University of Haifa

Department of Education, Government of Palestine, *Note on Education in Palestine, 1920–1929* (microfilm, Haifa University Library)

Deringil, S. 1999 *Ottoman Almanacs of the Arab Provinces, 1888–1892*, Buckinghamshire: Archives Editions

Doumani, B. 1995 *Rediscovering Palestine: Merchants and Peasants in Jabal Nablus, 1700–1900*, Berkeley and London: University of California Press

1999 'Rediscovering Ottoman Palestine: Writing Palestinians into History', in Ilan Pappe (ed.), *The Israel–Palestine Question*, London and New York: Routledge

Douwes, D. 1999 *The Ottomans in Syria, A History of Justice and Oppression*, London and New York: I. B. Tauris

Farsoun, S. and C. E. Zacharia 1997 *Palestine and the Palestinians*, Boulder: Westview Press

Firestone, Y. 1975 'Crop Sharing Economics in Mandatory Palestine', *Middle Eastern Studies* 11:1 (January) and 11:2 (April)

1990 'The Land Equalizing Musha' Village: A Reassessment' in Gad G. Gilbar (ed.), *Ottoman Palestine, 1800–1914: Studies in Economic and Social History*, Leiden: E. J. Brill

Firo, K. 1999 *The Druzes in the Jewish State*, Leiden: E. J. Brill

Flapan, S. 1987 *The Birth of Israel: Myths and Realities*, London: Croom Helm

Foucault, M. 1972 *Power/Knowledge: Selected Interviews and Other Writings 1972–77*, edited by Colin Gordon, New York: Pantheon Books

French, L. 1931 Reports on Agricultural Development and Land Settlement in Palestine, Jerusalem, December 1931

Gat, M. 1987 *The Jewish Exodus from Iraq, 1948–1951*, London and New York: Frank Cass

Gednizier, I. L. 1997 *Notes from the Minefield; US Intervention in Lebanon and the Middle East*, New York: Columbia University Press

Geertz, C. 1986 *Islam Observed: Religious Development in Morocco and Indonesia*, Chicago: Chicago University Press

Gerber, H. 1998 'Palestine and Other Territorial Concepts in the 17th Century', *International Journal of Middle East Studies*, 30:4 (November)

Gilbar, G. G. 1997 *Population Dilemmas in the Middle East: Essays in Political Demography and Economy*, London and New York: Frank Cass

Golani, M. 1998 *Israel in Search of War*, Brighton: Academic Sussex Press

Government of Palestine, *Report of Palestine Administration*, July 1920–December 1921

Government of Palestine, 1925 *Report of the High Commissioner on the Administration of Palestine, 1920–1925*

Gracia-Granados, J. 1948 *The Birth of Israel*, New York: Knopf

Gresh, A. 1988 *PLO: The Struggle Within: Towards an Independent Palestinian State*, London: ZED

Grossman, D. 1988 *The Yellow Wind*, Farrar, New York: Straus and Giroux

Gurney, E. W. 1920 *Hygiene and Disease in Palestine in Modern and Biblical Times*, London: Palestine Exploration Fund

Hadawi, S. 1967 *Bitter Harvest*, New York: New World Press

Al-Haj, M. 1987 *Social Change and Family Processes: Arab Communities in Shefar-A'm*, London and Boulder: Westview Press

Halpern B. and J. Reinharz 1998 *Zionism and the Creation of a New Society*, New York: Oxford University Press

Al-Haq Law in the Service of Man 1988 *Punishing a Nation: Human Rights Violations during the Palestinian Uprising, December 1987–December 1988*, Ramallah West Bank

Al-Husayni, J. 1930 'Palestine Today', *Journal of Central Asian Studies* 17:1

Haymson, A. M. 1918 'British Projects for the Restoration of the Jews in Palestine', *Journal of the American Jewish Historical Society* 26

1950 *Palestine Under the Mandate, 1920–1945*, London: Green Wood

Hechler, W. H. 1883 *The Jerusalem Bishopric*, London (no publisher)

Hilal, J. 1976 'Class Transformation in the West Bank and Gaza', *MERIP Reports*, No. 53

Hilterman, Y. 1990 'Work and Action, the Role of the Working Class in the Uprising' in J. R. Nassar and R. Heacock (eds), *Intifada: Palestine at the Crossroads*, New York: Prager

Hofnung, M. 1996 *Democracy, Law, and National Security in Israel*, Aldershot: Brookfield, USA: Dartmouth

Horowitz, D. and M. Lissak 1978 *Origins of Israeli Polity: Palestine Under the Mandate*, Chicago: Chicago University Press

Hourani, A. 1981 *The Emergence of the Modern Middle East*, London: St. Antony's/Macmillan Press

Hudson, M. 1969 'The Palestinian Arab Resistance Movement: Its Significance in the Middle East Crisis, *Middle East Journal*, 23:3 (Summer)

Hunter, F. R. 1991 *The Palestinian Uprising: A War by Other Means*, London and New York: I. B. Tauris

IDAN 1984 *Tel-Aviv in its Beginning, 1909–1934*, Jerusalem: Ben Zvi Institute

1999 *The Sacred Scrolls of Tel-Aviv*, Jerusalem: Ben Zvi Institute

Jad, I. 'From Saloons to Popular Committees, Palestinian Women, 1919–1989', in J. R. Nassar and R. Heacock (eds), *Intifada: Palestine at the Crossroads*, New York: Prager

Joint Parliamentary Middle East Councils Commission of Enquiry – Palestinian Refugees, 2001 *Right of Return*

Katz, Y. 1994 *The Business of Settlement*, Jerusalem: Magness Press

Kaufman, I. 1997 *Arab National Communism in the Jewish State*, Miami: University of Florida Press

Kaufman, M. (ed.) 1998 *The Magness–Philby Negotiations 1929*, Jerusalem: Magness Press

Khalaf, I. 1991 *Politics in Palestine: Arab Factionalism and Social Disintegration, 1939–1948*, Albany: State University of New York Press

Khalidi, R. 1986 *Under Siege: PLO Decision Making During the 1982 War*, New York: Columbia University Press

1997 *Palestinian Identity: The Construction of Modern National Consciousness*, New York: Columbia University Press

Khalidi, W. 1992 *All That Remains: The Palestinian Villages Occupied and Depopulated by Israel in 1948*, Washington: Institute for Palestinian Studies

Kimmerling, B. and J. S. Migdal, 1993 *Palestinians: The Making of a People*, New York: The Free Press

Kishk, A. B. 1981 'The Industrial and Economic Trends in the West Bank and the Gaza Strip', Beirut: UN Economic Commission for West Asia

Levi, M. J. 1966 *Modernization and the Structure of Societies*, Princeton: Princeton University Press

Levy, Y. 1997 *Trial and Error: Israel's Route from War to De-Escalation*, Albany: State University of New York Press

Lockman, Z. 1996 *Comrades and Enemies: Arab and Jewish Workers in Palestine, 1906–1948*, Berkeley: University of California Press

Lustick, I. 1980 *Arabs in the Jewish State: Israel's Control of a National Minority*, Austin, Texas: University of Texas Press

Mabro, J. (ed.) 1991 *Veiled Half-Truths: Western Travelers' Perceptions of Middle Eastern Women*, London and New York: I. B. Tauris

McCarthy, J. 1988 *The Population of Palestine: Population Statistics of the Late Ottoman Period and the Mandate*, New York: Columbia University Press

Mardin, S. 1993 'Religion and Secularism in Turkey', in Albert Hourani, Philip S. Khoury and Marcy C. Wilson (eds), *The Modern Middle East*, London and New York: I. B. Tauris

Masalha, N. 1997 *A Land Without a People: Israel, Transfer and the Palestinians 1949–85*, London: Faber and Faber

— 1999 'A Critique of Benny Morris', in I. Pappe (ed.), *The Israel–Palestine Question*, London and New York: Routledge

Masterman, E. W. G. 1918 'Hygiene and Disease in Palestine in Modern and in Biblical Times', *Palestine Exploration Fund Quarterly*

Mattar, P. 1988 *The Mufti of Jerusalem: Al-Haj Amin al-Husayni and the Palestinian National Movement*, New York: Columbia University Press

Meredith, D. 1975 'The British Government and Colonial Economic Policy, 1919–1930', *The Economic History Review*, 28:3

Mezer, J. 1998 *The Divided Economy of Mandatory Palestine*, Cambridge: Cambridge University Press

Middle East Institute 1984 *UNRWA and Peace in the Middle East*, Washington

Miller, Y. 1980 'Administrative Policy in Rural Palestine: The Impact of British Norms on Arab Community Life, 1920–1948', in J. Migdal (ed.), *Palestinian Society and Politics*, Princeton: Princeton University Press

Mogannam, M. E. T. 1937 *The Arab Women and the Palestine Problem*, London: Herbert Joseph Ltd

Meital, Y. 1997 *Egypt's Struggle for Peace: Continuity and Change, 1967–1977*, Gainsville: University Press of Florida

Morris, B. 1988 *The Birth of the Palestinian Refugee Problem, 1947–1949*, Cambridge: Cambridge University Press

— 1990 *1948 and After: Israel and the Palestinians*, Oxford: Clarendon Press

— 1993 *Israel's Border Wars, 1949–1956*, Oxford: Clarendon Press

— 1999 *Righteous Victims: A History of the Zionist–Arab Conflict, 1881–1999*, New York: Alfred A. Knopf

— 1999 'The Causes and Character of the Arab Exodus from Palestine: the Israeli Defense Forces Intelligence Service Analysis of June 1948', in I. Pappe (ed.), *The Israel–Palestine Question*, London and New York: Routledge

Nakhleh, K. 1975a 'The Goal of Education for Arabs in Israel', *New Outlook*, April–May

1975b 'The Direction of Local Level Conflict in Two Arab Villages in Israel', *American Ethnologist* 23 (August)

Nardi, N. 1945 *Education in Palestine*, Washington: Zionist Organization in America

Naval Intelligence Division 1943 *Palestine and Transjordan*

Newman, B. 1947 *Middle Eastern Journey*, London: Victor Gollancz

Nordau, M. S. 1941 *Max Nordau to His People, a Summons and a Challenge*, introduction by B. Netanyahu., New York: Published for Nordau Zionist Society by Scopus Publishing Company Inc

Owen, R. 1988 'The Economic Development in Mandatory Palestine, 1918–1948', in George T. Abed (ed.), *The Palestinian Economy*, London and New York: Routledge

Palestinian National Council 1989 'The Palestinian Declaration of Independence', *Journal of Palestinian Studies* 18

Palmer, A. 1993 *The Decline and Fall of the Ottoman Empire*, London: John Murray

Palumbo, M. 1987 *The Palestinian Catastrophe: The 1948 Expulsion of a People from their Homeland*, London and New York: Quartet

Pappe, I. 1988 *Britain and the Arab–Israeli Conflict, 1947–51*, London and New York: St. Antony's/Macmillan Series

1994a 'Jordan between Hashemite and Palestinian Identity' in J. Nevo and I. Pappe (eds), *Jordan in the Middle East: The Making of a Pivotal State*, London: Frank Cass

1994b *The Making of the Arab-Israeli Conflict, 1948–1951*, New York and London: I. B. Tauris

1995a 'An Uneasy Co-existence: Arabs and Jews in the First Decade of Statehood' in I. Troen and N. Lucas (eds), *Israel: The First Decade of Independence*, New York: State University Press

1995b 'A Text in the Eyes of the Beholder: Four Theatrical Interpretations of Kanafani's *Men in the Sun*', Contemporary Theatre Review 3:2

1997 'From the "Politics of Notables" to the "Politics of Nationalism": The Husayni Family, 1840–1922', in M. Maoz and I. Pappe (eds), *Middle Eastern Politics and Ideas: A History from Within*, London and New York: I. B. Tauris

1999a 'Breaking the Mirror: Oslo and After' in Haim Gordon (ed.), *Looking Back at the June 1967 War*, Westport: Prager, pp. 95–112

1999b *The Israel/Palestine Question*, London and New York: Routledge

1999c 'Were They Expelled?: The History, Historiography and Relevance of the Refugee Problem', in G. Karmi and E. Cortran (eds), *The Palestinian Exodus, 1948–1988*, London: Ithaca

2001 'The Tantura Case in Israel: The Katz Research and Trial', *Journal of Palestine Studies* 30:3

2003 'The Israeli Perspective of the 1958 Crisis', in R. Louis and R. Owen (eds), *The Crisis of 1958*, London and New York: I. B. Tauris (forthcoming)

Patati, R. 1957 'The Dynamics of Westernization in the Middle East', *The Middle East Journal*, 9:1

Peretz, D. 1993 *Palestinians, Refugees and the Middle East Peace Process*, Washington: US Institute of Peace Press

Pirie-Gordon, H. (ed.) 1919 *A Brief Record of the Advance of the Egyptian Expeditionary Force (July 1917–October 1918)*, London: His Majesty's Stationery Office

Plascov, A. 1981 *The Palestinian Refugees in Jordan, 1948–1957*, London and New York: Frank Cass

Porath, Y. 1974 *The Emergence of the Palestinian Arab National Movement, 1919–1929*, London and New York: Frank Cass

Qanu, J. 1983 *The Land Conflict in Palestine*, Givat Haviva: Institute For Arab Affairs

Quataert, D. 1994 'The Age of Reforms', in H. Inalcik and D. Quataert (eds), *An Economic and Social History of the Ottoman Empire, 1300–1914*, Cambridge: Cambridge University Press

Ravitzky, A. 1986 *The Roots of Kahanism: Consciousness and Political Reality*, Jerusalem: Shazar Library

Rouhana N. and A. Ghanem 1999 'The Democratization of a Traditional Minority in an Ethnic Democracy: The Palestinians in Israel', in I. Pappe (ed.), *The Israel–Palestine Question*, London and New York: Routledge

Roy, S. 2001 *The Gaza Strip: The Political Economy of De-Development*, Washington: Institute for Palestine Studies

Russell, M. 1985 *Palestine; or The Holy Land*, London: Darf Publishers Limited (new impression)

Said, E. W. 1994 *The Politics of Dispossession*, London: Chatto and Windus
      2001 *The End of the Peace Process: Oslo and After*, New York: Vintage

Sayigh, R. 1979 *Palestinians: From Peasants to Revolutionaries*, London: Zed Books

Sayigh, Y. 1997 *Armed Struggle and the Search for State*, Oxford: Oxford University Press

Schama, S. 1978 *Two Rothschilds and the Land of Israel*, New York: Knopf

Scholch, A. 1986 'Was there a Feudal System in Ottoman Lebanon and Palestine', in D. Kushner (ed.), *Palestine in the Late Ottoman Period: Political, Social and Economic Transformation*, Leiden: E. J. Brill
      1993 *Palestine in Transformation, 1856–1882; Studies in Social, Economic and Political Development*, Washington: Institute of Palestine Studies

Seale, P. 1992 *Abu Nidal: A Gun for Hire*, New York: Random House

Segev, T. 2000 *One Palestine: Jews and Arabs Under the Mandate*, New York: Metropolitan Books

Sella, A. 1986 'Custodians and Redeemers: Israeli Leaders' Perceptions of Peace', *Middle Eastern Studies* 22:2

Shafir, G. 1989 *Land, Labor and the Origins of the Israeli–Palestinian Conflict*, Cambridge: Cambridge University Press

Shalev, M. 1984 'Labor, State and Crisis: An Israeli Case Study, *Industrial Relations* 23:3

Shalim, A. 1988 *Collusion Across Jordan*, Oxford: Columbia University Press

Shamir, R. 2000 *The Colonies of Law: Colonialism, Zionism and Law in Early Mandate Palestine*, Cambridge: Cambridge University Press

Shamir, S. 1989 'The Collapse of Project Alpha' in Wm. R. Louis and R. Owen (eds), *Suez 1956: The Crisis and its Consequences*, Oxford: Clarendon Press

Shapiro, Y. 1976 *The Formative Years of the Israeli Labour Party: The Organization of Power, 1919–1930*, London: Sage Publications

Shehadeh, R. 1988 *Occupier's Law: Israel and the West Bank*, Washington: Institute for Palestine Studies

Shemesh, M. 1988 *The Palestinian National Entity, 1959–1974: Arab Politics and the PLO*, London and New York: Frank Cass

Shenhav, Y. 1999 'The Jews of Iraq: Zionist Ideology, and the Property of the Palestinian Refugees of 1948: An Anomaly of National Accounting', *International Journal of Middle Eastern Studies*, 31:4

Shepherd, N. 2000 *Ploughing Sand: British Rule in Palestine, 1917–1948*, New Brunswick, N. J.: Rutgers University Press

Shlaim, A. 1988 *Collusion Across Jordan*, Oxford: Columbia University Press
  1999 *The Iron Wall; Israel and the Arab World*, New York and London: W. W. Norton and Company

Shohat, E. 1988 'Sepharadim in Israel: Zionism from the Standpoint of its Jewish Victims', *Social Text*, 19, 20

Sirhan, B. 1975 'Palestinian Refugee Camp Life in Lebanon', *Journal of Palestine Studies*, 4:2

Smelser, N. J. and S. M. Lipset 1966 *Social Structure and Mobility in Economic Development*, Chicago: Aldine

Smith, B. 1993 *The Roots of Separatism in Palestine: British Economic Policy, 1920–1929*, Syracuse: Syracuse University Press

Smith, P. A. 1984 *Palestine and the Palestinians, 1876–1988*, New York: St. Martin Press

Smooha, S. 1981 *Israel: Pluralism and Conflict*, London: Routledge

Sofer, S. 1988 *An Anatomy of Leadership*, Oxford: Blackwell Publishers

Spafford-Vester, B. 1950 *Our Jerusalem: An American Family in the Holy City, 1881–1949*, Garden City: Doubleday

Sprinzak, E. 1986 *Gush Emunim: The Politics of Zionist Fundamentalism in Israel*, New York: American Jewish Committee, Institute of Human Relations

Stein, K. 1984 *The Land Question in Palestine, 1917–1939*, Atlanta: University of North Carolina State

Sternhell, Z. 1998 *The Founding Myths of Israel: Nationalism, Socialism, and the Making of the Jewish State*, Princeton: Princeton University Press

Swedenburg, T. R. 1995 *Memories of Revolt: The 1936–1939 Rebellion and the Palestinian National Past*, Minneapolis: University of Minnesota Press

Szyliowicz, J. S. 1973 *Education and Modernization in the Middle East*, Ithaca and London: Cornell University Press

Tamari, S. 1981 'Building Other Peoples' Homes: The Palestinian Peasant's Household and Work in Israel', *Journal of Palestine Studies*, 11:1 (Autumn)

1990 'The Revolt of the Petit Bourgeoisie: Urban Merchants and the Palestinian Uprising', in J. R. Nassar and R. Heacock (eds) *Intifada: Palestine at the Crossroads*, New York: Prager

Tibawi, A. L. 1956 *Arab Education in Mandatory Palestine*, London: Luzac

1986 *British Interests in Palestine, 1800–1901*, Oxford: Oxford University Press

Tsimchoni, D. 1979 'The Arab Christians and the Palestinian Arab National Movement during the Formative Stage', in G. Ben-Dor (ed.) *The Palestinians and the Middle East Conflict: Studies in their History, Sociology and Politics*, Tel-Aviv: Turtledove Publishing

Turki, F. 1972 *The Disinherited: Journal of a Palestinian Exile*, New York: no publisher

UNRWA 1951 Annual Report

UNRWA 1984 *A Brief History, 1950–1982*, The Agency: Vienna and Milton Viorst

UNRWA, 1991 Situation of Palestine Civilians under Israeli Occupation: Gaza Strip, March–May

Usher, G. 1996 'Closures, Cantons, and the Palestinian Covenant', *Middle East Report*, 199

Wallerstein, I. 1990 'Culture is the World System – a Reply to Boyne', in Mike Featherstone (ed.) *Global Culture: Nationalism, Globalization and Modernity, A Theory, Culture and Society Special Issue*, London, Newbury Park: Sage

Yazbak, M. 1998 *Haifa in the Late Ottoman Period, 1864–1914: A Muslim Town in Transition*, Leiden: E. J. Brill

Yiftachel, O. 1997 'Israeli Society and Jewish–Palestinian Reconciliation: Ethnocracy and its Territorial Contradictions', *Middle East Journal*, 51 (Autumn)

Ziyad, A. A. 1993 'Hamas: A Historical and Political Background', *Journal of Palestine Studies*, 22:4 (Summer)

1994 *Islamic Fundamentalism in the West Bank and Gaza*, Bloomington: Indiana University Press

Zureik, E. 1979 *The Palestinians in Israel: A Study of Internal Colonialism*, London and New York: Routledge

1980 'Reflections on Twentieth Century Palestinian Class Structure', in Khalil Nakhleh and Elia Zureik (eds), *The Sociology of the Palestinians*, London: Croom Helm

## SOURCES IN ARABIC

Abu Ghazzalah, A. n. d. *The National Education in Palestine During the British Mandate*, Acre: Al-Aswar

Abu Izz al-Din, S. 1929 *Ibrahim Pasha in Syria*, Beirut (no publisher)

Al-Budairi, M. 1980 *The Development of the Arab Workers' Movement in Palestine: Historical Introduction and Collected Documents*, Beirut: Dar Ibn Khaldun

Darwazeh, I. M. 1986 *Memoirs and Notes: A Palestinian Century*, Vol. 1, Damascus: Samed

Hala, M. 1974 *Palestine and the British Mandate, 1922–1939*, Beirut (no publisher)
Al-Hut, N. B. 1981 *Political Leaderships and Institutions in Palestine, 1917–1948*, Beirut: Institute for Palestine Studies
Al-Khalidi, A. S. 1925 'The Ottoman Education System', *Majalat Dar al-Mua'limin*, 1 (November)
Manna', A. 1995 *'The Notables of Palestine at the End of the Ottoman Period (1900–1918)'*, Beirut: Institute of Palestine Studies
Massarwa, R. 1983 *A Station Called Beirut*, Acre: Al-Mussawar
Qasmiya, K. (ed.) 1975 *Fawzi al-Qawqji's Memoirs*, Beirut: PLO Publication
Al-Safari, I. 1937 *Palestine between Mandate and Zionism*, Jerusalem (no publisher)
Sakakini, I. 1975 'The Palestinian Entity, 1964–1974', *Shuun Filastyinia*, 41, 42 (January–February)
Al-Tamimi, M. R. and M. al-Bahjat 1914, *Vilayet Beirut: The Southern Part*, Beirut: Al-Iqbal
Yehoshua, Y. 1974 *The History of the Arabic Press in Palestine: The Ottoman Period, 1908–1918*, Jerusalem: Hebrew University Press

## SOURCES IN HEBREW

Adler, R. 1986 'The Administration and the Problem of Tenants in the Wadi Hawarith Affair, 1929–1933', *Haziyonut*, 11
Agmon, I. 1994 'Women and Society: Muslim Women, the Shar'i Court and the Society of Jaffa and Haifa under Late Ottoman Rule (1900–1914)', doctoral thesis, Hebrew University
Amitai, Y. 1988 *The United Workers' Party (Mapam) 1948–1954: Attitudes on Palestinian–Arab Issues*, Tel-Aviv: Tcherikova Publishers
Asaf, M. 1970 *Arab–Jewish Relationships, 1860–1948*, Tel-Aviv: Mifalei Tarbut Ve-Hinuch
Ben Zvi, Y. 1936 *The Ben-Zvi Papers*, Tel-Aviv: Government Publication
Bernstein, D. 1987 *A Woman in Eretz Israel*, Tel-Aviv: Ha-Kibbutz Ha-Meuhad
Cohen A. et al., 1993 *Jews in the Muslim Court: Society, Economy and Communal Administration; The Eighteenth Century*, Jerusalem: Yad Ben-Zvi
Colbi, S. P. 1969 *Christianity in the Holy Land, Past and Present*, Tel Aviv: Am Hasefer
De Vries, D. 1999 *Idealism and Bureaucracy: The Roots of Red Haifa*, Tel-Aviv: Ha-Kibbutz Ha-Meuhad
Frumkin, G. 1954 *The Life of a Judge*, Tel-Aviv: Dvir
Gilad Z. (ed), 1957 *The Palmach Book*, Tel-Aviv: Ha-Kibbutz Ha-Meuhad
Greenberg, L. L. 1995 'The Arab-Jewish Drivers' Union Strike, 1931: A Contribution to the Critique on the National Conflict Sociology', in I. Pappe (ed.), *Jewish–Arab Relations in Mandatory Palestine: A New Approach to the Historical Research*, Givat Haviva: Institute for Peace Research
IDF Publications 1964 *The Book of the Alexandroni Brigade*, (Tel-Aviv)
Israeli, R. (ed.) 1988 *Ten Years of Israeli Rule in Judea and Samaria*, Jerusalem: Magness

Kalev, H. D. 1999 'The Wadi Salib Riots', in Adi Offir (ed.), *Fifty to Forty-Eight: Critical Moments in the History of the State of Israel*, Jerusalem: Van Leer Jerusalem Institute

Katinka, B. 1961 *Then and Now*, Jerusalem: Qiryat Sefer

Kazanelson-Shazar, R. 1930 *The Speeches of Women Workers*, Tel-Aviv: Council of Women Workers, Am Oved

Klausner, I. 1960 *Opposition to Herzel*, Jerusalem: R. Mas

Kutab, E. 1992 'The Participation of the Palestinian Woman in the Intifada', in S. Sivirski and I. Pappe (eds), *The Intifada: An Inside View*, Tel-Aviv: Mifras

Lifshitz, O. 1987 *Self Defeating Conquest*, Tel-Aviv: Mapam Publication

Makover, R. 1984 *Administration and Government in Palestine, 1917–1925*, Tel-Aviv: no publisher

Mezer, Y.and O. Kaplan, 1990 *The Jewish and the Arab Economy in Mandatory Palestine: Product, Employment and Growth*, Jerusalem: Mossad Byalik

Naor, M. and A. Levinson, 1984 'Who were the 66 Founders of Tel-Aviv?', in IDAN *Tel Aviv in its Beginning, 1909–1934*, Jerusalem: Ben Zvi Institute

Nini, Y. 2000 *Were You There, Or Was it a Dream?* Tel-Aviv: Am Oved

Offir, A. (ed.) 1999 *Fifty to Forty-Eight: Critical Moments in the History of the State of Israel*, Jerusalem:Van Leer Institute

Pappe, I. 1989 *A Profile of a Knifer*, Givat Haviva: Institute for Peace Research

Ram, H. 1996 *The Jewish Community in Jaffa: From Sepharadic Community to Zionist Center*, Jerusalem: Karmel

Reiter, Y. 1989 'An Assessment of the Reform in the Muslim Waqf Institution in Israel – the Waqf in Acre', in *The New East*, 32:125–128

Rupin, A. 1968 *Chapters of my Life*, Part 2, Tel-Aviv: Am Oved

Segev, T. 1991 *The Seventh Million: The Israelis and the Holocaust*, Tel-Aviv: Keter

Shaked, M. 2000 'The History in Court and the Court in History – the Verdict in the Kastner Case and the Narratives of Memory', *Alpyim* 20

Shehadeh, R. 1984 *The Third Way*, Tel-Aviv: Mifras

Sivirsky, S. 1981 *Deprived and Not Under-Developed: The Relationship between Mizrachim and Ashkenazim*, Haifa: Mahbarot

Sivirsky, S. and D. Bernstein 1993 'Who Worked in What, for Whom and for What? The Economic Development of Israel and the Making of the Sectarian Labour Distribution', in Uri Ram (ed.), *The Israeli Society: Critical Aspects*, Tel-Aviv: Breirot

Sluzki, Y. 1954 *The Book of the Hagana*, Tel-Aviv: Am Oved

Tamari, S. 1992 'The Palestinians in the West Bank and the Gaza Strip: A Sociology of Dependence', in S. Sivirski and I. Pappe (eds), *The Intifada: An Inside View*, Tel-Aviv: Mifras

Washitz, Y. 1947 *The Arabs in Palestine*, Merhavia: no publisher

Wigoder, S. and M. Widoger 1999 'The Matzpen Movement', in Adi Offir (ed.), *Fifty to Forty-Eight: Critical Moments in the History of the State of Israel*, pp. 195–204

Yehoshua, Y. 1981 *Jerusalem in Days of Old*, Vol. 3, Jerusalem: R. Mass

Yehudai, N. 1997 'Economic Cooperation Between Palestinian Arabs and Jews as a Possible Pattern for Relations for the Two National Communities in a State of Conflict, 1920–1930', MA Thesis submitted to Haifa University

### SOURCES IN GERMAN

Kahle, P. 1912 Gebräuche bei den Moslemischen Heiligtümern in Palastine, *Palalstina Jahrbuch* (1912)
Kober, A. 1968 *Samuel Gobat: Von Juradorf nach Jerusalem*, Basel: Gute Schriften

### SOURCES IN FRENCH

Baron, X. 1977 *Les Palestinians: Un Peuple.* Paris (no publisher)
Zureik, E. 1997 'Refugies: Etat des lieux (1ère partie)', *REP*, 11 (nouvelle serie) (Spring)

# Glossary of Names

**Abd al-Nasser, Gamal** (1918–70). Born in Bani Mur near Asyut. In 1939 as a young officer helped to create the group that would form the core of the Free Officers Association. Captured by the Israelis in the 1948 war. In 1951 became a colonel and planned the 1952 coup. President of Egypt (1956–70) and pursued a pan-Arabist policy with the cause of Palestine at its centre.

**Abdul Aziz II** (r. 1861–76). Ottoman Sultan of the Tanzimat period.

**Abdul Hamid II** (1876–1908). Effectively last Sultan of the Ottoman Empire. At first aligned himself with the reformists but then turned towards pan-Islamism and pan-Ottomanism.

**Abdullah, ibn Husayn** (1882–1951). Born in Mecca. Initiated into political life by his father. Appointed Mecca's representative in the Ottoman parliament of 1912. In 1914, conspired with the British in Egypt to prepare revolt. In November 1920 went to Ma'an in Transjordan threatening to retake Syria from the French, but settled for a kingdom there. Annexed the West Bank as part of prior agreement with the Jewish Agency in the 1948 war and was assassinated by a Palestinian in 1951.

**Abu Gosh, Mustafa** (1800–64). Born in Kafar Anab near Jerusalem. Leading sheikh of the Jerusalem mountains in the first half of the nineteenth century and head of the Yamani faction in that area.

**Abu Iyad (Salah Khalaf)** (1939–91). Born in Jaffa but expelled to Gaza with his family in 1948. From there moved to Cairo where he became one of Fatah's founders and considered second to Yasser Arafat until his murder in January 1991 by unknown assassins.

**Abu Jihad (Khalil al-Wazir)** (1935–88). Born in Ramleh (Ramla) whence his family was expelled to Gaza in 1948. Like Abu Iyad, considered to be one of the founders of Fatah, and Arafat's lieutenant. Murdered by the Israelis in April 1988. Led military wing and operations of Fatah.

**Abu Mazin (Mahmoud Abas)** (1933–). Born in Safad but expelled with his family in 1948. While a young businessman in Qatar became an early member of Fatah. From 1983 responsible for PLO connections with Israeli peace groups. Had strong ties with the Soviet Union where he spent some time. Took significant role in the Oslo accord, and in the Palestinian Authority, becoming its Prime Minister for a few weeks in 2003.

**Abu Musa (Mahmoud Said Musa)** (1931–). Born in Jerusalem. Rose to fame by leading an anti-Arafat Fatah faction in May 1983 while commander of the Fatah Yarmuc brigade. Protested against a host of military appointments decided upon by Arafat and against the new contacts with Jordan.

**Abu Shabib, Fatima.** Local Palestinian saint known for her healing abilities both during her lifetime and after her death.

**al-Afghani, Jamal al-Din** (1839–97). Born in Afghanistan. Early reformer of modern Islam. Inspired Sultan Abdul Hamid II to veer towards pan-Islamism as means of keeping Ottoman Empire intact. Later moved to Egypt where, together with Muhammad Abduh, sought synthesis between Islam and modernity.

**Ahad Ha'Am (Hebrew for 'One of the People')** (1895–1927). Pen name of Ahser Ginsburg, who was born in the Ukraine. Grew up as a brilliant student of the Jewish Halacha. In 1886 joined 'Hovevi Zion' but developed his own particular ideas of 'Spiritual Zionism'. Called for the creation of a spiritual and not political Jewish centre in Palestine.

**Ahronson, Aharon** (1876–1919). Born in Romania. In 1882 immigrated to Palestine. His father was a founder of Zichron Yaacov. Organized pro-British spying network in WWI. Died in a mysterious air crash in 1919.

**Allenby, Edmond (Viscount)** (1861–1936). As young English officer served in the South African war (Boer War) in the late nineteenth century. Served in France in the First World War. In 1917 appointed commander of British Expeditionary Force to Palestine, becoming first military governor of occupied Palestine. In 1922 became high commissioner to Egypt.

**Alon (Paikovitz), Yigal** (1918–80). Born in Kefar Tavor. Commander of the Palmach and Minister in several Israeli governments. From 1948 was a Labour Party leader until his death in 1980. In 1960 went to St. Antony's College, Oxford, but did not finish his studies.

**Aloni, Shulamit** (1929–). Born in Tel-Aviv. After years of activity in the Labour Party she founded in 1973 the Civil Rights Movement in Israel.

Minister of Education 1992–94. Known for her constant struggle for civil and human rights in Israel, for which she won the Kreisky Prize in 1985.

**Alterman, Nathan** (1910–70). Born in Warsaw. Immigrated to Palestine 1925. Leading poet and essayist close to the labour movement. Died 1970.

**Arafat, Yasser** (1929–). Born in Jerusalem and educated in Cairo. While in Kuwait (1957–1960), founded Fatah movement, remaining its official leader to today. Leader of the PLO (1968–93) and President of Palestinian Authority (1993–2003).Won Nobel Prize in 1994 for his participation in the Oslo Agreement. Besieged in his compound in Ramallah since April 2002.

**Argov, Shlomo** (1929–2003). Born in Jerusalem. Civil servant in the Israeli Foreign Office. Ambassador to London in the early 1980s. An attempt on his life provided the pretext for the Israeli invasion of Lebanon in 1982.

**al-Arif, Arif** (1891–1973). Born in Jerusalem. As a young man, recruited into Turkish army and captured by the Allies. After First World War was a founder of the Palestinian national movement, supporting at first the concept of Greater Syria and then of an independent Palestine. Joined Mandate administration and meanwhile wrote some of the most important history books on Palestine. In 1963, appointed director of Rockefeller Museum in Jerusalem.

**Arlosaroff, Haim** (1899–1933). Born in Ukraine but grew up in Germany. Immigrated to Palestine 1924. Edited several local Hebrew newspapers. In 1931 ran the political department of the Jewish Agency, its foreign ministry, and was assassinated in 1933 in Tel-Aviv by revisionist extremists who were never apprehended.

**al-Asad, Hafiz** (1930–2000). Born in Ladhakiya, Syria to an Alwaite family. His career began in the Syrian air force where, as a high ranking officer, he joined the Ba'ath party and rose to its leadership in 1968. Took over the regime in 1971 and became Syria's president until his death in 2000. Led Syrian army in the 1973 war and signed disengagement agreements with Israel in 1974.

**Awad, Mubarak** (1954–). Palestinian peace activist who tried unsuccessfully to introduce Gandhi's non-violence methods into Palestinian resistance to occupation of West Bank and Gaza Strip. Expelled by the Israelis just before the first uprising in 1987.

**Baidas, Khalil** (1874–1949). Born in Nazareth. One of Palestine's early novelists and a teacher admired by the first generation of national leaders.

**Balfour, Arthur James, 1ˢᵗ Earl Balfour** (1848–1930). Entered parliament in 1874 as Conservative member. In 1886 held his first position in the government and was Prime Minister (1902–1905) and Foreign Secretary (1916–19). In this position, he issued his declaration of support for a Jewish homeland.

**al-Banna, Hasan** (1906–49). Born in Ismailiya, Egypt, and founded the 'Muslim Brotherhood' in 1928. Assassinated by Egyptian secret service in 1949. His brother opened the branch of the movement in Palestine in the 1940s.

**Barak, Ehud** (1942–). Born in Kibbutz Mishamer Hasharon. Joined the Israeli army in 1959. After 35 years in army, where he reached the highest rank of Chief of General Staff, he entered politics in 1996. Became Israel's Prime Minister in 1999 and lost the 2001 election.

**Begin, Menachem (Wolfowitch)** (1913–92). Born in White Russia, led the Beitar movement in Poland (right-wing Zionist youth movement) and immigrated to Palestine in 1942. From 1943 to 1948 led the Irgun, engaged in guerrilla warfare against the British and in terrorism against the Palestinians. Led right-wing opposition to Labour Party until 1977 when he was elected Prime Minister; a position he held until 1982 when the Israeli fiasco in Lebanon ended his career.

**Beilin, Yossi** (1948–). Born in Tel-Aviv. After journalistic career joined the Labour Party and became its spokesperson 1977–84. Served in ministerial positions in several Labour governments from 1988. Joined Meretz in 2003 and lost his parliamentary seat. One of the Oslo accord architects.

**Ben-Gurion, David** (1886–1973). Born in Plonsk, Poland. Emigrated to Palestine in 1906 and advocated Zionist socialism. Career started in 1920 as general secretary of the Histadrut, or General Federation of Workers in Palestine. Founded the Labour Party, Mapai, in 1930, and became chairman of the Jewish Agency executive in 1935. Prime Minister of Israel 1948–53 and returned to power 1955–63. Headed his own party, Rafi, until 1970, when he retired for good from the Knesset and political life.

**Ben-Zvi (Shmishelvitz), Izhak** (1884–1963). Born in Ukraine. Immigrated to Palestine in 1907 and became a founder of the Zionist socialist movement. Helped to found Hashomer movement in 1908 and throughout Mandate wrote history books on Palestine. A leader of the Yishuv. Israel's second president (1952–63).

**Bernadotte, Count Folke** (1895–1948). Born in Sweden. President of Swedish Red Cross. UN mediator in 1948 war and assassinated by the Lehi in September 1948.

**Beshara, Azmi** (1956–). Born in Nazareth. In the 1990s became a leading political figure in the Palestinian community inside Israel. The founder of Balad, the Democratic National Party, which won three seats in the 2003 election. Served in the Knesset since 1996.

**Blyth, George Francis Popham** (1830–1914). Bishop of Jerusalem.

**Bowman, Humphry** (1879–1965). Head of Education Department during Mandate (1920–1935).

**Burg, Yosef** (1909–99). Born in Germany. Immigrated to Palestine in 1939. Leader in the Religious Zionist movement. A minister in almost all the Israeli governments until 1986, mostly as interior minister.

**Cohen, Aharon** (1910–). Born in Beserbia. Immigrated to Palestine 1937. A leader of Mapam and its principal expert on Arab affairs. Ran the party's electoral campaign in 1949 but left it in 1950 for what he considered anti-Arab orientation. Wrote many history books on the Middle East. In 1958 was found guilty of spying for the Russians. Tried in 1960 and sentenced to five years imprisonment, but released in 1963.

**al-Dajani, Hassan Sidqi** (c.1890–1938). Journalist, lawyer and politician from Jerusalem. Founder in 1919 of Muntada al-Adabi. Also a founder of the Liberal Party in 1930. A Mua'ridi and secretary of the Nashashibi's Difa' Party. Head of the Arab Car Owners and Drivers' Association. Murdered in 1938 probably by the Mufti's people.

**Darwish, Abdullah Nimr** (1958–). Born in Kafar Qassem. Founder of the Islamic movement in Israel in the 1980s and the leader of its southern wing.

**Dayan, Moshe** (1915–81). Born in Palestine. Joined the Hagana in his youth. Lost an eye while on a British mission in Vichy-occupied Lebanon in 1941. One of the founders of the Palmach, the commando units of the Hagana, and a general commanding Jerusalem area then the North. Chief of Staff in

1953 and during the Suez Campaign. Resigned from the army in 1958 and joined Ben-Gurion's Rafi until 1966. Led Rafi into alliance with Mapai to form present-day Labour Party in 1968. Israeli minister of defence during the 1967 war and a national hero, but lost prestige during the 1973 war. Foreign Minister in Menachem Begin's first government (1977–79) and was instrumental in bringing about Camp David accord between Israel and Egypt.

**al-Darawshe, Abd al-Wahab** (1940–). Founder of first Arab party among the Palestinian minority in Israel in 1988, after serving for a long time in the Labour Party.

**Eichmann, Adolf** (1906–62). Born in Germany. High ranking Nazi official and a mastermind behind extermination of Jews. Caught by the Israeli Mossad in 1962, brought to Israel, tried and executed.

**Eshkol, Levi** (1895–1969). Born in the Ukraine. Immigrated to Palestine in 1913. Member of the Hagana High Command. Minister of Agriculture 1951–52, Minister of Finance 1952–63. Third Prime Minister of Israel, 1963–69.

**Eytan, Refael** (1929–). Born in Moshav Tel-Adashim. Israeli Chief of General Staff 1978–83. Founder of Zomet, a right-wing party. Served as a minister in right-wing governments 1989–92 and 1996–99.

**Farouq** (1920–65). King of Egypt 1936–52. Born in Cairo. Deposed 1952 by Egyptian Free Officers and exiled to Italy.

**al-Faruqi, Shuqri Taji** (1882–1953). Born in Ramleh (Ramla). President of the Arab-Ottoman solidarity party in 1910. A leading figure in the Mu'arada.

**Faysal, ibn Husayn** (1885–1933). Born in the Hejaz, third son of Sharif Husayn of Mecca. Headed Arab revolt army and assisted in occupation of Damascus. King of Greater Syria (1918–20) and then of Iraq (1921–33).

**Galilli, Israel** (1911–86). Born in Ukraine. Immigrated to Palestine 1915. Early recruit to the Hagana and became its head (1946–48). Member of the Knesset and Labour governments from 1954 to 1977.

**Glubb, Sir John Bagot** (1897–1986). Commander in Chief and founder of the Arab Legion of Jordan from 1938 until his dismissal by King Hussein in 1956.

**Gobat, Samuel** (1799–1879). Born in Basel, Switzerland. In 1846, after a long missionary career, was appointed Bishop in Jerusalem. Remembered particularly for his role in education and in construction of modern hospitals all over the country.

**Goren, Shlomo** (1917–94). Born in Poland. Immigrated to Palestine 1925 and joined the Hagana 1936. The army's Chief Rabbi from 1948, after which he was the fourth Ashkenazi Rabbi of Israel. As such became spiritual leader of the Gush Emunim movement.

**Habash, George** (1925–). Born in Lydda. In his youth the family moved to Jaffa. Studied medicine in Beirut but moved after the Nakbah into political activity. In 1951 founded al-Qawmiyyun al-Arab, a pan-Arabist movement with branches all over the Arab world and a base in Amman. In 1967 founded the Popular Front for the Liberation of Palestine. From 1984 led opposition to Yasser Arafat because of the latter's *rapprochement* with Jordan, and created the rejectionist front in Damascus, but after 1987 returned to closer cooperation with Fatah in the PLO. Resigned after the Oslo accord. His successor moved to the West Bank and was assassinated by the Israelis after the outbreak of the second intifada.

**Habibi, Emil** (1922–96). Born in Haifa. Joined the Communist Party in his youth and edited its daily paper, *al-Itihad*, in the 1970s. Communist member of the Knesset. Known all over the Arab world as a novelist.

**Hacohen, David** (1898–1984). Born in Russia. Immigrated to Palestine 1907. Served in Turkish army in WWI and British army in WWII. Leading figure in the Hagana and in shaping policy towards Palestinians within the Labour Zionist movement. Member of Knesset in early years of Israel and also Israeli ambassador to Burma.

**Halevy, Benjamin** (1910–96). Born in Germany. Immigrated to Palestine 1933. As vice president of the regional court in Jerusalem presided over Kastner's trial. In early 1970s was a member of the Knesset for Gahal and joined Dash, the movement for change led by Yigal Yadin in 1977, before retiring.

**Hammad, Haj Tawfiq** (1863–1934). Born in Nablus. Served in Ottoman regional administration at a young age. Supported Abdul Hamid against reform. Became mayor of Nablus shortly before outbreak of WWI. Founder of the Christian–Muslim societies. Member of executive committee of Palestinian congresses. Joined Ahali party in early 1930s.

**Hammer, Zevulun** (1936–88). Born in Haifa. Member of the Knesset for the Mafdal from 1969 and early leader of Gush Emunim movement. Mafdal's leader in the 1980s when he served as Israel's Minister of Education.

**Hankin, Yeshosua** (1865–1945). Born in Ukraine. Immigrated to Palestine 1882 and was mainly responsible for vast land purchases in the north of Palestine.

**Harel (Halperin), Isar** (1912–2003). Born in Russia. Immigrated to Palestine 1930. Served for the Hagana in the Mandate police force. First head of the Shabak (1948–52) and then head of the Mossad. Resigned 1963 due to personal feud with Ben-Gurion and served for very short time as adviser on national security to Levi Eshkol.

**Hassan II, Muhammad** (1929–2000). King of Morocco from 1946.

**Hawatmeh, Naif** (1935–). Born in al-Salt in Jordan. Involved in politics through al-Qawmiyyun al-Arab and edited its paper *al-Hurriya*. Together with Habash founded the PFLP in 1967. In 1969 left and founded a more leftist organization, the PDFLP. Rejoined Habash briefly in the rejectionist front but supported Arafat and the more pragmatic stream after 1988.

**Hawihi, Talal** (1970–87). Born in Beit Hanun, Gaza. First casualty of the first intifada.

**Herzl, Theodor** (1860–1904). Born in Budapest. After an unsuccessful career as a playwright became a journalist on *Die Presse*, an Austrian daily. In 1895 he developed his ideas about Zionism and the need to colonize Palestine with Jewish finance and European blessing. Founded and headed the Zionist movement until 1903. Suggested Uganda as an alternative to Palestine.

**Herzog, Haim** (1918–97). Born in Dublin. His father was the Chief Rabbi of the Jewish community in Ireland. Immigrated to Palestine in 1936 and immediately joined the Hagana. During WWII headed British intelligence in northern Germany. In 1950s and early 1960s was chief of military intelligence in Israel. Became very popular as a radio commentator during the days leading to the 1967 war. First military governor of occupied East Jerusalem and later the West Bank. In the 1970s was Israel's ambassador to the UN. President of Israel from 1983 until his death.

**Hoffmann, Christoph** (1815–94). Born in Germany. In 1856 founded with friends the Templars movement for the Christian colonization of Palestine. In 1868 led the first settlers to Palestine and founded several colonies there.

**Hourani, Albert** (1915–97). Born in England to a Lebanese family. In 1946 he represented, as a young scholar from Oxford, the Palestinian case before the Anglo-American commission of inquiry. He returned to scholarly life and became one of the greatest historians of the Middle East.

**Husayn, Saddam** (1937–). Born in Tikrit, Iraq. Joined the Ba'ath party in 1957, and helped lead a Ba'ath coup in 1968. In 1979 became president of Iraq, running it as a cruel dictatorship. Led his army into two unsuccessful wars, one with Iran which lasted eight years (1980–88), and one with the West (1991). In the 1991 Gulf War, his army fired missiles into Israel. His regime was toppled by US-led invasion in April 2003. His whereabouts unknown at time of writing.

**Husayn ibn Ali, Sharif** (1852–1931). Born in Mecca. Became the Guardian of the holy cities of Mecca and Medina in 1908. Led the Arab revolt with his sons in WW1, after receiving promises by the British, in the Husayn–McMahon correspondence, to allocate much of the eastern Arab world to his dynasty. Became king of the Hejaz in 1916 but had to leave after the Saudis captured his seat in 1924. Spent the rest of his life with his son Abdullah in Jordan.

**al-Husayni, Abd al-Qader** (1907–48). Born in Jerusalem. Studied Chemistry in the American University of Cairo. Organized the youth national activity in the early 1930s and was a military commander in the revolt of 1936. Head of the paramilitary army al-Jihad al-Muqaddas and was killed in action in April 1948.

**al-Husayni, Amin** (1895–1974). Born in Jerusalem to its leading notable family. Served in Turkish army during WW1. After the war became active in al-Nadi al-Arabi and supported the idea of Greater Syria. For a while served under Amir Faysal in Damascus. After fall of Faysal's kingdom, was elected Grand Mufti of Palestine and president of the Supreme Muslim Council in 1922. Became the acknowledged leader of the Palestinian national movement and led the revolt against the British in 1936. He had to flee, and in exile during WWII tied his fate to the Italians and the Germans. After the war could not return to Palestine and remained in exile until his death in 1974 in Beirut.

**al-Husayni, Faysal** (1940–2001). Born in Baghdad while his father, Abd al-Qader, was in exile. Founding member of the Palestinian student movement late 1950s and joined Fatah early 1960s. Founded the Arab Studies Society in 1979 in the Orient House before being recruited to politics by the outbreak of the first intifada. His office became the seat of the local Palestinian leadership. With the Palestinian delegation to the Madrid conference and a minister for Jerusalem in the Palestinian Authority after the Oslo accord was signed. Died in unclear circumstances while visiting Kuwait.

**al-Husayni, Isma'il** (1860–1945). Born in Jerusalem. Head of his family in the late nineteenth and early twentieth centuries. Rose to high posts in the provincial and central Ottoman governments and developed education, in particular for girls, in Jerusalem. His private home became the famous Orient House.

**al-Husayni, Jamal** (1892–1982). Born in Jerusalem. Studied medicine in the American University in Beirut. After WWI became active, alongside the Mufti, in the Majlisiyyun Party. Member of the Arab Higher Committee and served as its 'foreign minister'. Became an active chairman of the committee after the Mufti's exile. After 1948 worked as a consultant in Saudi Arabia.

**al-Husayni, Kamil** (c.1842–1921). Born in Jerusalem. Was the Hanafi Mufti of the city when the British occupied Palestine and made him the Grand Mufti of Palestine.

**al-Husayni, Musa** (1853–1933). Born in Jerusalem. Held several significant posts in the Ottoman provincial service. Appointed mayor of Jerusalem in 1918 just before the British occupation, but was sacked by the British in 1920. Became the admired grandee of Palestinian nationalism and took part in demonstrations, despite his age, alongside young people.

**al-Husayni, Taher II** (1842–1908). Born in Jerusalem. First Hanafi Mufti to issue fatwas against Zionist colonization.

**Hussein, ibn Talal** (1935–2000). King Hussein of Jordan. Born in Amman to the son of King Abdullah. Became king in 1953 and had to deal with several attempts to overthrow him. Clashed directly with the PLO in 1970. In 1985 was reconciled with the PLO and in 1988 gave up his dream of a greater Jordan by ceding the West Bank. Died of cancer in 2000.

**Ibrahim Pasha** (1789–1848). Born in Eastern Macedonia. Probably the adopted son of Muhammad Ali. Led the invasion and occupation of Syria and Palestine in 1831 and remained its ruler until 1840. Introduced legislative, agricultural and administrative reforms and quelled the 1834 Palestinian rebellion against him.

**Jabotinsky, Zeev (Vladimir)** (1880–1940). Born in Odessa, Russia. Joined the Zionist movement in 1903 after the pogrom in Kishneiv. In 1909 worked for the movement in Istanbul. Gifted orator and writer. In WWI conceived the idea of a Jewish legion which he himself joined, fighting alongside Britain. In 1918 came to Palestine and devoted his time to organizing military capability for the Yishuv. In 1923 left the central body of the Zionist movement due to the leadership's consent to exclude Transjordan from the Palestine Mandate. The Herut movement regards him as its spiritual founding father.

**Jamal Pasha** (1872–1922). Born in Istanbul. Joined the Young Turks in 1908 and became one of the leaders that took over the regime in 1912. One of his tasks was the military governorship of Palestine during WWI, where he persecuted Palestinians and Jews suspected of working with the British enemy. In 1918 he escaped to Berlin and was a fugitive until he was assassinated in the Balkans.

**Kahana, Meir** (1932–90). Born in New York. Founded the Jewish Defence League in 1969. Immigrated to Israel in 1971 where he founded the Kach movement, a racist party that called for the enforced expulsion of Palestinians from Palestine. Entered the Knesset but his party was outlawed. Murdered in New York in 1990.

**Kanafani, Ghassan** (1935–72). Born in Acre and expelled with his family to Lebanon. Joined the PFLP and became the editor of its paper *al-Hadaf*. A poet and a novelist whose work presents the plight of the refugees. Assassinated by the Israelis in Beirut.

**Kapan, Eliezer** (1891–1952). Born in Russia. Immigrated to Palestine in 1920. Became 'finance minister' of the Jewish Agency and an important leader in Mapai. Member of the first two Israeli Knessets.

**Kastner, Israel Rudolf** (1906–57). Born in Budapest. As a leader of the Hungarian Jewish community negotiated their safety with Adolf Eichmann. Immigrated to Israel in 1946. In 1955, while on the Mapai list for the Knesset, he sued a Jew who had claimed he was a Nazi collaborator. Judge Benjamin Halevy's verdict was that Kastner had sold his soul to the devil. He was acquitted, but was assassinated in 1957.

**Kazanelson, Berl** (1887–1944). Born in Russia. Immigrated to Palestine 1909. A socialist idealist, he at first refused to join a particular socialist Zionist group and called for the unification of the labour movement in the Yishuv. Founded the agricultural union and in 1919 founded Ahdut Ha'Avoda. Editor of *Davar* from 1925 and with the publishing house Am Oved.

**al-Khalidi, Ruhi** (1864–1913). Born in Jerusalem. Served in the domestic and diplomatic services of the Ottoman Empire. Devoted much of his time to writing essays and novels. One of the first Palestinian representatives in the 1908 and 1912 Ottoman parliament.

**al-Khalidi, Yusuf Diya** (1829–1902). Born in Jerusalem. Educated in English missionary schools. Speaker of the first Ottoman parliament in 1876 and the representative there for Jerusalem. Held high posts in the provincial Ottoman service. Appointed mayor of Jerusalem in 1899 and served in this position until his death.

**Khalil, Ahmad** (1914–75). Born in Haifa. Studied in the American University of Beirut. Appointed a judge by the British. Governor of Nablus during Jordanian rule of the West Bank. In the early 1970s opened a private law office in Amman.

**Kook, Zvi Yehuda** (1891–1992). American Rabbi who spent much time in Israel from the 1950s to the 1970s. Principal ideologue of Gush Emunim, declaring that it would be heresy and sin to retreat from the occupied territories, and passed a Halachic injunction that settlement in the occupied territories was a religious duty.

**Levin, Hanoch** (1943–99). Born in Tel-Aviv. One of Israel's leading playwrights. In 1970 wrote the cabaret the 'Queen of the Bath', one of his many strong satires on Israeli militarism and occupation.

**Lilienblum, Pinchas** (1843–1910). Born in Lithuania. Writer in Hebrew who was one of the leading lights in the Jewish enlightenment. Joined Hovevi Zion in 1881 and became its secretary in 1884.

**MacDonald, Ramsey** (1866–1937). Born in Scotland. Moved to London in 1884 and helped to found the Labour Party in 1900. Won a seat in the House of Commons in 1906. Prime Minister for a short period in 1922 and then again from 1929 to 1931.

**Magnes, Yehuda** (1877–1948). Born in the USA. A Rabbi of the reform movement there. Active in WWI in the American pacifist movement. Immigrated to Palestine in 1921. First president of the Hebrew University in 1925. Founder of Brit Shalom.

**McMahon, Sir Henry** (1862–1949). High Commissioner to Egypt (1914–16). Negotiated with Sharif Husayn the future of the Arab Middle East.

**Meir (Meirson), Golda** (1898–1978). Born in Russia and grew up in the USA. Immigrated to Palestine in 1921. Active in the Histadrut and ran its political department. In 1946, when Sharett was arrested by the British, became head of the Jewish Agency's political department and hence its foreign secretary for a time. Negotiated with Abdullah before the 1948 war. Israel's envoy to Moscow in the early 1950s. Played a major role in founding the new Labour Party in 1968 and became Prime Minister in 1969. Resigned in 1974 over role in the 1973 fiasco.

**Mi'ari, Muhammad** (1939–). Born in Birweh, Galilee. Among the founders of al-Ard and founded in 1984 the Progressive List for Peace, the first Palestinian-orientated party in Israel. In the Knesset until 1988.

**Mozkin, Leo** (1867–1933). Born in Russia. Founded the Zionist student movement in Berlin in 1889. Active in the pursuit of equal rights for Jews in Russia. In 1905 became an ardent Zionist and president of various conferences of the World Zionist Organization.

**Muhammad V** (1910–61). Last Sultan of Morocco under the French domination who became the first king of independent Morocco in 1955.

**Muhammad Ali** (1769–1849). Born in Macedonia. Tobacco merchant who became an Ottoman officer in Egypt. Took over the province in 1805 and built a mini empire that included Palestine for a time. Introduced wide range of reforms which formed the basis of modern Egypt.

**al-Nashashibi, Fakhri** (1900–42). Born in Jerusalem. A leading figure in the Mu'arida and assassinated in Baghdad by unknown killers.

**al-Nashashibi, Raghib** (1881–1951). Born in Jerusalem. Graduated from the engineering school in Istanbul. Very successful career within the Ottoman administration. Elected to the Ottoman parliament 1914. Member of the all-Syrian conference in 1919. Mayor of Jerusalem 1920–34. Founder and leader of the Defence Party of the Mu'arida. In 1949 was appointed minister for refugees in the Jordanian government and served in various ministerial roles until his death.

**Navon, Yossef** (1852–1934). Born in Jaffa. Member of one of the leading families in the Old Jewish community. An entrepreneur who developed the railway and hotels with local notables and foreign investors. Went bankrupt in 1894 and left Palestine. Died in Paris.

**Netanyahu, Benjamin** (1949–). Born in Tel-Aviv. A BA in architecture and an MA in business management took him first to the world of business.

In 1988 he joined the Likud Party and ascended quickly, first as ambassador to the UN, then deputy foreign minister, then Prime Minister (1996–99). He was again foreign minister in 2001–03 and finance minister in 2003.

**Peel, William Robert Wellesley (Lord)** (1867–1937). Member, later chair, of London County Council. Elected as unionist member of Parliament. After First World War, became under-secretary of state for war, and in 1922 secretary of state for India. Shortly before his death headed Royal Commission of Inquiry to Palestine.

**Peres (Perski), Shimon** (1923–). Born in Poland. Immigrated to Palestine 1934. Began career as purchaser of arms for the young state of Israel. Founder of military and nuclear industries. From 1959 he first served Rafi and later Labour in several ministerial posts. In 1974 he stood for the first time for Prime Minister. He joined Likud in two unity governments (Labour–Likud) in 1984 to 1988 and replaced Rabin for a short while after the latter's assassination in 1995. Awarded Nobel Peace Prize for his role in the Oslo accord.

**Pinsker, Leon** (1821–91). Born in Russia. Famous as military and later civilian doctor around Odessa. Contributed to the Jewish enlightenment in the 1860s. Became a Zionist in the 1870s as a result of the pogroms and was the founder of the Hovevi Zion movement.

**Qadafi, Mu'amar** (1941–). Officer in the Libyan army who staged a military coup in 1969 and has been in power ever since.

**Qasim, Abd al-Karim** (1914–1963). Born in Baghdad. Officer in the Iraqi army in 1938. Battalion commander in the Iraqi forces in 1948 in Palestine. In 1958 was elected chair of the 'free officers' movement, which overthrew the Hashemite regime. Overthrown in a coup by the Iraqi Ba'ath Party in 1963 and executed.

**al-Qassam, Izz al-Din** (1895–1935). Born in Syria. After participating in the Syrian revolt in 1925 he moved to Haifa and became a preacher in the al-Istiqlal mosque, where he called for the removal of the British and Zionist presence from Palestine. He believed in armed struggle and holy war and practised his ideas with a group of devoted warriors until his death in a clash with the British in 1935. He is a martyr worshipped today by the Hamas movement, which named its military wing the Izz al-Din al-Qassam Battalions.

**al-Qawuqji, Fawzi** (1897–1974). Born in Lebanon. After participating in the Syrian revolt joined the Iraqi army in the 1930s. Volunteered in the 1936 Palestine revolt and returned as commander of the Arab Salvation Army in 1948.

**Rabin, Yitzhak** (1922–95). Born in Jerusalem and grew up in Tel-Aviv. Joined the Palmach in 1941. Commander of the Harel Brigade in the 1948 war. Remained in the army and rose to be Chief of General Staff and led the army to victory in 1967. After leaving the army, he was Israel's ambassador to Washington. Became Prime Minister in 1974 and again in 1992. Assassinated in 1995 for his determination to carry out the Oslo accord with the Palestinians.

**de Rothschild, Baron Edmond** (1854–1934). Born in France to one of the richest families in Europe. In 1883 received most of the Zionist colonies under his auspices until he transferred them to their own autonomous company in 1900.

**Rupin, Arthur** (1876–1942). Born in Germany. Immigrated to Palestine 1908. Led the project to turn the Yishuv into a modern society. In addition to his political activity, he founded the sociology department in the Hebrew University.

**al-Said, Nuri** (1888–1958). Born in Baghdad. Founder of the al-Ahd movement of Arab officers in the Turkish army. In 1916 joined the Arab revolt. First Chief of General Staff of Iraq, appointed 1921. Later became Minister of War, and Prime Minister in 1930. As such led the way with Egypt for the creation of the Arab League in 1944. Ardent supporter of Anglo-Iraqi treaty which brought about his demise in 1958.

**Salameh, Hassan** (1907–48). Born in Qula near Lydda. Joined Abd al-Qader al-Husayni's army, al-Jihad al-Muqqadas, in 1934. Commander of the Lyyda area in the 1936 revolt. As a commander of the Palestinian paramilitary force was killed in June 1948 in Ras al-Ayn.

**Samuel, Sir Herbert (later Viscount)** (1870–1963). Born in Britain of wealthy Anglo-Jewish family. Activist in Liberal Party from young age. Elected to Parliament 1902, and in government positions from 1906. Home Secretary in 1916 and began to take active interest in idea of a Jewish homeland in Palestine. First ever Jewish member of Cabinet and first High Commissioner to Palestine (1920–25). Afterwards elected to House of Lords, where he led the Liberal Party.

**al-Sakakini, Khalil** (1880–1953). Born in Jerusalem. At a young age emigrated to America where he failed as a businessman. Returned to Palestine in 1908 and organized an Arab revolt within the Orthodox Church, to which he belonged. Mainly interested in education and founded several private schools in Jerusalem. High ranking official in the Mandate educational system and active in the Palestinian congresses. Left in 1948 for Cairo.

**Shamir (Yizranizki), Yitzhak** (1915–). Born in Poland. Immigrated to Palestine 1935. Active in the Irgun. In the Mossad 1955–1965, and then joined Gahal. Served in several ministerial positions for Likud from 1977 until he became Prime Minister in 1983. Was joint Prime Minister with Peres 1984–88. Once more Prime Minister 1989–92.

**Shapira, Haim Moshe** (1902–70). Born in Russia. Immigrated to Palestine 1925. A principal activist in the Mizrahi movement in Palestine. Wounded in 1957 by a bomb thrown into the Knesset. As Mafdal representative, served on all the Israeli governments from 1949 until his death in 1970.

**Sharett (Chertock), Moshe** (1894–1965). Born in Russia. Immigrated to Palestine in 1912 where his father settled in a Palestinian village. In 1920 studied economics at London University. In 1933 became foreign minister of the Yishuv, heading the Jewish Agency political department. He was Israel's first foreign minister in 1949 and Prime Minister 1954–55. Represented the dovish school of thought against the hawkish policies of Ben-Gurion.

**Sharon, Ariel** (1922–). Born in Kefar Malal, Palestine. Served in the Alexandroni unit in the 1948 war. Founded commando unit 101 in the early 1950s, which carried out retaliatory missions against Palestinian targets. As commander of the southern region he helped win the 1973 war. In 1977, after foiled attempts to run alone for the Knesset, he founded Likud. Was minister of agriculture, of housing and of defence until the Kahana Committee found him indirectly responsible for the Sabra and Shatilla massacres. Served in several ministerial posts until becoming Prime Minister in 2001 and 2003.

**al-Shuqairi, Ahmad** (1907–80). Born in Tibnin in Lebanon. His father had been exiled by the Ottomans from Acre, where he was the Mufti. In 1916 Ahmad returned to Acre. He was active in the Istiqlal Party and served on the Arab Higher Committee of 1946. After the Nakbah he went to Saudi Arabia and represented that country in the UN. With the support of Gamal Abd al-Nasser he was chosen as Palestine's representative to the Arab League. From there he founded the PLO and became its first chairman until he was ousted by the Fatah in 1968.

**al-Shuqairi, Asad** (1860–1940). Born in Acre. Graduated from al-Azhar University. Elected to the Ottoman parliaments of 1908 and 1912. Appointed Mufti of the Fourth Ottoman Army during WW1. Founded the Liberal Party in 1930 and supported the Mua'rida factions.

**Tabenkin, Yizhak** (1888–1971). Born in Russia. Immigrated to Palestine 1912. A founder of Poalei Zion party, Ahdut Ha'Avoda, in 1919 and the Histadrut in 1920. Ideological father of the Kibbutz Mehuad movement. A founder of Mapai in 1930. In 1948 he helped to found Mapam but rejoined the Labour Party in 1968. In that year he established the movement for Greater Israel, adding secular voices to the religious nationalists who demanded the annexation of the occupied territories.

**Taha, Sami** (1916–46). Born in Arrabeh near Jenin. Grew up in Haifa and worked in the Chamber of Commerce there. Soon after founded the Arab Workers Union in 1930. Assassinated in 1946.

**Tamir (Kazanelson), Shmuel** (1923–87). Born in Jerusalem. Joined the Irgun in 1938. One of the founders of the Herut party in 1948. Left the party in 1952. Defended Greenwald in the Kastner trial and turned Kastner into the accused. Returned to Herut in 1965. In 1967 established a new centrist party that joined the Likud in 1973 and then joined Dash in 1977.

**al-Umar, Dahir** (1686–1776). Born in Safad. A Galilean sheikh who challenged successfully the Ottoman rule in Palestine. He began by occupying Acre in 1749 and ruled most of Western Palestine, apart from Jerusalem, while establishing alliances with Egypt and Russia. However, at the age of 90, he succumbed to a new Egyptian wish to reconcile with the Empire. He is also considered the builder of the new city of Haifa.

**Usishiqin, Menachem** (1863–1941). Born in Russia. In 1885 was chosen as the secretary-general of all the Zionist associations in Moscow. Elected 1887 as a delegate to the Hovevi Zion movement. Until 1919, visited Palestine several times and founded the teachers' union there. He immigrated in 1919 after representing the Zionist movement at the peace conference in Versailles. In 1923 he was appointed head of the Jewish National Fund and was active in land purchase and colonization.

**Webb, Sidney (Lord Passfield)** (1857–1947). Born in London. With his wife joined the socialist group the Fabians in the early 1880s. In 1895 they helped establish the London School of Economics and the secondary school system. They joined the Labour Party in 1900. In 1929 Webb was elevated to the peerage and appointed Secretary of State for the colonies, in which capacity he published the 1930 White Paper that curbed the Zionist project somewhat.

**Weizmann, Ezer** (1924–). Born in Tel-Aviv. Served in the RAF in WWII. First commander of the Israeli Air Force. Joined Likud in 1977 and served as Minister of Defence, facilitating the Israeli–Egyptian peace. Served as Israel's seventh president from 1993 to 1999.

**Weizmann, Haim** (1874–1952). Born in Russia. In 1899 gained a PhD in Chemistry and lectured from 1904 at Manchester University. Became active in Zionist politics in 1901 and led the anti-Uganda faction in 1903. Helped the British army to develop new kinds of explosives in WWI. In 1918 immigrated to Palestine and became head of the World Zionist Organization in 1920. Israel's first president in 1948.

**Wingate, Orde** (1903–44). Born in India. Served the British Empire from 1929, first in the Sudan where he was found to be a maverick army strategist. In 1936 he moved to Palestine and became an ardent Zionist, helping the Jewish community to develop defensive and offensive strategies for the survival of the Zionist project. He fought bravely in Burma in WWII and died in an aeroplane crash.

**Yasin, Shaykh Ahmad** (1937–). Born in Majdal and expelled in 1948 to Gaza where he worked as a teacher and preacher. Founded with Israel's blessing the Islamic Centre and University in Gaza in 1973. Transformed the Muslim Brotherhood in 1988 into Hamas, whose spiritual leader he became. Detained in 1989 by the Israelis and released.

**Yosseff, Dov** (1890–1970). Born in Canada. Immigrated to Palestine 1921. Member of the Jewish Agency executive in the last years of the Mandate. Military governor of Jerusalem in the first half of 1948. Appointed Minister of Supply (1948–50), supervising the special rationing regime, *Zena*. Served in other ministerial posts until 1955, when he became bursar of the Jewish Agency.

**Yossef, Ovadia** (1920–). Born in Baghdad. Immigrated to Palestine 1924. In 1945 became a judge in the rabbinical court. For a short time was deputy Chief Rabbi of Egypt. Became in 1968 Sepharadi Rabbi of Tel-Aviv, and in

1973 chief Sepharadi Rabbi of Israel. In 1984 he founded the Shas movement and became its spiritual leader.

**Zayad, Tawfiq** (1935–94). Born in Nazareth. A poet who won mayorship of Nazareth in 1975. The leader of the Communist Party and of Hadash until his death. Led the struggle against land confiscation in Galilee.

# Glossary of Terms

*A'ayan* (noble families)   The notable Muslim urban families of Palestine

*Ahdut Ha-Avoda*   Zionist Socialist Party established in 1919; together
with another party, Ha-Poel Hazair, founded Mapai in 1930, the
Labour Party that dominated Israeli politics until 1977. Another
Ahdut Ha-Avoda was founded in 1944 as a left wing of Mapai but
left to found Mapam in 1948, the second-largest socialist party in Israel

*Ahuzat Bayit*   Zionist neighbourhood established north of Jaffa in 1909
which became Tel-Aviv in 1910

*Alawites (Nusserieis)*   Ofshoot sect of Ismaili' Shiities, which borrowed
much from Christianity and resides mainly in Syria, Turkey and
Lebanon

*Alexandroni Brigade*   One of the Hagana brigades in the 1948 war

*Aliya*   Jewish immigration to Palestine and later Israel

*Alpha Plan*   Anglo-American peace plan for settling Arab–Israeli conflict
in post-1955 era, with no tangible results

*Arab Higher Committee*   Leadership of the Palestinians during the
Mandate (1934–1948)

*The Arab Legion*   The Jordanian Army. Founded in 1920 by Glubb Pasha
and played a crucial rule in 1948 war

*Arab Salvation Army*   Paramilitary force established in Syria at end of
1947, consistiing of volunteers from all over Arab world, and trained in
order to save Palestine. At beginning of 1948 its units infiltrated
Palestine. Consisted of two battalions, one headed by Fawzi al-Qawqji
and the other by Adib al-Shishaqli. Commander was an Iraqi general,
Ismail Safwat

*Arab Union of Workers*:   Established 1930 to protect rights of Palestinian
workers

*Al-Ard*   Political movement of Palestinian minority in Israel, founded
around a publication of that name calling for the partitioning of

Palestine according to Resolution 181. Outlawed by Israeli Supreme
Court and its members arrested and some exiled in 1964

*Ashkenazi* (Old Hebrew for a German). A Jew immigrating from the
West to Palestine

*Awqaf* (sing. *Waqf*) Religious Islamic endowments

*Awqaf dhuri* Private religious endowment

*Ba'ath Party* (Arabic for 'renaissance') Pan-Arabist party founded in
Damascus in 1947. Shared power in Syria in 1953, when Adib
al-Shishaqly came to power. In 1957 opened branches in the Arab world,
the most successful being in Iraq, where it became the ruling party.
Took control of Syria in 1963 and has been the ruling party ever since

*Badaliya* Tax paid by Jews and Christians in the Ottoman Empire as a
substitute for conscription

*Balfour Declaration* On 2 November 1917, the British Foreign Secretary
sent a letter to Lord Rothschild, promising the establishment of
national home for the Jews in Palestine, without prejudicing the rights
of the indigenous population

*Beitar* Zionist youth movement established in Eastern Europe by Zeev
Jabotinsky in 1919. In Israel it became the youth movement affiliated to
the Likud and right-wing parties adhering to the concept of Greater
Israel (a Zionist domination of the whole of Palestine). Its emblem
shows an even greater aspiration as it includes Jewish control over
Jordan

*Biluim* Zionist settler movement established after the 1881–1882 wave of
pogroms in Russia

*Bnei Akiva* Youth movement of the religious national movement in
Israel

*Brit Shalom* Jewish group founded in 1925 to promote better
understanding between Jews and Arabs in Palestine. Proposed
establishment of a bi-national state in the land. It dissolved in 1940

*Christian–Muslim Association* The first national association of the
Palestinians, founded in 1918

*Dinar* Currency of several Arab countries including Jordan

*DoP* (Declaration of Principles) Document signed by the PLO and
Israel on 13 September 1993, marking the beginning of the Oslo process

*Al-Fatah* One of the first pan-Arab national associations, founded in
Paris in 1911. Acted secretly in the Ottoman Empire

*Fatwa* Religious judgement pronounced by a mufti

*Fida'i* (pl. *fida'iyyun*) (Arabic for a warrior willing to sacrifice his or her
life) Palestinian guerrilla fighter in the 1950s and 1960s

*FLN*   National Liberation Front in Algeria founded in 1954 to lead the country to independence; remaining dominant political force in the state

*Gahal*   Political bloc headed by Menachem Begin and uniting in 1965 the Herut Revisionist Party and the Liberal Party

*Green Line*   The 4 June 1967 borders (originally the armistice lines drawn after the 1948 war) between Israel and the areas it occupied in the 1967 war (the West Bank, the Gaza Strip and the Golan Heights)

*Gush Emunim*   (Hebrew for 'community of believers') Formed in February 1974 to advance the settlement of the West Bank and the Gaza Strip and work for its annexation to the state of Israel. A religious national movement which had the support of the right-wing secular forces in Israel

*Ha-Avoda*   (Hebrew for 'labour').' Political alignment between Mapai and Mapam in 1969 and dissolved in 1984

*Hadassa*   Zionist women's association in America founded in 1912. One of the biggest women's associations in the world, focusing on raising money for Israel

*Haffiyye*   Ottoman secret police in the days of Abdul Hamid II

*Hagana*   (Hebrew for 'defence') Founded in the 1920s as the defence force of the Yishuv. Main Jewish underground until 1948 when it became the Israeli Defence Force together with the Irgun and the Stern Gang (Lehi)

*Halacha*   The Jewish religious law

*Haluzim*   (Hebrew for 'pioneers') Collective name given to early Zionist settlers

*Hamas*   (Arabic acronym for Movement of the Islamic Resistance) Radical Islamic movement founded in 1988 during the first intifada. Its military wing, Izz al-Din al-Qassam, was engaged in a guerrilla and terror campaign against Israel from 1988

*Hanafi*   One of the four schools of thought in the Islamic Sunni law. Considered the most prevalent (including in Palestine) as it is the most flexible as to time and place. Named after its founder, Abu Hanifah (died 767)

*Ha-Parasha*   (Hebrew for 'the affair') The Lavon affair was a scandal breaking in Israel following the exposure of a Jewish network of espionage and sabotage in Egypt operated by the Israeli secret service in 1954. The echoes of the affair, and especially the question of Ben-Gurion's involvement in it, affected the Israeli political system until 1963 and contributed to Ben-Gurion's fall

*Haram*    Holy Islamic site open only to Muslims

*Haram al-Sharif*    The area with the al-Aqsa mosque and the Dome of
the Rock on Temple Mount in the Old City of Jerusalem

*Hashemite*    Clan ruling Mecca and Medina in 1908, headed by Sharif
Husayn. His descendants ruled Iraq until 1958 and still rule Jordan
today

*Herut Party*    Replaced the Zionist Revisionist Party led by Jabotinsky.
Herut was founded in 1948 and was led by Menachem Begin until it
merged with the Liberal Party and became Gahal in 1965 and Likud in
1973

*Hezbollah*    (Arabic for 'Party of God') Shiite radical movement founded
in 1988 and both a political party and paramilitary organization

*Histadrut*    General Federation of Workers established in Israel in 1920

*Hovevi Zion*    (Hebrew for 'Lovers of Zion') Society for the colonization
of Palestine 1881–1896 mainly in Russia. Legally registered in Russia in
1890 but was expelled and moved to Palestine in 1891

*Intifada*    (Arabic for 'shaking off') Palestinian uprising against the Israeli
occupation, the first in 1987 and the second in 2000

*Irgun Zevai Leumi* (Irgun)    (Hebrew for National Military
Organization) Founded 1937 by David Raziel with the aim of
establishing a Jewish state all over Palestine (including Transjordan).
Menachem Begin became its head in 1941. Blew up King David Hotel
in 1946 and was heavily involved in terrorist attacks against the
Palestinian population. During the 1948 war became part of the IDF
and committed the Dir Yassin massacre; dissolved later that year

*Islamic Jihad*    Militant Islamic movement in the occupied territories that
split to form the Muslim Brotherhood movement in the occupied
territories in 1986. First attack on Israeli troops took place in 1986, and
since the mid-1990s has employed human suicide bombers in its
struggle against the occupation

*Al-Istiqlal*    Political party in Palestine founded in 1932 calling for the
establishment of an Arab state in Palestine within a united Arab world.
Disappeared effectively in 1941

*Izz al-Din al-Qassam*    Brigades forming military wing of Hamas

*Jabha*    (Arabic for 'the Front') Democratic Front for Peace and Equality,
known also by its Hebrew acronym Hadash. A political party founded
in 1977 by the fusion of the old Communist Party (Rakah) with
non-Zionist factions and individuals in Israel

*The Jewish Agency*    Established in 1929 as the informal government of
the Jewish community. Officially formed to assist Jewish immigration,

but in effect ran the Yishuv. After 1948 most of its functions were passed to the Israeli government. Since 1971 has coordinated Israel's relationship with the Jewish communities around the world

*Kapos* Jews appointed by the Nazis as guards in the concentration camps during the Holocaust

*Knesset* (Hebrew for 'assembly') Israeli parliament, first elected in January 1949. It has 120 members

*Lajant al-Tawjih* (Arabic for 'steering committee') In 1981 this informal body of young leaders in the West Bank tried to lead people against the occupation but was severely repressed by the Israeli army

*La-markaziayya* (Arabic for 'decentralization') One of the first pan-Arab national movements, founded in Beirut in 1912 and active in Egypt. Called for the adaptation of the Austro-Hungarian model to the Arab-Ottoman reality of the day

*Likud* (Hebrew for 'cohesion') Parliamentary bloc representing the right wing parties in Israel, formed in September 1973. First won election in 1977 and has been in power, apart from 1992–1996, since

*Little Triangle* Area between Hadera and Afula, consisting mostly of Palestinians. Ceded from the West Bank and annexed to Israel as part of the armistice agreement signed between Israel and Jordan in April 1949

*Ma'arach* (Hebrew for 'alignment') Labour Party became the Ma'arach in 1969 when it formed an alliance with Mapam. It changed its name again to Labour (Ha-Avoda) in 1984 when Mapam left it and became independent once more

*Mafdal* Hebrew acronym for national religious party. Founded in 1956 by merger of two religious Zionist movements: Ha-Poel Hamizrachi and Hamizarachi movement. It was the spiritual home of the Gush Emunim movement and served in most Israeli governments

*Majlis* (Arabic for 'assembly') Used for describing various councils in the local and national history of Palestine

*Majlissiyun* (Arabic for 'council members') Supporters of coalition headed by the Grand Mufti Amin al-Husayni and his party

*Mandate* Form of self-rule granted by the League of Nations for countries deemed unable to gain full independence. Guise for colonial ambitions curbed by the American insistence on respecting the right of self-determination in the post-WWI world

*Mapai* Hebrew acronym for the party of Eretz Israel's workers. The main Zionist socialist party, established in 1930. Became the Ma'arach in 1969 and then Ha-Avoda, Labour, in 1984

*Mapam* Hebrew acronym for the United Workers Party. Established in 1948 as a Zionist party left of Mapai. Joined its old rival in a new party, Ma'arach, in 1969 but left in 1984. Had own kibbutz movement until the mid-1990s. In 1990 joined forces with the civil rights movement of Shulamit Aloni and her party, Raz, to form Meretz, the left Zionist party

*Mazpen* (Hebrew for 'compass') Small group and first anti-Zionist activists in Israel, founded in the mid-1960s

*Mizrahi* (Hebrew for 'easterner') Collective name for Jews coming from Arab countries to Israel and who struggled against discrimination and deprivation. Since the 1970s the Mizrahim make up over half the Jewish population

*Mossad* (Hebrew for 'institute') Full title is Institute for Intelligence and Special Missions. The Israeli CIA, so to speak. Created in 1951 with similar mission to its American counterpart

*al-Mu'arada* Opposition parties to the Majlisiyyun led by Nashashibis

*Mufti* Muslim cleric passing judgements (*fatwa*) according to Islamic law. Politicized by the British both in Egypt and in Palestine where the Muftis were regarded as heads of the Muslim community

*Al-Muntada al-Adabi* (Arabic for the 'Literary Club') One of the first Palestinian national groups, founded in 1918 and calling for Palestinian independence

*Al-Muqawwama* (Arabic for 'resistance') Collective name given to guerrilla warfare conducted by several Palestinian organizations 1948–1968

*Musha'* Rural form of collective land ownership on a rotating basis common in Palestine and intact until the early twentieth century

*Muslim Brotherhood* First and largest political Islamic group in the Arab world. Founded in 1928 in Egypt by Hasan al-Banna. Its members volunteered to fight on behalf of the Palestinians in 1936 and in 1948. In early 1940s opened branches in Palestine and Transjordan. After the 1967 war, its leader, Ahmad Yassin, was allowed to re-establish the movement as a counter force to the Fatah. It later split into the Islamic Jihad and Hamas (Yassin became the latter's spiritual head)

*Mutawali* Guardian of Muslim endowment

*Al-Nadi al-Arabi* (Arabic for the 'Arab Club') Founded in 1918 and first national group among the Palestinians advocating creation of Greater Syria. Dissolved after 1921 and became Arab national party affiliated to the Husaynis

*Al-Nakbah* (Arabic for 'catastrophe') Term used by the Palestinians and the Arab world for the 1948 war

*Nazihun* (Arabic for 'uprooted') Term for Palestinian refugees from the areas occupied by Israel in the 1967 war and used to distinguish between them and the Laji'un (the refugees) of 1948

*Ohalim* (Hebrew for 'tents') Protest movement of Mizrahi Jews emerging in Israel in the 1970s demanding renovation and rehabilitation of urban slums where most of them lived

*The Palestinian Authority* Title of body running the legislative and executive affairs in the occupied territories according to the 1993 Oslo accord. Its president has been Yasser Arafat. Became ineffective as result of the second intifada in 2000

*Palmach* (Hebrew acronym for the 'Striking Platoons') Commando units of the Hagana founded in 1941

*PDFLP* Popular Democratic Front for the Liberation of Palestine. Splinter group that left the PFLP in 1969, headed by Naif Hawatmeh. Left the mother organization due to ideological disputes about the role of Marxism and Maoism in the struggle for the liberation of Palestine

*PFLP* Popular Front for the Liberation of Palestine. Founded by George Habash in 1967 as an agglomeration of several small groups merging with al-Qawmiyyun al-Arab. Loyal to Soviet Union and its brand of Marxism-Leninism and led way in the opposition to the Fatah and Arafat from 1984 onwards

*PLO* Palestine Liberation Organization. Founded June 1964 by the Arab League in Jerusalem as body representing Palestinian struggle for independence. Its traditional leadership replaced by the Fatah movement headed by Yasser Arafat and thereafter identified with Palestinian struggle for statehood, the right of return, and against the occupation

*PNC* Palestinian National Council. Parliamentary body of the PLO, its approx. 400 members include delegates of the various Palestinian political factions as well as professional organizations

*The Palestine National Fund* Ministry of finance of the PLO

*Poalei Zion Small* (Hebrew for the 'Left Workers of Zion') Splinter group in Poalei Zion movement founded in 1919. Mother movement was founded in 1900 in Minsk, Russia, and was the first Zionist socialist movement

*Qawmi* (Arabic for 'nationalism') Term referring to pan-Arabist nationalism

*al-Qawmiyyun al-Arab*   (Arabic for the 'Arab Nationalists') Pan-Arabist
   movement founded in 1951 by George Habash and operated all over
   the Arab world (in Jordan it consisted mainly of Palestinians). It had
   no formal organization but the avowed purpose of toppling
   reactionary Arab regimes. Most of its members joined the PFLP
   in 1969
*Qeren Ha-Qayemet Le-Israel*   (Hebrew for 'Perpetual Fund for Israel')
   Also known as Jewish National Fund (JNF). Major arm of the World
   Zionist Organization for the purchase of land and Jewish settlement in
   Palestine since 1905. Principal actor in the further settlement of Jews on
   land left by expelled Palestinians in 1948
*Qirsh*   Turkish unit of currency
*Samed*   (Arabic for 'endurance') PLO welfare organization
*Sanjaq*   Sub-district in the Ottoman Empire
*Sepharadi*   (Hebrew for 'person living in Spain') Collective name given
   to Jews from Arab countries coming to Israel
*Shabak*   (Hebrew acronym for the 'General Secret Service') and also
   known as Shin Bet (acronym for 'Security Service') Israel's domestic
   secret service, founded in 1948. Targeted at first the Palestinian
   minority and Jewish leftists. The brunt of its activity moved to the
   occupied territories in 1967
*Shas*   (Hebrew abbreviation of 'Guardian of the Torah') Founded by
   ultra-orthodox Mizrahi Jews who broke away from Agudat Israel, the
   major ultra-orthodox party. Headed since by Rabbi Ovadia Yossef.
   Called for creation of both a theocracy in Israel and for equal rights for
   Mizrahi Jews. Did extremely well in all election campaigns between
   1988 and 2000
*Shari'a*   Islamic law
*Shaykh (pl. Mashayikh)*   (Arabic for 'grandee') Usually referred in
   Palestine to rural or nomadic notables or heads of guilds
*Shiite*   (Arabic for 'parties') Sect that split from orthodox Islam in the
   seventh century. There are no Shiites in Palestine, but they are the
   dominant group in southern Lebanon
*Shinui*   (Hebrew for 'change') Centrist political party founded in 1974.
   Gradually joined forces with liberal and left Zionist groups to form
   Meretz in 1990, the principal left Zionist party, but left in 1996 and
   became a significant factor in the political scene in the first years of the
   twenty-first century
*Shuhada al-Aqsa*   Military wing of the Fatah movement during the
   second intifada

*Sijjil*   Shari'a court records, an invaluable source of information on the social history of Palestine through the centuries

*Stern Gang*   (Lehi – Hebrew acronym for the 'freedom fighters of Israel'). Zionist terrorist group founded by Abraham Stern in 1939, a former Irgun leader killed by the British in 1942. Responsible for assassination of UN mediator Count Bernadotte. One of its leaders, Yitzhak Shamir, was intermittently Prime Minister between 1983 and 1992

*Supreme Muslim Council*   Founded in 1922 to run Muslim affairs during the Mandate. Its president until its dissolution during the 1936 Arab revolt was Amin al-Husayni

*Sykes-Picot Agreement*   May–October 1916. Anglo-French agreement for the division of control of the eastern Middle East in the post-Ottoman period. The Russians consented to this division of spoils which divided the Middle East into political entities most of which exist today

*Tabur Amliyeh*   Forced-labour units recruited by the Ottomans for public works and during war

*Tanzimat*   Ottoman reform movement beginning in 1839 and ending in 1876. Major effort to modernize Ottoman Empire

*Tapu*   Register of land and property in the Ottoman Empire. Still used in Israel for registration

*Tawaqim*   (Arabic for 'teams') Groups that sat in the Orient House in Jerusalem in the wake of the Madrid Conference preparing the infrastructure for a future Palestinian state

*UAR*   United Arab Republic. Official name of Egyptian–Syrian union 1958–1961

*Ulama*   Collective name for religious clerics, hierarchy and learned community in Muslim societies

*UNRWA*   United Nations Relief and Works Agency for Palestinian Refugees in the Near East. Established by the UN General Assembly in 1949 to serve first as a transitory body for finding work for refugees until a solution was found. Soon turned into the major employer and relief provider for the refugees in the camps, where still they remain today

*UNSCOP*   United Nations Special Committee on Palestine. Inquiry commission established by the UN General Assembly in February 1947 for finding a solution to the Palestine question. Adopted a majority report for dividing Palestine into two states with an economic union. The report became UN Resolution 181 on 29 November 1947

*Usrat al-Jihad*   (Arabic for 'Jihad family') Original name of Islamic movement in Israel in the early 1980s

*Vaad Leumi*   (Hebrew for 'National Committee') National assembly of the Yishuv that became the Knesset in 1949

*Village Leagues*   Rural association established by Israelis in the early 1980s to counterbalance the PLO. Failed to serve their purpose

*Vilayet*   Regional district in Ottoman Empire

*Wahhabiyya*   Muslim Sunni movement of Islamic fundamentalism that emerged in the Arabian Peninsula in the mid-eighteenth century. Called themselves the Muwahidin, 'those who believe in God's unity'. Challenged Ottoman rule successfully in the peninsula and joined forces with the Saudi family in the twentieth century, taking over the Hejaz from the Hashemites

*Wailing Wall*   Holiest site for Judaism in Jerusalem on what is the western wall of the Temple Mount

*Wakil*   (Arabic for 'agent') Representative of land owner in land transactions and ownership

*Watani*   (Arabic for 'nationalism') Refers to local nationalist sentiment

*World Zionist Federation*   Founded in 1907 as pan-Zionist association of all Zionist bodies in the world. Democratic political body. Anyone can join by paying the Shekel, the annual tax, and then has the right to vote for the Zionist Congress. The Congress is run by an executive committee. After 1948 lost much of its significance

*Yesh Gvul*   (Hebrew for 'There is a Limit') Movement of Israeli soldiers refusing to serve in the 1982 Lebanon war, and later extended to those refusing to serve in the occupied territories

*Yishuv*   (Hebrew for 'Settlement as well as Community') Collective name for Jewish community during the Mandate

*Zena*   (Hebrew for 'austerity') Austerity regime that included rationing in early 1950s Israel

# Index